Film Theory and Contemporary Hollywood Movies

Film theory no longer gets top billing or plays a starring role in film studies today, as critics proclaim that theory is dead and we are living in a post-theory moment. While theory may be out of the limelight, it remains an essential key to understanding the full complexity of cinema, one that should not be so easily discounted or discarded.

In this volume, contributors explore recent popular movies through the lens of film theory, beginning with industrial-economic analysis before moving into a predominately aesthetic and interpretive framework. The Hollywood films discussed cover a wide range from *300* to *Fifty First Dates*, from *Brokeback Mountain* to *Lord of the Rings*, from *Spider-Man 3* to *Fahrenheit 9/11*, from *Saw* to *Memento* and *Kill Bill*. Individual essays consider such topics as the rules that govern new blockbuster franchises, the "posthumanist realism" of digital cinema, video game adaptations, increasingly restricted stylistic norms, the spatial stories of social networks like YouTube, the mainstreaming of queer culture, and the cognitive paradox behind enjoyable viewing of traumatic events onscreen.

With its cast of international film scholars, *Film Theory and Contemporary Hollywood Movies* demonstrates the remarkable contributions theory can offer to film studies and moviegoers alike.

Warren Buckland is Reader in Film Studies at Oxford Brookes University. His authored and edited books include *Puzzle Films*, *Directed by Steven Spielberg*, *Studying Contemporary American Film* (with Thomas Elsaesser), and *The Cognitive Semiotics of Film*. He also edits the *New Review of Film and Television Studies*.

Film Theory and Contemporary Hollywood Movies

EDITED BY

WARREN BUCKLAND

Routledge
Taylor & Francis Group

NEW YORK AND LONDON

First published 2009
by Routledge
270 Madison Ave, New York, NY 10016

Simultaneously published in the UK
by Routledge
2 Park Square, Milton Park, Abingdon, Oxon OX14 4RN

Routledge is an imprint of the Taylor & Francis Group, an informa business

© 2009 Taylor & Francis

Typeset in Spectrum MT by Keyword Group Ltd.
Printed and bound in the United States of America on acid-free paper by
Walsworth Publishing Company, Marceline, MO

Library of Congress Cataloging in Publication Data
Film theory & contemporary Hollywood movies / edited by Warren Buckland.
p. cm.
Includes bibliographical references and index.
1. Motion pictures—Philosophy. 2. Motion pictures—United States. I. Buckland, Warren.
II. Title: Film theory and contemporary Hollywood movies.
PN1995.F4667 2009
791.430973—dc22
2008043558

ISBN 10: 0-415-96261-7 (hbk)
ISBN 10: 0-415-96262-5 (pbk)
ISBN 10: 0-203-03076-1 (ebk)

ISBN 13: 978-0-415-96261-2 (hbk)
ISBN 13: 978-0-415-96262-9 (pbk)
ISBN 13: 978-0-203-03076-9 (ebk)

contents

illustrations

figures

tables

acknowledgments

I wish to thank Edward Branigan and Charles Wolfe for commissioning me to edit this volume. They also offered advice on this project from its beginnings through to the end, and presented me with valuable comments on my introduction.

All the contributors have provided me with in-depth papers that reflect their current research interests. They have been patient with my queries and requests for revisions and modifications. In addition, Thomas Elsaesser, Eleftheria Thanouli, and Yannis Tzioumakis offered feedback on my introduction. My colleagues at Oxford Brookes (Alberto Mira, Yoko Ono, Paolo Russo, and Daniela Treveri-Gennari) have created a working environment congenial to carrying out research.

Finally, I would like to thank Eun Young Kim for her moral and emotional support during the completion of this volume.

introduction

w a r r e n   b u c k l a n d

> *Theory has not vanished: it is in disguise. It plays hide and seek.*
> *(Francesco Casetti, 44)*

film theory

Debates on the status of theory—especially in the humanities—over the last few decades were largely dominated by ecological and evolutionary metaphors of theory's "life cycle." Theory was presented as a natural, organic body—but one in "decline" or being kept artificially alive in the university, like a zombie (Boyd), or is an abject ghost (Cohen). Or the body called "theory" was simply dead and we are attending its wake (Bové). Theory's demise was also expressed using mechanistic metaphors: theory had run out of steam (Latour) or, like a large and inefficient corporation, had been downsized (Stow), was in chaos (Kirby) or is on the scrap heap (Losee). We are therefore in an age of post-theory (Bordwell and Carroll), or after theory (Cunningham; Eagleton). David Rodowick has written an elegy for Film Theory—the most visible and privileged of all humanities theories. But Rodowick wants to liberate theory from the scientism of cognitive and analytic approaches to film, and renew the need for a philosophy of the humanities.[1] Francesco Casetti entertains three reasons for film theory's apparent demise: "there is no more theory because there is no more cinema" (35); cinema "has never existed as such" (37); and "the third reason for the weakening of film theory may be found in the weakening of the social need for 'explanation'" (39)—that is, postmodernism has weakened theory by rejecting master narratives and rationality itself. The result, however, is not theory's disappearance; instead, theory is (in Casetti's words) merely in disguise, playing hide and seek.

In *Shakespeare After Theory* David Scott Kastan is more positive about theory's invisibility: "The great age of theory is over," he writes, "but not because theory has been discredited; on the contrary, it is precisely because its claims have proven so compelling and productive" (31). Kastan's is a measured voice amongst the gloom. Theory, he argues, is a success story. It has been absorbed into the fabric of the humanities to such an extent that it has apparently disappeared. But what has happened is that scholars no longer feel the need (for the most part) to wear their theories on their sleeves (making them less vulnerable to postmodern critiques). Theory's realm has expanded to such an extent that it constitutes the horizon line, has become part of the ordinary background assumptions informing all manner of humanities scholarship. In literary studies Kastan, for example, readily admits his hard core historical studies of Shakespeare are inflected with theory. In film studies, theory has become part of the routine activity of studying the cinema. Gill Branston notes that "theory, always historically positioned, is inescapable in any considered practice" (30).

Let's briefly remind ourselves of some of the points of contention that have surrounded film theory (this list is not meant to be exhaustive). Theorists:

- use abstract, reductive concepts that are too general (and organize those concepts into binary oppositions: mind/body, intellect/emotions, spirit/flesh, universal/particular, language/image, telling/showing);
- are uncritical, complacent and dogmatic in their reliance on theoretical doctrines (when they should be relying on data);
- live under the misguided assumption that film theory can be explicitly political;
- cannot distinguish between theory and interpretation;
- maintain theory under a cloak of political correctness;
- make excessive claims;
- use arcane, difficult terminology;
- over-intellectualize their material (to the detriment of experiencing actual films and real emotions); and
- make unrealistic claims.

We shall consider just a few of these criticisms.

To criticize film theory for its abstract, reductive concepts is to ignore its historical positioning. The initial stage of any theoretical activity involves a narrowing of focus—the simplification (abstraction and idealization) of what is being studied. Simplifying is the necessary first step in constructing a theory. The early stages of theory-building are governed by attempts to obtain the maximum amount of simplicity by studying only the essential or major or proximate or likely determinants of a particular domain. But as research progresses, those determinants deemed inessential and irrelevant at the early stages take on a greater importance, and make the research domain complex, in the negative sense that the theory cannot successfully subsume important factors within its framework. For research to progress, this "negative complexity" must be translated into "positive complexity"— the theory must expand to take into account these additional factors. In the 1960s, semiotic film theory (a branch of what has variously been called "contemporary film theory," "modern film theory," or "*Screen* theory")[2] by design is narrowly focused: it followed the simplicity principle and attempted to reduce, by as much as possible, the negative complexity of film, by limiting itself only to the study of those characteristics thought to be specific to film—a system of underlying codes (that is, absent structures and causes that confer intelligibility upon individual films). This process of simplifying eventually and inevitably led to a crisis, as the so-called inessential phenomena left out of the initial study take on importance. In the 1970s *Screen* theory embraced positive complexity by incorporating within its semiotic framework Marxism and psychoanalysis. These theories studied additional absent structures and causes, such as ideology, society, and the unconscious, resulting in its theory of "subject positioning." In its turn, this theory exhausted itself, writes Casetti, because it fell "victim to its own rigidity and repetition." That is, "during the 1990s, it became clear that this paradigm gave rigid responses to diverse and fluctuating situations. It was not able, in other words, to provide responses to the questions which began to be posed" (34–5). The theory of subject positioning could not handle the new level of negative complexity—areas of research excluded from initial formulations of subject positioning theory (such as ethnicity, class, nationality, positive roles for female spectators, the active spectator), which scholars identified as important in the late 1980s and in the 1990s.

Research progresses, therefore, by addressing the incompleteness of a theory. Research also progresses through the identification of theoretical contradictions and inconsistencies. In regards to overcoming these faults, there are three possible responses: the theory can be (1) corrected (assuming the contradictions, etc., arose from errors or mistakes); (2) supplemented (preserving what is correct while eliminating what was contradictory by introducing new concepts, sometimes from other disciplines); or (3) discarded in favor of another theory or new, non-theoretical paradigm.

Film scholars overuse option 3. From the perspectives of analytic philosophy and cognitivism, David Bordwell and Noël Carroll argue that localized, middle-level (or piecemeal) theories, based on scientific thinking (study of the unknown in nature using causal, falsifiable models), should replace what they regard as the monolith of humanities-focused *Screen* Theory (with a capital T), and envisage an open dialog among theorists with the hope that theory will advance through dialectical exchange. In its turn, Rodowick's "Elegy for Theory" offers a fundamental response and challenge to Bordwell and Carroll's scientific attitude to film theory. This attitude, Rodowick argues, downplays ethical evaluation, plus the study of sense, meaning, and internal investigation. "What we need after theory," he writes, "is not science, but a renewed dialogue between philosophy and the humanities" (100).

Bordwell and Carroll's scientific approach and Rodowick's call for a philosophy of the humanities, offer powerful alternatives to *Screen* Theory. But option 3 has been misused as well. Attempts to discard previous theories are suffused with "present mindedness," a failure to understand concepts historically. Sam Wineburg writes that:

> We discard or just ignore the vast regions of the past that either contradict our current needs or fail to align easily with them . . . . We are not called upon to stretch our understanding to learn from the past. Instead, we contort the past to fit the predetermined meaning we have already assigned to it. (6)

Tomas Kemper manifests this lack of historical understanding of Christian Metz's film semiotics in a book review article. He writes:

> Clearly reading the writing on the wall in the semiotic soiree of contemporary French intellectual life, Metz translated his cinephilia into the lingua franca of the times, namely, the theory and jargon of semiotics, fully immersing his study in a thorough reading of the now notorious linguist Ferdinand de Saussure and his linguistic pedigree—the work of Chomsky, Barthes, Eco, and a veritable alphabet soup of theoretical terms and propositions. (143)

Here we merely need to note Kemper's shallow understanding of film semiotics. If he wants to attack structuralism or semiotics, why not examine its neo-Kantian assumptions, for example.[3] That is, why not present some penetrating insights backed up with historical research, rather than merely offer the reader a weak critique whose force is based on a few superficial words such as "jargon," "notorious," and "alphabet soup."[4]

Kemper is unable to offer penetrating insights or historical research because he suffers from "present-mindedness." He does not engage with the historical contexts from which Metz's theories emerged, or understand the problems to which his research was a response. He does not stretch his understanding to learn from the past; instead, he contorts the past. He wears his ignorance on his sleeves. To understand any theory, a critic needs to comprehend it from the inside, in its own historical context, understand the questions to which the theory is an answer, rather than judge theories only in terms of whether they meet present needs, or conform to current values and norms.[5]

Let's look at another example. The concept of "suture," developed (by Jean-Pierre Oudart, Stephen Heath, and Daniel Dayan) during the early phases of Lacanian-inspired psychoanalytic film theory, was key to subject positioning theory, but was quickly tossed aside before it had time to develop. In its initial theorization, Oudart, Heath, and Dayan presented suture in reductive, abstract, idealized terms. To continue using that initial formulation of the theory today would be unproductive. But Branigan's recent discussion of the concept considerably refines and extends it: "The theory of suture," he writes, "attempts to explain how a separation between various framed parts in a film is overcome in order to articulate a coherent, unified filmic expression" (*Projecting*, 133–4). He identifies what he takes to be the nine successive stages of suture (previous formulations only identify two), each stage representing the spectator's changing awareness—his/her alternating attention between absorption in the Imaginary and awareness of the Symbolic. Branigan confines his exhaustive description to Oudart's analysis of one shot in *The General* (Keaton, 1926). After presenting these nine successive stages (135–6), Branigan redescribes them entirely in terms of framing: the spectator's awareness moves from the nonframed, to the unframed, framed, deframed, and then the reframed (in the subsequent shot) (136). Here we witness Branigan updating, reformulating, and supplementing an incomplete concept, making it less abstract and reductive and more germane and relevant.

Another criticism leveled at theory is its proliferation of abstract terminology. Film theorists certainly weren't the first to commit this sin. There's a precedent in the hermeneutic style of writing, in which Anglo-Saxon writers (such as Frithegod, Lantfred, and Wulfstan) enriched their monosyllabic vocabulary with polysyllabic Latin and Greek words (especially after the Norman invasion of Britain in 1066). That some humanities scholars did not constrain their use of abstract terminology (due to another Norman invasion, this time of the USA in 1966[6]) does not in itself invalidate film theory; it merely means that a number of apprentice scholars in both the UK and USA were seduced by the theoretical paradigm. (A little knowledge is still a dangerous thing.) Jean-Michel Rabaté notes that theory can be seductive. With theory, he argues, one can make "grandiose pronouncements" with an apparent "lack of rigor" (quoted in Stow, 195), or can invent terms without due consideration for precision or accuracy. But such a misuse of theory is no different than driving your BMW at 80 miles an hour in a 30 mile an hour speed zone. We cannot blame the car for such behaviour, but we can penalize individual drivers. (In film theory there are, admittedly, a large number of drivers who go over the speed limit.)[7]

In general terms, film theory (like all theory) is a form of speculative thought that aims to make visible the underlying structures and absent causes that confer order and intelligibility upon films. These structures and causes, while not observable in themselves, are made visible by theory. The ultimate objective of film theory is to construct models of film's non-observable underlying structures in an attempt to explain the nature of film (the "system of codes" of film semiotics; the "Absent One" of suture theory, and so on). The absence of causes in their effects is the precondition for the theoretical activity of modeling. Film theorists from different fields model different sectors of film's non-observable underlying structures, depending on the absent causes they examine: unconscious, ideological, economic, cognitive, neurobiological, and so on. Academic film studies has created a specialized theoretical vocabulary around the cinema in order to talk about the structures underlying films. This vocabulary represents the film theorist's unique way of seeing and thinking, which exceeds the immediate, common sense view of films (their consumption as harmless entertainment) and begins to ask a set of questions that common sense has no need for. Film theorists are experts who ask seemingly strange and difficult questions about films. And theory itself is difficult because the invisible structures are unknown (although not unknowable), and the terminology used to describe and explain them does not have readily apparent referents. (The problem with film theory terminology is primarily a problem with the indeterminacy of reference, as well as the inappropriate mapping onto film of metaphors from domains outside film theory.)

One response to the difficulty of theory is to argue that, because film is a popular medium, it should be discussed only on a popular level. One only needs to read David Weddle's misguided attack on film theory in the *Los Angeles Times* (2003) to witness this retreat to a populist position of anti-intellectual nostalgia.

Film theory, then, is a system of interrelated hypotheses, or tentative assumptions, about the unobservable nature of reality (a reality assumed to be a regular, economical, cohesive structure underlying chaotic, heterogeneous observable phenomena). It unveils the scope and limits of human reasoning and, done well, can encourage us to question our collectively held values.

contemporary hollywood movies

So far I have simply argued that theory (in all its various, heterogeneous guises) is still prevalent in film studies, even though it no longer has a starring role, or top billing, and may have changed its identity through an alignment with science or philosophy. I'll now turn to the way theory has informed and continues to shape one of the dominant areas of film studies research since the 1990s—classical and contemporary Hollywood movies.

Serious study of Hollywood has galvanized around three trends: (1) the aesthetic; (2) the interpretive; and (3) the industrial-economic (or media industry studies). The aesthetic approach was initiated by the auteurism of *Cahiers du cinéma* (Hillier, ed.), Andrew Sarris, *Movie* magazine (Cameron; Perkins) and *Monogram*. The aesthetic became marginalized in the late 1960s as *Cahiers* turned to interpretive analysis, which in turn influenced *Screen* theory in the 1970s. In *The Classical Hollywood Cinema*, Bordwell, Staiger, and Thompson rejected interpretive analysis and instead combined in depth industrial-economic analysis with astute aesthetic analysis. Although the authors defined classical Hollywood filmmaking as covering the period 1917–1960, in chapter 30 (367–77) Bordwell argued that, through the assimilation of innovations, the classical style continues to dominate contemporary Hollywood filmmaking (which makes, as he says, 1960 a fairly arbitrary cut-off point).[8] Since then, an intense debate has centred around the periodization of contemporary Hollywood as a classical or new/post-classical practice (see Smith, *Theses*; Kramer; Elsaesser and Buckland, 26–79, for overviews). Thomas Schatz and Sean Cubitt continue the debate in this volume.

Aesthetic and especially interpretive analyses continue to dominate the study of contemporary Hollywood (e.g., Wood; Ryan and Kellner; Collins, Radner, Collins; Willis; Elsaesser and Buckland). Other studies stick to industrial and economic paradigms (Schatz; Balio, ed., part IV; Prince; Wasko; McDonald and Wasko, eds.); while others offer a mix of industrial and aesthetic (Hillier; Wyatt; Neale and Smith, ed.; Lewis, ed.; King; Stringer, ed.; Miller et al.; Buckland, *Spielberg*). The present volume begins with an industrial-economic analysis before moving into a predominately aesthetic and interpretive framework, centred on three areas: "New Practices, New Aesthetics"; "Feminism, Philosophy, and Queer Theory"; and "Rethinking Affects, Narration, Fantasy, and Realism."

New Practices, New Aesthetics. The volume opens with seven papers that examine new filmic practices and technologies, and the new aesthetics they have generated.

Thomas Schatz uses media industry studies to continue his penetrating examination of contemporary Hollywood cinema (see, for example, "New Hollywood" and "Conglomerate Hollywood"). In the present volume he investigates "the combined impact of conglomeration, globalization, and digitization" on contemporary Hollywood and American independent filmmaking. He delineates the "rules" that govern new blockbuster franchises, and presents a case study of the Spider-Man franchise, and a coda devoted to the wrangles behind the production of *The Hobbit*.

Sean Cubitt returns to the question that (as I pointed out above) has dominated the study of contemporary Hollywood cinema—periodization, of how different contemporary Hollywood is from classical Hollywood. Cubitt notes that "the question of periodisation is... not about a paradigm-shift but rather about a resurgent tendency in Hollywood and its alloyed entertainment trades" (such as theme park rides, computer games, comic books, TV shows, fan sites, toys) to represent the baroque. Cubitt argues that the classical and the baroque (or neo-baroque) are not binary opposites, for "both are cultural dynamics whose histories are braided together." Films such as *Van Helsing* (2004) and *300* (2006), he argues, braid together neo-baroque and classical elements.

William Brown argues that contemporary cinema is posthumanist not only on the level of content (with its themes of human extinction), but also on the levels of form and production. The digital is posthumanist, Brown argues, to the extent that it (especially in the form of invisible digital special effects) "presents the impossible to us *as if it were possible.*" Moreover, this sense of posthumanism does not involve the loss of something uniquely human, but makes humanity's reinvention possible by overcoming its limitations through technology. Brown uses his discussion of the digital to develop a theory of "posthumanist realism" in contemporary cinema, a theory that explains those moments where the "camera" (no longer a physical object, but, in Edward Branigan's term [2006], a projected hypothesis) performs an "impossible" and continuous shot. Brown analyzes examples from *War of the Worlds* (2005), *Panic Room* (2002), and *Fight Club* (1999).

Douglas Brown and Tanya Krzywinska use the concepts of transmediality, convergence, and adaptation to examine the increasingly important synergy that has developed over the last decade between the film and digital games industries. The authors argue that "games and movies have both shared and divergent features. A heightened awareness of these and their implications become apparent when addressing adaptations of games to films and films to games." They offer an informative survey of this synergy (from one of the earliest movie tie-ins, *Raiders of the Lost Ark*, to the latest, such as *Spider-Man 3* and *Pirates of the Caribbean: at World's End*), focusing on how games and films have been adapted to each other's media specificity.

K.J. Donnelly investigates the fusing of sound effects, ambient sound, and music in contemporary cinema, focusing on the "collapse of the space between diegetic sound and non-diegetic music" in *Saw* (2004). He sees this collapse as reflecting a breakdown between the film's "conscious" and its "unconscious," a collapse, he argues, which can be found beyond his favored genre, the contemporary horror film.

Barry Salt employs the scientific-based methods of statistical style analysis, which he has been developing for over 30 years, to determine the stylistic norms governing contemporary American films. He selects 20 films from the year 1999 and collects data on their stylistic parameters, including average shot length, shot scale, camera movement, reverse angles, and point of view shots. One conclusion he reaches is that contemporary American films are now being made according to increasingly restricted stylistic norms.

Calling to mind Michel de Certeau's distinction between a map and an itinerary (or the notion that narrative involves the transformation of general, abstract place into a particular, realized space), Thomas Elsaesser goes beyond the cinema to investigate one of the dominant sites of the Web 2.0 social networks—YouTube. He asks what "spatial stories" do these social networks tell, "once a user decides to engage with their dynamic architecture, [and] lets him/herself be taken to different sites, spaces and places, not by the logic of an individual character's aims, obstacles, helpers and opponents... but by the workings of contiguity, combinatory and chance." The individual *flâneur*'s route through these electronic social networks is marked by "key-words or tags, tag-clouds or clusters of such key-words, embedded links, user's comments, and of course, one's own 'free' associations." Elsaesser offers one such journey through YouTube, starting with a Honda car ad and ending on domino toppling contests via Rube Goldberg conventions and the Pythagoras Switch.

Feminism, philosophy, and queer theory. Philosophy, feminism and queer theories have continued to gain critical authority in the humanities in the last decade. One important issue they have grappled with is how to conceptualize the body's materiality. The New Lacanians (most notably Slavoj Žižek and Joan Copjec) focus on the Imaginary and the Real instead of concentrating on the Imaginary and the Symbolic in their analysis of sexual difference. In contrast, rather than appeal to the Real, which risks locating sexual difference at the pre-discursive level (biological essentialism), philosopher Judith Butler has continued to remain on the level of the Symbolic to define the performativity of gender. In her contribution to this volume, Saša Vojković draws upon Butler's *Bodies that Matter* to examine Tarantino's transcultural universe in *Kill Bill:* Vol. 1 (2003) and Vol. 2 (2004)—a universe marked by cultural exchange and influence between Asian and Western cinemas. Vojković argues that *Kill Bill* represents a fictional world where the Lacanian "Law-of-the-Father" does not hold. "If psychoanalysis is to be brought into a productive relation with the emerging changes on the cultural screen," she argues, "we need to explore the possibility of reworking the symbolic universe."

Harry M. Benshoff begins his chapter to this volume by noting that an unprecedented number of lesbian, gay, bisexual, and transgendered characters have appeared in movies beginning in the 1990s. He asks: "what does all this signify about our current understanding of (homo)sexuality and the American film industry? Does the mainstreaming of gay and lesbian culture and concerns necessarily mean its commodification and depoliticization?" After reviewing queer film theory and queer films from the last 20 years, he brings these questions to bear on Ang Lee's *Brokeback Mountain* (2005).

9

He argues that the film "uses the tools and methods of queer theory to critique the dominant institutions and subject positions created within white, Western, heteronormative discourses."

Film scholars not persuaded by psychoanalytic or Marxist film theory but equally dissatisfied with the scientism of cognitive film theory and analytic philosophy have in recent years turned to the French philosopher Gilles Deleuze and his two cinema books (*The Movement Image* and *The Time Image*). Deleuze is not a film theorist in the commonly accepted sense, for he theorizes *with* rather than *about* the cinema. What seems to have drawn him to the cinema is the relation of bodies, matter, and perception, seen as a traditional philosophical problem, and in the twentieth century most vigorously explored by phenomenology. David Martin-Jones presents a lucid and accessible outline of Deleuze's theory of the Movement-Image, the Time-Image, and of minor cinema. Martin-Jones challenges the assumption that Deleuze is primarily applicable only to classical Hollywood and European art cinema, by analyzing a contemporary mainstream American film (*Fifty First Dates* [2004]) and an independent film (*The Doom Generation* [1995]). He argues that *Fifty First Dates*, especially in the way it represents time and memory, falls between the movement-image and the time-image. He views *The Doom Generation* through the concept of minor cinema, highlighting the film's subversive sexual politics.

Rethinking Affects, Narration, Fantasy, and Realism. Cognitive film theory shares with *Screen* theory a focus on the interface between film and spectator. But whereas the *Screen* theorists examined the way a film addresses unconscious desires and fantasies, the cognitivists analyze "normative behavior such as perception, narrative comprehension, social cognition, and the experience of garden-variety emotions such as fear and pity" (Plantinga, 20). Carl Plantinga argues that cognitive film theory should not be identified exclusively as a sub-branch of cognitive science. Instead,

> one might say that cognitive film theorists tend to be committed to the study of human psychology using the methods of contemporary psychology and analytic philosophy. This can be an amalgam of cognitive, evolutionary, empirical, and/or ecological psychology, with perhaps a bit of neuroscience and dynamical systems theory thrown in the mix. (21–2).

Plantinga notes that the study of the way film elicits emotions has been one of the key areas of research in cognitive film theory (see, for example, Smith, *Engaging Characters*; Tan; Plantinga and Smith [eds.]; Smith, *Film Structure*). In his chapter for this volume, Plantinga continues this research through a study of *Titanic* (1997). He aims to "show that cognitive film theory can help identify the affective appeals that *Titanic* offers and relate those to the audience pleasures in its viewing." That viewing experience offers a paradox, in that the film represents traumatic events, so how can it be popular and enjoyable? He uses cognitive theories of emotion to address this paradox.

Like Plantinga, Volker Ferenz also draws upon cognitive and affective theory (especially that of Edward Branigan and Murray Smith), but he uses it to add some much needed clarity and precision to the topic of unreliable narration in the cinema. He examines the conditions under which spectators resort to inferring an unreliable narrator, and offers an informative study of unreliable character-narrators in *The Usual Suspects* (1995), *Fight Club* (1999), and *Memento* (2000).

Using *The Lord of the Rings* films as his case study, Martin Barker transforms the academic study of fantasy in the cinema, previously limited to psycho-analytic film theory (see Cowie, chapter 4), into an empirical research project. He asks: "how do people go about being audiences for a film that they regard as 'fantasy'?" He explores several ways of thinking about fictional fantasy, and asks how each "embed within its concepts and theories definite ways of conceiving 'the audience', and through these conceptions the cultural roles they variously attribute to fantasy." He outlines different types of empirical research into fantasy audiences before detailing his extensive *Lord of the Rings* project. "At the heart of the project," Barker writes,

> were three questions: (a) what does film fantasy mean and how does it matter to different audiences across the world?, (b) how was the film's reception in different contexts shaped by its origins as a very English story, celebrating its filming in New Zealand with money and backing from a Hollywood studio?, and (c) how was the film prefigured in different country contexts, and how did this play into the film's overall reception?

His *Lord of the Rings* project provides detailed answers to these questions, some of which are summarized in his chapter for this volume.

In the final chapter, Ian Aitken uses contemporary philosophical realist concepts to develop an intuitionist realist approach to Michael Moore's *Fahrenheit 9/11* (2004). The intuitionist realist approach, separate from a cognitive or rational model, "conceives of aesthetic objects such as documentary films as consisting of a network of theoretical categories which provide both descriptions of the subject as problematic and provisional accounts of cau-sality." Aitken provocatively argues that Moore frequently undercuts his own political intentions in *Fahrenheit 9/11* through qualifying and confounding his claims, through equivocation, and by creating conflicting orientations. For example, in his analysis of the film's prologue, Aitken writes that: "the *sheer assortment and quantity* of empirical visual portrayals succeeds both in under-cutting the commentary and authorial intentionality of *Fahrenheit 9/11*, and qualifying the underlying theoretical imperatives of the film."

The contributors to this volume not only demonstrate theory's continued explanatory relevance to the study of contemporary cinema; they also begin to reveal that theory has reached a point where it begins to open up hybrid spaces—spaces between binary oppositions: the classical/post classical cinema; the human/posthuman; diegetic sound/non-diegetic music; the analogue of aesthetics/its digital quantification; map/itinerary (based on contiguity, combinatory and chance, with tag-clouds as one's only guide); signification (the Symbolic)/the material body; the pairings homosexual-marginal/heterosexual-central; a productive space between the movement-image/the time-image; the apparent rationality of cognition/apparent irrationality of emotion; together with a new vocabulary that emphasizes porous boundaries—such as the transcultural and transmedial. Perhaps these hybrid spaces, as Homi Bhabha argues, "emerge in moments of historical transformation" (2) and represent "in-between" states (29) of impure unstable identities and shifting boundaries. The contributors to this volume demonstrate that, although theory has become established, constitutes the horizon line, it has not become stagnant. Its objects of study continue to expand and proliferate.

notes

1. Rodowick refers specifically to the cognitive-analytic scientism of Bordwell and Carroll (eds.) and Allen and Smith (eds.). Malcolm Turvey responds to Rodowick's paper. Rodowick looks to Stanley Cavell as a model for a philosophy of the humanities: "In my view, Cavell's work is exemplary of a philosophy of and for the humanities, particularly in his original attempt to balance the concerns of epistemology and ethics" (106).

2. For a rational reconstruction of film semiotics, see Buckland ("Film Semiotics"). For a brief summary of "Screen theory", see Buckland ("Screen Theory") and Rosen. For detailed first-hand accounts of Screen theory, see Willemen; MacCabe; Nash.

3. See also Eagleton, who takes cultural theory to task for failing to address several fundamental questions:

> Most of the objections to theory are either false or fairly trifling. A far more devastating criticism of it can be launched. Cultural theory as we have it promises to grapple with some fundamental problems, but on the whole fails to deliver. It has been shamefaced about morality and metaphysics, embarrassed about love, biology, religion and revolution, largely silent about evil, reticent about death and suffering, dogmatic about essences, universals and foundations, and superficial about truth, objectivity and disinterestedness. This, on any estimate, is rather a large slice of human existence to fall down on. It is also, as we have suggested before, rather an awkward moment in

> history to find oneself with little or nothing to say about
> such fundamental questions. (101–2)

4. For a detailed account of the historical, cultural, and institutional conditions of humanities theory, including structural linguistics, structuralism, and semiotics, see Niilo Kauppi, and Ian Hunter, "History of Theory" and "Time of Theory."
5. Developing a balanced view of any discourse from the past involves seeking

> to achieve the conflicting dual states: . . . steering a course
> between the arch sin of judgements reached through a
> state of present-mindedness, and legitimately employing
> the interpretive advantages of an aerial view of conceptual
> developments. (Keith Smith, 6).

6. This is the date of the "The Language of Criticism and the Sciences of Man" conference held at Johns Hopkins University, generally regarded to be the "originary" moment of French structuralism's arrival in the USA. The papers of the conference (by Derrida, Barthes, Lacan, etc.) were collected in Richard Macksey and Eugenio Donato (eds.).
7. Eagleton defends the abstractness of theoretical terminology in chapter 4 of *After Theory* (especially 75–80). "You can be difficult without being obscure," he writes. "Not all wisdom is simple and spontaneous" (77).
8. Bordwell has maintained that the classical style has "intensified"—but not fundamentally changed—since the 1960s ("Intensified Continuity;" *The Way*). Similarly, Thompson argues that classical storytelling techniques persist in contemporary Hollywood.

works cited

Allen, Richard, and Murray Smith, eds. *Film Theory and Philosophy*. Oxford: Oxford University Press, 1997.

Balio, Tino, ed. *The American Film Industry*, revised edition. Madison: University of Wisconsin Press, 1985.

Bhabha, Homi K. *The Location of Culture*. London: Routledge, 1994.

Bordwell, David. "Intensified Continuity: Visual Style in Contemporary American Film." *Film Quarterly* 55.3 (2002): 16–28.

——. *The Way Hollywood Tells It: Story and Style in Modern Movies*. Berkeley: University of California Press, 2006.

Bordwell, David, and Noël Carroll, eds. *Post-Theory: Reconstructing Film Studies*. Madison: University of Wisconsin Press, 1996.

Bordwell, David, Janet Staiger, and Kristin Thompson. *The Classical Hollywood Cinema: Film Style and Mode of Production to 1960*. New York: Routledge, 1985.

Bové, Paul. *In the Wake of Theory*. Hanover: Wesleyan University Press, 1992.

Boyd, Brian. "Theory Is Dead—Like a Zombie." *Philosophy and Literature* 30.1 (2006): 289-98.

Branigan, Edward. *Narrative Comprehension and Film*. New York: Routledge, 1992.

——. *Projecting a Camera: Language-Games in Film Theory*. New York: Routledge, 2006.

Branston, Gill. "Why Theory?" *Re-Inventing Film Studies*. Ed. Christine Gledhill and Linda Williams. London: Arnold, 2000. 18–33.

Buckland, Warren. "Film Semiotics." *A Companion to Film Theory*. Eds. Toby Miller and Robert Stam. Oxford: Blackwell, 1999. 84–104.

13

———. "*Screen* Theory." *The Critical Dictionary of Film and Television Theory.* Eds. Roberta Pearson and Philip Simpson. London: Routledge, 2001. 392–3.

———. *Directed by Steven Spielberg: Poetics of the Contemporary Hollywood Blockbuster.* New York: Continuum, 2006.

Butler, Judith. *Bodies That Matter: On the Discursive Limits of "Sex."* New York: Routledge, 1993.

Cameron, Ian, ed. *The Movie Reader.* New York: Praeger, 1972.

Casetti, Francesco. "Theory, Post-Theory, Neo-Theories: Changes in Discourses, Changes in Objects." *Cinémas* 17.2–3 (2007): 33–45.

Cohen, Tom. "Along the Watchtower: Cultural Studies and the Ghost of Theory." *MLN* 112.3 (1997): 400–30.

Collins, Jim, Hilary Radner, and Ava Preacher Collins, eds. *Film Theory Goes to the Movies.* London: Routledge, 1993.

Cowie, Elizabeth. *Representing the Woman: Cinema and Psychoanalysis.* London: Macmillan, 1997.

Cunningham, Valentine. *Reading After Theory.* Oxford: Blackwell, 2002.

De Certeau, M. *The Practice of Everyday Life.* Trans. Steven Rendall. Berkeley: University of California Press, 1984.

Deleuze, Gilles. *Cinema 1: The Movement Image,* trans. Hugh Tomlinson and Barbara Habberjam. Minneapolis: University of Minnesota Press, 1986.

———. *Cinema 2: The Time Image,* trans. Hugh Tomlinson and Robert Galeta. Minneapolis: University of Minnesota Press. 1989.

Eagleton, Terry. *After Theory.* London: Allen Lane, 2003.

Elsaesser, Thomas, and Warren Buckland. *Studying Contemporary American Film: A Guide to Movie Analysis.* London: Arnold, 2002.

Hillier, Jim, ed. *Cahiers du cinéma: 1950s: Neo-Realism, Hollywood, New Wave.* Cambridge, MA.: Harvard University Press, 1986.

Hillier, Jim. *The New Hollywood.* London: Studio Vista, 1992.

Hunter, Ian. "The History of Theory." *Critical Inquiry* 33 (2006): 78–112.

———. "The Time of Theory." *Postcolonial Studies* 10.1 (2007): 5–22.

Kastan, David Scott. *Shakespeare After Theory.* London: Routledge, 1999.

Kauppi, Niilo. *The Making of an Avant-Garde: Tel Quel.* Berlin: Mouton de Gruyter, 1994.

———. *French Intellectual Nobility: Institutional and Symbolic Transformations in the Post-Sartrian Era.* Albany: State University of New York Press, 1996.

Kemper, Tomas. Review of Edward Branigan, *Projecting a Camera. International Journal of Communication,* 1 (2007): 143–8, at http://ijoc.org/ojs/index.php/ijoc/article/viewFile/182/93 (accessed April 15 2008).

King, Geoff. *Spectacular Narratives: Hollywood in the Age of the Blockbuster.* London: I.B. Tauris, 2000.

———. *New Hollywood Cinema: An Introduction.* London: I.B. Tauris, 2002.

Kirby, David. "Theory in Chaos." *The Christian Science Monitor.* January 27 (2004): http://www.csmonitor.com/2004/0127/p11s01-legn.html (accessed April 15 2008)

Kramer, Peter. "Post Classical Hollywood." *Oxford Guide to Film Studies.* Eds. John Hill and Pamela Church Gibson. Oxford: Oxford University Press, 1998. 289–309.

Latour, Bruno. "Why Has Critique Run out of Steam? From Matters of Fact to Matters of Concern." *Critical Inquiry* 30.2 (2004): 225–48.

Lewis, Jon, ed. *The New American Cinema.* Durham: Duke University Press, 1998.

Losee, John. *Theories on the Scrap Heap. Scientists and Philosophers on the Falsification, Rejection, and Replacement of Theories.* Pittsburgh: University of Pittsburgh Press, 2005.

MacCabe, Colin. "Class of "68: Elements of an Intellectual Autobiography, 1967–81." *Theoretical Essays: Film, Linguistics, Literature*. Manchester: Manchester University Press, 1985. 1–32.

McDonald, Paul, and Janet Wasko, eds. *The Contemporary Hollywood Film Industry*. Oxford: Blackwell, 2007.

Macksey, Richard, and Eugenio Donato, ed. *The Structuralist Controversy: the Language of Criticism and the Sciences of Man*. Baltimore: Johns Hopkins University Press, 1970.

Miller, Toby, Nitin Govil, John McMurria, and Richard Maxwell. *Global Hollywood 2*. London: BFI, 2004.

Nash, Mark. "The Moment of *Screen*." *Screen Theory Culture*. Hampshire: Palgrave Macmillan, 2008. 1–27.

Neale, Steve, and Murray Smith, ed. *Contemporary Hollywood Cinema*. London: Routledge, 1998.

Perkins, V.F. *Film as Film*. Harmondsworth: Penguin, 1972.

Plantinga, Carl. "Cognitive Film Theory: An Insider's Appraisal." *Cinémas*, 12.2 (2002): 15–37.

Plantinga, Carl, and Greg Smith, eds. *Passionate Views: Film, Cognition, and Emotion*. The Johns Hopkins University Press, 1999.

Prince, Stephen. *A New Pot of Gold, 1980–90*. New York: Charles Scribner's Sons, 1999.

Rabaté, Jean-Michel. *Future of Theory*. Oxford: Blackwell, 2002.

Rodowick, D.N. "An Elegy for Theory." *October* 122 (2007): 91–109.

Rosen, Philip. "*Screen* and the Marxist Project in Film Criticism." *Quarterly Review of Film Studies* 2.3 (Aug. 1977): 273–87.

Ryan, Michael, and Douglas Kellner. *Camera Politica: The Politics and Ideology of Contemporary Hollywood Film*. Bloomington: Indiana University Press, 1988.

Sarris, Andrew. *The American Cinema: Directors and Directions, 1929–1968*. New York: Dutton, 1968.

Schatz, Thomas. "The New Hollywood." *Film Theory Goes to the Movies*. Jim Collins, Hilary Radner and Ava Preacher Collins, eds. London: Routledge, 1993. 8–36.

———. "The Studio System and Conglomerate Hollywood." *The Contemporary Hollywood Film Industry*. Paul McDonald and Janet Wasko, eds. Oxford: Blackwell, 2007. 13–42.

Smith, Greg M. *Film Structure and the Emotion System*. Cambridge: Cambridge University Press, 2003.

Smith, Keith. *Lawyers, Legislators and Theorists: Developments in English Criminal Jurisprudence 1800–1957*. Oxford: Clarendon Press, 1998.

Smith, Murray. *Engaging Characters: Fiction, Emotion, and the Cinema*. Oxford: Clarendon Press, 1995.

———. "Theses on the Philosophy of Hollywood History." Steve Neale and Murray Smith, eds. *Contemporary Hollywood Cinema*. London: Routledge, 1998: 3–20.

Stow, Simon. "Theoretical Downsizing and the Lost Art of Listening." *Philosophy and Literature* 28.1 (2004): 192–201.

Stringer, Julian, ed. *Movie Blockbusters*. London: Routledge, 2003.

Tan, Ed. *Emotion and the Structure of Narrative Film: Film as an Emotion Machine*. Trans. Barbara Fasting. Mahwah: Lawrence Erlbaum, 1996.

Thompson, Kristin. *Storytelling in the New Hollywood: Understanding Classical Narrative Technique*. Cambridge, MA.: Harvard University Press, 1999.

Turvey, Malcolm. "Theory, Philosophy, and Film Studies: A Response to D.N. Rodowick's 'An Elegy for Theory'." *October* 122 (2007): 110–20.

Wasko, Janet. *How Hollywood Works.* London: Sage, 2003.

Weddle, David. "Lights, Camera, Action: Marxism, Semiotics, Narratology." *The Los Angeles Times Magazine.* 13 July 2003.

Willemen, Paul. "Remarks on *Screen.*" *Southern Review* 16 (1983): 292–311.

Willis, Sharon. *High Contrast: Race and Gender in Contemporary Hollywood Film.* London: Duke University Press, 1997.

Wineburg, Sam. *Historical Thinking and Other Unnatural Acts.* Philadelphia: Temple University Press, 2001.

Wood, Robin. *Hollywood From Vietnam to Reagan.* New York: Columbia University Press, 1986.

Wyatt, Justin. *High Concept: Movies and Marketing in Hollywood.* Austin: University of Texas Press, 1994.

new practices,

new aesthetics

new hollywood,

new millennium

o n e

t h o m a s   s c h a t z

This essay is a sequel of sorts to "The New Hollywood," which first appeared in *Film Theory Goes to the Movies*, a lively collection published in 1993 that was intended, as the title exhorts, to bring film scholarship within shouting distance of contemporary Hollywood films and filmmaking. That volume was well received and helped fuel the growing interest in media industry studies, which gauges the complex interplay between media production (and media products) and the myriad forces that both shape and, in rare cases, are shaped by that production. My own work has continued along these lines, focusing mainly on the film industry in the late 1980s and 1990s as the New Hollywood steadily morphed into Conglomerate Hollywood. The focus here is on the film industry in the early 2000s, a period that in my view has proved to be quite distinctive, due particularly to the combined impact of conglomeration, globalization, and digitization—a veritable tri-umvirate of macro-industrial forces whose effects seem to intensify with each passing year.

It remains to be seen whether the early 2000s qualify as a distinct his-torical period—"millennial Hollywood," if you will—but even without the benefit of greater historical distance we can distinguish significant changes in the contours and overall configuration of the industry. Consider this brief inventory of industry developments during the past decade that mark either key advances over or distinct departures from the New Hollywood of the 1990s:

- the culmination of an epochal merger-and-acquisition wave and the consolidation of U.S. media industry control in the hands of a half-dozen global media superpowers;
- the related integration of the U.S. film, TV, and home entertainment industries into a far more coherent system than had ever existed before;
- the enormous success of DVD, both as a source of revenues for the studios (and their parent conglomerates) and also as a transformative technology for the home entertainment industry generally;
- the surging global film and TV markets, which have proved to be as susceptible to Hollywood-produced entertainment as the domestic media markets;
- the emergence of a new breed of blockbuster-driven franchises specifically geared to the global, digital, conglomerate-controlled marketplace, which spawn billion-dollar film series installments while also serving the interests of the parent conglomerate's other media-and-entertainment divisions;
- the annexation of the "indie film movement" by the media conglomerates, providing a safe haven for a privileged cadre of filmmakers while leaving the truly independent film business in increasingly desperate financial straits;
- the rapid development of three distinct film industry sectors dominated by three different classes of producers—the traditional major studios, the conglomerate-owned indie divisions, and the genuine independents—which generate three very different classes of movie product.

The transformative effects of these and other industry forces have grown steadily more acute, reaching an apparent culmination in 2007—or so it seems from the vantage point of this writing in mid 2008. Here again, only time and a broader perspective will tell us whether the past year was indeed a pinnacle of sorts, perhaps even a watershed, or simply another step in the industry's inexorable post-millennial transformation. In any event, Hollywood saw a remarkable number of singular developments and definitive events in 2007. These included record box-office revenues in both the U.S. and the worldwide marketplace, propelled by a run of franchise blockbusters like *Spider-Man 3*, *Shrek the Third*, and *Transformers* that cleared a billion dollars within a year of release, setting a new benchmark for the major studios commercially.[1] Their affiliated "indie divisions" garnered all the critical praise with hits like *No Country for Old Men* and *There Will Be Blood*, resulting in an unprecedented drubbing of the majors in the post-season Oscar ceremony. Meanwhile the scores of genuinely independent producer-distributors, which released well over half of all theatrical films in the U.S., suffered their worst year ever both commercially and critically, as the independent sector threatened to implode. Thus 2007 was positively Dickensian in its best-of-times/worst-of-times polarity, underscoring the fact that the story of modern Hollywood is a tale of two industries, and that conglomerate ownership has become the deciding factor in a studio's prospect for survival, let alone success. Indeed, while conglomeration has been the structural imperative of the movie industry for the past two decades, not until the early 2000s did it fully coalesce—with enormous consequences not only Hollywood but for the U.S. media industry at large.

conglomerate hollywood in the new millennium

The most salient development in contemporary Hollywood has been the formation of the so-called Big Six media conglomerates and their hegemony over the American film (and TV) industry (Epstein; Schatz, "Conglomerate Hollywood"). This modern conglomerate era crystallized in the mid-1980s when News Corp purchased 20th Century Fox and launched Fox-TV, and it culminated with the 2003 buyout of Universal Pictures by General Electric (GE) and subsequent creation of NBC Universal. At that point a cartel of global media giants—Time Warner, Disney, News Corp, Sony, Viacom, and GE—owned all six of the major film studios, all four of the U.S. broadcast TV networks, and the vast majority of the top cable networks, along with myriad other media and entertainment holdings including print publishing, music, computer games, consumer electronics, theme parks, and resorts. Conglomerate control of Hollywood is exercised primarily via ownership of the traditional major studios—i.e., Warner Bros., Disney, Universal, 20th Century Fox, Columbia (Sony), and Paramount (Viacom)—and in fact the term Big Six is used in the trade press to refer to both the major studios and their parent companies. The studios are situated within the conglomerates' "filmed entertainment" divisions, which produce content for both the movie and TV industries, and operate in close cooperation with the "home entertainment" divisions, which play a vital role in film industry fortunes due to the impact of DVD on the home-video industry.

Key to the conglomerates' hegemony and their financial welfare in the early 2000s has been the strategic integration of their film and TV operations in the U.S., by far the world's richest and most robust media market, as well as their collective domination of the global movie marketplace. In terms of their U.S. film and TV holdings, consider the figures in Table 1.1 from *Advertising Age*'s annual report on the 100 leading media companies in 2006.

Table 1.1 2006 Net U.S. media revenue (all figures in $ billions)

Company	[total revs][1]	movies[2]	TV[3]	cable	other[4]	TOTAL
Time Warner	[44.2]	2.91	.4	6.97	2.92	13.20
Disney	[34.3]	2.67	5.39	6.76	1.22	16.04
News Corp	[28.6]	2.95	5.12	3.85	1.53	13.45
NBC-Universal	[16.2]	1.76	6.53	2.92	1.65	12.86
Viacom-CBS	[25.8]	1.98	6.46	6.60	2.21	17.05
Sony	[71.5]	3.22	–	–	.87	4.09[5]

[1] Worldwide parent company revenues.
[2] Includes theatrical and home video/DVD revenues.
[3] Network and TV station income.
[4] Includes TV series production, distribution, licensing and syndication.
[5] Sony figures apply to filmed content production only. According to Sony of America's "Corporate Fact Sheet" (online at http://www.sony.com/SCA/corporate.shtml) the company's US sales for the 2006–07 fiscal year were $18.9 billion.

While movie-related revenues represent a relatively modest portion of the conglomerates' overall U.S. media income, it's important to note that the studios' worldwide movie-related income in 2006 (according to the Motion Picture Association) was $42.6 billion (Hollinger). This indicates well the significance of overseas markets for Hollywood films, as well as the explosive growth of the foreign and home-video markets in the early 2000s. While domestic box-office revenues remained fairly steady from 2002 to 2007 at $9 billion to $10 billion per year (roughly twice the 1990 total), foreign box office steadily climbed from $9 billion to $18 billion. That growth is expected to continue due to the economic development of foreign markets as well as the studios' coordination of domestic and international release—an effort that has been greatly facilitated by the fact that both the U.S. and overseas markets are fundamentally hit-driven, and are driven by the same studio-produced blockbusters. From 2002 to 2007, Hollywood's top ten releases averaged an astounding 25.6 percent market share domestically and a 25.5 percent market share worldwide. During the same period, the top 25 box-office hits captured 45 percent of the domestic market and 41.2 percent of the market worldwide, grossing $9 billion to $10 billion per year.

Meanwhile the home-video sector grew at an even faster pace due to the impact of DVD, which was introduced as a movie-delivery system in 1997 and enjoyed the most rapid "diffusion of innovation" in the history of technology (Taylor; Sebok). The main reasons for the success of this new digital format were, first, the unprecedented alliance between the Hollywood film industry and two adjacent industries, personal computers and consumer electronics; and second, the decision to abandon the VHS-era rental model in favor of a conglomerate-controlled "sell-through" strategy that returned a far greater portion of home-video revenues to the studios. In 2002, home-video revenues reached a record $20.3 billion, with DVD surpassing VHS for the first time ever and sell-through surpassing rental (Hettrick). The surging home-video industry reached $24 billion in 2004 and since then has leveled off in the $23–24 billion range, with the major studio-distributors consistently capturing the lion's share of that market in sell-through DVDs. In 2006, fully 45 percent of the studios' $42.6 billion in worldwide revenues mentioned above came from home video, and even top hits were routinely generating more revenue in DVD than in the domestic or foreign theatrical markets (Hollinger). This was most pronounced with CG effects-laden blockbusters like *Transformers* and *300*, huge box-office hits that saw even greater returns on DVD than in either the domestic or foreign theatrical market. Another interesting trend involves idiomatic hit comedies like *Wild Hogs*, *Knocked Up*, *Superbad*, and *Hairspray* that do not "travel well" in terms of foreign box office but did extremely well on DVD.

Most of the studios' DVD income is generated by current releases, although another crucial (and largely unanticipated) revenue source involved classic films and popular TV series, compelling the studios to make their entire libraries available on DVD. During the earlier VHS era, Disney was the only studio to exploit the extended shelf-life of its classic films. Indeed, Disney's climb from struggling mini-major to industry power in the 1980s was based primarily on the savvy repackaging of its library for home-video sale. The other studios followed suit in the DVD era, although Disney remains far ahead of the pack in the home entertainment market generally, including its revamped "straight-to-video" strategy. In 2007, the top 100 DVD releases included reissues of *Peter Pan* (1954) and *The Jungle Book* (1967), along with new direct-to-DVD films extending its classic Cinderella franchise and its recently launched High School Musical franchise, which has been a huge hit on both the Disney Channel and on DVD. The DVD revenues for these four Disney releases alone totaled $312 million.

The substantial returns from their TV and DVD pipelines have induced the studios to treat theatrical release as a "loss leader" in the commercial life span of their movies. In other words, Hollywood's major producer-distributors have developed a deficit-financing strategy whereby movies are expected to operate at a loss during theatrical release, ultimately recovering their production and marketing costs and turning a profit in the subsequent TV and home-video markets—and via the parent company's other media divisions as well, from books and records to videogames and theme park rides. The reasons for this deficit-financing strategy are altogether obvious. First, a movie's theatrical release and massive ad campaign establish its value in all other media markets. Second, TV licensing and DVD are far more profitable because the production and marketing costs—which ranged from $75 million to a quarter-billion dollars per film (more on this below)—are largely if not completely absorbed via theatrical revenues. Third, on a more abstract level, this strategy discourages competition, since film producers outside the conglomerate realm lack the financial leverage and ensured access to the marketplace enjoyed by the studios.

This deficit-financing strategy was facilitated by the conglomerates' broadcast and cable TV "pipelines"—for all but Sony, that is, which has been an outlier among the Big Six in its lack of significant TV holdings. This is not to say that the other five are structurally alike, and in fact each conglomerate's media-and-entertainment holdings outside the film and TV arena differ significantly. But the other five conglomerates do have similar profiles within the film-TV sector—including Time Warner, whose lack of a U.S. broadcast TV network is offset by its massive Turner Broadcasting division (whose acquisition was announced in 1995 within weeks of Disney's purchase of ABC), and also its development of HBO into the leading pay-cable network. TW has also kept pace with the other conglomerates in TV series production and distribution, another area in which Sony has lagged behind.

While the other conglomerates were acquiring media outlets, Sony has developed a very different strategy of media integration focusing on hardware-software synergy—i.e., on the coordination of its massive consumer electronics operation with U.S.-based content suppliers like CBS Records and Columbia Pictures. Sony has pursued this strategy not only in its filmed entertainment and consumer electronics divisions, but in its "computer entertainment" division as well. Sony is light years ahead of the other media conglomerates in the manufacture and sale of interactive games and game consoles, and it involves its three major divisions—Sony Pictures Entertainment, Sony Electronics, and Sony Computer Entertainment—in the development of entertainment franchises. Sony has tentatively pursued pipeline opportunities in recent years, most notably in a 2004 partnership with Comcast to acquire MGM/UA (Sorkin). This allied Sony with the top U.S. cable TV company (and a leading Internet service provider as well), while augmenting its film library and providing access to several dormant franchises—including James Bond, resulting in one of Columbia's top hits in 2006, *Casino Royale*. But Sony's overriding strategy continues to be the pursuit of hardware-software synergies, best evidenced by its 2007 introduction of Blu-ray, a high-definition (HD) DVD technology that Sony owns and controls, and that it hopes to establish as the worldwide standard for the "next generation" home video system (Hall; Fritz). In bucking the cooperative spirit of DVD's initial launch in 1997, Sony was willing to risk the kind of format war (with arch-rival Toshiba) that plagued the VCR's introduction in the late 1970s—a war that Sony lost. Sony seems to have prevailed, although it remains to be seen whether hi-def DVD displaces the current system. If and when that occurs, Sony's control of home video technology—and the license fees it collects for all discs and players sold—will help offset its lack of TV pipelines and will bring this perennial outlier into a closer rapport with the other media conglomerates.

hollywood filmmaking in the new millennium

Despite its outlier status and singular integration strategy, Sony's operations within the feature filmmaking realm have been quite consistent with the rest of the Big Six. Indeed, a key development in the new millennium has been the increasing uniformity of the conglomerates' filmmaking operations, particularly in terms of the major studios' intensified blockbuster efforts and the annexation of the independent film sector by the conglomerate's so-called indie divisions. The former is in many ways more important due to the sheer commercial success of the movie-driven global entertainment franchises. With each passing year since the late 1990s the studios' compulsive pursuit of franchise-spawning blockbusters has become more acute—and more successful—as the film industry at large has become more blatantly hit-driven on a global scale, and more intently focused on the coordination of the domestic, foreign, and home-entertainment markets. Meanwhile, the industry powers responded to the surging independent film movement of the 1990s by strategically expanding their own filmmaking operations in that arena, either by acquiring successful independents or launching subsidiaries geared to art films, imports, and other "specialty" productions.

Consequently Hollywood filmmaking by the early 2000s was increasingly geared to three distinct industry sectors wherein three different classes of film producer were creating three very different classes of product. The top tier, so to speak, comprises Hollywood's six traditional major studios—Warner Bros., Disney, Paramount, 20th Century Fox, Universal, and Columbia—whose filmmaking operations are closely tied to (and determined by) the structure and strategies of the parent conglomerate. The prime objective of these studios is the production of franchise-spawning blockbusters budgeted in the $100–$250 million range that are targeted at the global entertainment marketplace and are designed to operate synergistically with the parent company's other entertainment-related divisions. The next tier includes the conglomerate-owned film subsidiaries—the indie and specialty divisions like Fox Searchlight, Focus Features, and Sony Pictures Classics that produce more modestly budgeted films in the $30 million to $50 million range for more specialized and discriminating audiences. The bottom tier includes the truly independent producer-distributors, literally hundreds of companies that supply over half of all theatrical releases, usually budgeted in the $5 million to $10 million range (often far less), and that compete for a pitifully small share of the motion picture marketplace, due largely to the proliferation of the conglomerate-owned film subsidiaries.

To get a sense of the impact of these indie subsidiaries on contemporary independent American film, consider the transformation—and fundamental segregation—of that industry sector over the past decade (as gleaned from data provided by the MPA and Nash Information Services).

In 1995, the six major studios captured 80 percent of the U.S. theatrical market and the conglomerate-owned subsidiaries captured another 11 percent, most of it going to Disney's Miramax and Time Warner's New Line, two recent acquisitions still operating with contractually assured autonomy. The only other active subsidiaries at the time were Sony Pictures Classics and New Line's art-film subsidiary Fine Line, and the total indie subsidiary output was 79 films, roughly half that of the majors. Contrast that with 2005, when the six conglomerate-owned majors released 133 films while their 14 indie subsidiaries released 126 films, and together they captured over 95 percent of the theatrical market. Meanwhile, the number of independent releases grew from some 240 per year in the 1990s to well over 300 (and over 400 in both 2006 and 2007). The number of independent distributors grew from a few dozen in 1995 to well over a hundred a decade later, nearly half of which (64 of 138 companies) released only a single film. That year the domestic box office totaled $8.84 billion and the top two films alone—the latest Star Wars and Harry Potter installments—captured 7 percent of the market. In other words, as is typical of millennial Hollywood, the top two studio blockbusters alone generated more box office in 2005 than all of the 300-plus independent films combined. This disparity is even more severe in ancillary markets. Films produced by the conglomerate-owned studios are assured of domestic theatrical release and an attendant marketing campaign, and they are assured of access to subsequent markets as well. Most of the 300–400 independent films per year, conversely, were released with little or no marketing leverage and thus with meager prospects after theatrical release.

The deepening class divisions and class structure of contemporary Hollywood became remarkably acute by 2007. In sheer economic terms that was the movie industry's best year ever, with the conglomerate-owned companies enjoying record revenues in both the domestic and worldwide theatrical markets ($9.63 billion and $26.7 billion, respectively), while home video and TV provided the lion's share of their film-related profits. Business for the major studios was particularly strong, as all six surpassed $1 billion in domestic box-office revenues for the first time ever—which was an all-time record for four of them (McClintock, "Six"; McNary, "Foreign"). All of the majors released 20–25 films in 2007 with the notable exception of Warner Bros., which released 33, while Time Warner minimajor New Line released 14 (prior to its demise in early 2008, which will be discussed below). The average domestic box-office gross per release for the six major studios was $52.5 million, although averages mean relatively little in a sector that relies so heavily on "tentpole" hits—i.e., the top two or three runaway hits that generate most of a studio's revenues and thus prop up the entire studio operation. Remarkably enough, the top three releases for all six major studios (and New Line) returned roughly one-half of their domestic box-office revenues. The number-one release in each case was a franchise blockbuster that generated roughly one-fifth of the studio's total domestic revenues. The majors all dabbled in the mid-range and indie markets via pickups or special deals with top talent and leading independent producers, as with Paramount's *Sweeney Todd*, Warner's *Michael Clayton*, and Disney's *Apocalypto*, but their in-house production efforts focused primarily on high-cost, high-stakes franchise blockbusters.

While the major Hollywood powers enjoyed unprecedented prosperity in 2007, the true independents responsible for some 60 percent of all releases suffered their worst year ever due to over-production and intense competition from the conglomerate-owned indie divisions. Out of some 130 independent distributors in 2007, only four—Lionsgate, MGM, the Weinstein Company, and Goldwyn—enjoyed any real success at the box office, with nearly two-thirds of their releases (45 of 71) grossing at least $1 million. The eight other prominent independents, including Freestyle, ThinkFilm, Magnolia, and Roadside Attractions, were far less successful; in fact three-quarters of their releases (80 of 108) failed to return even $250,000 at the box office. A few independents operated successfully in small but relatively secure markets—IMAX, for instance, as well as Eros and Yash Raj, which release Indian films in the U.S.—while the other 115 or so companies failed to generate any significant business at all.

The most successful independent in 2007 was Lionsgate, which enjoyed its best year ever in terms of domestic box office ($372 million on 22 releases) and market share (3.9 percent). Currently the last of a vanishing breed of independent "mini-major," Lionsgate is in a class by itself in contemporary Hollywood. The studio is on a par with the majors in terms of output and market reach, but astute enough to eschew the mega-budget realm; and is at the same time more productive, eclectic, and financially viable than the conglomerate-owned indie divisions. It has steadily climbed to the top of the independent heap since 2000, when (as Lions Gate) its total gross was just $30 million and its market share 0.4 percent—well behind indies like USA Films and Artisan that were later absorbed by the conglomerates or fell by the wayside. In 2007, 17 of its films grossed over $20 million domestically, and its diverse release slate included franchise horror films (*Saw IV*, *Hostel II*), African-American comedies (*Why Did I Get Married*, *Daddy's Little Girls*), a Michael Moore documentary (*Sicko*), a martial arts film (*War*), an ambitious star-laden Western (*3:10 to Yuma*), a teen comedy (*Good Luck Chuck*), a CG animated film (*Happily N'Ever After*), and a live-action film based on a toy line and videogame (*Bratz*). In a clear indication of its distribution prowess, these ten films grossed $330 million domestically, nearly $150 million overseas, and $250 million on DVD. Lionsgate released only one "art film" in 2007, *Away from Her*, which was a critical if not a commercial hit, earning Oscar nominations for Julie Christie's performance and writer-director Sarah Polley's screenplay.

The conglomerate-owned indie-film sector was dominated by eight subsidiaries in 2007—Fox Searchlight, Focus Features (NBC Universal's indie division), Miramax (post-Weinstein, still a Disney company), Paramount Vantage, Sony Pictures Classics, Sony Screen Gems, Warner Independent, and another TW subsidiary, Picturehouse—which together released 83 films and averaged just under $10 million per release in domestic box-office returns. As a rule, these companies handled domestic distribution themselves while relying on their major studio counterpart for international distribution and on their parent company's home entertainment arm for DVD release. This complicates matters considerably regarding their relative autonomy within the conglomerates' filmed entertainment divisions—thus the off-hand reference to these companies as "the Dependents"—although the upside of conglomerate ownership in terms of production funding and marketing muscle apparently outweighs these constraints. Moreover, the role of top executives like James Schamus at Focus and Tom Bernard and Michael Barker at Sony Classics is to protect the interests and autonomy of their production operations and ensure the creative freedom of top filmmaking talent.

In this sense the conglomerate-owned subsidiaries have provided a safe haven for Hollywood's indie auteurs, and particularly for established writer-directors who are firmly ensconced in the indie-division sector—a privileged class that includes Joel and Ethan Coen, Paul Thomas Anderson, Pedro Almodóvar, Alexander Payne, Ang Lee, Wes Anderson, David O. Russell, Gus Van Sant, and Todd Haynes. Sustaining a filmmaking lineage dating back to the international art cinema of the 1960s and the Hollywood renaissance of the 1970s, these indie auteurs have managed to make films on their own terms thanks to their own distinctive talents, the support of indie-division executives and independent producers like Scott Rudin and Steven Soderbergh, and a conglomerate-era industrial machine that effectively ensures these filmmakers creative freedom (and continued employment) as long as they control costs and satisfy their ardent but highly discerning audiences. Thus the conglomerates' indie divisions are subject to their own brand of tensions between art and commerce, and are valued for the prestige and critical cache they provide the parent company, as well as the revenues.

These tensions were never more pronounced than in 2007, when the indie divisions reversed a decidedly subpar year with a succession of holiday season hits, notably *No Country for Old Men*, *There Will Be Blood*, *Juno*, and *Atonement*. This late-year surge was scarcely surprising, given the tendency to gear the release of quality indie films to both the holiday season and the upcoming awards. The strategy paid off handsomely in 2007, as these and other indie-division hits received an unprecedented number of Academy Award nominations in December that further enhanced their market value. Prospects improved even more on Oscar night in late February, when the voting members of the Academy displayed a pronounced bias against the major studios and in favor of the conglomerate-owned indies. "The Oscars have become the Independent Spirit Awards on a bigger budget," *Newsweek* critic David Ansen aptly observed in a preview of the event (Ansen). As Ansen anticipated (he correctly predicted all eight of the top awards), the indie subsidiaries thoroughly trounced their major studio counterparts across the board. In the high-profile top categories—best picture, director, actor, actress, supporting actor and actress, original and adapted screenplay—indie-division films won seven of eight awards, four of which went to *No Country For Old Men*. The trend extended to the craft categories (cinematography, editing, sound, etc.), where the major studios' vastly higher budgets invariably translate into superior production values if not better films. But here too the indies dominated, with 28 of 46 major craft nominations and six of ten Oscar wins.

The only 2007 studio release to receive significant Oscar attention was Warner Bros.' *Michael Clayton* (with seven nominations and one win), although it was scarcely a major studio film. Independently financed and produced, *Michael Clayton* was later picked up for distribution by Warner due in part to the studio's long-standing relationship with the film's co-executive producers George Clooney (who also starred) and Steven Soderbergh. *Michael Clayton* marked the directorial debut of writer Tony Gilroy, who previously scripted the Jason Bourne series for Universal, and it was budgeted at a relatively modest $21 million, which by Gilroy's estimate was one-fourth of what it would have cost a major studio. "I also got final cut," he told *Variety*. "I wouldn't have gotten that on a studio picture." *Michael Clayton*'s success won Gilroy a writer-director assignment on a big-budget thriller at Universal—where he certainly will not get final cut, nor will he enjoy the degree of creative control he had on *Michael Clayton* (Frankel).

The "Oscar snub" of the major studios' 2007 films was big news both inside and outside the industry, especially in light of the blockbuster hits that propelled Hollywood to its best box-office year ever. One could argue that the voting members of the Academy were collectively in denial regarding the economic realities of the industry, although the fact is that the year's box-office behemoths, topped by new installments of the Spider-Man, Shrek, Harry Potter, and Pirates of the Caribbean series along with the "instant franchise" blockbuster, *Transformers*, scarcely warranted recognition for their artistry—or even their technical merits, for that matter, considering the routine rebooting of their CG effects menus. Indeed, the Academy seemed to share with the critical community the view that the major studios were in an altogether different business than their indie-subsidiary counterparts, and one that seems increasingly indifferent to quality filmmaking by traditional Hollywood standards.

franchise blockbusters: the rules of the game

The business of the major studios is making and selling franchise-sustaining blockbuster hits—i.e., calculated megafilms designed to sustain a product line of similar films and an ever-expanding array of related entertainment products, all of which benefit the parent conglomerates' various media-and-entertainment divisions. Hollywood has been a hit-driven industry from day one, of course, and since the postwar era it has been increasingly wed to a blockbuster ethos. The franchise mentality has intensified during the conglomerate era, and in the new millennium it has gone into another register altogether due to the combined effects of digitization and media convergence, which have significantly impacted both production and formal-aesthetic protocols, and due also to the effects of globalization as Hollywood fashions its top films for a worldwide marketplace.

Millennial Hollywood is dominated by some two-dozen active franchises, plus another dozen or so single-film franchises—most notably Pixar's computer-animated films (*Monsters Inc.*, 2001; *Finding Nemo*, 2003; *The Incredibles*, 2004; *Cars*, 2006; *Ratatouille*, 2007). In fact Pixar's remarkable run of animated hits, along with its complex, highly conflicted relationship with Disney, well indicate the changing stakes of blockbuster filmmaking in the conglomerate-controlled, franchise-obsessed, CG-driven era. Pixar began as the computer imaging division of Lucasfilm before breaking away in the 1980s, and after struggling to survive was bought by Apple co-founder Steve Jobs in 1986 for a mere $10 million (Price). Jobs struck a three-picture deal with Disney in the early 1990s when the studio was surging to industry dominance via huge animated hits like *Beauty and the Beast* (1991), *Aladdin* (1993), and *The Lion King* (1994). Disney's animation division was run by Jeffrey Katzenberg, a strong proponent of traditional hand-drawn, cel-based animation, and put little stock in Pixar's efforts to develop a computer-generated 3-D format. All that changed when Pixar's debut feature, *Toy Story*, became a major hit in 1995, one year after Katzenberg left Disney to create DreamWorks with Steven Spielberg and David Geffen. Disney's animation division then began a rapid decline while Pixar hit its stride with *A Bug's Life* (1998) and *Toy Story 2* (1999), which like *Toy Story* were directed by Pixar's resident visionary John Lasseter, who thereafter supervised creative operations on all of its films. Thus in a paradigm shift of truly historic proportions, Pixar supplanted Disney (which financed and distributed its films) as Hollywood's top animation studio.

In the early 2000s, the Pixar-Disney alliance was in serious turmoil due to deal terms that, in Pixar's view, unreasonably favored Disney, and due also to a clash of cultures between the companies and a clash of personalities between Jobs and Disney CEO Michael Eisner. After Eisner's departure in 2005, his successor Bob Iger renegotiated the deal, resulting in Disney's purchase of Pixar in 2006 for $7.4 billion (Britt). But despite all the turmoil, the alliance flourished for two main reasons: first, Disney had decades of experience handling precisely the kind of G-rated, family-targeted animated features that Pixar produced; and second, Disney was singularly adept not only at marketing Pixar's films but transforming them into multi-purpose entertainment franchises far beyond what Pixar could have done on its own. Consider the franchising of *Cars*, a solid hit released in June 2006 with combined theatrical and DVD revenues of over $700 million, which in two years generated an astonishing $5 billion in the sale of related retail products. Current plans to expand the franchise include a nationwide ice-skating tour, theme-park attractions in Disney's global chain of parks and resorts, and perhaps most importantly, the 2012 release of *Cars 2*, with a plot devised specifically for the international marketplace (Barnes). This reverses a long-standing Pixar prohibition against sequels, which had been an ongoing sore spot with Disney. But it comes as no surprise in light of the growing competition in the computer-animation realm as well as the indisputable economic logic of series production.

What Pixar has had to recognize is that in today's Hollywood a blockbuster series is the consummate renewable resource—a product line that can be strategically regenerated to sustain and actually increase its yield. This marks an important change from the 1980s and 1990s, when movie sequels and series invariably meant steadily diminishing financial returns. Now series installments routinely outperform their predecessors, a trend that has intensified along with the expanding global marketplace and the crucial added value of DVD returns. The trend has been increasingly pronounced since 1999 and the enormous success of *The Matrix* and the rejuvenated Star Wars series (after a 16-year hiatus). Since then, six franchises have come to comprise fully one-half of the top 50 all-time worldwide box-office hits while racking up billions in cumulative revenues, and in each case the strategic development of the series itself along with the larger industry forces (globalization, digitization, et al.) have created entertainment systems that have steadily expanded into veritable sub-industries unto themselves. In terms of box-office revenues alone, Hollywood's elite half-dozen franchises have generated the following returns as of 2007:

Franchise	*worldwide box-office revenues*
Star Wars redux (1999, 2002, 2005)	$2.4 billion
Harry Potter (2001, 2002, 2004, 2005, 2007)	$4.5 billion
Lord of the Rings (2001, 2002, 2003)	$2.9 billion
Shrek (2001, 2004, 2007)	$2.2 billion
Spider-Man (2002, 2004, 2007)	$2.5 billion
Pirates of the Caribbean (2003, 2006, 2007)	$2.7 billion

One reason for the studios' record box-office in 2007 was the fact that four of these top franchises released new installments, all of which surpassed $1 billion in theatrical and DVD revenues within a year of release.

Moreover, three of these films—the Shrek, Spider-Man, and Pirates installments—were the strongest commercial hits to date for their respective franchises in terms of worldwide theatrical and DVD returns, despite being the weakest to date in terms of critical response. *Transformers* surpassed the billion-dollar mark as well in 2007, while another seven films cleared a half-billion dollars in combined box-office and DVD revenues, including new installments of the James Bond, Jason Bourne, and Die Hard series. Most of these second-tier franchise films featured adult protagonists and were targeted toward somewhat more discerning and mature audiences than the top performers, interestingly enough. And like the Mission: Impossible and reactivated Superman and Batman cycles in 2006, the Bourne, Bond, and Die Hard films were singled out by critics for such antiquated qualities as character development and human drama—as well as their spectacular CG effects and action sequences, which are now the sine qua non of blockbuster hit films.

While computer effects and action are essential to conglomerate-era blockbusters, they are scarcely the only rules that apply. The film industry's development in the early twenty-first century has been fundamentally wed to a new breed of blockbusters whose narrative, stylistic, technological, and industrial conventions have coalesced into a veritable set of rules governing the creation and marketing of Hollywood's "major motion pictures." These rules include the following:

- The film should exploit or expand an established entertainment franchise, which might exist initially in any number of forms—a classic children's story, a traditional fairy tale, a comic book or graphic novel, a TV series, even a theme park ride or a toy line.
- Regardless of its original form, the narrative source should provide not only a story property but also a piece of intellectual property whose copyright can be owned or controlled by the studio (or its parent company).
- The story should be amenable to continuation, with the film-to-film story line employing serial qualities that center on its principal character(s) rather than some external plot.
- The long-term story line should focus on an individual central protagonist.
- The protagonist should be male.
- The male protagonist should be an adolescent or an utterly naïve man-child.
- The protagonist should be a loner, either by choice or by circumstances, but one who is also forced by circumstances to perform some (preferably heroic) social function.
- The protagonist in the course of each film (and regardless of his heroic credentials) should develop from a relatively weak, ineffectual, or

compromised character into one who seizes the initiative and (re)asserts his heroic role.

- The hero should inhabit a Manichean universe of light and dark, good and evil, with the pervasive forces of evil embodied in one or more powerful antagonists.
- The hero should in some way mirror the antagonist(s)—perhaps via an alter-ego or an assumed identity—and thus he should confront both an external struggle against evil and also an internal struggle against his own "darker side."
- The story should provide dazzling computer graphics and effects-driven action scenes at regular intervals that are carefully calculated in terms of their frequency, intensity, and adaptability to other digital media platforms.
- The action scenes should include violent, even deadly clashes, but the violence should be sufficiently stylized and artificial to ensure a PG or PG-13 rating.
- The film should build to a climactic confrontation and a "happy ending" in which the hero prevails—but not to a degree that eliminates the prospect for sequels.
- The film also should include a "love story" as a secondary plot line, but one that is strictly non-carnal, and one that is not fully resolved at film's end.
- The story should take place in a world that is internally coherent but highly complex, and that is by design too expansive to be contained within a single film—and thus solicits further elaboration in subsequent films and in other media forms as well.
- This principle of further elaboration pertains to story materials as well, including software and effects, which should be designed for use in other media iterations.
- The monstrous antagonist and various secondary characters should have bizarre and fantastic qualities that can be enhanced via digital effects and readily exploited in subsequent (licensed) incarnations in other media.
- A successful franchise might secure stardom for its principal character(s), but top stars should not be cast in continuing roles in order to control costs, minimize creative interference, and encourage long-term participation.
- This same principle applies to filmmaking talent—particularly directors with indie-film credentials whose stature might be used to market the film.
- Coherent plotting and engaging characterization are important aspects of individual franchise films, but far less so than in "one-off" (self-standing, non-series) films. In franchise filmmaking, the primary concerns are, paradoxically, the integrity of the core narrative and its viability for expansion into an intertextual, transmedia system.

Hollywood's top franchises follow these rules with remarkable fidelity, to the point of comprising a veritable genre unto themselves. Other franchises follow many (if not most) of these rules as well, but we should note a number of important distinctions due to factors such as source material, the primary market and target audience, and the nature and range of transmedia reiterations. One key distinction, as indicated above, involves the age and relative sophistication of the protagonist—and by extension the intended audience. From Jason Bourne to the rejuvenated Bond and Batman series, the second-tier franchises clearly limit their audience reach and commercial appeal by investing in more complex character development and dramatic conflict—not only within individual series installments but through the series at large. Thus the individual films tend to be more internally coherent and character driven—more classical, if you will—and less likely to be designed with a videogame or a theme park ride in mind. The films are often more complex thematically and politically as well, although they invariably default to a reductive celebration of rugged individualism, technical ingenuity, and masculine superiority. We might also note the obvious ties to Hollywood's hardboiled detective and rogue-cop traditions in the Bourne, Bond, Mission: Impossible, and Die Hard franchises, among others. From Sam Spade to Jason Bourne, Hollywood has celebrated the heroic loner at odds with both the outlaw element and the authorities (including his superiors), the accomplished killer with his own moral code whose fiercest challenges often come from the institutional and political machinery that created him.

The superhero and fantasy franchises geared to younger and less sophisticated audiences tend to portray society generally in a more positive light and to see both the world and its inhabitants in simple (if not simplistic) binaries of light and dark, good and evil. Disorder in these worlds is invariably the result of human volition, of evil-doers who abuse or misuse power, and the restoration of order can only be attained through the intervention of the superhero—who also has his dark side to deal with. This is all quite predictable and formulaic, of course, and thus the primary selling point of each series installment tends to involve the satisfaction of viewer expectations by reproducing the "original" experience on the one hand, and enhancing that experience via entertaining, hyper-destructive villains and improved CG effects on the other. Along with these "production values," the marketing of the film and its integration with the key ancillary versions of the story (computer games, print or TV series, etc.) are crucial to the ongoing success and currency of the franchise.

the case of spider-man

The conglomerate's major studios and their related entertainment divisions—home video, gaming, print and music publishing, licensing and merchandising, and so on—have refined this process to a remarkable degree. Consider Spider-Man, a quintessential conglomerate-era media franchise controlled by Sony (via an ongoing licensing deal with Marvel Comics) whose current configuration was propelled by the 2002 block-buster movie hit, *Spider-Man*, produced by Sony-owned Columbia Pictures, which has become a multi-billion-dollar movie series and a crucial compo-nent of Sony's global media-and-technology operations, while both Sony and Marvel continue to expand the franchise in an array of media formats (Graser). The current film cycle was of course pre-sold by countless itera-tions in various media dating back to the origination of Spider-Man by Marvel Comics' Stan Lee in 1962. Those myriad versions did not include a live-action Hollywood film, however, which meant that Sony and Columbia could effectively re-originate the story, tailoring it to current industry conditions and to their own interests—a process that would become more focused and acute as the franchise evolved.

The series-spawning film was a major breakthrough for Sony because, in the words of chairman John Calley prior to its release, "This company has always suffered from not being able to market a franchise film" (Grover). *Spider-Man* changed that, firmly establishing the Sony franchise in the "popular imagination" while generating $822 million in worldwide box-office revenues. Much of the film's $140 million budget was spent on its visual design and special effects, conceived and realized by literally hun-dreds of artists and technicians under the supervision of John Dykstra. The CG effects were truly spectacular and, like the "bullet-time" technique in *The Matrix*, set new standards for CG rendering of action and airborne scenes. *Spider-Man* made stars of both Tobey Maguire and director Sam Raimi, whose prior work had been in the indie-film realm—with Raimi's success reinforcing the growing trend (also spurred by *The Matrix*) of indie directors taking on blockbuster franchises. The story itself is a straightfor-ward re-telling of the Spider-Man origin myth: high-school nerd Peter Parker is bitten by a radio-active spider, giving him super-human powers, and the murder of his uncle and father-figure Ben (Cliff Robertson) com-pels him to become a vigilante superhero in a crime-ridden modern metropolis. The antagonist is a familiar comic-book foe, the Green Goblin (Willem Dafoe), the villainous alter-ego of entrepreneur Norman Osborn who turns "mad scientist" when his military weapons project goes awry, and who also happens to be the father of Peter's best friend Harry (James Franco). Both boys are smitten with classmate Mary Jane (Kirsten Dunst), who provides the ongoing love interest for a superhero hopelessly torn between love and duty. The story culminates in Peter's full assumption of his Spider-Man role in a climactic battle with the Green Goblin, whose death wins the enmity of son Harry, and in an epilogue Peter spurns Mary Jane's affections due to his newfound (and troublesome) role as modern superhero.

These open-ended storylines provided the impetus for *Spider-Man 2*, in which the angst-ridden superhero battles Harry (transformed into the New Goblin) and another familiar Marvel foe, Doctor Octopus (Alfred Molina), a quasi-sympathetic mad scientist in the mold of Harry's father. Peter continues to struggle with his role and identity as Spider-Man, and also with his affections for the equally long-suffering Mary Jane. The film was critically well received despite its by-the-numbers plotting and characterization, although like its predecessor, *Spider-Man 2* failed to garner even an Oscar nomination in any of the major categories (best picture, director, actor, screenplay, etc.). But the film clearly delivered in terms of action and spectacle, with the increased budget—reportedly in the $250 million range including marketing and distribution costs—upping the ante in terms of visual effects and earning the series its only Academy Award to date, which went to CG wizard John Dykstra, aptly enough (who left the series after this second installment). *Spider-Man 2* fell just short of the first installment at the box office ($784 million worldwide) but did better business on DVD—including a record 6 million units sold in its first day on the market. Sony also was more aggressive in exploiting the licensing potential of the franchise, particularly in terms of videogames, and it effectively used the films to exploit its own computer-entertainment and consumer-electronics endeavors. Most significant here was Sony's decision to "bundle" both the film and the videogame with its new PlayStation2(PS2) system, helping it become the best-selling game console in 2005 (Zaun).

Sony intensified those efforts with *Spider-Man 3*, an awesome feat of marketing and media synergy and a solid commercial success, despite its relatively weak critical reception (only 44 percent positive reviews by top critics, according to Rotten Tomatoes.com). It was the top box-office hit in the U.S. in 2007, grossing $336 million, with foreign revenues of $554 million. DVD income quickly surpassed $100 million, thus yielding a theatrical and home-video total of over one billion dollars in 2007 alone. The DVD take would have been higher, but Sony opted to bundle an HD version of the film with both its new high-definition PS3 game console and its Blu-ray DVD player. The film's release involved a global marketing campaign, starting in April with a world premiere in Tokyo, followed by a European debut in London and a U.S. premiere at the New York Film Festival (Schilling). The film "went wide" on a record 4,253 screens in the U.S. on May 1, and within a week was playing in 177 territories worldwide. The film set records both in the U.S. and worldwide in its opening weekend, generating an astounding $382 million globally—thus realizing 40 percent of its entire box-office take in the first three days of release. The *Spider-Man 3* videogame was released on May 4, with multiple game developers issuing literally dozens of different versions of the story/game on Sony's PS3, Microsoft's

Xbox 360, Nintendo's Wii and DS systems among others (Mohr). The film's DVD release was equally strategic in terms of Sony's concurrent Blu-ray campaign, further enhancing the franchise's visibility and underlining its enormous value as a marketing tool (Ault).

While Sony's marketing campaign for *Spider-Man 3* was clearly a success, the movie itself is a confounding, hyper-active muddle. Like its ensemble of split-personality characters, *Spider-Man 3* manifests a dual identity as both a feature film and a big-screen videogame, and the results are most unsatisfactory in terms of narrative coherence and character development. This may explain the film's poor critical reception, and in fact many of the critics who reacted favorably to *Spider-Man 3* treated it as something other than a movie—primarily as a playful CG spectacle geared to teens and gamers, or as a purposefully extravagant promo for Sony's next-generation digital wares. The story sets Peter/Spider-Man against Harry/New Goblin (who veers in this installment from foe to friend to foe to friend before his climactic demise to save Spider-Man), along with Flint Marko/Sandman (Thomas Haden Church) and Eddie Brock/Venom (Topher Grace). What's more, an extraterrestrial "symbiote" crashes to earth and inexplicably attaches itself to our hero, creating a dark side for both Parker and Spider-Man. Thus the middle portion of the story focuses on a black-suited Spider-Man who rejects the social and moral code of the "real" Spider-Man, and also an obnoxious version of Peter modeled quite amusingly after John Travolta's character in *Saturday Night Fever* (1977)—a reference that is likely lost on the film's target audience. The film careens wildly from one plot line to another, all of which ultimately collide in a spectacular 13½ minute finale. This is the sixth CG-driven action scene in the film, which recur like clockwork—quite literally, at intervals of 16:15, 16:15, 16:30, 17:00, 19:00, and 29:00 in the course of the film. All told, fully 33:00 of the film's running time of 2:15:00 is devoted to action scenes of one sort or another, including the "birth scenes" of both Sandman and Venom.

The weakness of the story undoubtedly contributed to *Spider-Man 3*'s fast fade at the box office, although the film did well enough to join the billion-dollar club in 2007 along with two other lackluster franchise films, the new Shrek and Pirates of the Caribbean installments. This would appear to be Conglomerate Hollywood's version of Gresham's Law, as inferior franchise films succeed their quality predecessors in the studios' inevitable efforts to standardize product, minimize risk, and maximize revenues. Indeed, the studios have all but eliminated financial risk in the high-stakes arena of blockbuster filmmaking thanks to their increasingly adept facility for franchise formulation, their parent companies' collective control of the crucial U.S. marketplace and their overall domination of global markets as well, and an apparently insatiable worldwide appetite for Hollywood-engineered entertainment.

coda: time warner, new line, and *the hobbit*

In December 2007, as the major studios' record revenues were being tallied and the indie division hits were taking off, a long-running, high-stakes industry dispute was finally resolved—with consequences that speak volumes about the current state of the industry and thus provide an illuminating postscript to our assessment of millennial Hollywood. The dispute itself involved filmmaker Peter Jackson and New Line CEO Robert Shaye, whose three-year legal wrangle had effectively stalled the potent Lord of the Rings franchise—a matter of considerable concern to Time Warner, which also faced the impending conclusion of its Harry Potter franchise. Warner Bros. plans to extend the Potter series by splitting its adaptation of J.K. Rowling's seventh and final Potter novel into two films, inspired by New Line's similar plan to extend the Rings franchise via a two-film adaptation of *The Hobbit*, J.R.R. Tolkien's fictional precursor to his Rings saga (Garrett). But those plans were on hold due to the Jackson–Shaye squabble with its incessant legal proceedings, which raised some provocative questions about corporate authorship, intellectual property, and the implicit connections between a film franchise and its purported auteur.

Like most modern franchises, The Lord of the Rings has a long, complex history—in this case dating back to the Tolkien novels themselves (written in the 1940s and published in the 1950s) and extending through multiple screen versions. Jackson initiated the current cycle as an individual film at Miramax in the mid-1990s, but as the size, scope, and development costs increased, the Weinsteins began looking for a partner or perhaps a buyer. The prospects included New Line, which like Miramax was a conglomerate-owned, quasi-independent mini-major that had been producing increasingly ambitious and expensive features to compete with the major studios; and like Miramax, New Line was struggling to keep pace. In 1998 Bob Shaye, an inveterate risk-taker since founding New Line in the 1960s, decided to take on the entire production. It was Shaye's idea to do the Rings films as a trilogy, like Tolkien's novels, and to produce them simultaneously to keep the total cost of Jackson's ambitious enterprise in the $300 million range. Jackson and his key collaborator (and wife) Fran Walsh produced out of their own facilities in New Zealand, which were substantially expanded to accommodate the project. Thus Shaye was staking New Line's future on an untried three-film franchise and the talents of a relatively obscure independent filmmaker working halfway around the world. The gamble paid off, of course, as the Rings trilogy emerged as a model franchise for the global, digital age. Released in consecutive holiday seasons in 2002, 2003, and 2004, the series returned global box-office revenues of $868.6 million, $926.3 million, and $1.13 billion, respectively, with the final installment reaching the number-two all-time global hit behind *Titanic* (1997), and sweeping the Oscars in early 2004 with a record 11 wins (Kristin Thompson).

In the wake of that third mega-hit, however, Shaye made the fatal mistake of feuding with Jackson over his profit participation deal and derailing the franchise. When Shaye inexplicably refused to submit to an audit in early 2005, Jackson abandoned work on *The Hobbit* and sued New Line (Waxman, "Identity Crisis"). Finally in December 2007 after two and a half years of increasingly public acrimony, which eventually reached the executive offices at Time Warner, the lawsuit was settled (for undisclosed terms) and *The Hobbit* films were green-lighted with Jackson and Fran Walsh attached as Executive Producers for a $40 million fee (Fleming). Jackson was not available to direct, significantly enough, due to his collaboration with Steven Spielberg on *Tintin*, a multi-film, digital-cinema project in Jackson's WETA Digital plant in New Zealand, which thanks to New Line and the Rings films had displaced LucasFilm and ILM as the world's foremost digital facilities. But despite Jackson and Walsh's other obligations and their relegation to executive producer status on *The Hobbit*, their manager assured *Variety* that "the films will be made with the same level of quality as if they were writing and directing" (Halbfinger). That preposterous claim underscored Jackson's status as a name-brand franchise auteur, although it was scarcely supported by the quality of Jackson's most recent film, the ponderous *King Kong* (2005), nor by the fact that Sam Raimi was being touted as a possible director for the Hobbit films.

The tenor of the director search changed, however, when Guillermo del Toro emerged as a serious candidate. The news hit the national press in February 2008 within days of the Academy Awards, as *No Country for Old Men* and *There Will Be Blood* were reasserting the primacy of American independent film and as the Coens and Paul Thomas Anderson were being heralded as exemplary indie auteurs. Del Toro himself had enjoyed similar praise a year earlier, when *Pan's Labyrinth* (*El laberinto del fauno*, 2006), released in the U.S. by the Time Warner indie subsidiary Picturehouse, was lighting up the independent circuit. Written and directed by del Toro, *Pan's Labyrinth* was a brilliant amalgam of fantasy horror, historical drama, and political morality play that won widespread acclaim and multiple Oscars, and whose $37.6 million gross made it the most successful Spanish language film in U.S. box-office history. The film also put the Mexican-born del Toro on the map as an indie auteur, although like Raimi and Jackson he had already made a name for himself in the independent cult-horror realm with films like *Cronos* (1993) and *Mimic* (1997). But del Toro had major studio experience as well, most notably as writer-director of the two *Hellboy* films (2004 and 2008) and as a creative force behind the franchise's expansion into video games and animated TV series.

The Hobbit films promised to put del Toro in another league altogether, of course, and he readily seized the opportunity. While a *Variety* headline gushed "Oscar directors shun studio shackles," del Toro was negotiating a deal that would shackle him to a studio for the next four years—although not to Bob Shaye at New Line (Frankel). In a curious irony, del Toro's negotiation of the Hobbit deal directly paralleled a massive overhaul of Time Warner's filmmaking operations. In February 2008, as serious negotiations with del Toro got underway, Time Warner announced its decision to "merge" New Line with Warner Bros.—meaning the New Line brand would persist while most of its 600 employees, including Shaye, were fired. The del Toro–Hobbit deal closed in late April, and then just two weeks later TW announced that it was closing down Picturehouse and Warner Independent (Hayes and McNary, "New Line," "Picturehouse").

Del Toro was circumspect about these developments, focusing instead on his relocation to New Zealand, where he planned to work closely with Jackson and Walsh on the Hobbit films, scheduled for release in 2011 and 2012. Despite his distance from the "front office," however, the Warner-controlled New Line is likely to cut del Toro far less slack than Jackson enjoyed under Shaye. And although del Toro will report to an executive at New Line, he ultimately will be dealing with Time Warner CEO Jeff Bewkes and Warner Bros. president Alan Horn, who now control New Line and its leading asset, the Rings franchise, and who jointly decided to dismiss not only Shaye but also Bob Berney, the head of Picturehouse, who had been del Toro's chief ally on *Pan's Labyrinth*.

The Time Warner restructuring caught the industry off-guard but was scarcely surprising in the larger scheme of things. "The complete withdrawal of Time Warner from the increasingly dicey specialty game represents a significant moment in filmdom," wrote *Variety*'s Dade Hayes and Dave McNary, suggesting that it made little sense to risk its heavy output of innovative films when franchise blockbusters had become such a safe bet—especially for Time Warner, which got into the indie-specialty division game relatively late and was doing so well with its franchise blockbusters (Hayes and McNary, "Picturehouse"). Responding to the restructuring, the *Los Angeles Times*' Patrick Goldstein aptly described Warner Bros. as "totally clueless about the independent film business" but unmatched in the franchise arena: "Warner is Hollywood's version of an ad agency—it markets tentpole brands such as 'Batman,' 'Superman' and 'Ocean's Thirteen'—no studio has managed a franchise better than the way Warner has handled 'Harry Potter'."

Warner is indeed Hollywood's premier franchise factory, although it's important to note that this hard-won industry status came by way of both breakthrough hits and equally significant misses, best exemplified perhaps by its two-decade run of Batman films. The 1989 Time-Warner merger and concurrent release of the franchise-spawning *Batman* marks a true industry watershed—a tipping point that sent both conglomeration and blockbuster filmmaking into another register. Batman became the definitive 1990s franchise, but for all the wrong reasons. Warner Bros. squandered that extraordinary asset by replacing the visionary director Tim Burton with the more "commercial" Joel Schumacher and opting for an audience-friendly treatment in the third and fourth installments, which derailed the series for nearly a decade. Warner regained its franchise footing with the Matrix and Harry Potter series, although it was Jackson's dark and stylized treatment of the Rings trilogy that confirmed the Burton–Schumacher lesson and convinced the studio to replace Chris Columbus on the Potter series with more individualistic, innovative directors (Alfonso Cuarón, Mike Newell, and currently David Yates) to enhance the style and complexity of its signature franchise. In fact all of the "tentpole brands" that Goldstein lists are currently assigned to directors with indie-auteur credentials—including Christopher Nolan on Batman, Brian Singer on Superman, and Steven Soderbergh on the Ocean's series—which clearly have been crucial to their success.

Del Toro continues that trend, and in a sense advances it in that like Nolan he was hired as a hyphenate writer-director—a rare role for studio franchise directors these years, which should give del Toro a greater degree of creative control and authorial responsibility. The enormous success of Nolan's regeneration of the Batman series suggests that in the right creative hands, even a long-dormant franchise represents an eminently renewable resource. Whether this refutes Gresham's Law of franchise filmmaking is an interesting question, since Nolan's Batman series revival—or "rebooting," in an apt industry term—is so distinct from the 1990s cycle. Indeed, the top global box-office hit of summer 2008 prior to the record-setting release of *The Dark Night* was the plodding fourth installment of Lucas and Spielberg's Indiana Jones saga after a two-decade hiatus, which reinforced with a vengeance both the renewable-resource dimension and Gresham's Law of franchise filmmaking.

The New Line episode also underscores the fact that under current industry conditions "major independent" is a contradiction in terms, and that it is now all but impossible for an independent to compete with the majors. Soaring production and global marketing costs, media consolidation, and conglomerate control now require even the most successful independents to either align themselves with one of the six major studios, as in the Paramount–DreamWorks and Disney–Pixar alliances, or to radically lower their sights, as in the case of Lionsgate, MGM, the Weinstein Company, and Miramax. The latter, downsized by Disney after the Weinsteins left in 2005, hit its stride in 2007 with the indie hits *No Country for Old Men* and *There Will Be Blood*, both co-produced with Paramount Vantage. Indications are that New Line will follow the same route as Miramax, reverting to indie subsidiary status and the kind of mid- to low-budget films that both companies produced in the 1990s before they began challenging the majors. That also would put New Line in much the same relationship with Warner Bros. that Vantage has with Paramount and Miramax with Disney, whereby the subsidiary enjoys reasonable autonomy in terms of project development and production, but is under the sizable thumb of its major-studio counterpart in terms of marketing and distribution.

One final lesson of the Hobbit episode is that these corporate and business relationships involve human relationships as well, and that the complex play of personalities often plays a key role in the fate of these alliances. This includes not only top executives—Iger and Jobs in the Disney–Pixar alliance, for instance, or Bewkes and Shaye in the Warner–New Line contretemps—but also top filmmakers like Peter Jackson and Sam Raimi, who as franchise auteurs effectively become production executives as well. This dates back to Lucas and Star Wars, although the stakes have risen exponentially since then, to a point in fact where the Rings franchise and Peter Jackson were more important to Time Warner than New Line and Shaye. It's also worth noting that Warner Bros. president Alan Horn was co-founder of Castle Rock, a successful independent acquired by Time Warner along with New Line in the mid-1990s. While Horn clearly was able to adapt to TW's conglomerate culture and to the radically changing arena of studio filmmaking, Shaye never abandoned his independent ethos and never came to terms with New Line's corporate home or with the executives who controlled his company's destiny.

conclusion

Time Warner's decision to retain New Line as a brand and a distinct production unit indicates the conglomerate's ongoing if weakening commitment to the movie industry's now-entrenched Hollywood–Indiewood split. But the consolidation of marketing and distribution under Warner Bros. poses an obvious threat to New Line's autonomy and also, on a deeper level, to the vital tension between the movie industry's two dominant modes of production—the major studio and indie division operations—that has been the core quality and in many ways the saving grace of millennial Hollywood. This fundamental symbiosis is rapidly changing throughout the movie industry, due more than anything else to the enormous success of the studios' franchise blockbusters. The Time Warner consolidation was the result of pressure from stockholders (and Wall Street) to increase efficiency, and the same sense of fiduciary responsibility—i.e., the basic obligation of a publicly held company to operate in the best interests of its stockholders—might induce any one of the conglomerates to maximize profits and minimize risk by concentrating only on high-yield blockbusters and shedding its indie film division as a luxury it cannot afford.

But the conglomerates are unlikely to slough off their indie divisions for two basic reasons. The first is that Hollywood like all cultural industries requires new talent and new ideas, which under current conditions are far more likely to emerge from the indie realm than the major studios. The second is that the indie film sector is sufficiently robust to be rationalized on commercial as well as aesthetic grounds—at least for the conglomerate-owned indie divisions. This second point scarcely pertains to the genuine independents, however, which face extinction due to the conglomerates' control of the marketplace and the daunting competition from their indie subsidiaries. Thus the three-tiered mode of film production and corresponding industry sectors that coalesced over the past decade are on the verge of radical reformulation, as the truly independent sector implodes and as the autonomy of the conglomerate-controlled indie sector is further compromised. The only recourse for true independents is to reinvent themselves, and in fact that opportunity for reinvention is at hand as digital technologies transform not only the delivery and the experience of media but the production and consumption of media content as well. Online social network sites and video sharing sites now engage over half the U.S. "youth market" on a daily basis—including the movie industry's key demographic of young males, who are also driving the enormous growth of the videogame industry (with revenues of $18 billion in 2007, up 43 percent over 2006) (Fritz, "Videogame"). Meanwhile Internet use by adults tends to favor better educated, higher-income types, who also comprise the key market for indie films.

This is scarcely news to Hollywood, of course, which has been struggling for decades with the transition from old media to new. Predictably enough, the independents' 2007 market collapse and subsequent Time Warner restructuring led to a series of appeals from various indie-film veterans, notably Warner Independent founder Mark Gill and Picturehouse president Bob Berney, to overhaul their market strategies with an eye to digital delivery (A. Thompson). But the independents have been remarkably slow to exploit new media technologies, which only exacerbates their problems—particularly as the major studios and their parent companies rush headlong into the uncharted realm of digital cinema, digital delivery, and media convergence. Sony remains the clear leader here, thanks to the strategic coordination of its film, computer entertainment, and consumer electronics divisions (Siklos). Sony's Spider-Man franchise provides a case in point in terms of a movie-driven franchise, but this convergence is occurring on multiple fronts. Consider the recent launch of MGS4, "Metal Gear Solid 4: Guns of the Patriots," the seventh installment in a blockbuster videogame franchise that is rife with "cinematics" and extended linear narrative sequences, and thus melds movies and videogames in a very different context. MGS4 was the first in the series developed exclusively for Sony's PlayStation 3 (Blue-ray, HD) platform, and like the Spider-Man films was "bundled" with the PS3 (Schiesel). That enhanced sales of the console, although it kept the game from reaching the blockbuster stature of Halo 3, which generated $300 million in the U.S. alone during its first week on the market in September 2007, and Grand Theft Auto IV, another hyper-cinematic game that generated over $400 million in its opening week in

April 2008 (Fritz, "Halo"; *"Blu-ray"*). Meanwhile Sony is revamping its PS3 console to deliver Internet movie downloads, and is equipping its Bravia HD TV sets with an "Internet video link" to facilitate VOD (video on demand), which has long been the holy grail of the digital era (Stone).

This latter innovation involves a partnership with Amazon.com, whose new VOD service includes a library of 40,000 movie and TV series titles. Other new media powers like Microsoft, Google, and Apple are partnering with Conglomerate Hollywood as well, as the industry faces a wholesale transformation in the delivery and consumption of filmed entertainment. Thus if the old saw that whoever controls distribution controls the industry still applies, then the current media-and-entertainment power structure is in for even further realignment. Hollywood, still the world's consummate content supplier, undoubtedly will survive yet another industry transformation. Whether "the movies" will survive as an art form, a distinct cultural commodity, and the driving force in the global entertainment machine is another question altogether—and one that sorely needs to be addressed. Just as filmmakers and distributors at all levels need to rethink their work and their industry in this age of global media, digital convergence, and conglomerate control, so also must film and media scholars.

note

1 The financial data throughout this essay, unless indicated otherwise, are culled from three principal sources: The Numbers, an online data service provided by Nash Information Services available at http://www.the-numbers.com/; Box Office Mojo, available online at http://www.boxofficemojo.com/; and the Motion Picture Association of America, whose annual reports on all phases of the film (and filmed entertainment) industry can be requested online at http://www.mpaa.org/researchStatistics.asp. There are scores of other movie-related data services and sources available, including annual box-office and production reports from *Variety* and *The Hollywood Reporter*, which have been consulted as well. But these three have proven to be the most consistent, comprehensive, and reliable.

works cited

Advertising Age. "100 Leading Media Companies" (2007 edition). Available online at http://adage.com/datacenter/article?article_id=106352.

Ansen, D. "Ansen Forecasts the Oscars." *Newsweek.com*, February 21 (2008).

Ault, S. "'Spider-Man 3' spins Blu-ray debut." *Variety*, August 2 (2007).

Barnes, B. "Disney and Pixar: The Power of the Prenup." *The New York Times*. June 1 (2008).

Britt, R. "Disney, Pixar Agree to $7.4 Billion Deal." *The Wall Street Journal/Market Watch*, January 24 (2004).

Epstein, E.J. *The Big Picture: The New Logic of Money and Power in Hollywood.* New York: Random House (2005).

Fleming, M. "'Hobbit' Back on Track as Twin Bill." *Variety*, December 18 (2007).

Frankel, D. "Oscar Directors Shun Studio Shackles." *Variety*, February 5 (2008).

Fritz, B. "'Halo' Nabs $170 Million on First Day." *Variety*, September 26 (2007).

——. "Video Game Biz has Epic 2007." *Variety*, January 17(2008).

——. "Sony's Blu-ray Gamble Pays Off." *Variety*, March 3 (2008).

——. "'Grand' Videogame Breaks Record." *Variety*, April 15 (2008).

——. "Sony's Wooing Hollywood for PS3." *Variety*, June 26 (2008).

Garrett, D. "Last 'Potter' to be Split in Half." *Variety*, March 12 (2008).

Goldstein, G. "Indie Boxoffice Down But Not Out." *The Hollywood Reporter*, January 7 (2008).

Goldstein, P. "Why Warner Bros. Closed its Specialty Divisions." *The Los Angeles Times*, May 12 (2008).

Graser, M. "Spider-Man Helps Marvel Climb High." *Variety*, November 5 (2007).

Grover, R. "Unraveling *Spider-Man's* Tangled Web," *Business Week*, April 15 (2002).

Halbfinger, D.M. "Master of 'Rings' to Tackle 'Hobbit'." *Variety*, December 19 (2007).

Hall, K. "Sony's Blu-Ray Breakthrough." *Business Week*, January 8 (2008).

Hau, L. "New Line, Warner Bros. to Merge Operations." Forbes.com. February 28 (2008).

Hayes, D. and McNary, D. "New Line in Warner's Corner." *Variety*, February 28 (2008).

——. "Picturehouse, WIP to close shop." *Variety*, May 8 (2008).

Hettrick, S. "Home video industry bounds past $20 billion mark." *Video Business*, January 10 (2003). http://www.videobusiness.com.

Hollinger, H. "MPA Study: Brighter Picture for Movie Industry: All-Media Revenue from Pics up 8% to $42.6 bil." *The Hollywood Reporter*, June 15 (2007).

McClintock, P. "Six major studios top $1 billion." *Variety*, January 1 (2008).

——. "MPAA: Specialty films see rising costs." *Variety*, March 5 (2008).

McClintock, P. and Thompson, A. "Spielberg, Jackson Team for 'Tintin'." *Variety*, May 14 (2007).

McNary, D. "Foreign box office hits record levels." *Variety*, January 1 (2008).

——. "Guillermo del Toro to Direct 'Hobbit'." *Variety*, April 24 (2008).

Mohr, I. "'Spider-Man 3' Sets Records." *Variety*, May 4 (2007).

Price, D.A. *The Pixar Touch: The Making of a Company.* New York: Knopf (2008).

Schatz, T. "The Studio System and Conglomerate Hollywood." *The Contemporary Hollywood Film Industry.* Eds. P. McDonald and J. Wasko. Malden, MA: Blackwell (2007).

——. "The Return of the Hollywood Studio System," *Conglomerates and the Media.* Erik Barnouw, et al. New York: The New Press (1997).

Scheisel, S. "Making a Game That Acts Like a Film." *The New York Times*, July 5 (2008).

Schilling, M. "'Spider-Man 3' Debuts in Tokyo." *Variety*, April 16 (2007).

Sebok, B. *Convergent Hollywood, DVD, and the Transformation of the Home Entertainment Industries.* Unpublished PhD dissertation. Austin: The University of Texas (2007).

Siklos, R. "Media Frenzy: One Crisis After Another, but Sony Shares Keep Surging." *The New York Times*, April 29 (2007).

Sorkin, A.R. "Sony-Led Group Makes a Late Bid to Wrest MGM from Time Warner." *The New York Times*, September 14 (2004).

Stone, B. "Amazon Plans an Online Store for Movies and TV Shows." *The New York Times*, July 17 (2008).

Taylor, J. *DVD Demystified*, 2nd edn. New York: McGraw-Hill (2001).

——. *Everything You Ever Wanted to Know About DVD.* New York, NY:

McGraw-Hill (2004).

Thompson, A. "Indie Sector on Shaky Ground." *Variety*, June 26 (2008).

Thompson, K. *The Frodo Franchise: The Lord of the Rings and Modern Hollywood.* Berkeley: University of California (2007).

Waxman, S. "For New Line, an Identity Crisis." *The New York Times*, February 19 (2007).

Zaun, T. "Sony's Profit Surges on Strength of 'Spider-Man 2'." *The New York Times*, October 29 (2004).

the

supernatural in

neo-baroque

hollywood

s e a n   c u b i t t

A pallid sepia sky covers the battlefield of Thermopylae. The warriors are caught in poses of utter stillness, blood sprays over them, and detonations hurtle past their shields. Time spurts forward then curdles into slow motion. An execution scene: the blade falls and a general's head rolls through the air, its last expression of grim pain etched on its face. As the camera follows it down, the executioner has vanished to give way to a whole new scene, an elephant in battle order. The visual language of Zack Snyder's adaptation of Frank Miller's graphic novel *300* (2006) owes a great deal to both the Hong Kong fight movie, with its struck poses and characteristic shifts from rapidity to stillness, and to the graphical style which Miller in turn seems to derive in part from the Japanese *manga* tradition, with its graphical matches, strong lines, typical use of blocks of black and white, and its asymmetric, frequently triangular compositions. Snyder's film springs to life in the battle sequences (the background drama taking place in Sparta is sluggish and unconvincing) which provide, to pun on Eisenstein, a montage of affects. A particularly startling example, which appeared in trailers and derives directly from the graphic novel, shows the silhouettes of the Spartans driving a Persian force over a cliff, a blast of sunlight outlining their figures as they fall in slow motion. A cut, and we are looking down the precipitous cliffs watching their fall in real time. The camera tilts upwards to show the Spartans gazing at their beaten foes on the rocks below. We realise the camera is positioned in mid air. We are in the place of the dying and the dead.

The restricted palette of the film—bronzes, sepias and clarets, blacks, greys and whites—emphasizes this graphical look rather like the even more restricted palette of another adaptation from Miller, Roberto Rodriguez' *Sin City* (2005). While many of the dramatic scenes set back home in Sparta retain classical shot-reverse-shot editing, and while the narrative respects the classical Aristotelian story arc, something has changed. Leonidas, king of the Spartans, has nothing to learn, no character development. Nor does his wife, nor any of the numerous villains. The one character who changes at all is the grotesque rejected by the Spartans who betrays them. But in the visual language of the film, all villains are grotesque in some form or other, and one feels that he has merely revealed his true nature rather than changed. The longueurs of the narrative sequences are swept away in the battle scenes, where every blow is treated with respect and humour, characteristics lacking from the story elements. The vocabulary of post-punk S&M costumes and of Frank Frazetta monsters are the attraction: storytelling is a sideline. Though perhaps not every viewer knows in advance that the 300 Spartans are doomed, the satisfaction of the image rests on the simplest possible emotional response: revenge, a motif running through so many of contemporary Hollywood's drama and action films.

Much discussion of contemporary Hollywood cinema takes as its key theme the question of whether a new form has emerged. Classicism appears as a quality of Hollywood from Griffith, or at least the feature films of the early 1920s, through to the 1960s. In the late 1970s, the blockbuster successes of Lucas and Spielberg serve as milestones for the emergence of a new, quite stable system somehow different from the earlier period. The question is: how different? For David Bordwell, the answer appears to be, not very:

> This . . . compromise between deep space and selective focus typifies mainstream style today. The eclecticism introduced at the end of the 1960s and canonised in such films as *Jaws* and *The Godfather* seems to have become the dominant tendency of popular filmmaking around the world. (Bordwell 259).

These are modulations of the classical system, of course, but its fundamentals remain in place. For others something more dramatic has occurred. Angela Ndalianis' (2004) influential book on the subject addresses Hollywood in the context of its proliferating subsidiary or amalgamated industries: theme park rides, computer games, comic books, TV shows, fan sites, toys. Ndalianis singles out five central characteristics of the neo-baroque as an entertainment régime: serial form (including the elaborate relations between originals and copies or remakes within and across media); intertextual labyrinths (also an emphasis of Klein's [97–115]); hypertextual navigation as a mode of narrative engagement; spectacle and immersion; and the transcendental role of the technological sublime. The baroque, she argues, is not a binary opposite to classicism. Rather both are cultural dynamics whose histories are braided together. Walter Benjamin (82) made a similar point: Romanticism appears as a temporary resolution of their dialectical relationship. Norman Klein (113) goes as far as to include the *Odyssey* in his compendium of baroque texts. The question of periodization is then not about a paradigm-shift but rather about a resurgent tendency in Hollywood and its alloyed entertainment trades towards the characteristics outlined above. Certainly some films—and some quite unexpected ones—are deeply classical in character: the locked-off camera and classical *découpage* of Ridley Scott's *Kingdom of Heaven* is a prime example, from a filmmaker whose *Gladiator* otherwise fits many of Ndalianis' observations very closely. As we have seen in the case of *300*, neo-baroque and classical elements can share the same movie. In what follows I want to build on Ndalianis' observations, with a particular focus on Hollywood feature films, and in light of some changes that have become clearer since she wrote.

The notion of the present moment as a neo-baroque emerged in English during the 1990s, perhaps in reaction to the suggestion that the digital arts represented a "new Renaissance," characterized by a reunion of science and art, otherwise pulled apart since the days of Leonardo da Vinci. What first appeared as an amusing play on words, soon demonstrated its critical potential. Writing under Franco, the Spanish historian José Antonio Maravall (1986) had proposed a reading of the Baroque which would be applicable to the conditions of Franco's Spain: a regime of counter-reformation, a collusion of Church and State towards absolutism, and a culture characteristically intricate, labyrinthine, spectacular and populist to the point of vulgarity. Latin Americanist John Beverley (1993) read the similar stylistic excesses of the Latin American Baroque as symptoms of a crisis of power, a crisis brought about by the very ambition of absolute rulers, a crisis with deep echoes of our own period. The same theme appears in Norman Klein, who asserts: "Today the Baroque heritage (including the special effects world) supports transnational power under the cloak of entertainment" (Klein 115). Omar Calabrese (1992) used the term "baroque" as a synonym for postmodernity, an analogy which also appeared in Christine Buci-Glucksmann (1994), who delved into the opaque depths of Walter Benjamin's work on the German baroque (1977) to discover a strand of the grotesque and irrational working through Western civilization, emerging into the raw light of day in the Baroque of the Trevi Fountains, for example, and re-emerging in Surrealism, and in the taste for the extreme in contemporary culture. The idea has some traction among designers[1] and web artists,[2] to the extent that the concept may be becoming a self-fulfilling prophecy. To understand what might be intended by it, we need to pass first to a brief characterization of the seventeenth-century baroque.

the baroque and neo-baroque

The time of the Counter-Reformation witnessed an outpouring of conspicuous waste, of staggering, awe-inspiring spectacle. It was the era that invented the modernity of maritime empires, overseas colonies, North and South. It was the age that perfected the archetypal media of modernity: the map, the filing-cabinet and double-entry book-keeping. It was an epoch of power expended in a vast apparatus of propaganda—the very word derives from the Office for the Propagation of the Faith in Rome. It was the age of the Inquisition, of institutionalized torture justified by the goal of maintaining stability. The baroque was also an immensely playful period: a play of liquid and fluid shapes, of the irruption of the natural into the artificial and vice versa, the play of fountains and *trompe-l'oeil*, the play of practical jokes, an era of great comedies. That comedy, in Jonson, Molière and Calderón, plays endlessly on the risk of failure and the exposure of frauds: the baroque was "like postmodernism today, at once a technique of power of a dominant class in a period of reaction and a figuration of the limits of that power" (Beverley, 64). Our era likewise is dominated by displays of power and wealth, by an apparently insatiable cruelty, and by an immense (and immensely pleasurable) playfulness. The neo-baroque is as addicted to games as the old baroque, and indeed as its inspiration in the Roman Empire—whence the success of *Gladiator* (2000), a film that has the honesty to revel in the violent games it depicts, avoiding the hypocrisy of earlier sword-and-sandals epics. In Scott's movie, playfulness and cruelty are reunited in an account of the madness of absolute power. Like the older epoch, the neo-baroque's central concern appears to be with the approximation to absolute power, and the anxiety which that approximation conjures up as its dialectical counterpart: absolute disorder.

Stylistically, the neo-baroque like its predecessor is characterized by excess, by spectacle, and by the elaboration of decoration to the point where it takes over from the structural principle to become the characteristic formal property of cultural production. Eco (1986) observes that mediaeval allegory constructed a systemic anchorage for meaning, yet at the same time opened the floodgates for the proliferation of possible meanings for any given emblem, to the point at which it risked that bad infinity which for millennia defined and perhaps still defines the abyss for Western thought. As long as allegory could be restricted, as in Dante, to a rigourous hierarchy, the problem could be repressed. But by the seventeenth century, that hierarchy had ceased to be manageable, and the harmony and proportion governing levels of meaning began to fall apart. Proliferating resemblances, metamorphoses, symbolizations, emblematizations, connotations, reverberations, baroque allegory stood at the brink of an abyss where any sign could signify anything. The crisis explored by critics of the baroque from Benjamin (1977) to Beverley (1993) is a crisis of the excess of signs. Confronted by the hyper-inflation of symbolism, the baroque (like the Victorians after them) would pile symbol upon symbol in an attempt to control the turbulence of meaning. But ever and again the flood of signs would find a route around the desired effect, and demand a further set of symbols, another layer of interpretations. Lacking the grounding of a shared lexicon and grammar, the baroque arrived at that *mise-en-abyme* of meaning that the mediaevals had so assiduously avoided.

The neo-baroque proliferation of signs drains the meaning out of any single instance of symbolization. Where once the rose belonged to a hierarchy stretching from the female genitals to the *rosa mystica*, now "a rose is a rose is a rose." At the same time, however, a rose and its depiction are of one kind, whether we prefer to label that kind "sign," "representation," "data" or "commodity." The fundamental interchangeability of signs, representations, data and commodities undermines the attempt to ground an image of a rose in its signified, its referent, its truth or its use-value. Without such anchoring, each image is ephemeral, swiftly substituted with another, and another, in a sprawling and unruly connectivity. Digitization accelerates this substitution, and adds a new interconnection between the signifying chains of semantic, database and economic structures. At once isolated by scientific objectivism and connected to infinite networks of signifiers, symbols no longer gather meaning around them, but proliferate connections to centrifugal streams of equivalent data. The superficiality and intertextual wit of postmodernism are, in this sense, responses to the baroque's greatest challenge: the challenge of constructing and maintaining meaning.

Neo-baroque cinema responds to this double challenge—the draining of substance from the individual iconic image and the consequent proliferation of connections. It increases its own rate of substitution in the rapid editing that begins with Peckinpah, and in the increasingly frequent use of graphical matches to emphasize and counteract the instability of the content of the frame. At the same time it develops extraordinary techniques for combining substitutions into single sequences. The rise of steadicam and the perfecting of crane technologies encourage fluid navigation through scenes rather than *découpage*. Multi-layered soundtracks enabled by digital recording, Dolby noise reduction (essential in compiling complex layered sound effects) and theatrical systems like Lucasfilm's THX encouraged both extreme separation of sound (Fincher's *Se7en* [1995]) and the use of wall-of-sound effects (Bay's *Transformers* [2007]). Composition in depth, once the preserve of Bazinian realism, allowed filmmakers to stack interest across the field of vision through faster film stocks and digital compositing, a technique which encouraged viewers to purchase high-quality DVD versions of films in order to see everything layered into the visuals, from set-dressing to multiple planes of action. Here the isolation of elements in space and their combination into symbolic chains fleeing outward from the central action form a new kind of dialectical image. In some extreme examples (such as the surface of the asteroid in *Armageddon* [1998]), visual space veers towards the indecipherable, inducing the kind of disorientation previously reserved for the horror genre. To control such chaos, characters gifted with a kind of spatial omnivoyance or extended proprioception populate narratives from *Desperado* (1995) to *Daredevil* (2003). Narrative is supplemented with semantic structures built on the accumulation of signifier upon signifier, resulting in a pattern-making aesthetic characterized by the modularization and spatialization of narrative, particularly apparent in the closing scenes of *The Usual Suspects* (1995). A recurrent motif in the construction of central characters is their deep isolation, bordering on narcissism: the examples of *Gladiator* and *The Matrix* (1999) are far from unique.

These technical features—graphical composition and graphical matches, navigation, soundscaping, depth of field and staging in depth, disorientation, proprioception, pattern-based narration and isolation—suggest that the neo-baroque is a fundamentally spatial aesthetic. Time presents itself as the process of deriving order from the assembled elements, in a process in which, however, the goal is a spatial one, so that time appears only as the deferral of a spatial conclusion, the solved puzzle. In an aesthetic in which neither the single image nor the chain of substitutions can contain the proliferation of connections, such solutions, for example in the notice board that spatializes the clues deployed in the narrative of *The Usual Suspects,* can only demonstrate the continuing absence of a concluding truth. In its stead, neo-baroque space offers itself for the immersion of the spectator in the spectacle, much as the old baroque drew the faithful into rapt contemplation of immense *trompe l'oeil* ceilings. This immersion is itself an allegory: in the old baroque an allegory of redemption; in the new, of a satisfaction that comes from bathing in the apogee of consumerism, the lifestyle.

The allegory of immersion reduces the narrative conviction of familiar cause–effect structures, limiting them to pattern-making functions, or disregarding them entirely. The old structure of causation—the past causes changes in the present—becomes the neo-baroque "cause" which lies in the future. Themes of predestination proliferate, from Neo learning that he is the One to Frodo's resignation to his fate in *The Return of the King* (2003). A characteristic of this narrative in which nothing occurs (the character merely discovers what has always been the case) is its problematic construction of good. While we might surmise that early twenty-first century audiences are too sophisticated for white-hat morality, evidence to the contrary comes in the formal properties of protagonists who, in a surprising number of instances, are portrayed as innocents: hobbits, Captain Jack Sparrow, Harry Potter. Kant notes somewhere that innocence is a splendid thing, but doesn't keep well, and tends to be misled. Such is no longer the belief of Hollywood, where innocence is a state that, for example in the figure of *X-Men*'s (2000) Wolverine, forgives a great deal of sin. Yet innocence is in a certain sense merely given, rather than achieved. It is a weak form of good. The good, in fact, has abdicated its place in the centre of Hollywood morality. Innocence is too weak to build an ethics upon. Instead, the ethical universe of the neo-baroque is grounded in the fight against absolute evil. In a fundamentally Manichaean universe, evil has a far more solid existence than the good in contemporary Hollywood (Bather): the satanic Dark Lords, Dark Sides, and He-who-must-not-be-nameds; the gallery of snarling, depraved villains from *Die Hard* (1988) to *300*'s Xerxes. In neo-baroque Hollywood, evil needs no backstory, no explanation, not even the cod-Freudianism of the 1950s. It can be assumed: it simply is. The absolute existence of evil deprives antagonists of character arcs: they cannot change. It also indicates a deep-seated anxiety in US popular culture concerning the nature of power. If innocence is the only good (as in "innocent victims"), and evil is absolute, who is to fight the evil? Who indeed is going to look into the pit? Evil is the first and central trope of the neo-baroque's supernatural.

Universal's early 1930s cycle of horror films, including *The Mummy* (1931), *The Invisible Man* (1933), *Frankenstein* (1931) and *Dracula* (1932) are clearly classical. The distinctive symmetry of classicism, the adherence to plotting and cutting regimes, the concentration on character psychology: such features distinguish them as products of the classical studio system. The evocation of nameless and unnatural violence in these early talkies depended on reaction shots. In a typical example from the Universal cycle, Boris Karloff's reanimated mummy Im-Ho-Tep is seen blinking awake before a cut to his victim, the young Oxford scholar, whose hysterical laughter is the only real token of violence. The mummy's exit and the horror it implies is left to the imagination, traced only by a trailing bandage dragging across the floor. These distinctly brief films (running between 68 and 72 minutes) are nonetheless staged and cut at a relaxed pace when compared with their late-century remakes, notably Barry Sommers' cycle *The Mummy* (1999), *The Mummy Returns* (2001) and *Van Helsing* (2004) which run at between 120 and 129 minutes. The 1930s films nonetheless permit themselves leisurely dialogue reassurance from fatherly experts, and to contemporary tastes sluggish exposition of what has already been made apparent by the action. Such rational explanation coincides with the conclusion of the narrative. At the same time, however, the 1930s cycle makes frequent recourse to the *deus ex machina* in order to complete the story, in the case of the 1931 *Mummy* the intervention of Anubis in the person of a statue in the Cairo museum. Such unmotivated interventions—unmotivated that is by any previous scenes or dialogue—are no longer deployed in the ostensibly post-classical era of Sommers' re-readings of genre classics (nor indeed in Coppola's *Bram Stoker's Dracula* [1992] or Verhoeven's reversioning of *The Invisible Man* as *Hollow Man* [2000]). Barthes' old memorandum, that a gun revealed in a drawer must always be fired, did not hold of the Universal cycle: a previously unopened drawer could always be opened at random to reveal a gun at the crucial moment. To that extent, chance and even the occult were always at the behest of the good. These melodramatic elements of classicism (Altman) have drifted from the side of the good towards the side of evil: the consolidation of American power now sees the random as anarchy, and in spectacular terms as demonic. The neo-baroque monster has recourse to chance: the hero is far more likely to rely on permutations of the logic of evil. In this sense the more recent variations on the motifs are more, not less classical. As Ndalianis (3) observes, "a film like *Jurassic Park* is not only a classical narrative, but a 'superclassical' narrative": the neo-baroque is even more likely to demand of scriptwriters a neat introduction and resolution of plot mechanisms and an even simpler (and less developmental) construction of characters' goals.

van helsing

Sommers' follow-up to the successful *Mummy* films, *Van Helsing*, seems extravagant even by these standards. After taking two films to restore one 70-minute programmer, the new film batters three tales—Frankenstein, Dracula and the Werewolf—into its central narrative, after a prologue involving Dr Jekyl and Mr Hyde. In the eleven minute sequence comprising Van Helsing's arrival at the village and the battle with Dracula's brides, an opening shot follows Van Helsing and his friar into the village on a dolly. A short dolly in and longer dolly back advance in front of Van Helsing and the friar as they walk into the village, in a shot wide enough to show the menacing crowd that is forming behind them. This shot establishes the preternatural capacity to sense danger which is a characteristic of the neo-baroque hero, a 360-degree perception that subordinates the world to the hero and places the hero at its centre. This centrality will then power the action sequence, as the camera swirls in 360-degree pans following Van Helsing's line of fire at the flying brides.

The village square is never entirely established, however. Although an early dialogue is cut shot-reverse-shot, no true establishing shot lays out the geometry of the scene. The exception is the establishment of the stone cross and its plinth next to a well as the centre of the surrounding open space and buildings: suggesting that the polar coordinate system used extensively in computer graphics dominates the construction, rather than classical rules of orientation. The action begins with a sudden focus pull from close up on Gypsy princess Anna Valerious (Kate Beckinsale) to the mountains and rooftops revealed behind her as she ducks, and the three brides diving down towards the spectator. A few frames in, the camera zooms in on the face of the bride, the set element also zooming in, deformed as in a fish-eye lens to emphasize the speed and aggression of the attack, until the lead bride's face fills the frame. A brief reverse angle on Van Helsing pulls at an upward angle of 30 degrees or so, cutting to a Cablecam shot (equipment now used extensively in TV coverage of field sports) accompanying the diving brides, a shot which sways on its own axis as if banking from side to side with the flying monsters. At the bottom of the dive, the lead bride again fills the screen, the camera swirling over her head, the background lost in a blur of motion and wings, then hurtling upward ahead of her to leave a panoramic shot of the villagers scrabbling for cover, and Anna still safe on the edge of the well just off the centre of the frame. We cut to a second POV shot of the fleeing attackers, the well now upper right of centre. The camera flies again on cables extending several hundred feet into the air above the set. Such movements into the screen space, and the extensive use of the top and bottom of the screen to add new vistas, correlate with Ndalianis' observation that "The baroque's difference from classical systems lies in its refusal to respect the limits of the frame that contains the illusion" (25). The organization of screen space through navigation rather than establishing shots and the 180 degree rule is not disorienting: it suggests that orientation itself is not important; so much so that when we rediscover a cow that has been flung into a building in the fight standing on a second-floor balcony and mooing querulously, the return to an orientational composition strikes us as a joke.

The sequence combines location shoots, blue-screen, wire-work, motion capture and digital effects (notably the skies which, during the location shoot, were obstinately sunny) and digital compositing, including effects such as shadows for the superimposed attacking brides, and a digital cow. But classical editing still occurs, even in these action sequences. The village square battle continues with another 360 degree pan shot circling our protagonists, stopping with a cut to the fallen Van Helsing. We cut to a reverse angle of Anna's reaction, back to Van Helsing's eyeline match, and back to Anna in brisk fashion, but this last shot dramatizes the breakdown of *découpage* in the neo-baroque: with the aid of wirework, Anna is snatched by one of the brides and hurtles away from the close-up into the air—a vertical exit whose drama arises from its abrupt departure from the normative codes of classicism. The sequence of reverse-shots starts to establish a recognizable pattern only to interrupt it, so that the second shot of Anna occurs not as a continuity shot but as a graphical match of her first close up, graphical not only in the cinematic but in the comic book sense of the term. After three shots of the trio—bride, Anna and Van Helsing— suspended in mid-air, we cut to the human couple falling to earth, Anna on top. A reverse shot from above shows Van Helsing's reaction to her sexually-connoted position astride his neck; we cut to a side-on angle as he rolls on top of her, the shot continuing as she rolls back on top of him in what is clearly a competition for sexual dominance. The sudden mood swing, from peril to sexual encounter, swings instantly back to action. Such encounters are not unusual in the classical cinema, especially in film noir, a genre constantly quoted in the neo-baroque, and in German expressionism, which underlies noir, and is likewise a constant reference point for both the Universal series of the 1930s and the neo-baroque. It is a distinctive quality of the neo-baroque that such reference is incorporated into the shot itself, as if there were no way of holding its meaning to a narrative or even an ideological function, as in classical battle-of-the-sexes films.

Throughout the sequence, the camera is in constant movement, with locked-off shots occurring only rarely, for example in two shots showing a beam of sunlight, fatal to the attacking brides, over the valley where the village sits. But even in the lull that follows, the camera reframes constantly, as if following the generic characteristics of documentary, where camera movement is dictated by the actions of its subjects. *Van Helsing* seems here to have learnt from the incessantly mobile camerawork of Andrew Lesnie on *Lord of the Rings*: the only locked-off shot in the entire trilogy covers the transformation of Theoden in *The Two Towers* (2003). Deep focus and the long take have taken centre stage in a cinema of spectacle and illusion despite Bazin's attempts to secure those techniques for realism. In the same way this capture of documentary technique exhibits a quality of formal innovation which Bazin (26–7) had already expected when he articulated the necessary illusion integral to cinematic realism, and the generative contradiction which that produces: no technique is free of the temptation, indeed the internal necessity, of producing illusion, and when pursued for its own perfection, loses the reality it sought to grasp. Deep focus and the long take may have ushered in, with neo-realism, an epochal realism: in the neo-baroque they usher in an integral illusion. In a similar way, *découpage* no longer serves its classical function of orientation and coherence, not least when the reverse angles show relationships between CGI characters and actors, and do so not on the horizontal but on the vertical axis, as happens in several interchanges between Anna and the brides. A clearer example of modernist paradigms becoming neo-baroque pastiche—a "blank parody" in Jameson's terminology (17)—could scarcely be imagined.

the supernatural

This blankness echoes a line of Walter Benjamin's concerning the seventeenth century. Referring to the split between Catholic and Protestant, he reflects

> For all that the increasing wordliness of the Counter-Reformation prevailed in both confessions, religious

aspirations did not lose their importance: it was just that this century denied them a religious fulfilment, demanding of them, or imposing on them, a secular conclusion instead. (79)

Religious doctrine was safe from heresy, the old hallmark of mediaeval rebellion, because the baroque's rebellion, if there was one, was secular, and would not choose a religious form of expression.

> Since therefore neither rebellion nor submission was practicable in religious terms, all the energy of the age was concentrated on a complete revolution of the content of life, while orthodox ecclesiastical forms were preserved. The only consequence could be that men were denied all real means of direct expression. (Benjamin 79)

In the neo-baroque, the occult retains its allure, self-consciously regressive as in the recourse to ancient curses in *Van Helsing* (but see also the slave narrative of *Candyman* [1992], or the native American graveyard in *Poltergeist* [1982]). The City University of New York's *American Religious Identification Survey* (ARIS) conducted in 2001 found that 76.5 percent of US citizens identified as Christians, and a total of 81 percent identify themselves with a specific religion (Kosmin et. al. 2001). Supernatural motifs in the neo-baroque do not simply reflect the demographic it serves, but they do draw on the cultural competences of the US audience, not only for their popular cultural intertextual skills, but for the raft of beliefs and quasi-beliefs that fuel the imagination of the afterlife. At the same time, an economic imperative demands that features are not so Christian that they alienate the global marketplace (the domestic success of Gibson's *The Passion of the Christ* [2004] was an exception but its international performance was less stellar). The supernatural reappears as a hedged bet: in the subjunctive register of Mannoni's "I know, but all the same . . .," a Freudian denegation.

The place of the supernatural in contemporary society is a puzzle, as indeed it appears to have been for the first baroque. To judge from his ceiling at the San Ignazio in Rome, Pozzo shared the faith of his Order (he was a Jesuit) in the miraculous apotheosis of Saint Ignatius, founder of the Jesuit order who would form the vanguard of the Counter-Reformation. The artist of the equally overwhelming quadratura *Allegory of Divine Providence and Barberini Power* ceiling for the Palazzo Barberini, Cortona, must have known that the papal family of the Barberini was mired in hypocrisy. In both, anamorphosis gives the illusion of a perspective that does not exist, a column of air extending to infinity, a dome in *trompe l'oeil* on an otherwise flat ceiling. The revelation of divine truth is achieved through the strongest techniques of illusion: just as Bazin had noted of realist techniques in cinema. Faith and the lack of faith (or bad faith) are indistinguishable when both depend on illusion. The display of wealth, the piling of allegory upon allegory, the disappearance of the actual, the revelation of a wholly separate semantic universe with its own rules of gravity and perspective: these features return in the epoch of the Fremont Street experience, the Las Vegas arcade whose ceiling is lit by 200 hi-definition video projectors. The supernatural in the baroque was not a matter of the afterlife, but of an immanent realm just beyond the sublunary veil of the everyday. It was habitable; and it touched on the quotidian at every turn. Perhaps most of all, as Ndalianis notes, the everyday articulates with the immanent (if perpetually deferred) sublime through a technology which is itself an object of awe. This technically mediated beyond at once exists and does not exist.

Just so the supernatural of the twenty-first century. The demonic cowboy whose narrative opens *Ghostrider* (2007) is an emissary between worlds. As the voiceover begins the pre-credit tale of the Devil's bounty-hunter who outran the Devil himself, the camera tilts and pans down from a full moon past moonlit clouds to a horizon of buttes and mesas. As the edge of the rider's hat comes into the bottom right of the frame, the camera makes a sudden drop and a dolly back, from eye-level close-up to an upward long shot of horse and rider, a movement accompanied by a sweetener on the soundtrack, a sound like rain and distant thunder. The camera move and the sound are unnatural: they do not fit with the normal movements of either cinema or human vision, just as the sudden sound distinguishes itself from the musical score and the voice. These third elements, neither familiar technologies (camera, orchestra) nor familiarly human, are by now familiar markers of the entry of the supernatural. The tilt itself, relatively rare in classical Hollywood, especially when combined with dollying or tracking out and consequent refocusing, has become a signature move in the neo-baroque: a readiness to use top and bottom of the frame as well as the vertical edges which were familiar to the audience for classicism, which grew up on theatre wings. With its heritage of *deus ex machina*, of the Up of heaven and the Down of hell, its alternately devout desire for or sinister threat of revealing a world not bound to the earth's surface and the lateral pan of human scale and action, movement on the vertical axis has become an emblem of the supernatural.

In the neo-baroque supernatural, ancient beliefs in life after death persist along with elements of paganism, the belief that places retain at least the memory of the gods or people who once inhabited them. In the industrial revolution, the technological triumph over nature posited a new kind of "supernatural," an anti-nature: "the artifice of eternity" as Yeats expressed it. In the digital epoch, artificial life appears as a new order, the cybernatural (Cubitt). These imaginings of the otherworldly form deep strata in the contemporary. Secular belief in posterity still dominates; but the idea of lifelogging (Bell), for example, indicates a growing personalization of database logic whose extreme form is Moravec's idea of downloading consciousness into a machine (Moravec). This latest addition to the repertoire of supernatural orders rests, however, on older Christian beliefs in personal salvation, and deeper pagan beliefs in the immanence of supernatural forces in rivers, trees and mountains. The result, in Hollywood's syncretic version, is an ill-defined, diffuse hybrid of these, where monsters may emerge from the earth, from the beyond, from machines; and salvation may come from any of them.

Thus the characterization of the camera as a non-human player in the scene from *Ghostrider* overlays the conquest of nature with the imagination of a postnatural intelligence, while both draw on older well-springs of superstition. The fear of death is as ancient as sex and hunger, but like them it has its history. Just as sex is no longer a brute fumble in the dark but a centre of social rituals; and just as hunger is no longer assuaged by ripping animals apart with bare teeth; so the fear of death is answered age by age with new accumulations of fetishes and fantasies, rituals and commerce. Death itself changes its meaning, perhaps most tellingly from common fate to the existential loneliness of Heidegger's being-towards-death. The terrible weight placed on individuality in the modern world is matched by the dreadful responsibility to be faced in the final moments, when the meaning of a single life must be upheld.

The discretion surrounding this premise of the neo-baroque is perpetually tenuous. In Christopher Nolan's *The Prestige* (2007), the rival Victorian stage magicians Alfred and Robert confront each other for the last time. We have just seen Alfred die, yet here he is, shooting Robert. The reveal, surprising as it is, is more or less what we would expect: there is a rational if unusual explanation, one which explains, in a swift montage of flashbacks, a list of strange details, most of all the success of a particularly difficult trick. Alfred asserts the sacrifices that the trick, and indeed his career and life, demanded. The dying Robert reveals his own methods. He has used the maverick scientific inventions of Nicola Tesla, ostensibly as stage dressing. But now we learn a chilling fact. Each magician has lived a double life, doubled by their devotion to the illusion-making art of magic. Alfred's has the characteristics of explanatory logic; Robert's however is at once tragic and infernal. The distinctive feeling of the film arises from the realization that there is indeed a rift in reality where some other, quite different order of things arrives. Robert's stage trick conceals not an explanation but a deeper mystery. The techniques of illusion are not merely techniques: they make it possible that everything is illusory. Most of all, we are unclear, as are the protagonists, whether the Robert who dies is in any sense the "real" Robert. Without that reality, the reality of the self, what meaning can his death provide him with?

The illusion of individuality is a critical ideological task of capital. On it depends the regime of property, already in crisis in the Open Source movement; the self-discipline of crowds on which the risk management of our infrastructures depend (obedience to the rules of the road for example); the discipline of consumer lifestyle marketing, which addresses the individual agent of purchasing with the instruction to become the self you always were through the accumulation of the right commodities. Individualism is the reverse of the equally central task of maintaining (the illusion of) meaning. In this context death appears as the negentropic at its most absolute, and it is therefore not surprising that death should provide the structuring visual language of monstrosity, perversion, and the mode of absolute Evil on which what passes for a moral code in Hollywood fiction is premised. The nexus of terms includes death, dying, the dead, the undead, the immortal—those blessed or cursed with endless life, whether the shamanic figure of the Highlander or the monstrous vampire. Reality TV acts to maintain the ideological truth that "we are all individuals" by encouraging the eccentric, idiosyncratic and extravagant. Neo-baroque Hollywood plunges us into worlds where the capacity to act, to live, to die a justified death after a fulfilled life are all in doubt. The deaths of innocent victims is always "inexplicable" and "meaningless" in TV news and in life. While evil is clear and present, the immanent world beyond all appearances can frequently appear not as the fullness of the divine but a fatal emptiness.

The labyrinth which Ndalianis and Klein note as a characteristic of the (neo)-baroque can be understood not only as an outgrowth of the unanchored chain of signifiers seeking a perpetually absent goal, pursuing an absent but immanent unity through the labyrinth of connectivity. It can also be construed as reweavings of old tales in new patterns: patterns to ward off the boogie man, patterns to lace overt the dark secret: that the painted ceiling does not just hide the roof—it hides the void. This orgy of pattern-making is apparent in the *Pirates of the Caribbean* franchise, as indeed it is in other key franchise projects of the neo-baroque: *Star Wars*, *The Matrix*, *Harry Potter* and *The Lord of the Rings*, and indeed is if anything even more apparent in contemporary television dramas and their convergent web and wireless media, in a style inaugurated by *Twin Peaks* (1990–1) and carried to new heights with *Lost* (2004–). In all of these patterned narrations, the motif of the immanent supernatural is centre stage, whether played for comedy or for epic (the tragic mode is unavailable where narrative is haunted by predestination: those who are fated cannot live or die tragically).

the departed

Scorsese's *The Departed* (2006) does not seem at first glance to fit this populist mode, sitting as it does on the brink of arthouse/independent values. Adapted from the first of a trilogy of films made in Hong Kong characterized by intense mirrorings and symmetries, *The Departed* lays its cards on the table in an early sequence in which gang-boss Frank Costello (Jack Nicholson) advises the young Colin in the ways of the world, introducing the Latin phrase "Non serviam." Colin recognizes it as a quote from Joyce's *Portrait of the Artist as a Young Man*. What he does not recognize is that it is introduced by Joyce as the words of Lucifer at the moment of his rebellion against God: I shall not serve. The scene is shot in a garage, Costello in silhouette speaking in a quiet, husky voice, the voice of temptation. At the end of the sequence, as Costello asks what's the difference between a cop and a criminal, we have that typical graphical match: Costello's face at last in the light, the boy's face, and Colin's adult face. This is no longer the classical editing it refers to but a graphical montage, one in which it is not so much the passage of time as the assimilation of the fresh-faced boy into the ambit of Satan that is most apparent, as the last line of Costello's dialogue voices over the first appearance of his adult mole: "My boy."

Visual symmetries accumulate around the non-criminal world. We see the Catholic Church from an interior balcony in harmonious symmetry; the symmetry of ranked young police officers, even the bird's eye view of a football scrimmage. As we switch to the mirror story of Billy (Leonardo DiCaprio) during his brief legitimate career in the police, the symmetries are even stronger: a clock in full frame ticking towards nine o'clock. This simple dichotomy (symmetry of the just and sacred institutions, asymmetry of the criminal underworld) breaks down in minutes. Already many of the symmetrical compositions had featured focus pulls, dollies and zooms in or out. When the newly graduated Colin sits in the back of Frank's car framed by the seat backs in centre-frame, looking at his badge, we feel already the instability of the opposition, just as we will the opposition between good and evil. Billy's training is tracked in asymmetric steadicam; Colin's interview with undercover chief of operations Captain Queenan (Martin Sheen), conducted at attention, is in medium long shot, emphasizing the symmetry of the set; Billy's has him seated, in tighter framing, emphasizing the subtler asymmetries of the props behind him and his slightly skewed way of sitting. Frank's stooge Colin has no problem gliding into the hierarchy: Billy is treated to an interrogation which seems to frame him as the mole. Though the pair of displacements—Colin's gangster turned cop, Billy's cop turned gangster—are separated by months if not years, they appear as paired narratives in these intercut sequences. Colin moves into an upper-class neighborhood, to an apartment with a view of the statehouse; Billy is incarcerated on a trumped up charge to provide his cover. The good is bumbling, good-natured, good-humoured, like Colin's boss Captain Ellerby (Alec Baldwin); evil is direct, swift to action, rough-tongued, like Frank Costello's right-hand man French (Ray Winstone). The film speculates on a theme enunciated earlier by Brecht: the impossibility of being a good person in an evil time. Innocence in this world is no defence, even if, in the figures of various minor characters, it deserves to be defended.

The Departed is in many ways a realist film in the tradition of Renoir's work of the Popular Front period or Rossellini's and de Sica's after the war. It portrays a world, and traces in that world one of Scorsese's commonest authorial motifs, the pursuit of salvation. The funerals that run through the early part of the film indicate something curious about this world, however, something pointed to by the title. In many respects, the protagonists Billy and Colin are already dead. This is not just Boston: it is Purgatory. Like its source, Andy Lau and Alan Mak's hugely successful 2002 Hong Kong thriller *Infernal Affairs* (*Mou Gaan Dou*), Scorsese's film inhabits a world that is already doubled. Recognizably Hong Kong in its geography and architecture, *Infernal Affairs* is also set in the lowest circle of Buddhist hells from which it takes its title (Cameron and Cubitt). Just so the urban sociology of Boston, especially the Irish South Side and the conditions for migration to the wealthier, safer, cleaner North, frame the construction of a moral desert in a meticulously observed milieu. But place has ceased to have the kind of solidity it had for Renoir, de Sica and Rossellini. Pretending to be his lawyer, Colin interviews Costello's muscle Fitzy in a police holding cell. The shot-reverse-shot structure is interrupted first by a vertical shot of the mobile phone passed between them, then by another shot of a call being placed. The phone substitutes for the cell: we cut to a reaction shot from Billy in a remote location, then to another close up of a ringing mobile on a cluttered tabletop. French picks it up, but we get a wide shot of the room rather than a reverse angle. Cut back to Fitzy in the cell, speaking, and a reverse angle to Colin. Never having met Fitzy thus far except as a still in a slide show of gang members, we see him as Colin does, not as a man but a medium to get a message out to the gang that a raid is in preparation. The walls, the buildings, the geography are permeable; the phone not only connects, it blurs the old distinctions, geographical, professional, and ethical. *The Departed*, with its mix of fluid and static camerawork, its richer palette, its realism, is only partly a symptom of the neo-baroque; it is also a dissection of its moral landscape. The silent dialogue between Billy and Colin via their cell phones is the apogee of this misadventure.

Colin and Billy move towards their showdown. They cannot make an act of will, no act of will that could convert into action, no action that would change what awaits them. Klein observes the doubled experience of the neo-baroque that is enacted for us in and by *The Departed*:

> An audience goes from confusion to the realization that
> there is a program greater than themselves. . . . Part of our
> revenge against the system is the knowledge that it is filled
> with gimmicks. . . . So we imagine that our ontological

> awareness is a weapon against ideology, but in the end, we
> accept the epistemology as a truth (a democratising force),
> even a game about the truth. (Klein 328–9)

The technologies we live by we also see through, but seeing through them is part of them. The very attempt to understand the truth behind the neo-baroque is a neo-baroque move, because it ends up in a labyrinth of signification in endless chains, and because it hypostasises an immanent elsewhere where truth and meaning, even true individuality are available, but which is permanently deferred—as fate, as some other place, as the next signifier or the next. The supernatural in the neo-baroque stands in the position of the impossibly complete illusion of the ceiling which is no longer a ceiling, a story which is really a pattern, a cause that is actually an effect of the future, not of the past.

In *The Departed*, the neo-baroque is doubled or shadowed by the second great development in twenty-first-century media: the always-on wireless world. In the old baroque and the new, the immense and immersive spectacle engulfs the viewer-auditor, but also addresses them as individual—individual soul in the old, individual consumer in the neo. By contrast the wireless experience is primarily of isolation, but isolation in perpetual connectivity. The contradiction between immersion and connectivity, mirrors that between the sublime and the communicative. Since we know that the immersive experience is technically mediated, that there is a host of artisans behind the screen, and that the cinematic experience still has the legacy form of mass entertainment, we might describe it as the actuality of community with the illusion of isolation. The wireless experience, by contrast, offers the actuality of isolation and the illusion of community. This chapter has addressed only one side of a dialectic: the immersive. If there is to be another turn in the historical narratives traced here, that second half of the equation will have to be brought back into the analysis. Critically, only through an analysis of the relation between immersive and personalized media will we be able to reach a genuine understanding of the ways in which the supernatural—the discovery that we are constantly placed in the place of the dying and the dead—functions today. In a letter to Benjamin, Adorno described the problem of high and low as "the two torn halves of an integral freedom to which, however, they do not add up" (123). In an era in which high and low culture have been reconciled, not least in works like Scorsese's, the distinction between the spectacular, immersive, collective event experienced in profoundly individual form, and the intensely intimate third-screen portable device with its extraordinary potential for connectivity poses much the same problem in a new form. The neo-baroque cinema is only half of a story, even if it has the capacity to tell the whole of it.

notes

1. Joost van Gorsel contributes an animation at http://www.iconique.com/flash/design.html (accessed February 1 2008).
2. William Poundstone's *New Digital Emblems* at http://www.williampoundstone.net/ (accessed February 1 2008).

works cited

Adorno, Theodor W. "Letters to Walter Benjamin," 18 March 1936. *Aesthetics and Politics*. Eds. Ernst Bloch et al. London: New Left Books, 1977.

Altman, Rick. "Dickens, Griffith and Film Theory Today." *Classical Hollywood Narrative: The Paradigm Wars*. Ed. Jane Gaines. Durham, NC: Duke University Press, 1992. 9–47.

Bather, Neil. "Big Rocks, Big Bangs, Big Bucks: The Construction of Evil in the Popular Cinema of Jerry Bruckheimer." *New Review of Film and Television Studies*, 2.1 (2004): 37–59.

Bazin, André. "An Aesthetic of Reality." *What is Cinema?*, volume 2. Trans. Hugh Gray. Berkeley: University of California Press, 1971. 16–40.

Bell, Gordon. *MyLifeBits*, Microsoft research: http://research.microsoft.com/barc/MediaPresence/MyLifeBits.aspx, retrieved 6 October 2007.

Benjamin, Walter. *The Origin of German Tragic Drama*. Trans. John Osborne. London: Verso, 1977.

Beverley, John. *Against Literature*. Minneapolis: University of Minnesota Press, 1993.

Bordwell, David. *On the History of Film Style*. Cambridge, MA: Harvard University Press, 1997.

Buci-Glucksmann, Christine. *Baroque Reason: The Aesthetics of Modernity*. Trans. Patrick Camiller. London: Sage, 1994.

Calabrese, Omar. *Neo-Baroque: A Sign of the Times*. Trans. Charles Lambert. Princeton, NJ: Princeton University Press, 1992.

Cameron, Allan and Sean Cubitt. "Infernal Affairs and the Ethics of Complex Narrative." *Puzzle Films: Complex Storytelling in Contemporary Cinema*. Ed. Warren Buckland. Oxford: WileyBlackwell, 2009.

Cubitt, Sean. "Supernatural Futures: Theses on Digital Aesthetics." *Future Natural: Nature, Science, Culture*. Eds. George Robertson, Melinda Mash, Lisa Tickner, Jon Bird, Barry Curtis and Tim Puttnam. London: Routledge, 1996. 237–55.

Jameson, Fredric. *Postmodernism, or, The Cultural Logic of Late Capitalism*. London: Verso, 1991.

Klein, Norman M. *The Vatican to Vegas: A History of Special Effects*. New York: The New Press, 2004.

Kosmin, Barry A., Egon Mayer and Ariela Keysar. *American Religious Identification Survey*, 2001. http://www.gc.cuny.edu/faculty/research_briefs/aris.pdf. Retrieved 28 September 2007.

Maravall, José Antonio. *Culture of the Baroque: Analysis of a Historical Structure*. Trans Terry Cochran. Manchester: Manchester University Press, 1986.

Moravec, Hans. *Mind Children: The Future of Robot and Human Intelligences*. Cambridge, MA: Harvard University Press, 1988.

Ndalianis, Angela. *Neo-Baroque Aesthetics and Contemporary Entertainment*. Cambridge, MA: MIT Press, 2004.

man without a movie camera—movies without men

t h r e e

towards

a posthumanist

cinema?

w i l l i a m   b r o w n

the extinction of mankind?

To discuss "posthumanism" can be an emotional issue. For, it is easy to believe that posthumanism implies humanity's possible extinction, a prospect that without doubt causes consternation in any human reader. Within the context of critical theory, there are indeed some theorists who view mankind's development of intelligent machines and information superhighways as leading inevitably to the end of humanity. A prominent example is Friedrich Kittler, who argues that humans are merely a by-product in the development of ever more efficient processes of information exchange. Paul Virilio and Manuel De Landa, meanwhile, argue that humans are also potentially redundant in a world predicated upon surveillance technologies and war machinery (see also Johnston).

Whilst Virilio and Kittler (and, to a lesser extent, De Landa) are noteworthy for their pessimism, they are not alone in downplaying the fact that humanity has traditionally understood itself as playing a central role in the world. However, far from being necessarily a doom-mongering practise, posthumanism is better understood not as the end of humanity, but as the end of humanism—that is, posthumanism is precisely the belief that humans no longer play a central and binding role in reality. Advances in technology, astrophysics, neuroscience, biology and philosophy, as well as "[diverse] discourses [including] actor-network-theory, pragmatism, deconstruction, post-Darwinian accounts of evolutionary dynamics, post-Kantian versions of social constructivism, Foucault-inspired inquiries into knowledge/power, the Deleuzian 'body without organs'," all contribute to what Evan Selinger and Timothy Engström (564) term "the end of human exceptionalism." In other words, posthumanist discourse seeks to displace old, anthropocentric theories and practices with new, "posthuman" considerations of mankind and its creative endeavours, be they technological or artistic. With this in mind, we can find strands of posthumanist discourse that are not pessimistic at all. Computer scientist Kevin Warwick, for example, looks forward to becoming a "posthuman" cyborg—literally a being that is part-man and part-machine. Others feel that Warwick's literal self-transformation is not even necessary; mankind's daily interactions with intelligent machines already modify our traditional notions of human identity. N. Katherine Hayles, for example, believes that to interface with a computer already makes us posthuman (see also Hansen). Donna Haraway believes that the human-machine interface similarly makes of us "cyborgs," which redefine traditional gender definitions (masculine/feminine) and social relations. Such ideas can be seen as stemming from Marshall McLuhan, who believed that the media were "extensions of our nervous system." Whilst Gilles Deleuze and Félix Guattari (*Anti-Oedipus; A Thousand Plateaux*) also play a pivotal role in the development of posthumanist discourse, since they similarly argue that the use of machines sees the creation of a new "assemblage," which in itself has a new identity separate from our traditional conceptions of self. Deleuze and Guattari see the creation of assemblages not as the irredeemable loss of something uniquely human, but as the opportunity for endless self-recreation through the creation of ever-more complex and wonderful identities. In other words, by becoming posthuman—through a process of hybridization with not just machines but, potentially, with all that surrounds us—humanity can be set free from its own limitations. This does indeed mean letting go of our old "fixed" identity, but, for many theorists, there is something positive in embracing the limitless opportunities of always *becoming* other.

a cinema of extinction?

If posthumanism leads some to fear the end of humanity, then a post humanist cinema might be one in which this takes place—or at the very least threatens to. There is a host of films that certainly do reflect the potential extinction of our species. The threat might be alien (*Independence Day*, Roland Emmerich, 1996; *Mars Attacks!*, Tim Burton, 1996; *Starship Troopers*, Paul Verhoeven, 1997; *War of the Worlds*, Steven Spielberg, 2005); it might be a non-living threat from outer space—be it a meteorite collision (*Armageddon*, Michael Bay, 1997; *Deep Impact*, Mimi Leder, 1997) or the extinction of the sun (*Sunshine*, Danny Boyle, 2007); it might be on account of an ecological disaster (*The Day after Tomorrow*, Roland Emmerich, 2004; *The Core*, Jon Amiel, 2003); it might be as a result of a deadly virus (*Outbreak*, Wolfgang Petersen, 1995; *28 Days Later . . .*, Danny Boyle, 2002); it might be because humanity's own inventions, specifically robots, achieve artificial intelligence and decide to remove us from the planet (*The Matrix*, Andy and Larry Wachowski, 1999; *Terminator 3: Rise of the Machines*, Jonathan Mostow, 2003; *I, Robot*, Alex Proyas, 2004; *A.I.: Artificial Intelligence*, Steven Spielberg, 2001); or it may simply be because humans evolve into the "next" phase of evolution (*X-Men* and *X2*, both Bryan Singer, 2000 and 2003). Whatever the source of the threat, these films show us literal interpretations of a (potentially—in that more often than not the humans still "win the day") posthuman future. These films, regardless of their predominantly "happy" endings, can certainly be considered posthumanist, too, since they remind us that our place on the planet and/or in the universe is contingent and not fixed or guaranteed.

One might equally interpret a posthumanist cinema as either being a cinema that does not feature human characters (or in which humans are at the very least relegated to equal status alongside other life forms), or in which "humans" have become capable of transcending the laws of physics. Prime examples of the former group of course include the *Star Wars* films (George Lucas, 1977–2005) and the *Lord of the Rings* films (Peter Jackson, 2001–2003). The latter group includes superhero movies such as the *Spider-Man* films (Sam Raimi, 2002–2007), *Hulk* (Ang Lee, 2003) and the *X-Men* films (including *X-Men 3: The Last Stand*, Brett Ratner, 2006). By showing humans as "just another" (as opposed to a privileged) species, or, indeed, by showing humans as inferior to other "supermen," these films could be interpreted as posthumanist, for they similarly downplay mankind's "special" place in the universe.

Finally, there is a more complex *group* of films that similarly challenges a traditional humanist understanding of the world, and which suggests, somehow, that human identity is not fixed and/or stable. This group includes films in which characters turn out to be someone other than who they thought they were, "posthumous" films in which the protagonist realizes that he or she is dead (albeit still conscious), films in which characters discover that they are living within a simulation, and so on. Examples include *The Matrix*, but also *Total Recall* (Paul Verhoeven, 1990), *Being John Malkovich* (Spike Jonze, 1999), *eXistenZ* (David Cronenberg, 1999), *Fight Club* (David Fincher, 1999), *The Sixth Sense* (M Night Shyamalan, 1999), *Memento* (Christopher Nolan, 2000), *The Others* (Alejandro Amenábar, 2001), *Vanilla Sky*

(Cameron Crowe, 2001), *The Machinist* (Brad Anderson, 2004), and *Eternal Sunshine of the Spotless Mind* (Michel Gondry, 2004). These films can be deemed posthumanist for they suggest by turns that we have no physical reality, that physical reality is an illusion, that the world in which we thought we played such a key role is in fact a simulation, and/or that our "identity" is uniquely mental and not physical. By divorcing mind from body, these films undermine a traditional, "humanist" understanding of our position in the world/universe, and reveal that what we think we know about ourselves is in fact unstable/illusory. As such, many of these films rely upon "twists" and final "revelations" in order to reinforce the shattering of humanist illusions that the films portray.[1]

the extinction of cinema?

However, it is not just on the level of content that cinema can be deemed posthumanist. For, whilst many contemporary films might feature mutants, cyborgs, monsters, and other alien life forms that do not conform to our traditional and fixed notions of identity and gender (for more on this see Pisters), we can also see cinema as posthumanist on the level of production and, more specifically, on the level of form.

The absolute majority of the above films are defined by the use of digital technology to create photorealistic special effects in order to render these threats to humanity in a convincing manner—be these threats aliens or natural disasters. It is the same use of digital technology that has modified the entire nature of cinema, above all in Hollywood, but also, arguably, on a global scale. The extent of the change in cinema's being as a result of the increased use of digital technology—from its use in terms of sound, in terms of the image, and in terms of how the image is framed—has caused some theorists to declare the end of cinema (see, for example, Jon Lewis), or at the very least the creation of "new media" (Manovich, *Language*).

This "new" cinema *may* be deemed posthumanist if we are to understand traditional, analogue cinema as a predominantly human (and therefore humanist) medium (see Balázs, 262). Whilst analogue cinema features human characters faithfully captured by an analogue camera, digital cinema often involves the modification of the appearance of these human characters. This is most notable in the digital morph (for more on this, see, *inter alia*, Jenkins), but also, quite simply, in terms of "airbrushing" or changing facial expressions. What this means is that the characters that we see on film are a hybrid of "real" flesh and blood actors and digital imagery, meaning that they have become "posthuman" cyborgs, even if the characters that the actors play are supposed to be humans as we traditionally perceive and understand them.

The transition from analogue photography, which has traditionally been thought of as an indexical representation of what is placed before the camera (Bazin, *What is Cinema?* I, 14; also quoted in Prince, "True Lies"), to digital graphics, which can modify/embellish/falsify that reality—and *do so in a manner that the two, "false" and "real," become indistinguishable*—provokes a crisis in perception such that our (loosely humanist) faith in taking what we see to be real ("seeing is believing") has been irrevocably challenged. It might be obvious that a balrog does not exist in real life (as in the *Lord of the Rings*). It might also be obvious that New York has not really flooded (as happens in *The Day After Tomorrow*). But, when the same digital technology is used to modify the colors of a film, to add and/or remove details that are or are not desired by the director, to add digital crowds, an animal or even an entire human character (see Prince, "True Lies"; "Emergence"), then digital cinema (be it digitally modified analogue cinema or "cinema" created uniquely with computers) can be classified as posthumanist, or, at the very least, as anti-humanist. It should be noted that animated humans are still not quite realistic enough to pass for "real" humans (unless it has already happened and we have not yet noticed), but the mix of "real" and "virtual" elements, even on the level of color, suggests a cinema that is no longer an indexical representation of a reality that existed before the camera (even if that "reality" was part of a "fictional" world, i.e. a set), but rather a new, posthumanist reality, which possesses a new ontology that similarly raises questions about our old, "human" reality.

We shall return to the question of realism, but first I would like to highlight one further way in which digital technology helps to create a posthumanist cinema. Traditionally, the analogue camera has been thought to represent (the equivalent of) a human point of view, or, more precisely, has been equated to "seeing" or having an "eye" in the sense that (most) humans do. This simple equation of the camera's perspective with a human perspective is undermined, however, once digital technology allows filmmakers to dispense with the camera entirely. For, whilst digital technology can create all manner of effects and manipulate the captured contents of an image in any way that the director/graphic designer sees fit (creating a hybrid image of analogue and digital), a director/cinematographer can also use digital technology to enable the camera to do whatever she or he wishes. This can include the creation of impossible (i.e. impossible for humans as far as natural perception is concerned) viewpoints (be they of infinitely small objects or infinitely large ones), the creation of impossible "camera" moves (passing through walls, oncoming vehicles, and even human beings), or a combination of the two. The ability to do this renders cinema posthumanist for, not only do digital effects allow the spectator to see impossible creatures and events that challenge our humanist understanding of reality; but it also allows the spectator herself to adopt impossible (as far as human powers of vision and motion are concerned) viewpoints. The reason that these "impossible" "camera" moves are possible is because they dispense with the camera entirely. Instead, through Universal Capture and other techniques, an entire scene is digitized in 3D, subsequently allowing the filmmaker to "film" it in whatever way she or he chooses.

In other words, digital cinema is a cinema that can be made without cameras and it is a cinema that can be made without human characters or even actors. Misappropriating the title of Dziga Vertov's most famous film, therefore, digital cinema can involve a man *without* a movie camera and movies without men.

One might argue that cinema has not needed to involve a camera or human characters since its inception, especially if one considers the early tradition of spectacular cinema established by Georges Méliès and Dadasaheb Phalke, in which the role of human characters is downplayed in favour of "magical" beings such as the Man in the Moon (see Cubitt), or, indeed, the whole history of film animation, which need not involve cameras at all if, like Len Lye or Norman McLaren, one paints directly on to celluloid. (Lev Manovich [*Language*, 302] takes this argument one step further by saying that digital technology has transformed cinema into a subset of animation rather than the other way round, which has traditionally been the case). In addition, cinema has long since involved what Bordwell ("Camera Movement," 24) calls "forbidden movements" that "block an anthropomorphic reading, refusing it as an intelligible or likely surrogate for bodily movement," although he does confess that these are limited to animation and the American avant-garde.[2] However, wonderful though the achievements of Méliès and Phalke, Lye and McLaren, and the American avant-garde arc, digital cinema involves a move away from avant-garde cinema, where the construction of the image is brought to the fore, to the mainstream, where, in the services of "realism," the movements of the camera, even ones that are "forbidden," are hidden. Indeed, it is on account of digital cinema's *realism* (and not so much the way in which it draws attention to itself) that it truly challenges our traditional notions of not only what is possible and impossible, but also, and more fundamentally, of time and space. It is not simply by showing to us the impossible that digital cinema could be described as posthuman. This depiction of the impossible has been a trait of cinema throughout its history. It is because digital cinema presents the impossible to us *as if it were possible*, rather, that it takes on its full posthumanist significance.

Having established how digital technology provides cinema with the tools to become a "posthumanist" cinema, we shall now look at how this posthumanism paradoxically has its roots in the traditionally humanist notions of cinematic realism. If posthumanism is a term that provokes strong responses, then so too is realism, and I should be at pains here to establish the kind of realism to which I am referring; that is, quite simply (and paradoxically, given his inherent humanism), a Bazinian conception of realism as a rejection of the cut and a move towards the depiction of a continuous space and time.

Before analyzing this posthumanist (and "post-Bazinian") realism, the following should be made clear: if in fact posthumanism generally does not involve the extinction of mankind, but simply offers us a perspective on mankind such that we achieve a greater understanding of our own (contingent) position in the world/universe, it is because posthumanism is not a split or schism from humanism and/or the human. Posthumanism instead offers us this new perspective through a synthesis of the old and the new, in the same way that a cyborg is *both* human *and* machine (as opposed to either human or machine). Similarly, a posthumanist cinema is not a cinema created by a spectacular split or schism from old cinematic techniques—a point that I should take great care to emphasize (hence evoking Méliès, Phalke, Lye, McLaren, and the American avant-garde above). Rather, it is a cinema that involves old techniques *in conjunction with* new techniques; it is, as Manovich ("Image Future") has pointed out, a hybrid cinema that combines the two, but which, by combining the two, draws out the inherent potential for posthumanist thinking that has long since been overshadowed by cinema's "humanist" norms. As such, digital cinema has the *potential* to be a cinema without cameras and without humans (as exemplified by, say, *Final Fantasy: The Spirits Within*, Hironobu Sakaguchi/Moto Sakakibara, 2001—although this latter film is, obviously, an animation), even if, for the time being, digital cinema retains (the appearance of having used) traditional techniques.

a cinema of intensified realism

David Bordwell ("Intensified Continuity") has pointed out that contemporary Hollywood films employ a technique that he labels "intensified continuity." In his analysis of various recent films, Bordwell explains that, contrary to the expectation of greater spatial and temporal continuity raised by the use of digital cinema (i.e. through a lack of cutting), there is in fact as much if not *more* cutting (i.e. a greater number of shots) in contemporary Hollywood. Bordwell's analysis is thorough and correct. But, whilst there is arguably more cutting/shots in contemporary Hollywood cinema, this is done in the services of *continuity*, as Bordwell himself points out. Continuity, it must be noted, is a technique employed in the services of *realism*, of a sustained and continuous diegetic world (even if that world is, say, Tatooine, as per *Star Wars*). That is, if there is a continuity of time and space, a continuity established through visual and aural cues such as lines of sight, sound bridges, and the use of offscreen space, then we feel that the story unfolds in real time and in a single, homogeneous space—even if that space is in fact fragmented into multiple shots and angles.

In spite of Bordwell's analysis, in which he highlights the greater number of shots in contemporary cinema (even if this high number is "hidden" by the techniques of continuity), we should contend that digital cinema also involves greater continuity through the use not of cuts linking images but by *not cutting at all*. In his analysis of Steven Spielberg's *War of the Worlds*, Warren Buckland (*Spielberg*) elaborates an example of this apparently unbroken continuity: Spielberg presents to us a 150-second shot featuring Ray (Tom Cruise) and his son, Robbie (Justin Chatwin), who tries to calm his terrified sister, Rachel (Dakota Fanning). The scene takes place without involving (or appearing to involve) a single cut. It is not that Spielberg films this scene from a single angle and refuses to offer us an alternative perspective. Far from it; during the scene, the camera does not stop moving, instead circling the characters, moving both into and out of the moving vehicle as if it and/or the camera were made of thin air. Since this scene does not involve a cut, it presents to us a temporal continuity (we see the scene in "real time"), that lends to the scene a greater sense of realism (even if aliens have not yet attacked Earth in the "real" world). For, and in accordance with André Bazin's theory of cinema, realism is predicated upon temporal and spatial continuity.

Spatial continuity can be understood in two different ways: continuity within a single frame and continuity within a single shot (or, after Bordwell, across shots). Continuity within a single frame can be understood as follows: rather than showing dinosaurs in one shot and humans in another, Steven Spielberg is able, in *Jurassic Park*, to show dinosaurs occupying the same frame/space as and interacting with human characters. This means that both dinosaurs and humans share the same ontology (see Elsaesser and Buckland, 215–17), creating a sense of realism through continuity within the same frame. This realism is arguably a posthumanist realism, since not only does it challenge everyday human perception through the photorealistic depiction of a creature that we know not to exist (anymore), but it also shows humans sharing the same space with other species (thereby minimizing the prominence of the human characters, who must be shown in longshot, especially if they are to appear in frame with a giant brachiosaur). However, there is also spatial continuity within a single shot; that is, the "camera" moves through a continuous space to show the *form* of that space to a greater extent than through cutting.

We can perhaps better understand this by comparing the scene in *War of the Worlds* to other "in-car" scenes that feature characters driving in other of Spielberg's blockbusters. As Buckland (*Spielberg*) explains, *Duel* (1971), *Close Encounters of the Third Kind* (1977), and *Jurassic Park* (1993), feature "in-car" scenes and, in each Spielberg divides them into various shots from various different angles. Now, even if the "continuity" across the shots—be it in the form of engine hum, passing scenery, etc.—"matches," i.e. gives the appearance of continuity, each cut lessens the realism of the scene, because it fragments space (and time), whilst in human reality, we experience space (and time) as continuous. Of course, it is sometimes in Spielberg's interests to cut; by cutting away from a head-on shot that allows us to see through the rear windscreen (and behind the driver), Spielberg can deprive the viewer of the knowledge that a truck (*Duel*), a UFO (*Close Encounters...*) or a dinosaur (*Jurassic Park*) is following the vehicle—thereby making it all the more surprising when said truck, UFO or dinosaur appears. Similarly, Spielberg can create suspense precisely by allowing us to see the following truck, UFO or dinosaur, whilst the driver, also in shot, looks obliviously ahead (without checking his rear-view mirror). Because we know more than the respective drivers (Dennis Mann, Richard Dreyfuss and Sam Neill), in that we know that something/someone is following them when they themselves do not, we ask ourselves the question: will these drivers be able to notice the (potential) danger before it is too late? However, whilst the use of cutting to create suspense or any other effect is without doubt evidence of a filmmaker's skill, it still diminishes the realism/spatial and temporal continuity of the scene (and in fact self-consciously exploits its *falseness* in order to create a certain sensation in the viewer, namely suspense). Although the scene in *War of the Worlds* features no chasing aliens, Spielberg could easily create the same suspense by moving the camera around the car in a certain direction and at a certain pace, such that the imminent danger (if it existed) were either on- or off-screen at the appropriate moment, but all the while this effect would remain built into a single, continuous shot that would, through its very continuity, be more realistic (although, again, this is in spite of the fact that Hollywood does not so much seek to replicate everyday life, as create credible versions of extraordinary/"impossible" situations—here, an alien invasion).

The continuity of the shot makes it realistic, in that it depicts a continuous time and space, but this realism is also predicated upon something that is impossible for a physical camera. A film camera, given its bulk, cannot typically pass through the closed windows of a car, for it would have to smash through the windscreen and/or knock the door frame. If a real camera did this, the realism of the shot would be destroyed by our becoming aware that the camera was present. Although much of the scene in *War of the Worlds* was shot using a physical camera, the scene is segued together into a seamless whole (as opposed to one fragmented into different shots which are linked through cuts) through the use of digital technology. Thanks to the digital technology that links the shots into a single, homogeneous scene, Spielberg's latest car scene presents to us a space that is continuous, but not from the human perspective. For, neither a physical camera nor a human can pass through glass panes without smashing them. For physical cameras and for humans, space *is* fragmented by the solid, physical objects that fill it—be those objects window panes, cars, walls, mountains, or entire planets. By passing through one or any of these objects, this, and other scenes like it, suggest to us a non-human, or post-humanist, realism. By divesting the camera and/or the physical obstacle of its very solidity, digital cinema can present to us a continuous space; this continuous space is, paradoxically, realistic from the Bazinian point of view, but not realistic according to a human understanding of reality (we cannot do what the "camera" does).

There are numerous other examples of this in contemporary cinema.[3] Let us limit ourselves to two films, both by the same director. In *Panic Room* (2002), the "camera" can pass between the legs of a banister frame and through a keyhole. In *Fight Club*, the "camera" can move down through an office block, into a basement car park, towards a van, through a bullet hole in the rear window of the van, and into a close-up of a bomb. On another occasion, we learn that the apartment of the film's narrator (Edward Norton) has been destroyed due to a fire caused by a gas leak. As if it were the gas, the "camera" moves around the apartment, hugging the surfaces of the floor and tables. It approaches the refrigerator and moves behind it before reaching the ignition spark that turns the fridge on according to its timer. The apartment goes up in flames. On another occasion still, the "camera" drifts past an outsize Starbuck's coffee cup and various other bits of detritus before emerging from the inside of a waste paper bin and into the narrator's office. Each of these is a further instance in which the "camera" performs an "impossible" and continuous shot, a shot that is made possible by its having been finally put together not with a camera at all, but with a computer.

If more proof were needed of the posthumanist nature of these shots, then we need only consider the opening shot of *Fight Club*, in which the "camera" tracks backwards from the fear centre of the narrator's brain, through his scalp, down his face and then down the barrel of a gun that has been placed inside the narrator's mouth. Here, not just physical obstacles have been passed through, but so has an entire human. If these films suggest a posthumanist perspective thanks to their ability to pass through solid objects as if they were thin air, then, by passing through a human being, that human being is similarly reduced to the equivalent of "thin air." In other words, *Fight Club*'s narrator is not the privileged individual that we might normally associate with the main protagonist of a feature film. Rather, the narrator is simply another piece of undifferentiated space through which the "camera" can pass as easily as through "empty" space. This is fitting in a film in which the narrator discovers that "he" does not exist in the same way that he thinks he does. For, the narrator of *Fight Club* is also Tyler Durden (Brad Pitt), and we cannot rightly separate the two, even after Tyler has shot the narrator/himself in the head (since the final shot of the film involves a 6-frame insert of a penis, a practise that Tyler "himself" used to do, suggesting that "he" is still at large). In other words, if *Fight Club*'s narrator cannot tell what is inside ("himself") from what is outside ("other" people), then it is fitting that the "camera" also pays no respect to the narrator's supposedly physical boundaries (his flesh). Deprived of any material boundaries, the narrator/Tyler does not exist in any fashion to which we humans are used; the narrator finds "himself" a polymorphous identity in a posthumanist world.

The shots in *War of the Worlds*, *Panic Room* and *Fight Club* suggest a spatial continuity, in that the "camera" can pass through solid objects, including humans, as if they were thin air. These shots are also temporally continuous, in that they are single shots (they take place in "real time"). However, it will perhaps be best to provide further examples of how temporal continuity, established via a failure to cut, can also suggest greater realism than the fragmentation of scenes into different shots (even if these cuts are linked and make sense through the tropes of continuity editing). We can do this by comparing two scenes involving teleportation, the first from Jean Cocteau's *La belle et la bête* (1946) and the latter from Bryan Singer's *X2*. In Cocteau's film, Belle (Josette Day) dons the glove that the beast (Jean Marais) has given to her. This enables her to teleport from the beast's castle to her family home. We see her disappear from her bed in the beast's castle. The film cuts to what appears to be a wall in the castle, and from it emerges Belle. The shot is achieved by playing backwards an aerial shot of Belle lying horizontal on a sheet held taut over two supports, one either side of the actress. At the time of filming, gravity causes Belle to fall between the supports and to be engulfed by the sheet. When played backwards, the shot looks as though a vertical Belle emerges from the wall. This "magic" shot is accompanied by a third shot of Belle, standing vertically against the wall that the sheet was supposed to represent. Of course, while watching the film play forwards, we follow the logic of the sequence and see Belle emerging from the wall (only close analysis reveals how the effect was achieved). By contrast, in *X2*, Nightcrawler (Alan Cumming) infiltrates the White House in an attempt to send a pro-mutant political message to the President. Once detected, Nightcrawler teleports back and forth in order to fool and defeat security guards that are trying to stop him. We see Nightcrawler disappear, before reappearing elsewhere. Not only is it practically undetectable how the shot was done, but Nightcrawler appears, disappears and reappears *within the same, continuous shot*. Now, both scenes use artifice to give the impression of continuity; but if the quest for realism has involved a history of ever-more subtle ways of *hiding* the cut, then cinematic realism could potentially have reached its apogee thanks to digital technology, because the scene in *X2* does not so much hide the cut as not feature a cut at all. With all due respect to Cocteau (whose genius perhaps deserves even greater praise than Singer's given the ease with which digital effects can, allegedly, be deployed), the temporal continuity of/the lack of cuts during the teleportation in *X2* means that it achieves a greater level of realism (albeit that teleportation is, as yet, beyond the ken of human beings).[4]

In addition to the above, digital technology means that we can photorealistically travel in a single, continuous shot from deep space and into Planet Earth and vice versa—as happens in *Contact* (Robert Zemeckis, 1997) and *Event Horizon* (Paul W.S. Anderson, 1997) (for an analysis of these shots, see Ndalianis,155–6). It would appear, therefore, that there really are no obstacles to digital technology's ability to expand the language of cinema, not only in terms of what can photorealistically be depicted, but also in terms of how these things are depicted, for, by removing the camera from the filmmaking process, the filmmaker is free to show us anything from any angle (and for as long as she wants).

towards a supercinema

Neither spatial nor temporal *continuity* (or lack thereof) is new to cinema. André Bazin, in his analysis of the films of Jean Renoir and Orson Welles (*Renoir*; *Welles*), has emphasized the relationship between continuity and realism. Digital cameras can, of course, allow filmmakers to capture images that possess nearly the same resolution as an analogue 35mm camera and for longer than the typical, 10-minute reel. This arguably does provide "greater" realism through greater continuity, as exemplified by Alexander Sokurov's 96-minute, single-shot film, *Russian Ark* (2001), which was made using the Sony 24p high definition digital camera.[5] However, through a hybridization of old techniques (continuity) and new techniques (digital creations, manipulation of images, digitized sets, passing through walls, etc.), we do reach a "new" or (after Bordwell) an "intensified" realism that might also be described as posthumanist.

Scott McQuire asks why anyone would want to make a film solely on a computer. The question is an apt one, for there certainly remain limitations to what can and/or cannot be achieved with digital technology. However, McQuire's question is also short-sighted. If digital cinema is a hybrid of the old and the new (in the same way that a cyborg similarly combines the old and the new), it is, in part, only so because it chooses to be. All of the films discussed may contain instances of posthumanist spatial continuity, or instances of temporal continuity which, in a single, continuous and realistic shot, see creatures like Nightcrawler act in an impossible/"posthuman" manner. But these films do also contain numerous, perhaps more instances, of traditional filmmaking techniques, such as editing with cuts, etc. However, in theory there is nothing stopping a filmmaker from *never* cutting. In addition, in the same way that these films can make us rethink the conventions of characterization, or can dispense with the camera as we traditionally understand it (it is no longer a physical, recording object), so, too, could digital technology enable us to rethink the notion of frames and framing, and virtually any/every other aspect of films and filmmaking. Many of these films challenge traditional narratives (through twist endings, through convoluted chronologies, through our inability to tell what is "false" from what is "real," as well as more simply through the rise of the passive victim as opposed to the active hero[6]), but they do so by retaining enough of a traditional narrative for us to recognize how/why it is challenging that tradition. These films involve new techniques, but they also retain many traditional techniques that allow us to recognize the new for what it is. But this need not be so, and, if we are allowed briefly to speculate, the future might hold a "cinema" so different as eventually to be unrecognizable to the cinema that we know today, which has already been so profoundly changed by the advent of digital technology.

If we might make an analogy, traditional analogue cinema is like Batman. As Batman is a human trying to be a superhero, so too is analogue cinema a "human" art form that tries to hide its technical limitations (by hiding cuts through realist techniques of the sort praised by Bazin, including spatial and temporal continuity, continuity editing, and, of course, deep focus). Digital cinema, on the other hand, is a cinema that need not cut at all, and yet which employs techniques such as the cut in order to hide its potential for being so radically new as to be unrecognizable. In this sense, digital cinema is Superman, a superhuman pretending to be human, as opposed to Batman, who tries to be a superhuman but who is, at the last, all too human.

The notion of digital cinema as posthuman is rendered all the more interesting when we recall Manovich's dictum that the digital image is simply *colors changing in time* (*Language*). In other words, if we consider images in the same way that a computer does, the information that comprises the digital image is rendered simply as a series of pixels, each of which represents a certain color in a certain position. Whether each pixel is, when we see it onscreen, "part of" a human, a sky or a wall is, to the computer, irrelevant. Even when a digital film gives the appearance of cutting, it is still simply (fixed) pixels changing color (i.e. *colors changing in time*; there is no "cut" at all). For the computer, therefore, a wall, a human, sky, an animal, a planet—each is simply pixels, with no pixel having greater or lesser prominence or meaning than any other. In yet another, but quite fundamental, way, the "pixelization" of all matter in order to create a digital image deprives that matter (even if it is "part of" a human) of all meaning beyond its immediate color value. From the perspective of the computer used to create it, therefore, the digital image is, once again, posthumanist in its tendency to democratize/not to distinguish between the supposed referents that it depicts (a tendency that does, of course, exist in analogue cinema, where images are in fact simply grades of light and shade on celluloid; but perhaps, as suggested below, the digital, posthumanist way of thinking applies not just to digital cinema, but to all cinema— simply digital technology drew out cinema's posthumanist characteristics and brought them into the open/the mainstream).

projecting a camera

Having looked at the various ways in which digital cinema can be considered a posthumanist cinema, especially because it involves humans without movie cameras and movies without men (or, at the very least, men deprived of their privileged position in the movies), we should turn our attention to a problem in film theory Edward Branigan highlights in his book, *Projecting a Camera*, before seeing whether his understanding of various problems involved in the discussion of the camera affect our argument for a posthumanist digital cinema.

Here, broadly speaking, Branigan explains how, when discussing the "camera" in the context of film, we often are talking at cross-purposes, since "camera" can mean different things in different contexts. In other words, the use of the term "camera" in the discussion of a specific film or of film in general reflects not so much a shared understanding of the camera asan absolute and fixed notion, but more how each discussant's mind works when thinking about a/the "camera" in the context of a film or film in general (*Projecting*, 60).

How we "project" different meanings of the word camera can perhaps most easily be conceptualized by remembering that, when we watch a film, we do not literally see a moving image, but a succession of still images in which *nothing* in fact moves. Therefore, when, watching a film (and discussing it), to talk of a "camera" (or even of "movement" or a "shot") is to *construct* these phenomena. In other words, we bring our own interpretations of these concepts from outside the literal cinema experience (which is the viewing of a succession of still images) in order to describe that experience. This can perhaps be understood most clearly when we consider that viewers are happy to overlook continuity errors, etc, in watching a film in order to follow a film's fiction (176); that is, we do not analyze what we literally see, but how we interpret what we see. In addition, it is worth bearing in mind that it is through prior knowledge of the outside world that we can recognize a human on a cinema screen, for this "human" is in fact constituted by light projected through colored celluloid.

If, when discussing cinema, we in effect "project" a camera (we apply our own interpretation of the word camera), this means that different people can use the word "camera" to refer to quite different ideas: my definition of camera is different from yours. Discussants might believe that there is consensus of definition when discussing a "camera," when this is in fact far from being the case, as Branigan so lucidly points out. Camera as a notion is therefore determined by how members of a community agree to confront physical reality (96). After Wittgenstein, Branigan sees projecting a camera as taking part in "language-games"; or, as Buckland ("Death," 311) puts it, Branigan points out "the multiple, contradictory, literal and metaphorical meanings of fundamental concepts in film theory." As a result, Branigan argues that

> a camera should be analyzed not *as* an identifiable *center* for
> a film (the private instrument of an Author) but, instead,

as a dispersed and depersonalized (impersonal) effect of watching a film. A camera comes into being—we are able to place it—as we discuss and appraise our reactions to a film. A camera will appear in many places, not just in the place occupied by the physical camera. . . . To frame a camera, we must understand the formal or informal language we use to see it. (*Projecting*, 18)

Branigan on occasion refers to various of the issues that we have raised in this chapter. For example, he feels that continuity editing "anthropomorphizes" a camera; that is, we attribute human characteristics to a camera/ believe that it provides us with a "human" point of view, but that "eccentric angles, swish pans, impossible camera positions . . . and impossible movements" (39) involve a non-anthropomorphic camera. Given our analysis of the "impossible shots" from *War of the Worlds* and *Fight Club*, we can see howcontinuity, a technique that surely inclines a viewer normally to anthropomorphize the camera, can in fact be turned against itself, allowing continuity not to reinforce this anthropomorphization, but to challenge it, suggesting not a humanist, but a posthumanist point of view.

Branigan believes that, by pointing out that we "project" a camera through language-games, he exposes the camera as being not a

real, physical object moving around in a profilmic or post-filmic reality in order to show the choices being made by an invisible observer . . . or else to relay no one's point of view. . . . Instead, film is rid of misleading and reductive anthropomorphisms. "Humanism" is relocated within a larger process whereby society fabricates meaning for itself according to prescribed conventions of behaviour, canons of interpretation, and accepted practices. The qualities that count as "human" would be defined through a given social system and not by an immutable, a priori conception of "human nature." (88)

Again, Branigan's argument that the camera is not a given but a linguistic construct reinforces our posthumanist *understanding* of digital cinema, in which there is no camera. For, Branigan, by considering the camera as not being a physical entity, reduces humanism to being a fabrication of society. Digital cinema, in which there literally is no camera, similarly forces us to rethink our understanding of cinema from a posthumanist perspective.

"In the present age," says Branigan

where each new form of digital media provokes a frantic search for its unique features, I believe that the lessons of Eisenstein remain pertinent. One should be cautious about

> focusing too quickly on physical characteristics, technology, and typical operations of a medium at the expense of radial sorts of connections to other "older" media. The reality status of a new medium is relative. (118)

Branigan is correct to raise this issue, and it is for this reason that it is important to understand the use of digital technology as involving not a complete split or schism from older, analogue cinema, but to understand that it continues to respect/obey the conventions of the analogue narrative (even though it does not need to).

Branigan continues:

> theorists of "new media" conclude that essential qualities of film cannot be photographic because new technologies make it impossible to tell the difference between a photograph and a computer-generated picture. Such arguments miss the point, because they are premised on the need for a perceiver to attain *certainty* in his or her judgments based on acts of perceiving. . . . When looking at an image, what is it that one is supposed to be certain of? A connection to the world, if it is to be true? I have been arguing that the physical connection of photography to the world is not the issue. A connection to the world may be causal (and thus truly representative, even "causal") in many ways *other* than "physical." And these other ways cannot be reduced to the physical. (181–2)

Here Branigan reminds us that digital cinema, in spite of its non-photographic nature, still looks like a photograph and contains images that we recognize as containing "humans," "walls," etc. However, to remember, after Manovich, that the digital image is simply *colors changing in time*, and that, to a computer, a digital image has no discernible contents (or even a physical reality), is to concur with Branigan: just because the digital image is not physically real, it still looks like reality. However, it is important for us to remember (from a posthumanist point of view) that these images are a false construct, in the same way that Branigan urges his readers to remember that the recognition of reality relies upon the viewer bringing prior knowledge and expectations of reality to the cinema-going experience.

Early in his book, Branigan writes:

> Once we reject the idea that "meanings" exist in the world, hidden inside objects and texts, the focus of inquiry will shift to the cognitive activities of a spectator: how we see objects *under descriptions* and how *interpretations* are made, how we "connect" and "go on." A film "text" then becomes a

81

(loose) collection of descriptions of an artifact . . . meaning and knowledge have a basis in the body. (21)

In other words, Branigan is correct to remind the film viewer that whatever "meaning" we attribute to a film is an interpretation on the viewer's part and not inherent to the film itself. By understanding the immaterial nature of digital cinema, in which there is no camera, we are made to reach the same conclusion: a digital film might look like a "normal" film, and we may use traditional words like "camera" or "shot" or "meaning" to describe it. But, in fact, and on account of its very immateriality (as well as its inhuman characters and "impossible" perspectives/camera movements), these are terms and interpretations that we bring to the film, but which are not inherent to it.

Whilst Branigan perceptively raises issues about the ways in which we have traditionally understood films, it would appear that the literal disappearance of the camera that potentially comes through the adoption by cinema of digital technology, can lead us to draw similar conclusions. That is: by realizing that we "project" a camera (a concept that is more readily graspable when we look at films that have been constructed without a camera), we can arrive at a posthumanist perspective on cinema. This posthumanist perspective is also made more readily graspable by the ways in which digital cinema often does, in its content, reflect the logic of the tools used to create it. For, by depicting the end of humanity, or worlds in which humanity's central place is downplayed, and by reflecting this content in its form, we can readily grasp the posthumanist perspective on film.

All the while respecting the likelihood that all use of terms and concepts involves "language-games" (something that is as true for Branigan as it is for this chapter), we might argue that, whilst Branigan's thesis is both rigorous and timely, digital cinema raises the same questions through its very nature—and perhaps more tangibly owing to the literal manner with which cameras, characters and traditional editing techniques can be dispensed. The potential similarities between Branigan's thesis and digital cinema as a literal phenomenon itself means that viewing *all* cinema from the posthumanist (or digital) perspective might, after Branigan, enrich our (understanding of our) understanding of cinema *tout court*, and not just digital cinema itself.

notes

1 One might also add that contemporary Hollywood sees a "crisis of action." In contrast to the classical Hollywood narrative, many films now do not so much feature narratives in which a human character chooses to undertake certain tasks/roles—overcoming adversity in order to reach his or her final goal. Rather, many contemporary Hollywood films, as Elsaesser and Buckland (271), after Deleuze, have pointed out, involve characters who find themselves passively the victims of a certain situation, to which they

must respond. This subtle, but noticeable reversal undermines the humanist conception of cinema, because it reduces humans from being causal agents to mere reagents, characters trapped in a scenario that was not of their own making. In other words, there is a shift from viewing humans as the primary motivators in stories, to seeing humans as victims of considerably greater forces against which we must subsequently struggle. Cubitt (251) similarly describes this as "heroic problem-solving."

2   Edward Branigan (*Narrative Comprehension*) also discusses ways in which the camera can occupy impossible positions thanks to the manipulation of the set (removing walls so that the camera can occupy a certain position). The point, however, is not so much that such practices are brand new, but that they are increasingly commonplace, which in turn draws out and adds emphasis to the potential for the posthumanist approach to cinema, an approach that itself might enhance and/or instruct our view of cinema/ open up new avenues for critical debate.

3   One might also think of the so-called Burly Brawl in *Matrix: Reloaded*, in which Neo (Keanu Reeves) fights many incarnations of Agent Smith (Hugo Weaving). As Manovich ("Image Future") explains, the use of Universal Capture here enables the entire scene (temporal duration) and set (space) to be digitized in 3D, thus enabling the "camera" to show us any perspective it chooses.

4   Perhaps it is appropriate here to emphasize that realism, as I employ the term here, is different from credibility. The intention here is not to say that we do not credit the Cocteau effect, nor even to make any claims for a "cine-literate" contemporary spectator who, used as she might be to "seamless" digital special effects, does not credit the Cocteau scene any more. Whether audiences now or in the past find/found the Cocteau or the Singer teleportations to be credible or not, that the Singer teleportation does not contain a single cut suggests, if we use Bazin (against himself), a greater level of realism by virtue of its continuity/lack of cuts.

5   Mention might also be made of Mike Figgis' 96-minute real time split screen movie, *TimeCode* (2000), shot on DV.

6   See endnote 1.

works cited

Balázs, Béla. "The Close Up." *Film Theory and Criticism: Introductory Readings*, 4th edition. Eds. Gerald Mast, Marshall Cohen, Leo Braudy. Oxford: OUP, 2001. 260–62.

Bazin, André. *What is Cinema?* Trans. Hugh Gray. Berkeley: University of California Press, 1967.

——. *What is Cinema?* Vol. *II*. Trans. Hugh Gray. Berkeley: University of California Press, 1971.

——. *Jean Renoir*. Trans. W.W. Halsey II and William H. Simon. London: WH Allen, 1974.

——. *Orson Welles: A Critical View*. Trans. Jonathan Rosenbaum. London: Elm Tree Books, 1978.

Bordwell, David. "Camera Movement and Cinematic Space." *Ciné-Tracts: A Journal of Film, Communication, Culture and Politics* 1:2 (Summer 1977): 19–25.

——. "Intensified Continuity: Visual Style in Contemporary American Film." *Film Quarterly* 55:3 (Spring 2002): 16–28.

Branigan, Edward. *Narrative Comprehension and Film*. London: Routledge, 1992.

———. *Projecting a Camera: Languages-Games in Film Theory*. New York: Routledge, 2006.

Buckland, Warren. *Directed by Steven Spielberg: Poetics of the Contemporary Hollywood Blockbuster*. New York/London: Continuum, 2006.

———. "The Death of the Camera: A Review and Rational Reconstruction of Edward Branigan's *Projecting a Camera: Languages-Games in Film Theory*." *New Review of Film and Television Studies* 4:3 (December 2006): 311–30.

Cubitt, Sean (1999). "Phalke, Méliès and Special Effects Today." *Wide Angle* 21.1 (1999): 115-130. Also available at http://muse.jhu.edu/demo/wide_angle/v021/21.1cubitt.html.

De Landa, Manuel. *War in the Age of Intelligent Machines*. New York: Zone Books, 1991.

Deleuze, Gilles, and Félix Guattari. *Anti-Oedipus: Capitalism and Schizophrenia*. Trans. Robert Hurley, Mark Seem and Helen R. Lane. London: Athlone Press, 1983.

———. *A Thousand Plateaux*. Trans. Brian Massumi. London: Continuum, 2004.

Elsaesser, Thomas, and Warren Buckland. *Studying Contemporary American Film: A Guide to Movie Analysis*. London: Arnold, 2002.

Hansen, Mark B.N. "Cinema Beyond Cybernetics, or How to Frame the Digital Image." *Configurations* 10 (2002): 51–90.

Haraway, Donna J. *Simians, Cyborgs and Women: The Reinvention of Nature*. New York: Routledge, 1991.

Hayles, N. Katherine. *How We Became Posthuman: Virtual Bodies in Cybernetics, Literature and Informatics*. Chicago: University of Chicago Press, 1999.

Jenkins, Henry. "The Work of Theory in the Age of Digital Transformation." *A Companion to Film Theory*. Eds. Toby Miller and Robert Stam. Malden, MA: Blackwell, 1999. 234–61.

Johnston, John. "Machinic Vision." *Critical Inquiry* 26:1 (Autumn, 1999): 27–48.

Kittler, Friedrich. *Gramophone Film Typewriter*. Trans. Geoffrey Winthrop-Young and Michael Wutz. Stanford: Stanford University Press, 1999.

Lewis, Jon (ed.). *The End of Cinema as We Know It: American Film in the Nineties*, London: Pluto Press, 2001.

McLuhan, Marshall. *Understanding Media: The Extensions of Man*. London: Routledge, 2001.

McQuire, Scott. "Digital Dialectics: the Paradox of Cinema in a Studio Without Walls." *Historical Journal of Film, Radio and Television* 19:3 (1999): 379–97.

Manovich, Lev. *The Language of New Media*. Cambridge, MA: MIT Press, 2001.

——— "Image Future." *Animation: An Interdisciplinary Journal* 1:1 (2006): 25–44.

Mast, Gerald, Marshall Cohen, and Leo Braudy (eds.). *Film Theory and Criticism: Introductory Readings*, 4th edition. Oxford: OUP, 2001.

Miller, Toby, and Robert Stam (eds.). *A Companion to Film Theory*. Malden, MA: Blackwell, 1999.

Pisters, Patricia. *The Matrix of Visual Culture: Working with Deleuze in Film Theory*. Stanford: Stanford University Press, 2003.

Prince, Stephen. "True Lies: Perceptual Realism, Digital Images, and Film Theory." *Film Quarterly* 49:3 (1996): 27–37.

———. "The Emergence of Filmic Artifacts: Cinema and Cinematography in the Digital Era." *Film Quarterly*, 57:3 (2004): 24–33.

Selinger, Evan and Timothy Engström. "On Naturally Embodied Cyborgs: Identities, Metaphors, and Models." *Janus Head* 9:2 (2007): 553–84.

Virilio, Paul. *War and Cinema: The Logistics of Perception.* Trans. Patrick Camiller. London: Verso, 1989.

———. *The Vision Machine.* Trans. Julie Rose. Bloomington: Indiana University Press, 1994.

Warwick, Kevin. *I, Cyborg.* London: Century, 2002.

movie-games

and

game-movies

four

towards an

aesthetics of

transmediality

douglas brown and
tanya krzywinska

Gilles Deleuze argues that the power of film lies in the close alliance between
the cinematic process and perceptual thought; film not only "puts movement in the image, it also puts movement in the mind" (366). In conjunction with the cinematic apparatus, which is as much perceptual as material,
audio and visual vocabularies working in the service of film,[1] become a
potent and flexible palette capable of generating a vast array of meanings
and emotions. Like film, digital games are screen-based, and as such utilize
many cinematic features, providing thereby one of the more basic and
formal reasons for the increasing numbers of movie-game tie-ins.

Digital games often employ aspects of cinema to make more meaningful and lend resonance to the activities undertaken by players in a game,
yet what defines games generally, distinguishing them from other media,
is that a game has to be played. This necessarily involves the player in
making choices that affect in some way the state of the game and that the
game responds to those choices. Many movie tie-in games highlight the
participatory nature of games in their advertising: "Live the Movie: Be the Hero"

(*The Lord of The Rings: The Return of the King*, 2003, EA Games/New Line Cinema); "Pack your bags and move to Middle-Earth" (*The Lord of the Rings Online*, Turbine, 2007); or even herald these sentiments in a game's title as with *Enter the Matrix*, backed up with the slogan "In the war to save Zion, what part will you play?" (2003, Shiny/Atari). This is a major claim, but an entirely valid one. It is not simply marketing rhetoric. Unlike any other media, in order to play digital games, players must read, predict and then respond correctly, or within certain preset parameters, to situations that arise moment-by-moment on screen and in the auditory field. This is necessary if a player is to progress, prosper and prevail—or, in other words, to retain a sense of agency within the tightly controlled, programmed spaces of games. It is the case with relatively simple casual games such as *Tetris* (1986, Spectrum Holobyte) as well as highly complex and time-consuming massively multiplayer online role-playing games like *The Lord of the Rings Online*. The player's relation to the game-screen can therefore be said to be dialogic and cybernetic.

Games are not afforded the spatial and temporal flexibilities of film however. This apparent loss is the price to pay for player agency, a sense of presence in a game space and the cybernetic circuit. Movies tend to offer a diverse range of visual entry points into a diegetic space, sometimes anchored to character in the case of the shot-reverse-shot, and at others completely disembodied as in the case of the establishing shot, plus a host of perspectives in between. Most films are then composed of a mosaic of differential shots ordered according to established convention to create some sense of continuity. This rhythm of shot types plays an important role in the aesthetic experience produced by film. In this equation the type of edits used to join shots together can signal the passing of time—a temporal ellipse might be signaled by a fade to black, for example. In many first and third person games that take place in a realized world across a range of platforms and game types, point-of-view and framing are anchored *directly* to the character whom the player controls. This is especially common in film tie-in games, where a given character is central to a franchise—or even in some cases embodies the brand (Spiderman, Batman, Superman, James Bond etc.). The camera is therefore controlled by the player, a feature that is also increasingly the case in so called "god" and strategy games (*The Sims* and *The Lord of the Rings: Battle for Middle-Earth* for example). Non-interactive cut scenes within individual games do however often utilize multiple points of view and editing, generally in the service of establishing place or situation. Cut scenes are not found in all games, and where present are rarely more than a few minutes in length, acting as support to and context for gameplay. In conjunction with the fact that many games take place in real-time, the point of view offered by games means that space and time in games are organized rather differently to that found in cinema. A further notable difference is that in a game context what is seen and heard on screen is dependent on what the player does (even if various cues and encouragement is given for wider exploration). While Hitchcock, for example, celebrates the way he can control very tightly the viewer's aesthetic experience, it is by contrast much less easy to control very tightly the minutiae of a player's gaming session. Games make capital from this difference, establishing the distinction of their medium. In different ways and to different degrees games offer various outcomes in response to players' actions and choices.

The pleasures of watching most fiction-based films designed to be consumed as entertainment can be said to lie in a luxurious submission to the dramatic journey that a given film orchestrates, which the spectator can do nothing to alter. Despite any desires or urges we may have to do so, we are forced to look on. As is the case with the novel, we are powerless to aid Boromir, should we wish, as he fights a horde of blood-thirsty Uruk-hai to his admittedly redemptive death in *The Fellowship of the Ring* (2001). By contrast, the pleasure (and sometimes almost unbearable unpleasure) of games lies in the progressive development, practice and mastery of the skills and knowledge of rules and physics necessary to act effectively within the game world. It is one thing to be caught up with the trials of a small group of endearing and fallible characters as they struggle heroically against the odds, our passage eased by the familiar and effectively expressive audio-visual vocabularies of Hollywood film. It is quite another to take up arms, to learn to be skillful, to make context sensitive choices, become embodied and thereby limit your perspective largely to your character's point of view, and to be able to explore at will a world that has been established for us in another media. These factors mean that games do in fact tell stories and provide experiences in rather different, yet still equally potent, ways to film.

To adapt Deleuze's point, digital games put movement in the image, movement in the mind, like film, but they also demand from players often precise, controlled physical movements that extend out from the physical into the virtual, where those real movements can be made more elaborate, excessive and meaningful in accordance with the imaginative world of the game. In various spheres games and movies have both shared and divergent features. A heightened awareness of these and their implications become apparent when addressing adaptations of games to films and films to games, particularly in the broader context of a culture industry that is becoming ever more intensively transmedial.

Movie-game ties-ins are often discussed generally using certain persistent rhetorics, often centered in some way on the notion of fidelity or quality. These values are the product of intricate social interactions, wherein taste and consumption are related to identity, power and social position. Such concepts can only operate through hierarchy, indeed they are produced by it. Dominant paradigms of taste affect patterns of consumption and thereby the economics of the contemporary entertainment industry—including the capacity therein to innovate, and even more fundamentally the interface between aesthetics, experience and psychology. As the new kid on the block, games generally, and not just "second-hand" tie-ins, are considered within some circles low-status, as if they are always uncomplicated and replicatory. Even the concept of "remediation" (Bolter and Grusin) which has been much used within contemporary Game Studies tends to underline replication rather than innovation. Games might have some growing up to do in terms of market and content, yet they are nonetheless the highly complex progeny of state-of-the-art screen and computing technologies. Even in their rawest, simplest or most exploitative form digital games are engaging players in ways that go beyond what is offered by cinema. While increasingly games are leading high profile franchises (Microsoft and Bungee's *Halo* or Blizzard's *World of Warcraft* for example), the medium often still suffers from the stigma of the movie tie-in, even where the adaptation to game format is artistically and neatly achieved.

movie-game growing pains: from commercialism to convergence

Videogame movie tie-ins have existed almost as long as videogames themselves. The crossover and commercial potential of the two markets was seized upon during the second generation of games machines, the *Raiders of the Lost Ark* tie-in game on the Atari 2600 in 1982 being a good candidate for the earliest direct movie-game tie-in. The relationship between games and movies has broadened ever since, with many exceptional commercial successes piggybacking a film's development, marketing and advertising to produce big profits for publishers and licensees with less of the cost and risk usually associated with the release of an original title. Movie inspired videogames have a fairly low reputation amongst dedicated gaming audiences, but this is balanced alongside significantly greater mass appeal, their connection to the hype or nostalgia generated by the movie boosting sales and diversifying audiences. There have been quite a few critical as well as commercial successes, however. *Goldeneye 007* (Rare, Nintendo, 1997), released significantly two years after the film, is generally considered one of the very best games on the Nintendo 64 console and more recently the *King Kong* (Peter Jackson, Universal, 2005) tie-in game received excellent reviews and its development was closely monitored by Jackson himself, as Kristin Thompson reports (250–3). These are as we show later exceptions to the rule, and by contrast some movie tie-ins have been disastrous failures, none more so than *E.T. The Extra-Terrestrial* (Atari, 1982), which went some way towards bankrupting Atari when the publishers assumed the game release would meet with the same popularity as Spielberg's classic. Market misconceptions have occurred in both directions, and game-inspired movies run the same risk when attempting to sell commercially solid gaming brands to an entirely different audience, as the critical failure of the movie based on that most lucrative and iconic of game franchises, *Super Mario Bros.* (Rocky Morton, Hollywood Pictures, 1983) attests. Major Japanese videogame publisher Squaresoft lost an estimated US$120 million[2] when they released the movie *Final Fantasy: The Spirits Within* (Hironobu Sakaguchi, Columbia Pictures, 2001) and it completely failed to draw in audiences, eventually forcing a merger with rivals Enix. In videogame spheres the "Final Fantasy" moniker and branding is sufficient to guarantee a hit.

The crossover potential for exciting, innovative adaptations of movies into games does exist, but in a hit-driven business like the games industry the stakes are so high that few companies are really willing to gamble on a movie license which may have been expensive in and of itself. However, compromises are emerging. Chief amongst these are diversified spinoff games which fall under the umbrella of the license but do not directly mimic the movie or replicate game-friendly scenes. *Star Wars: Starfighter* (Lucasarts, 2001) and *The Matrix Online* (Monolith/EON/Warner/Sega, 2005) provide two examples. As occurred with the *King Kong* game, planning communication between film creatives and game design teams earlier on in the movie development process is alleviating some of the problems that previously contributed to problems critics and gamers had with movie tie-ins. Film writers are even including some games in their screen narratives, as was attempted in the crossover between the *Matrix: Reloaded* (Wachowski Bros./Warner, 2003) movie and the *Enter the Matrix* game, where some scenes in the film only made complete sense if the viewer had completed the videogame, and vice-versa. The prequel to the *Pitch Black* series of films was developed as a game: *The Chronicles of Riddick: Escape from Butcher Bay* (Starbreeze Studios, 2004), and met with praise for playing to the strengths of both mediums. Presently, the cutting edge game design studio Oddworld Inhabitants is working on a simultaneous game and animated film release, where the two distinct works will be directly interrelated. Thus, narrative universes are forming as a result of commercial interests' desires to exploit the potential of franchises and spread the risks of innovation, and a creative desire to maximize their respective potentials. This is more commonly known as media convergence. Nonetheless short lead-in times and a lack of sufficient investment can lead to poorly realized games that lean for sales on enthusiasm for the franchise, even in the case of major studios like Disney. It should be noted that games associated with large well-established franchises still sell, and sell extremely well, because of brand recognition. *Spider-Man 2* (Activision, 2004) the official movie-game tie-in for the Playstation 2 for example sold 1.12 million copies in the US despite receiving mediocre reviews, demonstrating the power of the brand and the enthusiasm of that players have to inhabit a fictional world in this case in the skin of a superhero.[3]

Franchising and convergence therefore play important roles in game-movie and movie-game adaptations. Henry Jenkins claims that we are now living within a "convergence culture." He notes that this represents a shift in media ownership, with media conglomerates having "controlling interests across the entire entertainment industry," which is changing the way media is consumed (16). Convergence occurs at the levels of technology, content and commerce, providing a context within which certain cultural and industrial practices have emerged. The digital age has been celebrated for its capacity to offer more flexible and participatory media that empowers the consumer (see Kline et al. for rigorous critical analysis of such rhetorics), yet the rise of convergence has placed the "franchise" as central to the marketing strategies of many media and entertainment conglomerates. Risk splitting is often an active facet of this strategy. Targeting as many different markets as possible with the same Intellectual Property (IP) allows more opportunity for hits with less risk attached and it also can be used to maintain a brand's visibility. The movie-game is often just a single strand of this scattergun marketing approach. In a risk-averse industry, where in 2004 the average cost of producing a game title was $15 million and since then has undoubtedly grown (Thompson, 226), mainstream popular culture now features what was once the domain of the cult. This manifests as coherent fictional worlds that span a variety of media, and are often aggressively marketed across further media. The *Resident Evil* (Capcom, 1996) franchise for example exists in dozens of games spanning several genres on multiple platforms, an expanding series of movies, ongoing literary works in Japanese as well as seven English-language novels by S. D. Perry, a comic book series and several standalone graphic novels published by Wildstorm. However, the diegetic infrastructure of the worlds and storylines portrayed in these disparate media are designed to add up into a coherent whole, or at least not contradict one another. They are designed to maintain some form of driven, expanding yet unending macro-story more akin to the format of a soap-opera than a more directed, strictly literary equivalent. Within this broad context adaptation is no longer a marginal activity, instead it has become a major trend in popular culture. The *Warcraft III* (Blizzard, 2002) strategy game is adapted, indeed has evolved, into the *World of Warcraft* (Blizzard, 2005) massively multiplayer role-playing game, utilizing the same geography, vocabulary and several forms of character class. This new game's popularity (at time of writing the most subscribed to multiplayer online game there has been) inspires the *Warcraft Trading Card Game* spinoff. Some of this latest incarnation's playing pieces feed back into the parent product, allowing upgrades to players' characters in the online role-playing game. Novels and manga-styled comics have also been published that fill in back-story, tell stories of the various races and explain the complex histories that have lead up to the current state of affairs in the game world. The whole edifice is currently being adapted into a fantasy movie in the epic mould of the *Rings* trilogy. This commercial/creative alliance pushes the franchise across yet another media frontier and continues the exploitation of the single, yet inherently malleable piece of IP. An important factor here is that a game provides the "parent" text—an indication that games are attaining greater commercial authority and status. Following the path forged by myth and fan-fiction, adaptation in this case is geared by elaboration, proliferation and participation. Evolving worlds such as the *World of Warcraft* universe or the *Eve Online* (CPC, 2003) galaxy can find creators vying with fans and players, all eager to continue the narrative they feel a personal investment in and duty towards. The use of organized online forums, wikis and websites enables a whole range of fans to add their own material and express themselves through a given franchise. This generation of group fantasy has the potential to bring immense financial benefits to the creators, who can rest on the laurels that convergence allows them. They can still break even or make profit on film-inspired videogames which pay lip service to both the inspiration and the new medium.

reading, watching, playing games—pastword: fidelio

Theories of adaptation have then to be revised to fit the contours of this new, supposedly flatter in terms of access, multi-dimensional mediascape. This is not to imply that games render many of the issues raised in previous analyses of literature-to-film offerings completely irrelevant. Of central concern to many recent theories of adaptation is the way in which film adaptations of novels or stories are regarded as inferior. The valorization of the written word above all other media cited by Robert Stam as a reason for hostility towards film adaptations of novels is largely eschewed by the digital game. It would seem more generally that within the frontier-world of new media, the written word is either deified, a signifier of authority, or regarded as expressively and aesthetically narrow, an antique curiosity best placed often in neo-medievalized worlds in the form of flowing instructional text. In the case of Japanese role-playing games designed to be consumed worldwide words become a means of dealing economically with dialogue translation. Many games do include large amounts of written text, but it is largely audio and graphical realization that is emphasized in terms of development teams' focus and technological development of game-making tools. The audio-visual is also what is most rewarded by critical reception and reviews. Cinema rather than the novel is therefore positioned as an aesthetic benchmark against which games are measured. Often in reviews of movie-game tie-ins it is film that holds the valorized position rather than the written word, which ironically may dog the film simultaneously. All three media have the potential to retain thematic cohesion, and elements of themes or meanings inherent in the original text can, and are, presented from different angles in their adaptations. The best movie-games are able to communicate something new about their parent texts on a thematic level, rather than simply parroting the events of the film, as we suggest below, even though games that replicate scenes from a film are undeniably very popular. When maverick games designer Chris Crawford councils new design recruits to avoid the film tie-in at any cost, he notes an unfortunate clash between the goals of games and movies, particularly "star vehicles." Since movies tend to privilege the visual, it might appear to be the case that audiences take greatest pleasure in seeing characters (and stars) rather than wanting to *be* them. Using a fictional action star "Big Bob Broadshoulders," Crawford warns:

> The one thing you *don't* want to do is waste time and energy trying to get creative with the game design. . . nobody is going to purchase a Big Bob Broadshoulders game for the creativity of the game itself; they are buying it solely because of the brand. Any exertions you make to give them creative design are wasted; they don't want creativity, they want Big Bob. (172)

Thus, turning away from the film in an attempt to create a different experience can, according to this model, pose just as many pitfalls for the designer as parroting the parent medium. The fundamental distinction between the passivity of film viewing and the active engagement of game playing seems therefore to be something of a barrier to adaptation. Yet this view elides the complex processes of spectatorship and fantasy, there are, as is advocated by cine-psychoanalysis, multiple entry points into a text. Many tie-in games do allow the player to see the character/star in digi-talized form, but their status as object is not absolute, as is also the case in film. Instead in both films and games we also form often a fantasy based-identification, and not just empathy, with an appealing character; games encourage greater identification because we act through the character, even as that character inevitably retains some representational status.

Stam argues that the specific attributes of cinematic form lend new dimensions to the adaptation of a story or novel into film that alter substantially our experience of it (something we claim also rings true for games). He notes that in spite of this there is still a resistance to adaptations, surfacing in loaded rhetorical terms like "parasitism." His diagnosis of such resistance in relation to these two media lies in the way film realizes concretely in audio-visual terms what, when reading, occurs within the imagination of the reader. The modal differences between delivery of content via screen or text contribute much to both the disregard of the new and the valorization of the written word. It is assumed that film viewers are passive and allow the cinematic experience to overwhelm their receptive faculties, rather like taking a warm bath on a cold day, while the *reader* must utilize imagination in an active, enlivening and highly individual relationship with the text. Game players straddle, rather uneasily, the space between the confident literary reader and the affect-seeking cinema viewer. This discomfort is symptomatic of the hybrid nature of digital games and, as Crawford's dilemma illustrates, never more in the spotlight than in the case of the movie tie-in. Boundaries are thin, particularly when Google is just a couple of clicks away, and often players consult manuals or forums during play. Text-based objects and interfaces are found regularly within a game itself, which are co-present alongside a whole range of elements derived from other media (various types of television, CCTV, cinema, photography). Players are also required to "read" embedded and enigmatic audio and visual cues extremely attentively if they are to progress through a game and achieve a satisfying sense of agency. We would argue therefore that a game player's relationship to a game is even more intrinsically dialogic than the reader's relationship with the literary text or a film. A game requires constant inputs which demand a knowledge of its rules and patterns alongside repeated efforts at suspension of disbelief in order to generate engagement at the level of the imaginary, necessary to accrue some sense of "being" in the game world. Yet games do tend to climax with a passive, highly cinematic and spectacular movie, allowing the players to sit back and view in relaxed, passive comfort the outcome of their efforts. It is also often the case that in some games, the "Prince of Persia" series (Ubisoft 1989–) for example, the player is encouraged to chain together their character's actions to produce the type of fluid, seemingly effortless and forward-moving movement found in mainstream action movies (failure and death leading to repetition and stasis which might be associated with anti-illusionist cinemas). Cinema is clearly aspired to in these ways, yet straddling multiple modes is intrinsic to playing contemporary digital games.

In the case of any adaptation, including where games are in the equation, fidelity to the originary product is usually high on the agenda when spoken of and assessed by consumers and critics. This question of fidelity becomes more complex within the context of convergence culture however, as is evident in *The Lord of the Rings Online*. This game adapts not only Tolkien's novels but also has no choice but to adapt, at least at one remove, Peter Jackson's film trilogy. As a set of blockbuster "event" movies, the "Rings" films have been watched, and watched recently, by millions, fixing in the mind of many what characters and places look and sound like. Unlike EA's franchise games (*The Return of the King*, 2003; *The Two Towers*, 2002) and Microsoft's *The Battle for Middle Earth I & II* (2004, 2006), the official tie-in games to Jackson and New Line Cinema's Trilogy, Turbine's *The Lord of the Rings Online* could not draw obviously on the IP or on the assets of the films (props, digital assets such as motion-captures, models and textures, music, actor voices etc).[4] Cues are though taken in terms of the game's iconography, characterization, landscapes and musical modes, closely enough not to jar with the experience of Jackson's films yet not so close as to incur a lawsuit. The fact that the audio-visual dimensions of the game resemble more what has been realized in Jackson's films than Ralph Baski's film of 1978, which mixed analogue animation with live action, suggests that for those who would not class themselves fans, fidelity rests on what is freshest and foremost in the popular imagination. While it might be said that the novel and Jackson's films feature strongly in *The Lord of the Rings Online*, it also draws from further afield, on more general fantasy-based texts and artistic/design influences from a range of media, including board games and table-top role-playing systems as well as other gaming genres. Many players will primarily compare this online game not to the novel or even the films but instead to other online games they have played previously, specifically those with generic similarities. The core gameplay mechanic used, alongside the game interface, are adaptations and evolutions of a genre originally adapted from table-top role-playing game *Dungeons and Dragons*, and established commercially within the multiplayer online sphere by *Everquest* (SoE, 1999–), the constant reiteration and tweaking of a few core "genre" game models being standard practice in the risk-averse games industry. A regular conversation in in-game "chat" is how the game compares to Blizzard's *World of Warcraft*, for instance, and for these players this game will be regarded as an adaptation of this and other "fantasy" online games—but of course many of these texts are themselves in fact, and in a circular fashion, indebted to and in many ways adaptations of Tolkien's *The Lord of the Rings*. Judgements about fidelity and indeed innovation become a form of cultural capital that in turn reintroduces hierarchy back into the supposedly liberated and democratic domain of new media. After acquiring the licenses from the Tolkien Estate, the developers of *The Lord of The Rings Online* found themselves having to cater directly for zealous fans of the books, dedicated MMORPG genre gamers and a mass-market of moviegoers who knew no more about the IP of *The Lord of the Rings* than was expressed in Jackson's film trilogy. The grand adaptive challenge was to tell a story, build a world and craft an enjoyable gaming experience which all added up to something new out of these disparate adaptive materials.

Both Stam and Julie Sanders note the way that critical perspectives informed by structuralism and semiotics have shaped academic analyses of adaptation. With an emphasis on cultural artefacts as "texts," notions of authorship and originality become problematized. Reader-reception theory brought with it the notion of different interpretational and situational frames that further destabilized surety about textual meaning: Lara Croft for example has been read separately as aristocratic white colonialist, cyber-bimbo or empowering action heroine tailored to suit the tastes of a post-feminist generation. With the dislocation of authority that such theory entails, Kristeva's concept of intertextuality exemplifies the now commonly accepted notion that any text, no matter how innovative it might be considered, draws systemically and intrinsically on other texts. Within game studies there has been some resistance to the notion that games can be considered "texts," a term tainted for some by literary connotations that elide the ludological (that which is specific to games as closed systems). In what can be regarded as an inversion of the cultural elevation of literature, game scholars such as Espen Aarseth (1997, 2003), Markku Eskelinen (2001, 2004) and Jesper Juul have been intent on regarding games as *games*, and thereby attempting to "emancipate the study of computer games from literary theory" (Marie-Laure Ryan, 183); film theory is also regarded in the same vein by this hard core of "ludologist" scholars as deterimental to the study of games. Nonetheless other games scholars have found it useful to regard games as texts, precisely because of the multiple affordances they provide for meaning making (Carr; Atkins and Krzywinska).

That is not to say however that the meanings a game text generates are in any way stable, or that they are directly comparable to more traditional literary or cinematic texts. Games come in a wide range of formats and many variables are in play—some games offer linear progression, others are more open. Players may choose to run *The Lord of the Rings Online* on a low-spec computer that results in less detailed graphics while others choose a high-spec computer that permits high resolution graphics and audio without lengthening the time to process player actions. *Resident Evil 4* might be played on the GameCube or the Wii (where controls are radically different). *Final Fantasy 3* might be played on a clunky console or a sleek handheld Nintendo DS. *Tomb Raider Legend* could be experienced on a small 14 inch TV or a widescreen plasma monster. You might play in the skin of an Orc Warlock and I might inhabit a Night Elf Druid in *World of Warcraft*. We might have characters of entirely the same class, race and faction in that game while you raid high level dungeons and I just chat with my mates and meander around making potions. All these examples make for different experiences of playing the same game, altering thereby the properties we experience of the "text" or indeed the characteristics of the adaptation. Films and TV serials are also consumed differently according to hardware and the panoply of factors that govern our interpretational frames, but because games can be *played* in a range of different ways, they are, as we have said earlier, more pervasively dialogic.

the success factor

The typical movie-game adaptation has traditionally remained problematic for game critics because of production issues, the goals of the creators and the difficulty of adaptation to form. The release date issue is of such importance that it is worthwhile to divide movie-related games into "game of the movie" tie-ins, such as *Spider-Man 3* (Treyarch Invention/Activision, 2007), *Lord of The Rings: The Two Towers* (EA Games, 2002) or *Pirates of the Caribbean: at World's End* (Disney Interactive, 2007), and movie-inspired games which are not subject to these marketing rigors and are released long after the movie, *Die Hard Trilogy* (Probe/Fox: 1996), *Blade Runner* (Westwood/Virgin, 1997) or *Scarface: The World Is Yours* (Radical/Vivendi, 2006) are examples. Those in the latter category have far greater opportunity for critical success than the former, simply because they are able to function within a normal development schedule and boost sales by trading off of well known and relished IP. The former category has more direct commercial potential however, because of a bigger, immediate advertising "splash." The development cycle of games in the former category is often compressed into the much tighter constraints of a movie's gargantuan marketing schedule. Production problems run rife because, perhaps, of limited cooperation from a studio which may well have never worked with game developers before and movie executives more concerned with the maintenance of the brand than the critical value of this specific finished product. Thompson for example reports EA's *The Lord of the Rings* tie-in games suffered from several problems in this regard including lack of access to voice acting, no knowledge of how the film trilogy ended until shooting stopped, and the director's lack of interest in generic "hack and slash" games (251). IP and the film material itself can be jealously guarded and only certain amounts of footage released to developers during production. Actors and special effects designers can prove difficult to deal with or ambivalent when trying to insert some genuine crossover into the game, especially where this form of voice acting isn't included in an actor's film contract. The squabbles over the license alone can run over and leave the successful developers with very limited time to throw together a product which has a release date a few weeks before the movie release set in stone. Profit-hungry developers eager for guaranteed sales and cynical film marketing anxious to diversify the movie brand into every possible sphere contribute to the mediocrity of these direct adaptation movie-games.

For many who just want to be and see Jack Sparrow for a few hours before bedtime the issues that might be of concern to a dedicated and highly informed gamer are probably not apparent. For some it is enough to laugh at his quips, get him through various and heavily signalled key presses to produce some "Jackenisms," admire the replication of Johnny Depp's/Jack's off-balance shrugging movements, and to guide him through various situations, some of which replicate scenes from the films. At this level the game is just a bit of throw-away light-hearted fun that marries spectacle and swashbuckling, just as was the case with the movie. Though it appears on several other formats, the *Pirates of the Carribbean: at World's End* for the Wii offers an ostensible unique haptic innovation in that the

Wii controller is used to make the type of movements that one would if using a sword—rather than pushing buttons. This makes a literal hand/eye connection between the action the player does outside the game and what is seen to be happening within the game's diegetic world. This might be seen as just a novelty, but works to encourage the casual gamer into the position of being Jack by shrinking the gap between a real sword stroke action and the type of action the player has to make to perform that action (pressing the x button is less like that than swishing the controller). While for some players who might be invested in a notion of quality games, this might be regarded as covering up flaws in the game, such as the inability to manipulate the camera independently of character movement, for others the game provides an opportunity to escape into a fantasy realm without too much effort or technical knowledge. It also is of direct interest to these games' core market, which represents devotees of the movie rather than a specific strata of those who frequently buy videogames.

While it is the case that tie-in games play second fiddle to their parent movies in terms of investment and production, it is worth considering whether there is something about the form of games that resists the way that films are structured. Even movie-inspired games that don't simply replicate scenes generally fail to match the critical appeal of strictly game IP franchises like *Resident Evil, Metal Gear Solid* or *Grand Theft Auto*, which generate much of their appeal through mimicking the modes of movies successfully within the game form. Yet one game has garnered critical acclaim, winning a BAFTA award in 1998 and selling over eight million copies. That is Rare's *Goldeneye 007*.

There are several reasons why *Goldeneye 007* has classic status. Primarily, it was amongst the first console first-person shooter games to fully embrace analogue control in a 3D environment, allowing players greater immediacy and fluidity of movement within the gameworld, unlike many of its competitors at the time of release. The single player "campaign" was the feature that really stood out. Inspired more by the character of James Bond than the minutiae of the movie itself it took the form of a series of missions, some based on the movie, others based on the (post hoc) novelization. Short scenes from the movie are used to build up whole levels of the game, and the story reworked to fit into the new mould. Different difficulty levels catered not only for gamers seeking more challenge, but also deepened the extra-filmic content by providing new objectives. All of the memorable scenes from the film are included in the game, from the opening base-jump off the dam through to the final confrontation with villain Trevelyan on the satellite dish. Movie quotes are interspersed with dialogue written for the game, and actors' likenesses are used for the character models. Trademarks of the franchise are reworked to serve a directly ludic purpose, so Bond's ever evolving super-watch doubles as the game's pause menu, health meter and status screen. It also sometimes functions as a weapon, and designers incorporated abilities from several Bond movies rather than being held back and allowing only the functionality the gadget had in *Goldeneye* (directed by Martin Campbell, 1995). Each mission was preceded by written briefings from Bond's backup team. Reading through these alongside some familiarity with the movie provided direction on how to act "in character" during the level and cueing successful gameplay actions, although missions can be completed in various ways. The first-person framing reduces the gap between player and character, lending more profoundly therefore the agency of Bond to the player and in providing freedom of scope and multiple ways to achieve tasks the player can realize their own self-generated movie.

This game's development was neither hurried nor underfunded, and the underlying game engine was reused for multiple original IP titles, so it was more a case of this game finding its theme in the movie than attempting a direct adaptation from source. The game and franchise complement one another without needing to compromise, and as such the original features of the game were brought to the mass market via its connection with a very well-known, long-lived and therefore malleable franchise.

The *King Kong* movie tie-in achieved critical success by a different route, opting to forego many traditional ludic elements in an attempt to bridge the gap between cinematic and gaming experiences. Primarily a first-person shooter like *Goldeneye 007,* the game has no usual display of ammo, player health levels or inventory. Instead the display is completely clear and this information is accessed by audio-visual cues, the player character's remarking when ammunition is low and the screen turning red when he is injured. Containing all this information within the diegesis meant that several other sacrifices needed to be made. There are really only two types of simple puzzles in the game repeated to varying degrees of complexity, but this simplicity and immediacy means the learning curve is minor. A further upshot of this is that players new to the genre, which unusually for this game can include quite a sizable amount of the target audience, will have no trouble immersing themselves and becoming competent. Allowing a small set of actions and control possibilities allows players to focus their attention on the monsters and the tension that encountering them can generate. Players can only carry one missile weapon at a time and ammunition is scarce, pushing the game towards "survival horror," a gaming genre with even closer links to the cinematic. Players are rewarded for getting through these tougher sections by opportunities to play as King Kong in third person segments, reminiscent of the special effects sequences in the movie. During these scenes the power relationship is reversed and players can happily run amok over the beasts that have been terrifying them.

As with many film tie-ins, the game picks out its own path through the structure of the film, rewriting the story in minor ways as appropriate to fit the new setting where players control one of the central characters of the movie. Designers created an extremely short game which can be completed in around five or six hours by a player familiar with the genre, and by sacrificing game length to the rigours of the short release date window were able to add a high degree of polish to the content that went into the finished product, as well as providing the type of narrative immediacy that is often core to the experience of watching a film. The filmmakers and their special effects studio worked closely with the game development team, and Peter Jackson collaborated directly with the game's lead designer to ensure the experience retained a degree of parity with its cinematic counterpart beyond basic aesthetic similarities. This manifests itself in a level of graphical detail considered high at the time of release which is combined with high production values of the audio tracks and sound effects. The strength of the game lies in the way that it translates the affective power of the film into its both the audio-visual and the ludic qualities of the game. The sacrifices the design team had to make are likely to prevent the game from achieving the cult status of *Goldeneye 007*. The older game takes on the franchise in order to enhance elements of itself, while the newer game gives up some elements of the gaming experience in order to get closer to the cinematic mode.

To conclude, many of the debates and issues that are pertinent in addressing film adaptations are applicable to game tie-ins, but it is important not to flatten out the differences between media. Games are still regarded by some as a juvenile medium, awaiting the touch of a D.W. Griffiths, yet in fact even in the case of those simply produced to sell on the back of a Triple A movie, games are extremely sophisticated artefacts capable of telling stories in new ways. In this sense it is perhaps reductive to consider game tie-ins as simply adaptations. As Barry Atkins says the game version of Blade Runner allows "a player to have access to a third dimension that would only be made available through its remediation as a computer game" (89). To a greater or lesser, more simple or more sophisticated degree, most movie tie-ins bring a third dimension that allows the player to penetrate the space set up by the film, whether or not this experience lives up to a player's expectations or accords with their particular tastes and aesthetic values. As Atkins astutely notes "The actual playing of a computer game is almost entirely dependent on the basic process of asking 'what if?' that then adds the agency of the 'I' in the posing of the 'what if I?'" (88). It is in this that games display a profound difference to film, adding something new, even if in many ways cinema is still placed through both tie-ins and the reverence with which many but not all game designers hold it, in the position of parent text.

notes

1 Camera movement, framing, colour, lighting, editing, dialogue, style, sound, or lack of, and music, blocking, spatial organization, kinesics, alongside narrative and characterization.
2 US Domestic total gross $32.1m opposed to total production budget of $137m using data from http://www.boxofficemojo.com/movies/?id= finalfantasy.htm (accessed February 1 2008).
3 See http://en.wikipedia.org/wiki/List_of_best-selling_video_games (accessed February 1 2008).
4 See Kristin Thompson (224–56) for an account of the commercial and technical relationships between Jackson's films and EA game tie-ins.

works cited

Aarseth, Espen J. *Cybertext: Perspectives on Ergodic Literature*. Baltimore: Johns Hopkins University Press, 1997.

Aarseth, Espen J., Solveig Smedstad and Lise Sunnanå. *A Multi-Dimensional Typology of Games. Proceedings of the DiGRA Level Up Conference*. Utrecht 2003.

Atkins, Barry "Replicating *Blade Runner*." *The Blade Runner Experience: The Legacy of a Science Fiction Classic*. Ed. Will Brooker. London: Wallflower Press, 2005.

Atkins, Barry, and Tanya Krzywinska. "Introduction." *videogame/player/text*. Eds Barry Atkins and Tanya Krzywinska. Manchester: Manchester University Press, 2007.

Bolter, Jay David and Richard Grusin. *Remediation: Understanding New Media*. Cambridge, Mass.: MIT Press, 2000.

Carr, Diane. "Un-situated Play: Textual Analysis and Videogames." http://www.digra.org/hardcore/hc18/ (accessed February 1 2008).

Crawford, Chris. *Chris Crawford on Game Design*. Boston: New Riders, 2003.

Deleuze, Gilles, "The Brain Is the Screen." *The Brain Is the Screen: Deleuze and the Philosophy of Cinema*. Ed. Gregory Flaxman. Minneapolis: University of Minnesota Press, 2000.

Eskelinen, Markku. "The Gaming Situation." *Game Studies* 1.1 (July 2001): http://www.gamestudies.org/0101/eskelinen/ (accessed July 1 2008).

——. "Six Problems in Search of a Solution: The challenge of Cybertext Theory and Ludology to Literary Theory." *Dichtung Digital*, Brown University 2004: http://www.brown.edu/Research/dichtung-digital/2004/3/Eskelinen/index. htm (accessed July 1 2008).

Jenkins, Henry. *Convergence Culture: Where Old and New Media Collide*. New York: New York University Press, 2006.

Juul, Jesper. *Half-Real: Video Games between Real Rules and Fictional Worlds*. Boston: The MIT Press, 2005.

Kline, Stephen, Nick Dyer-Witherford and Greig de Peuter. *Digital Play: The Interaction of Technology, Culture and Marketing*. Montreal: McGill-Queen's University Press, 2003.

Kristeva, Julia. "The Bounded Text." *Desire in Language: A Semiotic Approach to Art and Literature*. Ed. Leon S. Roudiez. Oxford: Blackwell, 1980.

Ryan, Marie-Laure. *Avatars of Story*. Minneapolis: University of Minnesota Press, 2006.

Sanders, Julie. *Adaptation and Appropriation*. New York: Routledge, 2006.

Stam, Robert. "Introduction: The Theory and Practice of Adaptation." *Literature and Film: A Guide to the Theory and Practice of Film Adaptation*. Eds Robert Stam and Alessandro Raengo. Oxford: Blackwell, 2004.

Thompson, Kristin. *The Frodo Franchise: The Lord of the Rings and Modern Hollywood*. Berkeley: University of California Press, 2007.

saw heard

musical

sound design in

f i v e

contemporary

cinema

k . j .   d o n n e l l y

Film sound has seen some radical developments in both technological and aesthetic terms over the last thirty years or so. The traditional basic speaker system in cinemas in many cases has been replaced in many by a multi-speaker system which involves a significant spatialization of film sound allied to a remarkable improvement in sound definition. These changes augur an altered psychology at the heart of much new cinema, instilled by sound's increased importance for films.

> The sound of noises, for a long time relegated to the back-ground like a troublesome relative in the attic, has there-fore benefited from the recent improvements in definition brought by Dolby. Noises are reintroducing an acute feel-ing of the materiality of things and beings, and they herald a sensory cinema that rejoins a basic tendency of … the silent cinema.
>
> The paradox is only apparent. With the new place that noises occupy, speech is no longer central to films. (Chion 155)

Michel Chion points to technological developments in cinema that have had a notable impact on film aesthetics. Any movement from a speech-centred cinema to one that allows more prominence to "noise," is potentially a move from a cinema dominated by synchronized dialogue to one with significant amounts of asynchrony and sound as an effect in itself, be that through loud music or featured sounds.

The series of *Saw* I–IV (2004–7) demonstrates a situation where film music has an intimately close relationship with the film's overall sound design: where there is a convergence of sound effects, ambient sound and music. On the one hand, this might be attributed to the development of digital surround film sound and the corresponding importance of sound design in mainstream films. On the other, though, it might be accounted for by social and cultural aspects: there has been a gradual but exponential increase in the degree of ambient sound and ambient music over the past couple of decades. Sound effects are often less used to bolster a sense of verisimilitude than they are as an aesthetic effect, as, to all intents and purposes, music. Sound design in these films might be understood as essentially musical in nature, following a musical logic rather than any other.

The first film in the series, *Saw*, has a highly distinctive soundscape, which I will be discussing in this chapter. There is no solid demarcation between incidental music and sound design: consequently, sound effects can sound synthetic and music can sound like sound effects. The film has a very intimate relationship of sonic elements that makes it unconventional, although many recent films do not follow the dominant conventions of music-sound effects-dialogue atomization. The film's music was written and performed by first-time film music composer Charlie Clouser. Up to this point, he was known for his remixes of existing songs, adapting and rebuilding sonic material rather than "creating" as such. Hence, it might be possible to approach Clouser's work in the *Saw* films as an adaptation, a partial remix, of the sound world as a whole rather merely than the music alone. Clouser's music in the films is often unmelodic, unmemorable and anempathetic but focusing instead on texture and timbre and plays upon a confusion between what might be termed "film music" and "sound effects." The films wield sound often either explosively or in a disconcerting and semi-dislocated manner. Furthermore, *Saw* illustrates the assimilation of new technologies and new techniques and concomitantly different assumptions about cinema's diegetic world and the place of sound in this.

transformation

In certain recent films there has been a notable fusing of elements of the soundtrack, much as classical musicals fused music with dialogue (or more accurately we should use the term "voices"), some recent films have fused music with sound effects, creating a sonic continuum. Music in film has a significant interaction with other elements of the soundtrack as well as with the images, and one might even argue that its interaction with dialogue outweighs its interaction with images. In recent years, the development of converging digital sound technology has allowed sound designers to use musical software to enhance sound effects in films and allowed music composers to produce their own music incorporating elements of sound effects. Such developments, in line with technological convergence, aesthetic convergence and harmonizing platforms and industries has meant that music is no longer simply a "bolt-on" to films but integrated almost genetically on a conceptual level: instigating film titles and narratives, perhaps even having films as spin-offs from existing music, while continuing to inspire and articulate the most emotional and exciting moments of the overwhelming majority of films and other audiovisual media.

Technology has played an important part in recent developments in film sound and music, and technological determinism is always an attractive if too-easy answer. The availability of relatively cheap and easily programmed keyboard synthesizers at the turn of the 1980s led to an explosion of popular music and musicians premised upon the use of these instruments. This had a notable impact on films. In the 1970s, John Carpenter's scores for his own films sounded unique in their use of simple textures with monophonic synthesizers, but by the next decade they were sounding more like some of the contemporary pop music they had partly inspired. Greek keyboard player Vangelis came to some prominence for his scores for *Chariots of Fire* (1981) and *Blade Runner* (1982), and while rock keyboard players like Rick Wakeman and Keith Emerson had dipped their toes into film scoring, by the mid-1980s pop groups using drum machines and synthesizers were producing scores, such as Wang Chung's for *To Live and Die in L.A.* (1985). The revolutionary development from analogue to digital sound has had a notable impact on many aspects of cinema (Sergi 30), and on music and sound perhaps more than most other areas, allowing minute alteration and precise manipulation of all aural aspects. By the turn of the millennium, it was possible for musical scores to be constructed and fitted to a film on a computer screen at home, using AVID (or similar) and digital audio workstation (DAW) technology. Consequently, film makers like Robert Rodriguez are easily able to construct the scores for their films themselves, making film less of a collaborative medium, and making music less collaborative perhaps than ever. The elevation of the DAW has revolutionized music production, allowing easy construction of relatively high quality music on a home computer, although most of the top Hollywood film composers only use them for "mock ups" until the final recording with an expensive orchestra. However, the development of sequencing software has had a direct influence on the styles of music being produced in the popular music arena. Examples of the dominant types of software sequencer include Steinberg Cubase, Sony Logic, Ableton Live and

Propellerheads Reason. One of the central tenets of such computer technology is that music can be reduced to recorded components that are then processed, through audio enhancement/distortion and through the process of looping, where a passage of music is repeated verbatim. This latter aspect has been responsible for the proliferation of dance music in the 1990s that was developed in home studios, with an emphasis on the manipulation of sound samples, pre-recorded passages of music, which could be adapted, treated and woven together into a new musical composition. Such music technology instils an awareness of sound and ability to manipulate electronically. This encourages a "sound for sound's sake" approach focusing on the manipulation of sound on a basic level (e.g., reverb, filters, placing in stereo mix, etc.) more than the traditional virtues of composition enshrined in so-called "classical training" (harmony, counterpoint, orchestration, etc). This can lead to a confusion about what might constitute "music" and what might constitute "non-musical sound," and at the very least has challenged the limited concepts of music that were in wide circulation. Such technology is not only used by "musical" people but also by sound designers and editors, who use digital technology and techniques to "manipulate" sound effects the same way that composers use the same procedures to "compose" music. While on the one hand, composers are more aware of sound as an absolute than perhaps ever before, film sound people are approaching soundtracks in a manner that might be termed "musical," or at the very least betrays a musical awareness of the interaction of elements and their particular individual sonic qualities.

Saw evinces a unified and complex field of music and sound effects. This inspires a certain sonic (and audiovisual) complexity, while the more self-contained nature of the sound track inspires less in the way of extended passages of synchronization. One context for this is the use of digital electronics for both music and sound effects, which means that music increasingly is conceptualized in sonic terms (or at least in electronic terms of basic sound manipulation, dealing with concepts such as envelope, filtering, etc.). On the other side of the coin, there is an increasingly "musical" conceptualization of sound design in such films, where sound elements are wielded in an "artistic" manner, manipulated for precise effect rather merely than aiming to duplicate on screen activity. Consequently, the distinct psychologies of music and sound effects mix. There is a notable collapse of the *space* between diegetic sound and non-diegetic music. This manifests a collapse of mental space, between the film's "conscious" and its "unconscious." Rick Altman wrote about the differences between diegetic and non-diegetic music:

> By convention, these two tracks have taken on a quite specific sense: the diegetic reflects reality (or at least supports cinema's referential nature), while the [non-diegetic] music

> track lifts the image into a romantic realm far above the
> world of flesh and blood. (11)

In a similar manner, the unified field of sound merges these distinct channels, potentially mixing (by the film's terms) the objective and subjective, fantasy and reality, fixed perception and unstable reverie, conscious and unconscious, and not least, musical and communicational.

The convergence of music with ambient sound and sound effects contravenes the film tradition of solid demarcation between such elements. As I have suggested, sound design in films might be understood as essentially musical in nature. After all, sound designers use "musical software" and digital products designed primarily for the production of music (such as the industry standard ProTools). This has led to a more *aesthetic* rather than *representational* conception of sound in the cinema. For a long time, cinema sound was thought of in terms of clarity of dialogue and uncluttered but functional composition of diegetic sound elements. This is particularly evident in films which have recourse to technical as well as representational extremity, most notably in the horror film. The concomitant lack of synchronization in this equation adds up to a degree of mental uncertainty, emphasized by the film for the purposes of horror. At times, the *Saw* films seem to have soundtracks that have a dislocated nature, having become at least partially uncoupled from the image track of the film.

traditions

Film incidental music's effects includes eliciting and affirming emotion, clarification or provision of information (such as mood and setting), providing a sound bath that immerses the audience in the film world, as well as the more traditional functional aspects that include attempting to provide continuity across edits and joins between shots and time-spaces. As such, the score can also furnish a sense of, or emphasize filmic movement while also functioning to clarify and articulate a formal structure for the film (through punctuation, cadence and closure). Related structural functions might also include anticipating subsequent action in the film, and commenting on screen activities or providing a further symbolic dimension not evident in other aspects of the film. In separate writings, Noël Carroll (139), Jeff Smith (6) and Roy Prendergast (213–22) all quote a newspaper article where in the 1940s respected concert hall composer Aaron Copland posited five categories of film incidental music function. These functions are: "creating atmosphere, highlighting the psychological states of characters; providing neutral background filler, building a sense of continuity; sustaining tension and then rounding it off with a sense of closure" (28). Music has many material functions. It regularly has an enormous influence on the pacing of events and "emphasizing the dramatic line" (Burt 79). David Raksin notes that it was common to enter before the required emphasis, with what was called "neutral" music in the trade (in Burt 80), before being more emphatic with the music or making a specific musical effect. Such neutral music has given rise to pejorative descriptions of film music as "wallpaper" or "window dressing" which, perhaps in some cases, is justified. Music regularly performs an instructive role, creating meaning through representing ideas, objects and emotions. Indeed, it performs a primary role in eliciting emotional responses in the audience, and in providing consent for the audience's emotional responses.

Without assuming an unassailable cinematic ideal of sound and image in harmony, it should be admitted that in mainstream films sound overwhelmingly is functional. It works to elide itself as contract more than perhaps any other element of film. Some theorize that we perceive the diegetic world on screen as an unproblematic reality (on some level) (Kracauer 33–4), and sound is one of the principal elements that convince us that the space on screen is "real." After all, one might argue that most sounds in films exist essentially to bolster or "make real" the images we see on screen and the surrounding world we imagine. Consequently, when we see faces on screen talking we expect to hear what they are saying, when a car drives past we expect to hear those sounds corresponding. The fact that we hear a representation of those sounds, a convention allowing crisply-heard voices and unobtrusive car engine sounds rising then falling in pitch and volume, but not intruding on the important conversation, underlines just how conventional film sound is. Certainly, this is apparent if it is compared to the sounds recorded from an integrated microphone mounted on a home video camera.

However, having stated this, film sound still retains a principal function that is to guarantee the illusionistic world on screen. Random sound effects used in avant garde films might serve as an obtrusive reminder of the fabricated nature of film sound (and indeed synchronized cinema more generally), and point to our expectation of film sound to be merely a vehicle for the illusions on screen. Now this is a very different traditional function from that of music in films. Perhaps such a unity of sound effects and music might be approached as just moments of aesthetic effect, where sound effects are precisely sonic *effects*, such as the disconcerting noise from the attic early in *The Exorcist* (1973). This instance is not simply a sound—it is an emotional effect, more like an emanation from the Id, a manifestation of primary psychology. Such opportunities are opened by the recession of sound's representational function, which frees it to fulfil more in the way of direct emotional and aesthetic roles, in short, making film sound more like, or perhaps even a part of, the musical dimension of films. Consequently, great care can be taken with qualitative aspects of certain sounds—as the sounds have value in themselves rather merely than being conventionally representative of sounds from a small repertoire of stereotypical sounds (as remains the case in much television production).

Michel Chion discusses the new sonic space offered by directional multi-speaker surround sound as a "superfield," "which changes the perception of space and thereby the rules of [audio-visual] scene construction" (150). Although it retains much of tradition of monaural film, he insists that it is an extension of off-screen space and qualitatively different from previous sonic space, while similarly Philip Brophy uses the term "acousmonium" to articulate the new tactile and multidirectional space (38). Chion continues with his description:

> I call superfield the space created, in multitrack films, by ambient natural sounds, city noises, music, and all sorts of rustlings that surround the visual space and can issue from loudspeakers outside the physical boundaries of the screen. By virtue of its acoustical precision and relative stability this ensemble of sounds has taken on a kind of quasi-autonomous existence with relation to the visual field, in that it does not depend moment by moment on what we see onscreen. (150)

This new field is not simply one of dialogue and sound effects, but one where their interaction with music can be the key to its organization. This development has inspired a new aesthetics. According to Chion, Dolby multitrack favours passive offscreen sound, which works to establish a general space and permits more free movement for shots (and more of which are close ups) within that space, without any spatial disorientation of the viewer-auditor (85), although there is a corresponding tendency to keep speaking characters on screen as spatial anchors.

A further part of this process, evident in some films, is the convergence of music and sound effects, with a concomitant collapse of the strict demarcation between the two that reigned earlier. Of course, to a degree, it has always been impossible to fully and clinically separate musical score from sound effect. Music regularly has mimicked, emphasized or suggested certain sounds in the diegesis. Similarly, sound effects in films are regularly more than simply an emanation from the illusory diegetic world constructed by the film. They often have symbolic or emotional effects that outweigh their representational status. Indeed, it might be argued that much time and energy have been spent in attempting to approximate, or at least take inspiration from, the natural world, from birdsong to the rhythmic sounds of machinery. So, talking in terms of a solid distinction between the diegetic sound effect and musical accompaniment becomes difficult upon closer scrutiny and deeper thought. However, in terms of film production, there has been a relatively solid divide: musicians and composers produce music for film, and foley artists and sound editors are responsible for constructing a conventional series of sound effects to accompany on-screen action. The advent of digital sound technology and the relative accessibility of complex sound-treating equipment have had a notable impact on the production process. An early example of this was the development of special sound for *Evil Dead 2* (1987), where the sound of a rocking chair creaking was merged with sound recordings of a scream, using digital synthesizers to fuse the sounds on a genetic level. A more recent example of the process is *Resident Evil* (2002). The film begins with a voice-over narration accompanied by metallic and booming "non-musical" sounds, leading into a loop of one of the electronic themes Marilyn Manson wrote for the film as the action follows the events of a laboratory accident. Shortly afterwards, when protagonist Alice studies what appears to be her wedding photograph, we hear music that sounds like it was composed from various "non-musical" sound samples, in other words, re-organized and repeated shards of sound effects. Her contemplation is halted abruptly by a nearby door opening. Sonically, this involves a very loud and percussive sound matched to the image of an automatic door. Yet the consistency of the sound is certainly not at odds with the preceding music, firmly supplying the impression of a continuum of organized sound that is able to be more rhythmic and more melodic while retaining a foot in diegetic sound effects and ambiences.

Such a unified field of music and sound effects is evident in a good number of recent films, although this marginal tradition might be traced back to an origin in silent cinema, where the live music performed to accompany the film in many cases "did" the sound effects. This tradition is probably more evident in the film scoring tradition where music will mimic or suggest certain diegetic sound effects, even through they may well be present on the soundtrack anyway. There was a minor tradition of certain sound films having a sonic continuum that fully merged music and sound effects. Probably the best example is *Forbidden Planet* (1956), which had a soundtrack of "electronic tonalities" by Louis and Bebe Barron. For the purposes of film production this could not be credited as "music," and indeed, its origins in recordings of "cybernetic sound organisms" that were then collaged to fit the film evinces a process far removed from the dominant traditions of Hollywood film scoring. There a direct confusion of origins of sounds. Some of the electronic sounds appear to be functioning like incidental music, some clearly are synchronized with images on screen (such as the monster, for example). Others appear to be environmental, marking the ambience of the unfamiliar alien planet, and adding to the sense of the exotic and uncharted that the film represents. In his study of the sound and music for *Forbidden Planet*, James Wierzbicki notes that this was not an isolated case, and through traversing the membrane of conventional sound functions pointed to a new psychology:

> In contrast [with traditional orchestral scores of the time], electronic sounds in scores for many 1950s science-fiction films were strikingly non-traditional, and thus they tended to blur the long-standing boundary between non-diegetic underscore and diegetic sound effect. Electronic sounds did not simply accompany "foreign" narrative objectives; in many cases, they seemed to emanate directly *from* them. (26–7)

Similarly, Hitchcock's *The Birds* (1963) has a soundtrack that mixes sound effects and music. It contained no underscore in the traditional sense. Instead it used electronic "sound design" (apparently Herrmann's idea), which was recorded in Munich with experimentalists Remi Gassmann and Oskar Sala. Hitchcock's regular composer at the time, Bernard Herrmann was "advisor" and the final product, while using synthetic bird noises, remains related to the *musique concrete* produced by experimenters such as Pierre Schaeffer and Pierre Henry in the 1940s and 1950s. *The Birds'* sound design approached music as merely another element of the soundtrack and replaced a musical underscore with "sound effects," that nevertheless are fairly musical in their inspiration. While the soundtrack appears to represent bird sounds that match the action on screen, they are in fact produced electronically and only vaguely synchronized with the birds on screen. It might be more apt to characterize the soundtrack to *The Birds* as a continuum of ambient bird sounds most clearly in the sequences of bird attacks.

Another film that has a soundtrack that goes beyond simple sound effects and music is David Lynch's *Eraserhead* (1977), which makes particularly harrowing use of ambient sound in the background through the film. The sound design for the film, by Alan Splet, collaged industrial sounds, metallic noises, rumbles and wind into a disturbing and continuous sonic backdrop for the film's action. It is not unchanging and moves to the foreground at times. Arguably, it takes something from the general function of film scores, which provide a sonic backdrop and a vague mood for the action. The fact that these sounds were not easily classified as non-diegetic music meant that they were more satisfactorily accounted for as acousmatic sound effects: seemingly the sounds emanating from some dreadful but indistinct industrial machines somewhere in the distance. Indeed, Alan Splet's sound work was far more than merely recording and compiling sounds for use in films. An available 3-disc set, *Sounds From a Different Realm*, showcases Splet's work along with his collaborator Ann Kroeber. Some of the pieces are called "Unusual Presences" and illustrate the construction of nearly autonomous sound environments, some of which were used in David Lynch's films. Despite the collection nominally being a sound effects set, they manifest more a sustained, "canned atmosphere" rather than being simply "recorded sound effects" ready for general use.

film sound as music (and film music as sound)

The effect of a unified field of sound and music is the destruction of conventional use of sound in films, with a concomitant questioning of the relationship of sound to image. Certain contemporary films evince a unified sound design that conceives of the film's sound in holistic terms rather than as the traditionally separate music, dialogue and sound effects. Miguel Mera and David Burnand note:

> Modernism is inherent in the technologically enabled means of audio production in filmmaking that encourages the alliance of music and sound design as a recorded and edited form, and thus is at odds with the rehashed nineteenth-century orchestral scores typical of classic cinema, flown into the virtual orchestra pit of the movie theatre. (5)

Such films with a unified sound field deal with it in highly sophisticated terms. Sound effects are not simply about matching what the screen requires to verify its activities. Instead, sound effects can take on more of the functions traditionally associated with music, such emotional ambiences, provision of tone to a sequence or suggestions of vague connections. In short, film sound as a unified field has taken a high degree of its logic from music, and more specifically from music in films in the form of non-diegetic or incidental music. Films such as *Se7en* (1997) or *Ju-On: The Grudge* (2003) have notable sequences where sound could be construed as music or as sound effects. In both cases, the ambiguity is doubtless part of the general effect of the film. In *Donnie Darko* (2001), a voice (belonging to "Frank") appears in the night, telling Donnie to wake up. This is accompanied by deep ambiguous rumbles and what might be construed as supernatural sounds. It certainly is not easily recognizable as film score, but equally fails to identify itself as sound effects for anything in the diegetic world. There is a seemingly organic mixture of diegetic sound and music evident in the London underground-set *Creep* (2004). At the start of the film one of a pair of sewage workers disappears down a tunnel and as the other searches for him the soundtrack embraces deep sub-bass rumbles that are ambiguous as to whether they are diegetic or not. As his desperation grows, the music grows in volume, featuring metallic sounds and developing from the deep rumbles into a more clearly organized pattern, and thus more clearly becomes "music."[1] Like much of the film, this sequence exploits the dramatic and psychological possibilities of an extended range of bass tones available to 5.1 Dolby sound.

Indeed, since the advent of multi-track recording technologies in the 1960s, Dolby stereo and surroundsound in the 1970s and digital sound technology in the 1980s, soundtracks have become increasingly complex and sophisticated. Indeed, Elisabeth Weis points to the exponential expansion of sound resources indicated by the number of sound technicians working on recent films in comparison with the number on a film during the heyday of the Hollywood studio system (Weis). The division of labour is often quite precise, although the supervising sound editor or sound designer will tend to have dominion over all sonic resources. Many directors have a significant input to the final sonic character of their film, while ones like David Lynch also design the sound for their films. Film soundtracks are constructed with great care and creativity. Any attempt to approach the unified soundtrack as simply "sound effects" is doomed—doomed to banal answers. The only viable approach is from a musical point of view. After all, music has been the "science" of sound for a very long time, and it is clear that aesthetic impulses are highly significant in determining film soundtracks, rather merely than representational concerns (to make sounds match screen action).

Sometimes it seems easy to forget that for centuries we have had a theory of organized sound relevant to the cinema: music. Music is at heart about organizing sound events in time and some of its dominant concepts are highly evident in sonic organization in films. For example, the general ambience assigned to a space is conceived as "backing" to the "aria" or singing voice of dialogue. A more recent tradition has been concerned with making sound recordings into music: *musique concrete*, which developed in France after World War 2 and was based on the manipulation and distortion of sound recordings on magnetic tape. While it would be a massive reduction to suggest that it is similar to film sound, there nevertheless are shared points of interest and assumptions. It is hardly fortuitous that the primary theorization of film sound comes from an individual with a background in electroacoustic music and a training in *musique concrete*. Michel Chion has introduced a large number of terms and theories from this body of thought and praxis into the study of film. As one of the few areas to deal with sound, often in musical terms, *musique concrete* should be a stopping-off point (however brief) for any analysis of film soundtracks.

saw's musical sound

The *Saw* films centre upon the activities of the "Jigsaw Killer," a serial killer who is at pains to threaten or kill people in creative and imaginative ways apt to each individual. This involves a high level of invention, as well as meticulous planning leading to a tortuous route of potential escape for the protagonists of the films. The first film starts with two men coming into a basement of a deserted building, both handcuffed securely but with clues about possible escape (and redemption for their sins). It is notably based on an aesthetic of matching a sumptuous soundscape to what are often overwhelmingly static visuals. Apart from flashback sequences, the whole film takes place in one room. The soundtrack thus serves to provide some variation for the audience and remove the potential for boredom. While the narrative is gripping, the visuals are often quite pedestrian and the sound track's use of unusual timbres and unfamiliar activities compensates for this to a degree. Thus the limited diegetic space inspires a sonic drama of space, where the drama of aural elements encourages a feeling of space that is denied by the film's visual construction. The claustrophobia of the film is highly effective, but is enhanced or thrown into relief by a feeling of expanded space in the soundtrack. There is copious use of reverb and echo, which makes the film feel like it is taking place in a large arena of emptiness rather than an overlit basement room. This provides a striking mismatch of claustrophobic visual space with expansive and echo-laden sonic space: this mismatch is dramatic in itself. Furthermore, it makes for a psychological mismatch between the image track and the sound track which is further enhanced by the uncertain status of much of the sound (as being diegetic sound effect being non-diegetic music). The limited diegetic space forces sonic space's elevation in importance to the point where the film's sonic space manifests an expansion of experience, but simultaneously a fragmentation of the vaguely-coherent subject position of the spectator (as theorized long ago and far away). In *Saw*, the Jigsaw Killer hears (rather than sees) the proceedings throughout, unperceived by the two protagonists. The film could be characterized as a "point of audition sound" acousmonium for him (offering a sonic experience close to ours as the audience: could this be seen as an aural *Rear Window* [1954]?). Thus the spectator–auditor position in the film might be construed in this way to furnish the auditory equivalent of the person sitting in the film theatre.[2]

The film's music composer, Charlie Clouser, started off as an electronic music programmer, being involved in television incidental music before becoming known as a member of industrial rock group Nine Inch Nails and subsequently as a remixer for many rock groups, producing new versions of recordings that have a highly individual stamp on them.[3] Clouser joined the *Saw* project after director James Wan had used a number of Nine Inch Nails pieces in the film's temp track (Sacks). Clouser had been a member of that group in the mid and late 1990s. A background in electronic sound manipulation is advantageous for a film that requires something radically different from a conventional orchestral film score, and indeed, Clouser approached the score in a far from traditional manner. He was interested in using non-musical sounds, such as metallic clashing and banging, in

> sounds that might have originated in the sound effects. Subconsciously, I think almost sound as though these

might be unseen characters to attack, on the other side of the wall. . . . [There was also a concern with] [b]lurring the line, and having industrial sounds that spring from the background of the movie [which] might make the viewer less aware of the music as music and that more aware of the general sense of tension and anxiety we were trying to create. (Sacks)

Director James Wan wanted to use the score precisely as an effect, for psychological impact rather than merely for emotional impact. Clouser noted:

Usually, I don't try to use sounds that will clash against the sound design—doors slamming, gunshots, things like that. But because of the character of the music that James [Wan] wanted it would involve a lot of metal screeching and banging types of sounds, which were going to get in the way of the sound effects, so it was the skillful [sic] mix that kept everything together. (Clouser)

While the final mix may accommodate Clouser's sounds as well as sound effects, it works with similar sonic material in what appears to be a unified field of sound and music. It is little surprise that when asked to list influences on his work Clouser mentioned Louis and Bebe Barron, who provided the electronic sounds/music for *Forbidden Planet* (Clouser).

The likely main source of *Saw*'s temp track was Nine Inch Nails's 1999 double-album *The Fragile*, which included slow atmospheric music as well as more up-tempo and noisy songs. While Trent Reznor was (and remains) the principal player in the group, Clouser was a mainstay at this point. An indication of Clouser's importance for the textural and ethereal tracks is his sleevenote credit on the track *The Great Below*, for "atmospheres." The *Saw* scores are premised upon music as provision of atmosphere, although they might be characterized as a distinct alternation of non-musical sounds and spare synthesizer tones, with kinetic mechanical drum patterns, characteristic of certain industrial rock groups, particularly Nine Inch Nails. Clouser noted that he used the sections with energetic percussion patterns "to build adrenaline" (Sacks). These sections include the speeded up images of a man caught in razor wire, and for some of the "reverse bear trap" sequence, where a character has to beat a time limit to remove a piece of potentially fatal headware.

While the drum-based passages provide energy, much of the rest of the music is sparsely-textured. The type of music Clouser concentrated on focuses on the vertical aspect:

[Tracks] usually have a level of density, which is greater than most scoring cues, in terms of the number of things happening and how much attention you have to pay to them to decode it all. That kind of works against a lot of people coming from a record background when they're scoring because they wind up making it sound like a record and it might be too busy or too dense to serve as "background." (Clouser)

While many forms of music that work outside the cinema can be reined into films effectively, Clouser points to a concern with momentary texture and the vertical (momentary) aspects rather than the melodic or developmental. In fact, throughout, *Saw* tends to use emotionally "cold" sound/music, lacking any emotional warmth to the characters and being partially disconnected from proceedings. This lack of empathy can be related to Michel Chion's notion of "anempathetic music," where mechanical music or music that follows its own logic continues across emotional action without any care for matching its mood with that of the images (8). In *Saw*, the connection of sound to images can be vague and the music provides atmosphere and energy that match screen mood and action, but the music refuses to provide music that "connects" with the characters on an emotional level, refusing to take advantage of one of the principal functions of film music, which is to allow the audience to empathize with the characters on screen.

One aspect of Clouser's score that is instantly striking is the sheer variation of sounds in circulation. It utilizes a wealth of electronic tones as well as sounds derived from sound samples. However, it is nevertheless "scored" in the traditional sense. For example, it uses deep drones conventional to horror films and dramatizes and punctuates the voice of the Jigsaw Killer as it appears played on a tape. That Charlie Clouser conceived his music in terms of sound elements that would form a sonic foundation for each scene (Sacks), denotes a process closer to soundscape creation than to traditional film scoring. A sound art infusion to film is further evident in *Saw* in that Clouser's electronic score makes copious use of sounds originating with metal sound sculptures. These were Chas Smith's metal sculptures that were designed to be bowed and scraped to create sounds (Sacks). Clouser used recordings of these as raw material, manipulated in digital samplers but often retaining their original metallic sonic character.

Upon the two protagonists noticing a dead body lying on the floor between them, there is a series of shots of the body that include a revolving shot and close ups of the body's bloodied head and the gun clasped in its hand. Each shot appears regularly and is accompanied by a sonic "hit," making for a regular rhythmic pulse of sound and image. Matching the dramatic and unusual visual, the sound also acts unconventionally, including some reversed sounds and the music alternating between the front two speakers, a rarity in films and highly obtrusive sonic activity.

When Adam tries to get the tape player from the dead body's hand, a shot showcasing the tape player in the hand appears simultaneously with an echoed drum "hit," marking and synchronizing the action. In the wake of this, as Adam uses his shirt and some cloth to try to obtain the tape player, the music moves through a number of fairly distinct sonic passages: starting with a high, falling ethereal monody interrupted by a sound reminiscent of a distant train passing, then a short, high-pitched squeaky sound, then a deep drone (that sounds like an electronically treated male voice choir), a brief burst of repeated guitar feedback. Then, as Adam picks up the cloth to use, we have a synchronized metal sound, similar to that of a bowed cymbal, followed by echoed deep sounds (like a large water tank being hit). Sonically, this sequence seems very much a succession, which likely emanates from the ease with which contemporary digital technology encourages the use of sonic loops (particularly of the digital audio workstations [DAWs] and their ease of manipulating samples and musical "blocks"). This is further underlined by the moment when Adam finds a saw in a bag in the toilet cistern, which is accompanied by what sounds like heavily-echoed guitar feedback looped and repeated into a single musical figure.

Overall, *Saw* has sections with sparse dialogue, which therefore lack the most regular and clear lynchpin of synchronized sound and image. Furthermore, the fact that *Saw* is premised upon two characters (Lawrence and Adam) chained up in one room allows for dialogue without showing the speaking characters. The audience is aware of the spatial set-up and thus the camera has more freedom of movement. Chion notes that the development of the sonic "superfield" has erased the tradition of spatial scene construction in films through losing the requirement for establishing (and re-establishing) long shots,

> because in a more concrete and tangible manner than in traditional monoaural films the superfield provides a continuous and constant consciousness of all the space surrounding the dramatic action … such that the image now plays a sort of solo part, seemingly in dialogue with the sonic orchestra in the audiovisual concerto. (150–1)

The sonic aspect of *Saw* certainly evinces much variation, but also consistently uses sounds of obscure origin, such as drones, scrapes and loud bumps, all of which could be construed as diegetic sounds but more likely are non-diegetic, lacking any origin in the film world on screen.

To describe such sounds, with unapparent origins, Chion invokes the concept of the "acousmatic," a term initiated by Jerome Peignot but developed by Pierre Schaeffer, and defined as "… sound that one hears without seeing the cause" (Chion 71). The antonym of this is what Chion calls "visualized sound," as a correspondent with Schaeffer's notion of "direct sound" (with a clear origin). There is an essential ambiguity to such sounds.

Their origins are immediately obscure, although their source may be understood later. In psychological terms, such sounds are perceived as a potential threat in that they hang in uncertainty for the perceiver. In *Saw*, we hear much in the way of metal sounds that could possibly be diegetic. They certainly don't sound like traditional film score. But then there is no indication of any diegetic origin for these sounds. They question the status of the diegesis and, significantly, add to a sense of ambiguity of environment through confusion of sound and image. Similarly, there are regular bass rumbles (almost sub-bass rumbles) on the film's soundtrack. Are these diegetic? That information is never furnished by the film. The potentially disturbing effect of such ambiguous sound is discussed by Chion, who points to the essential ambiguity of such sounds. Their origins are immediately obscure, although their source might be understood later. In psychological terms, such sounds are perceived as a potential threat in that they hang in uncertainty for the listener.

As an aural counterpart to the rare "non-diegetic insert,"[4] we might wonder if recent cinema is wielding the "non-diegetic sound effect," which likely has the same ambiguity of acousmatic sound, although it sounds like it could emanate from the world on screen yet *cannot* be retrospectively understood and placed in the surrounding (diegetic) world. It indeed has lost its synchronization absolutely, in that there is no possibility of its matching the screen world and thus manifests an extreme of mental confusion and potential threat. The horror genre often has been premised upon the drama of off-screen space concealing the unknown, such as in films like Hitchcock's *Psycho* (1960). However, in *Saw*, these sounds not only are "offscreen," they are "off world."

They are sounds "from nowhere," occupying the same space as the film's non-diegetic music, which also emanates from an obscure space somewhere that is not existentially connected to the world represented on screen. Now, non-diegetic music is purely conventional, and as such does not invite direct questions about its origins. However, sound effects are anchored to screen representations. They provide the spatial and conformational aspects of activities on screen or nearby still in the diegetic world. From time to time, however, sound effects appear to come from outside the diegetic world, most notably in surreal or horror films. For example, in the remake of *The Fog* (2005), as DJ Stevie Wayne (played by Selma Blair) sits in her car, there are deep threatening sounds. Their status is ambiguous—they might be part of Graeme Revell's non-diegetic music, or they could be diegetic sounds of the mysterious fog itself. However, in all likelihood, they are non-diegetic sound effects.[5] This appears literally to be an occult aesthetic, yet such general "ambiences" function to immerse the audience in the film more effectively in sonic terms than might be available as a visual effect. There are highly-effective low-volume continuums, such as Freddy Kruger's basement in the *Nightmare on Elm Street* films, or in space ships such as the Starship Enterprise in the *Star Trek* films and television series. Rick Altman, McGraw Jones and Sonia Tatroe note that some Hollywood films in the 1930s had continuous low-volume "atmosphere sound," which had a function of "enveloping" the audience in a film's sonic space (352). Such "enveloping" is an effect of the extension of sonic space, which is a characteristic of surroundsound but also an effect of the degree of reverberation (or "reverb") evident on any recorded sound. In audio terms, reverb expresses "space" as the equivalent of showing open space visually. Furthermore, the use of electronic reverb, adding a sense of space around a recorded sound, might be seen as a prime signifier of sound as aesthetic in films rather than following any vague attempt to reflect the space represented visually on screen. Philip Brophy notes that, "psychoacoustically, reverb grants us an out-of-body experience: we can aurally separate what we hear from the space in which it occurs" (108). This inconsistency of sound space represented on the soundtrack and the expected sound ambience that would have emanated from the space represented on screen. This is not only evident in *Forbidden Planet* but also in films such as *Saw*. It illustrates a degree of mental separation emanating from the evident mismatch in *Saw* of expansive, reverb-drenched music and sounds, with an enclosed and circumscribed visual space. We might go further, and approach electronic reverb and echo as a manifestation of a state of mind more than it is a representation of anything. After all, it does not signify diegetic space but something beyond, an emotional and unconscious enveloping of sound. In his discussion of *Forbidden Planet*, Philip Brophy continues,

> Reverb is heavily applied to *Forbidden Planet*'s synthetic sound effects firstly to invoke the expansive opening of interplanetary frontiers, and secondly to invoke an imposing sense of size and space. At least fifteen centuries of European church architecture used reverb to conjure up thundering scale and omnipotent power; sci-fi movies followed suit with their own brand of technological mysticism and God-fearing morality. (108)

So, it is nothing to do with representing the world on screen and more to do with providing an effect and an emotional tone. Annabel Cohen notes that:

> The affective quality [of music] is consistent [with the diegesis]; the acoustical aspects of the music are not. Although the affective associations produced by the music seem to belong to the corresponding images, the sounds that produced those associations do not. Somehow, the brain attends to this affective meaning, while ignoring or attenuating its acoustical source. (373–4)

As registered earlier, the unification of sound effects and music conjoins the distinct psychologies of music and sound effects. The use of electronic echo and reverb marks a *musical* appropriation of sound space, unifying diegetic and non-diegetic sound as a psychological effect more than as a representational counterpart of the images on screen (and diegesis of recorded voices). Sound theorist David Toop points to the "... attraction to the synthetic mimicry of resonance, the structural potential of delays and the physicality of sound waves in enclosed space has evolved into a wider exploration of time, space and sound ..." (64). This quotation may have been aimed at a certain tendency in music, but is equally applicable to the use of sound in some films, films that are interested, one way or another, in exploring mental and psychological space. In other words, these films are *about* mental space, enabled by the sonic dimension of the film that is beyond representational functions.

conclusion

Of course, music and sound effects have always been mixed despite efforts to keep them separate. Film scores have regularly imitated diegetic sounds (as indeed has music habitually imitated the sounds of nature). However, in recent years there has been more in the way of radical confusion of score and sound effects. These two aspects of film sound, distinct since the coming of synchronized sound cinema, have converged and cross what once was a fairly impermeable membrane between these two sonic aspects. The personnel involved in their production often remain as distinct as they had in the heyday of the Hollywood studio system, but techniques and hardware have encouraged a convergence. Developments such as this need acknowledgement from those studying film. The increased depth of aestheticization evident in many recent film soundtracks renders many analyses that ignore their nuances little more than naïve descriptions of "what happens" in those films. Narratological concerns should allow for the fact that sound-dominated films are essentially sensual experiences.

Now, on one level, some of this discussion might seem naïve. Austere music might well sound like "sound effects" to the uninitiated. I am aware of this ——but there is a tradition of sound effects in film (and television, and video/computer games), and these recent scores/soundtracks engage those traditions more than they come from outside (from art music, for example). However, a number of recent films offer very rich sonic landscapes that work on their own independently of their film. This could be traced to the tradition of programmatic music, illustrating vistas and places through sound, a tradition reinvigorated by certain ambient music and new age music. There might also be an influence from sound art, which has been a burgeoning area of the art world over the past couple of decades. As a concrete instance, one artist relevant for discussion and who has crossed a number of boundaries is Brian Williams (usually known artistically as Lustmord). Starting in left-field rock music, some of his early recordings were of specific spaces (such as the Dunster Abattoir in Bangor and Chartres Cathedral on *Paradise Disowned* [1984]). He worked with experimental rock group SPK when they were using "found" metal percussion and he went on to produce regular recordings that sounded like they were inspired by horror film soundtracks. His 1990 album *Heresy* is seen as inaugurating the "dark ambient" (sub)genre, while albums such as *The Monstrous Soul* make copious use of horror film samples in their nightmarish soundscapes. Over the past decade or so, Williams has worked in Hollywood as a "musical sound designer," usually in collaboration with composer Graeme Revell (with whom he collaborated in SPK in the 1980s). Williams's role in films like *The Crow* (1994) was to provide certain sounds and ambiences that can be used in the film or in Revell's score. This suggests a unified sound design that is "musical" in its origin, as testified to by Williams's screen credit.

It is incontrovertible that the category of music has expanded to include much other sound. For instance, CDs of natural sounds, not just of singing whales, but recordings of natural landscapes, such as the Global Journey CD *Nature Recordings: Thunderstorm*,[6] not to mention the recorded soundscapes of sonic artists such as Hildegard Westerkamp. Such "soundscaping" is perhaps less to do with any attempt to objectively record a sound environment than it is to configure sound "psychogeographically" as personal and emotional landscapes. To a degree, this process might also be identified in some films, which aim to produce a mental and psychological aural landscape, as is the case in *Saw*.

Freed from a functional role, freed from the diegesis, and freely mixing with music, film sound is able to manifest a direct emotion, and a primary psychology. The tradition of sound mixing and construction developed by classical Hollywood and influential the world over was premised upon a solid demarcation of sound effects, dialogue and music, and with a concomitant clarity of purpose for each and the system as a whole. This appears to reflect a sense of clarity of purpose and solid understanding of the relationships between things in the world that mark protean American cinema of the time. By the same token, the collapse of consensus of sonic clarity might reflect social and political developments—perhaps the cultural confusion is a reflection of, or simply emanates from a social and political confusion. We can speculate about such "reflection," but what is beyond doubt is that there is a remarkable collapse of the *space* between diegetic sound and non-diegetic music. This manifests a collapse of mental space, between the film's "conscious" and its "unconscious," and perhaps not only between rational and irrational elements in such horror films but also in wider cinema.

notes

1 When protagonist Kate runs along the deserted underground train, the music consists of a rhythmic loop of treated metallic sounds that are more "sound effects" than "musical" in origin. This piece has notable similarities with some of Charlie Clouser's kinetic music in the *Saw* films.

2 Such as in other celebrated "sonically based" films like *The Conversation* (1974) or *Blow Out* (1981).

3 Clouser worked in television music with Australian composer Cameron Allen in the late 1980s before working with Nine Inch Nails and as a remixer. He worked on shows including *The Equalizer* and *Kojak*, and more recently on *Fastlane* and *Las Vegas*.

4 These are the proverbial shots of trains going into tunnels that allegedly implied sex scenes in silent films. They are likely apocryphal stories and the fodder of comedy. Probably the most famous non-diegetic insert is the intrusion of a shot of a bull being slaughtered at the violent riot concluding Eisenstein's *Strike* (1926).

5 A philosophical problem is posed by the notion of the non-diegetic sound effect. The concept of diegetic is itself highly questionable, being dependent on an assumption about the illusory world on-screen, made by an idealized audience member.

6 On Global Journey records, GJ3638, 2001.

works cited

Altman, Rick. *The American Film Musical*. London: British Film Institute, 1987.

Altman, Rick, McGraw Jones and Sonia Tatroe. "Inventing the Cinema Soundtrack: Hollywood's Multiplane Sound System." *Music and Cinema*. Eds James Buhler, Caryl Flinn and David Neumeyer. Hanover: Wesleyan University Press, 2000.

Brophy, Philip. *100 Modern Soundtracks*. London: British Film Institute, 2004.

Burt, George. *The Art of Film Music*. Boston: Northeastern University Press, 1994.

Carroll, Noël. *Theorizing the Moving Image*. Cambridge: Cambridge University Press, 1996.

Chion, Michel. *Audio-Vision: Sound on Screen*. Edited and translated by Claudia Gorbman. New York: Columbia University Press, 1994.

Clouser, Charlie. "Interview" at *ign.com*. http://music.ign.com/articles/562/562509p1.html (accessed 03/12/2004).

Cohen, Annabel J. "Film Music: Perspectives from Cognitive Psychology." *Music and Cinema*. Eds James Buhler, Caryl Flinn and David Neumeyer. Hanover: Wesleyan University Press, 2000.

Copland, Aaron. "Tip to the Moviegoers: Take Off Those Ear-Muffs." *The New York Times*, 6 November 1949, section six.

Kracauer, Siegfried. *Theory of Film: The Redemption of Physical Reality*. New York: Oxford University Press, 1960.

Mera, Miguel and David Burnand. "Introduction." *European Film Music*. Eds Miguel Mera and David Burnand. London: Ashgate, 2006.

Prendergast, Roy M. *Film Music: A Neglected Art*. New York: Norton, 1992.

Sacks, Rob. "Charlie Clouser's Scary Soundtrack for *Saw*" (interview with Charlie Clouser) in *NPR*'s "Day to Day," Friday 9 October 2004. http://www.nrp.org/templates/story/story.php?storyId=4132853 (accessed 15/11/2006).

Sergi, Gianluca. *The Dolby Era: Film Sound in Contemporary Hollywood*. Manchester: Manchester University Press, 2004.

Smith, Jeff. *The Sounds of Commerce: Marketing Popular Film Music*. New York: Columbia University Press, 1998.

Toop, David. *Haunted Weather: Music, Silence and Memory*. London: Serpent's Tail, 2004.

Weis, Elisabeth. "Sync Tanks: The Art and Technique of Postproduction Sound." *Cineaste*. 21.1–2 (1995): 42–48.

Wierzbicki, James. *Louis and Bebe Barron's* Forbidden Planet: *A Score Guide*. London: Scarecrow, 2005.

the

shape

of 1999

the stylistics of

american movies

at the end of the

century

b a r r y   s a l t

Why does it matter whether or not there is an objective description of the standard form of American commercial cinema in the here and now? Well, just for a start, there is surely something wrong when none of the reviews of Paul Thomas Anderson's *Magnolia* mention one of its major formal features, which is that it is conducted in very long takes by the standards of 1999. Amongst the hundreds of other films backed in one way or another by Hollywood studios appearing in that year, there is only one other film, Woody Allen's *Sweet and Lowdown*, which is filmed with long takes. That nobody mentioned the long take style in connection with *Sweet and Lowdown* is just slightly more excusable, as Woody Allen has been shooting films that way for many years. The fundamental principle of aesthetic judgement that is important in this context is that deviations from the norms of the period are important, and indeed potentially of artistic worth. If you can't handle this, then you are off in the egomaniacal world where nothing but "critical intuition" is used in dealing with art. So how does one deal with establishing objective descriptive standards for dealing with the mass arts of film and television?

how to do it

It should be obvious that the terms used for analyzing movies are those used by their makers in putting them together, and indeed that the only rational approach in general terms is for the analysis to reverse the construction process used in creating the work. Fortunately for my task, the basic components of film form have been constant for most of the past century, once they had been established in American cinema around the time of the First World War. In fact the American cinema has drawn the commercial cinema in the rest of the world along behind it stylistically ever since, up to the present.

I first proposed statistical methods for the formal analysis of both individual films and groups of films in 1968, and these proposals were first published in Salt ("Film Form"), and the first results of the program appeared the same year in Salt ("Statistical Style"). Much more of my results in this area, and also their application to critical considerations, can be read in Salt (*Film Style and Technology* and *Moving into Pictures*).

The easiest basic variable in film construction to obtain is what I call the Average Shot Length (ASL). The lengths of the shots making up films have been discussed from time to time by film-makers since at least 1912, though they have invariably done it in terms of the number of shots in particular individual films. This would be perfectly satisfactory if all films were exactly the same length, but they are not. All films are not even approximately the same length. Hence my introduction of the Average Short Length, which has since been taken up by other people interested in this matter.

Another obvious variable used in film construction is the Scale of Shot, or Closeness of Shot. This is measured by how much of the height of the actors in the foreground of the shot is visible within the frame. Again, this has been discussed by film-makers from at least as early as 1912. The descriptive terms used then were "French foreground" and "American foreground," followed shortly afterwards by the still-used term "close up." The terms I use are those current in the 1940's, and to be found in *The Five C's of Cinematography*, written by a Hollywood cameraman of the period, Joseph V. Mascelli. They are as follows: Big Close Up (BCU) shows head only, Close Up (CU) shows head and shoulders, Medium Close Up (MCU) includes body from the waist up, Medium Shot (MS) includes from just below the hip to above the head of upright actors, Medium Long Shot (MLS) shows the body from the knee upwards, Long Shot (LS) shows at least the full height of the body, and Very Long Shot (VLS) shows the actor small in the frame. (A shot which shows the head and shoulders of an actor sticking into the lower part of the frame with a yard of air above them does not count as a Close Up). In recent decades in film and television the vaguer term "Wide Shot" has come to replace the various kinds of Long Shot described above, but I am keeping to the earlier, more finely graded, terminology which was in use when I first became involved with film-making more than fifty years ago. If one wishes to use a different system of Scale of Shot in making a similar analysis to the one here, the results can still be compared with mine, as long as a definition is given of what each gradation of scale of shot corresponds to against the actor's height.

After counting the total number of shots in each category in a film, I then normalize or standardize the number to be the relative proportion there would be in an average 500 shots in the film. I round to the nearest integer in this operation. This is done to make an easy and clear comparison between the relative tendencies of different film-makers to use different Closeness of Shot. It would be possible to express the relative frequency of each type of shot as a percentage of the total number, but I am loath to go back and alter thirty years' worth of results to do this. (Also, you can easily convert to percentages if you wish, by dividing by five). Incidentally, the use of percentages almost demands that one begin to use decimal fractions in the results, which I think is unnecessarily messy.

Other basic units of film construction refer to the relation of shots to each other within scenes. These are reverse angles, which describe a shot taken in approximately the opposite direction to the preceding shot in the scene, and Point of View shots, which are shots taken exactly in the direction a character is looking in the preceding or succeeding shot. (The term originally used in the United States for what are now called "reverse angles," or often just "reverses," was "reverse scene," after such things began to appear in 1908. At that time they were always shot at a distance from the actors, but as the camera moved closer in, and was applied at more varied angles, and indeed the term "camera angle" itself came to be used, the expression shifted to "reverse angle." "Reverse shot" was occasionally, but far less frequently, used.) In my work, I count a cut as being one to a reverse angle (RA) when it changes the camera direction by more than 90 degrees. In other words, not all cuts between "singles" of two actors facing each other in the scene count as reverse angle cuts. The other basic quantity that I collect is the number of inserts used. That is, shots of objects, or distant scenes, either of which do not show an actor featured in the film story. I also include in this category such shots as a Big Close Up of an actor's hand going into their pocket, for these can be, and frequently are, shot with a stand-in. I express these three quantities as percentages of the total number of shots or cuts in a film.

As for camera movement, the categories I use are pan, tilt, pan with tilt, track, track with pan, track with pan and tilt, crane, and zoom. All of these are fairly self-explanatory, but it is worth remarking that my category of simple tracking shot includes only camera dolly movements in a straight line, including those sideways to the camera direction and subject, which is sometimes referred to as "crabbing." Any tracking on a curved path invariably contains panning movements as well. The zoom category, admittedly not strictly a camera movement, includes zooms made with simultaneous panning or tilting. Camera movements of small extent which are made to keep the actors well-framed as they move about a little are not counted, as these have been done effectively automatically by camera operators for the last eighty years at least, and are hence without significance. The same applies to small dolly adjustments of a foot or so made for the same reason. Camera movements are also normalized to the number per 500 shots for the film in question.

A few other people have taken up these methods over the last thirty years, first Harv Bishop in a stylistic comparison of the films of Peter Bogdanovich and certain other directors, then Michael J. Porter has applied similar methods in television analysis, and most recently, Warren Buckland has tested them on a couple of recent Hollywood films.

what to do it to

For this survey, I chose to work with films from 1999 because this is the most recent year for which I have been able to see large numbers of American films on British free-to-air television. (British television companies have an agreement with the major American film distributors only to show films that were released in the cinema in the UK at least three years previously). According to the International Movie Database (which seems to have fairly reliable data for recent years), there were more than 1000 American feature films released in 1999. (I am including films that are listed as American co-productions with another country by the IMDb, but I am excluding made for television feature films, and also "straight to video" features, not to mention feature-length documentaries and animated features). Ideally, in the search for a representative sample, one would make a random selection from these 1000 or so films, but not all of them are available on VHS cassettes or DVDs even in the USA. A rough check shows that those films that are available in these formats correspond fairly exactly to those for which at least ten people have registered a vote on the IMDb. This reduces the number to be considered to 671. A random selection of twenty films from this corpus using a random number generator produced the following list:

The Underground Comedy Movie
The Storytellers
Music of the Heart
Heart to Heart.com
Money Buys Happiness
The Curse
The Treasure of Pirate's Point
Hot Wax Zombies on Wheels
Point Doom
Palmer's Pick Up

Playthings
Coming Soon
Outside Providence
Cremaster 2
Storm
An Invited Guest
Scar City
Jesus' Son
Raw Nerve
The Distraction

How many of these have you seen, or even heard of? With titles like *The Storytellers* and *An Invited Guest,* some of these films are longing to be ignored. And would you really want to read my analysis of them? In any case, only *Jesus' Son* and *Music of the Heart* have been released in the UK. So I decided to limit myself to a selection from a smaller group of films about which rather more people had been interested in expressing an opinion. So I narrowed the corpus to those films for which at least 500 people had put in an opinion and vote on the IMDb. (As you can check for yourself, such opinions and votes are far from always being complimentary to the film concerned.) This gave me 179 films to select from, and these usefully happened to have a rough correspondence with the body of the American films from 1999 released on VHS or DVD in Britain. Making another random selection of 20 films from these produced the following list:

10 Things I Hate About You (Gil Junger)
Angela's Ashes (Alan Parker)
The Blair Witch Project (Myrick and Sanchez)
Brokedown Palace (Jonathan Kaplan)
Crazy in Alabama (Antonio Banderas)
Deep Blue Sea (Renny Harlin)
Detroit Rock City (Adam Rifkin)
EDtv (Ron Howard)
The Insider (Michael Mann)
Jakob the Liar (Peter Kassovitz)
Life (Ted Demme)
Love Stinks (Jeff Franklin)
Man on the Moon (Milos Forman)
The Mating Habits of the Earthbound Human (Jeff Abugov)
The Minus Man (Hampton Fancher)
The Sixth Sense (M. Night Shyamalan)
SLC Punk! (James Merendino)
Snow Falling on Cedars (Scott Hicks)
The Talented Mr. Ripley (Anthony Minghella)
Three to Tango (Damon Santostefano)

This seems to me to be a convincingly varied collection, though naturally, given the method of sampling, it contains no proper representation of the rather large amount of absolute rubbish in the original list of all US features from 1999. However, it does include representatives from the cheap end of production, with *The Mating Habits of the Earthbound Human* and *SLC Punk!* being clearly made for about one or two hundred thousand dollars, not to mention *The Blair Witch Project*. The quite representative balance of genres in the final sample also reminds us that extremely expensive mindless action films like *Deep Blue Sea* only form a very small part of American production, however much attention they attract, and however much money they take at the box-office. Well, actually not that much in the case of *Deep Blue Sea*. Minor points I discovered in this sample is that none of them contains a real car chase sequence, though *Detroit Rock City*, which is a very conventional teen rock-music comedy, does have a short highway car bumping duel. There is no genuine "art film" in my sample, though such things do exist in the total American production for the year, but *The Minus Man* and *SLC Punk!* are nudging the edge of this category. The other thing I notice in the sample is the relative absence of nudity and explicit sexual activity, even though such scenes could be justified by many of the scripts. In fact the only real nudity in the sample is in *Angela's Ashes*, and it is very brief at that. I think this may actually represent a trend which has been underway for a few years, with explicit representation of sexual activity now being increasingly exiled to the very bottom end of production, and in Britain, to television.

I have also included in the results the figures for two additional shows. These are the film *Dark City* (Alex Proyas) from 1998, because this has, as far as I know, the fastest cutting in American film up to the present,[1] and a piece of television drama from 1999, namely an episode from the soap opera *Melrose Place* (Richard Lang).

what we get

The first thing to look at is Average Shot Length (ASL). To put this in context, I present a historical survey of the trends in this variable in American commercial cinema since 1940, including all the latest figures I have collected (see Figure 6.1).

Over the last decade I have obtained many thousands more values for this variable, so the figures represented in the histograms here supersede those in my *Film Style and Technology: History and Analysis* (1992). The graphs cover the same six year periods used in that source, and as in the earlier survey, the class intervals are defined so that the height of the column or bar above the number five, say, represents the number of films with ASLs between 5.0 seconds and 5.9999... seconds. In the case of the 1994–99 period, for instance, this is 192 films. Any films with ASLs greater than 25 seconds

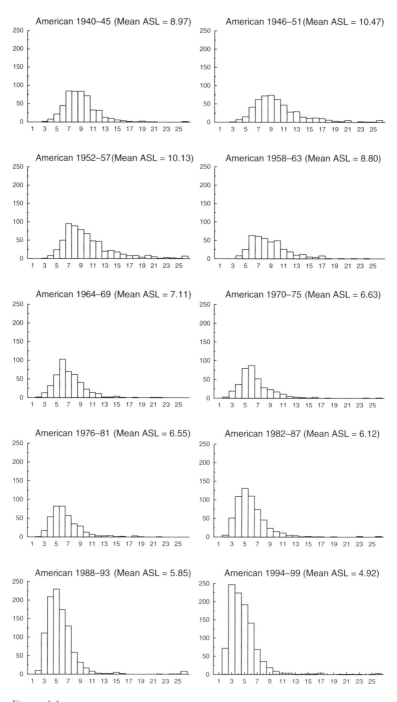

Figure 6.1

Historical survey of Average Shot Length (ASL) in American commercial cinema 1940–1999.

are lumped together in the column after the 25 second column. The total number of films recorded in the 1994–99 sample is 1035, whereas the period 1970–75 is represented by only 373 films. The other periods are represented by numbers of films between these two figures, and for the whole sixty years I am dealing with 5,893 films altogether. The number of films covered by each graph is proportional to the total area inside the columns (bars) of the histograms of that graph. The majority of these ASLs are taken for the complete length of the films concerned. My initial practice of being satisfied in some cases with the ASL for the first 40 minutes of a film was abandoned ten years ago.

The first observation about the general trend of change over this sixty years of American cinema is obvious. The cutting rate or number of shots has increased fairly steady over the period, and the measure of this, the ASL, has decreased. The position of the modal (or most common) value of the ASL can easily be seen to be moving leftwards from 9 seconds in 1946–51 to 3 seconds in 1994–99. Although it stands out clearly, the modal value is not the most accurate way of measuring the general trend, because its value is susceptible to the size of the class interval chosen. Preferable is the mean ASL for each period. This can be seen to be decreasing continuously from the high value of 10.47 seconds in 1946–51 to 4.92 seconds in 1994–99. The period 1946–51 was the peak of the adoption of the long take way of shooting films by a select group of Hollywood directors, though not by the majority. (Any film with an ASL of greater than 11 seconds will contain many long takes; that is, shots having durations of 30 seconds and above.) The long take school of directors were still hard at work in Hollywood through the 1950s, but then they began to be displaced by newer entrants to the profession in the late 1950s, and the mean ASL started to go down. The continual decrease was held up for a while in the 1970s by a bit of a return to shooting long takes, now using the zoom lens as well as tracking and panning as a means of keeping a shot going beyond the normal length.

At the other extreme, the first appearance of ASLs of less than 3 seconds in American sound cinema appears to be in 1968, with Daniel Haller's *The Wild Racers*, followed by Russ Meyer's *Cherry, Harry, and Raquel* in 1969. Through the 1970's there were a few more Russ Meyer films, and also a handful from Sam Peckinpah and George A. Romero. In the 1980s, there were slightly more action films such as the later *Rambo* and *Rocky* films, and also a few action horror films, that also had ASLs below 3 seconds. Then suddenly in the 1994–99 period the number of films with ASLs less than 3 seconds leapt to 72 films out of the sample of 1035. This development is accurately represented by two films in the twenty-film sample for 1999 that I am analysing in detail. These are *Deep Blue Sea* and *Detroit Rock City*, as you can see in Table 6.1.

Incidentally, the move towards faster and faster cutting in American cinema over the last fifty years has *not* been led by American television

Table 6.1 Average Shot Lengths, percentage of Reverse Angle cuts, percentage of Point of View shots, and percentage of Insert shots for the twenty-film sample from 1999

Title	Director	ASL	RA	POV	INS
10 Things I Hate About You	Junger, Gil	6.7	58	4	2
Angela's Ashes	Parker, Alan	3.9	31	4	10
Blair Witch Project, The	Myrick, D & Sanchez, E.	15.8	1	2	44
Brokedown Palace	Kaplan, Jonathan	5.8	50	6	6
Crazy in Alabama	Banderas, Antonio	5.4	45	8	8
Deep Blue Sea	Harlin, Renny	2.6	24	10	23
Detroit Rock City	Rifkin, Adam	2.2	25	5	11
EDtv	Howard, Ron	5.5	31	8	12
Insider, The	Mann, Michael	5.4	33	6	6
Jakob the Liar	Kassovitz, Peter	5.7	37	10	4
Life	Demme, Ted	4.5	55	6	2
Love Stinks	Franklin, Jeff	4.6	49	7	6
Man on the Moon	Forman, Milos	3.9	46	18	4
Mating Habits of the Earthbound Human, The	Abugov, Jeff	5.6	35	6	9
Minus Man, The	Fancher, Hampton	5.5	50	10	15
Sixth Sense, The	Shyamalan, M. Night	8.6	57	21	15
SLC Punk!	Merendino, James	4.2	38	3	7
Snow Falling on Cedars	Hicks, Scott	5.3	23	6	13
Talented Mr. Ripley, The	Minghella, Anthony	5.0	45	6	6
Three to Tango	Santostefano, Damon	3.7	61	5	6
Melrose Place	Lang, Richard	4.0	70	3	5
Dark City	Proyas, Alex	2.0	26	7	14

practice. I believe the pressure on time and expenditure in television production militates against the larger number of camera set-ups necessary to get a shorter ASL. In any case, I have a collection of results for television drama and comedy for the last fifty years, and these show that film cutting rates have always been faster than those in television. The part of this research relating to the last ten years can be read in Salt ("Practical").

Going back to the slow end of cutting, you can see from the distributions that in the 1990s there are now very few films indeed with an ASL greater than 11 seconds. I have previously suggested that for American films made after 1990, any having an ASL greater than 9 seconds falls into the "art film" category, though I now think that 10 seconds is a better dividing line. For the 1994–99 sample of 1035 films there are only 26 features with ASLs longer than 10 seconds. The only ones from 1999 amongst the 140 odd that I have so far seen, and having an ASL greater than 10 seconds, are *Sweet and Lowdown*, *Magnolia*, and *The Blair Witch Project*. Inside the sample, *The Sixth Sense* is flirting with the idea of being an art film, according to this criterion, with an ASL of 8.6 seconds. Otherwise, the majority of films in the sample (16 of them) have ASLs between 3 and 7 seconds, just like the vast majority of the films in my much larger sample for 1994–99.

One would think that eventually a limit will be reached in cutting rate, and we may be near it now. This limit is presumably imposed by the minimum length of comprehensible sentences in dialogue scenes, together with just how many reaction shots a dialogue scene will stand without looking ridiculous. There is no limit to how many shots a scene of pure action may be broken down into, but even the most mindless action film needs a certain amount of explanation in the dialogue as to the reason for all the bashes, crashes and explosions. However, we may already be seeing a new way of getting the effect of a cut without actually making one within a shot. For the last several years, many action films have scenes in which the lights that are ostensibly lighting the scene are flashing on and off during the course of the shots, which, particularly if these lighting changes are extreme, gives the effect of virtual cuts within the shot, because successive lengths of footage look so different to each other under the lighting changes. There are a number of examples of scenes with this technique in *Deep Blue Sea*, *Detroit Rock City*, and *Dark City*.

The complete tabulation of Average Shot Lengths, percentage of Reverse Angle cuts, percentage of Point Of View (POV) shots, and percentage of Insert shots for my twenty film sample from 1999 is given in Table 6.1.

There is not a great deal to be said about the percentages of reverse angle cuts in the films under consideration—they range from 21 percent to 70 percent, ignoring *The Blair Witch Project*, and all these values could have been found forty years ago. However, there are probably more films with RA percentages above 40 percent than there would have been forty years ago. In the very special case of the *The Blair Witch Project*, its basic feature that all its shots were taken by the two cameras used by the characters in it eliminates the possibility of reverse angles and POV shots, except under very special circumstances. That is, one of the characters has to be shown filming one of the others, and then there has to be a cut to the footage from their camera. This does happen a couple of times in the introductory scenes, but not thereafter. You might say that the fact that since all the shots in the movie are filmed by characters in the film, then that should make all of them POV shots, but my definition of a POV shot is one that represents what one of the characters shown in an adjoining shot sees, which accords with ordinary film nomenclature, and it is this definition that gives the result above.

The percentage of POV shots is in general below 10 percent for the sample, with the exception of two films. In *Man on the Moon* a great deal of the film is occupied with the protagonist performing on stage or television, watched by people who know him, so *The Sixth Sense* is the only truly exceptional case. Here, a proportion of the POV shots are assigned to the psychiatrist character after the prologue near the beginning of the main story, and also at its end. Those near the beginning seem to me misleading about the physical existence of the psychiatrist, since if we see his POV shots just like those of the real people in the film, this tends to imply that he exists, just like them. You might say that this goes with the treatment of the restaurant scene, in which his wife appears to reply to what he says, and which is equally deceiving of the film audience. But at least there are no shots of him done as POV shots from the viewpoint of the other characters. And it must be pointed out that the handling of "subjective" effects, including POV shots, has frequently been logically inconsistent, ever since such things first appeared in movies a hundred years ago. Also striking, in a negative way, is the low proportion of POV shots in *The Talented Mr. Ripley*, particularly if we contrast it with Alfred Hitchcock's treatment of a not dissimilar Patricia Highsmith novel, *Strangers on a Train*, fifty years before. In that case, 18 percent of the cuts are between one of a character and their POV, and, boy, are they working dramatically!

Insert shots are another aspect of "pure cinema," as Alfred was wont to put it (or basic filmic narration, if you want to be pretentious about it), and these are given due emphasis in some of the films. They are of course performing their suspense/thriller function in *Deep Blue Sea*, *The Minus Man*, and *The Sixth Sense*. *The Blair Witch Project* takes this kind of thing to what must be a new world record, eclipsing Fritz Lang's efforts of long ago. (Peaking at 27 percent Insert shots in *Das Testament des Dr. Mabuse* [1933]. For more details see my "Fritz Lang's Diagonal Symphony" in Salt, *Moving into Pictures*, 190–6.) Whether they would have worked just as well if there were rather less of them in *The Blair Witch Project* is an interesting question. In *Snow Falling on Cedars* the inserts mostly occur in the numerous arty "mental image" sequences.

how close we are

The proportions of shots of different scale (or closeness) for the films in my sample are presented in a series of graphs of the histogram variety (Figure 6. 2). I have grouped them on the page according to the degree of resemblance between their profiles. The degree of close resemblance between the Scale of Shot profiles for the first eight of the films, and also their resemblance to that for the *Melrose Place* television show is rather scary, particularly in contrast to the variety to be seen in the many results for the 1920s through the "High Hollywood" period of the 1930s and 1940s presented in my *Film Style and Technology: History and Analysis* (Salt). And of course this very heavy emphasis on the use of close shots is unparalleled in

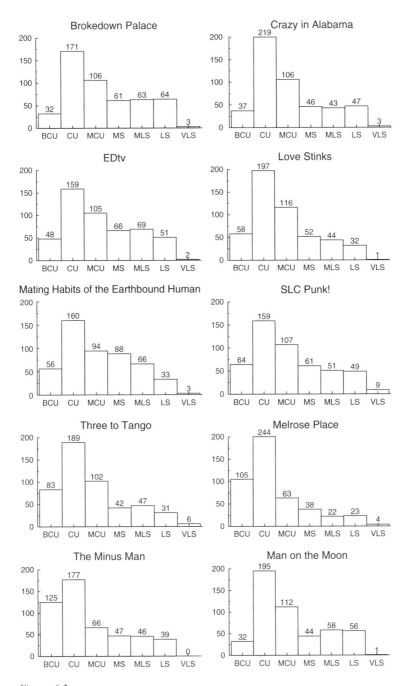

Figure 6.2

The proportions of shots of different scale (or closeness).

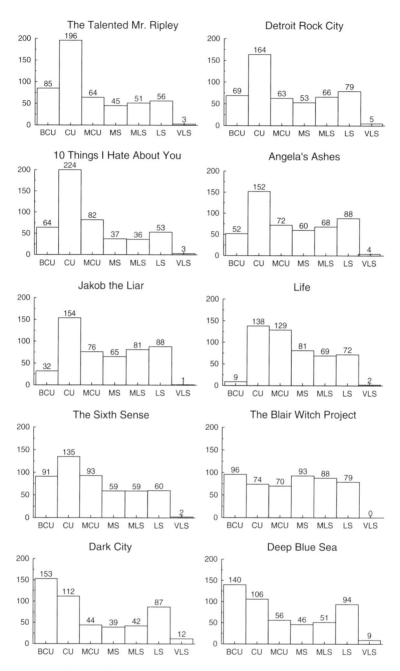

Figure 6.2 (*continued*)

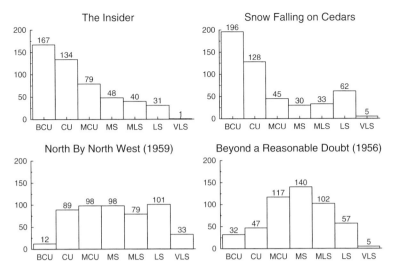

Figure 6.2 (*continued*)

the past. The first variant on what is clearly now a standard profile is represented by the group made up of *10 Things I Hate About You, Angela's Ashes, Detroit Rock City, Jakob the Liar,* and *The Talented Mr. Ripley.* In these films the large number of Close Ups (CUs) stand out above a more even background of the other scales of shot. One interpretation of this sort of profile is that the directors concerned are reluctantly paying lip service to the notion of "more Close Ups" by just going for that pure category alone. And it is noticeable that there are three non-American directors in this group—Alan Parker, Peter Kassovitz, and Anthony Minghella. On the other hand, Gil Junger and Adam Rifkin are purely American film-makers, the former having directed a large amount of commercial television before making *10 Things,* and Adam Rifkin having been involved with making low budget film junk for quite a while before getting a bit more money to make this film celebrating the band Kiss. So perhaps there is nothing in my interpretation. Milos Forman's *Man on the Moon* also has a fairly similar Scale of Shot profile.

Ted Demme's *Life* is the only film in the sample that has the kind of fairly even distribution across the Scale of Shot from CU to LS that was quite common once upon a time. This regressive feature may be due to Demme's inexperience in directing films. *The Sixth Sense* and *The Blair Witch Project* also have a pretty even distribution across the Scales of Shot, but in this case they have the equally heavy emphasis on Big Close Up so characteristic of recent times. *Deep Blue Sea* and *Dark City* push the emphasis even further onto Big Close Up, and at the other end of the scale onto Long Shots. They are both science fiction spectaculars, and the extra proportion of Long Shots against the middle range of closeness is to contain the spectacular

137

sets and their destruction and transformation that is so essential to these films' being. I wouldn't be surprised if further work showed that this profile was characteristic of other similar big budget films.

Incidentally, *The Blair Witch Project* has a number of peculiarities in framing, which are due to the desire of the makers to give the impression that it is the rushes of a real *cinéma vérité* film that were shot by the characters in it. As their fear and anguish grows, the framings become compositionally unbalanced, and indeed go so far as to be a crude sort of Dutch tilt framing even when they put the camera down onto some fixed surface to get a shot with themselves in it. These devices probably work in the usual expressive way for an unsophisticated audience, but a microsecond's thought should tell you that someone who can conquer their fear sufficiently to pick up a camera and film what is going on, will be certain to also get the shot reasonably well framed.

Finally we have two films which have the most extreme use of Big Close Up, *The Insider* and *Snow Falling on Cedars*, both of which have relatively inti-mate stories, which makes possible such large numbers of Big Close Ups, and both of which are intentionally pushing the envelope of commercially acceptable style. They also show the way that film leads television, for television shows do not get quite this close on the average, as indicated by the Scale of Shot distribution for the *Melrose Place* episode. (The pressure against television shows using very large amounts of Big Close Ups is that under the fast shooting regime of television, there is considerable danger of producing ugly looking pictures of the actor's heads in Big Close Up if a slight error is made in framing by the operator. In looser framings, slight framing errors do not draw attention to themselves quite so much.)

In the process of analysing these films with respect to Closeness of Shot, I realized that there has been a change in the standard framing of a head in Big Close Up, and also to some extent of ordinary Close Ups, over the last decade or two. Whereas Big Close Ups used to be framed cutting the figure at the neck at the bottom of the frame, and at the top of the head at the top of the frame, now it is more usual to include a bit of the shoulders, and cut through the forehead at the top, so leaving the closeness just the same, but substantially changing the look of the shot. That this change had passed me by up to the point of making this analysis is yet another illustration of the usefulness of these methods.

138

moving around the scene

There are characteristic variations in the use of camera movement amongst film directors, and I deal with this by counting the number of camera move-ments of various types in the films (Table 6.2). These are tilts, pans, panning and tilting simultaneously, tracking, tracking with panning, tracking with panning and tilting, crane movements, and zooming. (Yes, I know the last

Table 6.2 Camera movements for the twenty-film sample from 1999

Title	Pan	P w T	Track	T w PT	Crane	Zoom	Total
Blair Witch Project, The	24	79	24	152	0	31	310
Jakob the Liar	24	17	24	47	3	0	115
Brokedown Palace	22	23	19	30	10	0	104
Snow Falling on Cedars	28	30	22	18	5	0	103
10 Things I Hate About You	15	6	20	50	10	1	102
Dark City	25	11	22	7	35	0	100
Sixth Sense, The	9	11	46	26	5	0	97
Insider, The	26	11	21	34	2	2	96
Detroit Rock City	22	15	27	23	2	7	96
Crazy in Alabama	22	12	27	28	6	0	93
SLC Punk!	17	13	31	21	10	0	92
EDtv	18	11	29	20	3	5	86
Minus Man, The	26	21	13	20	3	0	79
Talented Mr. Ripley, The	17	15	19	25	3	0	79
Love Stinks	23	7	14	29	4	0	77
Deep Blue Sea	21	8	27	16	2	0	74
Life	16	3	19	24	4	0	66
Angela's Ashes	24	14	9	5	0	1	53
Man on the Moon	27	7	6	9	2	0	51
Three to Tango	10	7	15	14	2	0	48
Mating Habits of the Earthbound Human, The	28	5	9	4	1	0	47

of these is not actually a camera movement, but it changes the content of the frame during the shot, and I have to get it in somewhere.)

Although I actually collect all these categories, in this case I will consolidate some of them, so as to bring out the similarities and differences between the films more clearly. So I put both pans and tilts together in the category of Pans, and put the Tracks with Pans together with the Tracks with both Panning and Tilting. The films are ordered in terms of the total number of shots with camera movement per 500 shots. I do not distinguish the different methods of supporting the camera, so that hand-held tracking and Steadicam tracking go in together with the traditional tracking with the camera on a dolly.

One curiosity that leaps to the eye is the relatively uniform use of simple pans and tilts, which range between 15 and 27, with the exception of *The Sixth Sense* and *Three to Tango*. Apart from this, *The Blair Witch Project* is totally unique with respect to camera movement, as it is in other respects. Nevertheless, we can see that the different combinations of kinds of movement do make some distinctions amongst some of the films. It is possible to distinguish a definite low camera movement class, made up of *Angela's Ashes*, *Man on the Moon*, *Three to Tango*, and *The Mating Habits of the Earthbound Human*. The noticeably small use of camera movements in the first three of these is undoubtedly intentional, since their directors are all very experienced, but it is likely that *The Mating Habits of the Earthbound Human* has little camera movement because of the sheer lack of talent of its director, as well as his inexperience (proven by some dubious eye-line matches). Perhaps *Life*, from another inexperienced director, should be included in this group. Other things that stand out are the very large proportion of crane shots in *Dark City*, though this is not strictly part of our main sample, and the particularly large amount of tracking with a free head in *Jakob the Liar* and *10 Things I Hate About You*. In both of these cases, most of the tracking is actually done with a Steadicam, as it has to be nowadays when there is a lot of it, since laying tracks for a dolly is very expensive in terms of time and labour. No doubt Gil Junger was relishing the opportunity to set his camera free, for lots of tracking of any kind, and the Steadicam kind in particular, are not used in television studio work.

The other stand-out figure is the amount of straight-line tracking in *The Sixth Sense*. These movements are in general short in range, and slow, and a lot of them are also sideways tracks or crabbing movements, and most of them are done on quasi-static scenes. That is, they are not following the characters as they move around. The characters are sitting down, say, and the camera tracks slowly across behind one of them sitting on a sofa. This trick does not originate with M. Night Shyamalan, but he does it a bit more in *The Sixth Sense* than his contemporaries. Indeed, there is a smaller amount of this kind of short and slow tracking in *Snow Falling on Cedars* and *The Talented Mr. Ripley* in our sample. It could be claimed that it produces an expressive sense of unease in *The Sixth Sense*, but it just irritates me, here and elsewhere. The most adventurous of these films stylistically is *The Insider*, which uses a high amount of camera movement, with both moves on a dolly, and on a Steadicam, and also old-style hand shooting. There seems to be an expressively graded use of these techniques, from dolly to Steadicam to hand-held shots having an extra bit of wobble put on, and so intentionally producing a more and more agitated effect as we go through to the last of these.

Incidentally, there are some other films from 1999 and thereabouts which show the influence of the camera operating in the television show *NYPD Blue*. Waving the camera around for extra excitement is to be found extensively in *G.I. Jane* (1997), and in *Any Given Sunday* (1999) a new optical device was used in front of the lens on some shots to give the effect with a camera that was not being moved at all.

But the most striking device in *The Insider* is the use of out-of-focus effects. For instance, when Russell Crowe enters the room where the bosses of the tobacco company are meeting near the beginning of the film, the shot is a Close Up of the back of the head of the big boss, which is in sharp focus. Crowe is distant in the background and well out of focus, and he stays that way for the rest of the shot, even though he is the object of principal interest. There are also brutal focus pulls all the way from Big Close Up to Very Long Shot, and much play with messy bits of out-of-focus hair etc. obscuring parts of the frame in the foreground, in a thoroughly unconventional way.

Zooming is in general not used in our sample, at least in any noticeable way. (Some of these movies were filmed with a zoom lens on the camera to give a quick adjustment of the focal length when changing from set-up to set-up, and sometimes they have an occasional slight tightening or loosening of the framing due to a small change in the focal length within the shot, but I do not count that as a zoom, any more than I count a small pan or tilt for re-framing purposes.) Otherwise, we have a small number of zooms in *Detroit Rock City* in the final rock concert, where they naturally belong, and a similarly small number in *EDtv*, which is about actuality television, another habitat of the zoom. Otherwise, real zooming is mostly out nowadays, with one exception. This is a repetition of the "Vertigo" effect; that is, a simultaneous zoom and track in the reverse direction, so that the framing stays the same, but the internal perspective of the shot changes. This expressive device is used for comedy near the beginning of *10 Things I Hate About You*, and also almost invisibly near the beginning of *The Sixth Sense*, when the psychiatrist is staking out his prospective child patient. And I have seen this device used in these sorts of ways in other recent films. It has become a cliché.

the look of the picture

My casual impression of films from the last decade was that a large proportion of them had colour bias applied to all their scenes for expressive or stylistic purposes. But careful examination of the films in my sample just goes to show how wrong intuitive impressions can be, even for the expert eye. In fact, most of the twenty films have their shots fairly correctly balanced to white light, with the exception of the night exteriors, which are generally given the traditional bluish bias. The minor exceptions to this generalization are *Brokedown Palace* and *Life*, which have an orange or amber bias given to many day exteriors, presumably to suggest the heat of the Far East or the Deep South, and *The Insider*, which has a number of night interiors with a slightly warm tone. The major exceptions are *Angela's Ashes*, *Jakob the*

Liar, and *Snow Falling on Cedars*, all of which have had desaturation applied to all colours throughout. In the first two, this has presumably been done to emphasize the miserable conditions under which their characters exist, and in the case of the latter, to emphasize the pastness of the story, with a touch of the miserables as well. At a more technical level, there is a just noticeable variation in lighting style across the sample, with in the first place a varying degree of hardness (directionality) in the light applied to the interior scenes. This ranges from hard lighting on the figures in *Love Stinks* and *Life* through to very soft lighting on the figures in *The Minus Man* and *Man on the Moon*. Another variable is the amount of backlight used on the figures. This tends to be low, as usual nowadays, and is largely absent in *Jakob the Liar*, and completely absent in *Angela's Ashes*, which is truly exceptional in this respect. This film has much the most realistic lighting, with its poverty-stricken interiors lit by one or two fairly small soft sources just out of shot, with the level of light falling rapidly away to the walls of the sets, so that there is no separation of the figures from the background.

telling the story

Fourteen of these films tell their stories in the basic straightforward way that was standard fifty, and more, years ago. Of the rest, *Angela's Ashes*, *SLC Punk!*, and *Crazy in Alabama* are narrated in voice over by someone who appears in the film as their younger self, while *Life* is presented as a series of flashbacks told to an audience by an old participant within the framing scenes. *The Talented Mr. Ripley* is begun with a voice over by the protagonist regretting what he had done to initiate the action, but this does not reappear, so it doesn't really count as a narrated film. *The Mating Habits of the Earthbound Human* is presented as a documentary, with personal narration, made by some kind of extra-terrestrial being about the subject of the title. *Snow Falling on Cedars* is a mixture of flashback narration and memories framed by a trial scene. My impression is that the use of narration to power the story has become more common in the last couple of decades than it was fifty years ago, since a quick check on a list of films from 1946–51 shows less than 5 percent having narrated stories.

The other feature that I have noticed in these and many other recent films is the large number of them that use shots and sequences representing mental images in the minds of their characters. In *The Minus Man* scenes representing the imaginings of the protagonist are cut straight into the action, and *Life* has a sequence in which the verbally expressed fantasies of the leading characters are followed by a depiction of these fantasies, with the dialogue carrying back and forth between fantasy and reality in a fairly ingenious way. *SLC Punk!* has a couple of scenes in which the background behind the characters changes within the shot to represent their fantasies.

142

In *The Mating Habits of the Earthbound Human* there are fantasy scenes belonging to the human characters who are the subject of the film, which doesn't make much logical sense, and in *The Sixth Sense* the psychiatrist also has his mental images represented visually. *Crazy in Alabama* does not have any visual mental images, but it does have a voice inside the head of the female lead coming through on the sound track at times, presumably to convey her insanity. As for *Snow Falling on Cedars*, throughout this film, besides the conventional flashback sequences, there are also many brief flashes of images of objects from the characters' past cutting in unexpectedly. The combination of all this, together with the lack of much dramatic development in the framing trial scene of this film, almost reduces its narrative drive to zero, and sufficiently explains its commercial failure.

Single shots of unexpected content suddenly cut into the narrative have begun appearing in quite a number of films recently, and other notable examples from 1999 include the skies with lightning flash appearing gratuitously in the latter parts of Oliver Stone's *Any Given Sunday*. (Oliver Stone has had quite a bit of influence on the work of other directors, including in particular *Snow Falling on Cedars*, in this sample.) The most outlandish of the cut-ins from 1999 is the viewpoint of a spent bullet inside the guts of a wounded soldier in David O. Russell's *Three Kings*. Apart from showing-off, the point of these memory flashes and inserts is that they are another way of increasing the cutting rate a bit.

how good are they?

The most rational and objective criteria for evaluating aesthetic worth are, in order of their importance: 1. Originality, 2. Influence, 3. Success in carrying out the maker's intentions. Here, as in other respects, *The Blair Witch Project* stands out for its originality from conception to execution, and also its great commercial success scores some points under Criterion No. 3. The degree of commercial success counts for all these films, since none of them are art films, let alone avant-garde films, and their makers undoubtedly had commercial success in mind. The runner-up in originality is *Snow Falling on Cedars*, with its heavily worked mixture of flashbacks and mental images, closely followed by *The Insider*, with its novel play with focus, and then *SLC Punk!*. This last film uses a small array of New Wave style tricks, such as freeze frames, peculiar shots, jokey fake documentary sequences, and talking to the audience, besides the matted-in background transformations that I have already mentioned. Evaluating Criterion 3, success in carrying out the maker's intentions, depends on knowing what the maker's intentions are, and for recent films this is mostly fairly easy to find out if you want to. Indeed, statements on this usually form part of the press pack at the film's release. For instance, in the case of *Snow Falling on Cedars*, according to a conversation recorded by Chrisopher Probst in the *American Cinematographer,* Scott Hicks said:

> The whole film is about the process of revealing. Nothing is quite what it appears to be; therefore, you never give it all away at once, but instead gradually. That was our guiding principle in the overall design of the film. The story is told through the gradual unravelling of several different mysteries: what happened at sea, in the war, [and between] Hatsue and Ishmael. I wanted the film to move seamlessly through its different time frames, like a knife through a slice of cake. (Probst 98)

He more or less achieves this, but obviously the idea was pushed too far, for the audience rejection of it upset its makers, which shows that they were indeed concerned with audience reaction. This is unlike the directors of real art films, who tend to shrug off such reactions.

Something similar is the case with *The Talented Mr. Ripley.* Anthony Minghella is quoted by Jay Holben as saying that:

> The film is lit with warm hues that serve to collect what is innately gorgeous about the landscape, and completely contradict the rather purgatorial journey that we are being led on. Rather than present *Mr. Ripley* as a collection of monochrome and increasingly moody images full of presentiment, we decided it would be much more interesting to do absolutely the reverse, and lend the film a romantic look that would stand in counterpoint to the action. (57)

As I have noted above, there are other aspects of the form of this film that avoid the standard filmic expressive methods, so Minghella's approach, like that of Hicks, is surprisingly perverse for the maker of an expensive commercial film. It occurs to me that this is another tendency that has appeared in recent decades, along with various changes in subject matter that are outside my immediate concerns, such as the marked increase in cynicism and nihilism in film scripts. Incidentally, the previous film adaptation of this novel, René Clément's *Plein soleil* (1959), was equally photographed in high key throughout.

One can reasonably assume that the makers of the more ordinary of these films were intending to comply with the ordinary craft standards, and evaluating their success in doing this makes up part of the calculus of Criterion 3. So one can definitely mark down *The Mating Habits of the Earthbound Human* in this area. The quality of script construction by conventional standards also counts under the craft part of Criterion 3, and here it is worth commenting on a feature of *Jakob the Liar* which I have not seen mentioned in the reviews. This is that there are no dramatic developments stemming from the basic situation established at the beginning until about half-way through the film. This is of course a serious deficiency for most audiences. The rest of the films not discussed here are fairly equal in this respect.

Discovering the influence of a film has to wait for at least several years, and so it cannot be applied to the evaluation of these movies. A film's influence depends, of course, on the interest other film-makers have in it, both immediately, and in the longer term.

tricks of the trade

Ideally, the analysis should be done by recording the complete characteristics of each shot (scale, movement, length, etc.) in succession down the length of the film. This permits the most complete analysis of all the possible interrelationships between the variables. But although I initially tried this thirty odd years ago, I found that it took about three times longer than the method I have since used, except in a few special cases. This gives sufficient information for the general comparisons you see made above. The method used here collects each quantity sequentially over the length of the film, and even this method took about 35 twelve-hour days to analyse the twenty-one films dealt with in this article.

Up to this piece of research, I have always worked with prints of the films I was analysing, and indeed almost exclusively with 35 mm prints, and I worked with them on Steenbecks and other flat-bed editing machines. It would have been possible for me to get 35 mm prints of most of these films, but the costs to me of educational hire and transport would have been around £2,000, not to mention the labour of then lugging the cans up five floors of stairs to the editing department of the London Film School. So the analysis was done from DVDs and VHS tapes. I fed these into a non-linear editing system, in fact Adobe Premiere on an ordinary PC (though a cheaper NLE would do just as well), and while they were being digitized in real time, I recorded the camera moves from the window in the digitizing programme screen. For the experienced analyst, this is just possible to do in real time, even for the fastest cut films. Then I went more slowly through the film in the NLE programme, recording the Scale of Shot, which usually requires some stopping and starting and going back, particularly for the films with very short Average Shot Lengths. I also record the Inserts on this pass. Two more passes are necessary to get the numbers of reverse angles and POV shots. If I have a VHS tape I usually do this on a VHS recorder with a jog-shuttle control, as I can usually manage recording these last two quantities at high speed for most films. Alternatively, it is possible to do the complete analytical process entirely on a VHS recorder with a jog-shuttle control, as I have done when analysing television programmes in the past. For my analytical procedure the standard control system for DVD players is awkward to use when trying to work directly with the DVD disc.

There are important cautions to be made about the analytical process when working from tape recordings or DVDs of films. The first of these relates purely to the use of recordings made for the PAL television system. These are initially created from film prints that were shot at 24 frames per second when the original film were made, but are always transferred to the consumer medium at 25 frames per second. This means that their running time when played on PAL system devices is shortened by 4 percent of the original running time. This means that a correction factor has to be applied to the ASL by multiplying it by a factor of 25/24. I have applied this correction in the above results. No correction is necessary for NTSC recordings. More important is the question of Scale of Shot determination from video and DVD copies of films. For old Academy screen ratio films, both 16 mm copies and, even more so, video copies are cropped in all around the frame on transfer to a greater extent than the screen masking when they are shown in the cinema, or on a Steenbeck. The effect of this on the Scale of Shot is fairly slight, as it shifts a very small proportion of the Close Ups into the Big Close Up category, and an even smaller proportion of the more distant Shot Scales into the next closer category. Since all American feature films made since 1954 are intended to be masked to widescreen on projection, or are shot in one of the anamorphic 'Scope systems, or in a wide film system, the difficulty does not exist in quite this form for wide screen films. The problem is that films made since then which are shot "flat," i.e. with spherical lenses on the camera, may have the full Academy image that was invariably recorded on the negative for American films, transferred to video, and not masked in to the widescreen proportions that were intended to be seen in the cinema. Despite the fact that DVD transfers are virtually always given the correct masking, and there is an increasing trend to releasing VHS copies properly masked in to wide screen, this problem has received a new boost from the shooting of many films in Super 35. In this process, the camera exposes what is called the "full" aperture in the gate of the camera, which is equivalent to the old silent period aperture. This image on the original film is masked in to widescreen or even to 'Scope proportions by optical printing when making the release prints of the film.

Where possible, I used DVD copies when analysing the sample, and I also checked with the VHS copy of the same film where possible. This check showed that in the case of *Deep Blue Sea*, which was shot in Super 35, the VHS copy had been taken from the full frame, and the DVD copy, like the cinema prints, was taken from the middle of the original frame in 'Scope proportions. This meant that for any shot much more could be seen of the scene vertically in the VHS frame than could be seen in the DVD copy. That is, if I had analysed the VHS copy, I would have found that the film was shot from much further back than it really was, with respect to the intended cinema release framing. Another difficulty that can occur with films shot in Panavision, or other 'Scope systems (as opposed to merely being filmed with a Panavision camera), is that full frame VHS copies can be made by "scanning and panning" the 1:2.35 'Scope frame. A pan made across the 'Scope frame during the video transfer will show almost the true height of the frame, so creating no more of a problem than a video copy of an old Academy ratio film, but a scanning *cut* from one end of the 'Scope frame to the other, which sometimes happens, introduces an apparent extra cut into the film which wasn't there before. If there are a substantial number of these, this will affect the Average Shot Length slightly. Fortunately, the expert eye can detect most of them, but even I find I have missed some scanning cuts on re-examining a film. But to repeat, as long as you stick to DVD copies most of these difficulties can be avoided.

the last word

I believe this research has identified an increasingly restricted stylistic norm that has gripped most ordinary American commercial feature film making, using extremely fast cutting, and continuous close shooting, and I have described its essential nature. Substantial deviations from this stylistic norm are mostly, but fortunately not quite entirely, restricted to low budget film-making. And a number of other interesting and unexpected points have turned up along the way.

coda

If you check the latest results for the cutting rate in American films in this article against those in *Film Style and Technology*, you will notice some discrepancies. This is inevitable, given the relatively small samples that I had in

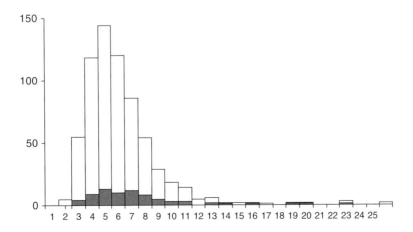

Figure 6.3

Average Shot Length of American films released between 1982 and 1987.

1992. To illustrate the effect of sample size, in figure 6.3 I reproduce a graph for the ASLs of American films released between 1982 and 1987, inclusive of those years.

This is based on the relevant histogram you can see in this article, but also includes the data from the histogram for the same period on page 283 of *Film Style and Technology*, which is recorded as short tinted bars on the graph. They are short because the sample size in 1992 was only 75 films, whereas the latest results are for a sample of 596 films. You can see that there is a general resemblance between the shapes of the two distributions, allowing for the difference in scale, and the modal (most common) values are about the same, in the range of 5 to 6 seconds. However, the early results give a mean Average Shot Length for the period of 8.4 seconds, whereas the mean Average Shot Length for the period calculated from the vastly larger present sample is 6.12 seconds. Closer inspection shows that the early small sample has relatively too many films in the range 7 to 9 seconds, which accounts for the error.

All this illustrates a basic fact about the reliability of estimating a variable (Average Shot Length in this case), which is characteristic of a population (the films), by selecting a sample from the population. My initial sample was not only small given the size of the population, which was in the area of 2,000 to 3,000 American feature films made from 1982 to 1987, but it was also definitely non-random. That is, it was taken from films that I *wanted* to see in those days. If it had been completely randomly selected, it would probably have got closer to the true value for the mean Average Shot Length, but not certainly, since there is an appreciable chance of even a random sample dragging in too many non-typical films, according to statistical sampling theory. Even though my much larger present sample is strictly speaking non-random, it results from my getting the Average Shot Length of every film I could possibly see on television over the last dozen years. In other words, it includes lots of rubbish. And given that it represents about a quarter of the population of American films for the period 1982 to 1987, it is probably pretty close to the correct value of the mean Average Shot Length for that period.

However, in this new twenty-first century, it is finally possible to get a truly random sample of the American films shot in any particular year, since every American film made and shown in a cinema will certainly have a DVD recording of it published a year or two after its release. And inevitably, within a year of writing "The Shape of 1999," there was a new fast cutting champion, which probably still holds the title. It was *Derailed* (2002), directed by Bob Misiorowski, and starring Jean-Claude Van Damme, and it has an Average Shot Length of 1.63 seconds. This film was clearly not a really big budget production, but Misiorowski got quite a lot of bang for his bucks by shooting in Eastern Europe. A great deal of *Derailed* was set on a train, and much of this footage was shot hand-held, which would have speeded up production considerably. Unlike the previous speed champions, there was not much attention to visual elegance in the shooting of this film, nor to tidy shot transitions; another casualty of budget restrictions.

note

1 A new winner in the fast cutting stakes has just been identified from the corpus of American films of 1999 shown in England. It is *End of Days*, directed by Peter Hyams. It contains 3875 shots in its 112.5 minutes running time, which is an Average Shot Length of 1.74 seconds. After studying it, I believe this record can and will be broken in later years.

works cited

Bishop, H.J. "A Medium Variable Analysis in Film: A Comparison of Bogdanovich with Ford, Hawks, Hitchcock and Welles." M.A. thesis in Journalism. University of Colorado at Boulder, 1985.

Buckland, W. "*Mise en scène* Criticism and Statistical Style Analysis." Thomas Elsaesser and Warren Buckland, *Studying Contemporary American Film: A Guide to Movie Analysis*. London: Edward Arnold, 2002. 80–116.

Holben, J. "Alter Ego." *American Cinematographer* 81.1 (2000): 56–71.

Mascelli, Joseph V. *The Five C's of Cinematography*. Los Angeles: Silman-James Press, 1998.

Porter, M.J. "A Comparative Analysis of Directing Styles in *Hill Street Blues*." *The Journal of Broadcasting and Electronic Media* 31 (1987): 323–34.

Probst, C. "Impeccable Images." *American Cinematographer* 81.6 (2000): 97–105.

Salt, B. "Film Form, Style, and Aesthetics." *Sight & Sound* 43.2 (1974): 108–9.

———. "Statistical Style Analysis of Motion Pictures." *Film Quarterly* 28.1 (1974): 13–22.

———. *Film Style and Technology: History and Analysis*. 2nd ed. London: Starword, 1992.

———. "Practical Film Theory and its Application to TV Series Drama." *Journal of Media Practice* 2.2 (2001): 98–113.

———. *Moving into Pictures: More on Film History, Style, and Analysis*. London: Starword, 2006.

An earlier version of this chapter was published in the *New Review of Film and Television Studies*, 2,1 (2004): 61–85.

tales of

epiphany and

entropy

paranarrative

worlds on

youtube

t h o m a s   e l s a e s s e r

the trouble with narrative

Film theory has always had particular problems with narrative. Was story-telling the cinema's manifest destiny, as an earlier generation of historians used to think, or does "early cinema," especially in the formula of the "cinema of attractions," prove the exact opposite? How medium-specific is narrative, given that it is generally recognized as a quasi-universal way of making sense of experience? Is (classical) narrative a mode of world-making or "totality-thinking" that reveals or reflects Western capitalism's political unconscious (in Fredric Jameson's sense)? Or can narratology, as a highly specialized and sophisticated trans-media discipline, manage to clarify the problems (e.g. levels of narration, enunciation, the role of the reader) that classical film theory, based as it was on linguistic models, failed to resolve?

Some of these questions now seem to belong to a by-gone age, a pre-history to our present that in several ways is hardly recognizable. Not only because, according to a wide-spread (but highly debatable) belief, narrative no longer matters in mainstream cinema, driven more by special effects and spectacular scenes than story-telling skills and careful plotting. It is the concern with media-specificity that now seems especially antiquated, given the general belief in intermediality and remediation, and the faith or fears surrounding "convergence." Also long gone is the ambition that (structural) linguistics might provide the master code by which to read all products of culture, from literary texts to films, from advertisements to fashion. And there is "interactive narrative" and "database narratives": two oxymorons now occupying pride of place in the discussions, thanks to the commercial success, aesthetic possibilities and conceptual challenges enjoyed by computer games.

Today, then, a more anthropological, but also technologically inflected approach to narrative seems to prevail, according to which narrative is only one, culturally very specific, way of storing, organizing, retrieving and accessing data in time, and that other modes are both possible and may even be more desirable. Narrative now tends to be seen as a special instance of the "archive" or—in the case of film narrative—be regarded as the all-but-defeated rival for quasi-universality and cultural superiority when competing against the (computer- or video-) game. In the anthropological sense, narrative is still a central organizing principle, functioning according to specific compositional rules, "scripts" or "programs," some of which are mapped on large-scale "life" patterns, such as birth, maturity, death, or on the idea of the journey, the quest or the initiation. In the case of myths, narratives have the cultural or religious function, either bricolage fashion (if one follows Lévi-Strauss), or by other taxonomies and coding processes of natural phenomena (if one follows George Lakoff), to represent the origins of the universe, and our place and purpose within it: narrative as one of the "interfaces" between "man" and "his" God(s) . . .

My aim is less exalted, but this essay is nonetheless concerned with the changing function of narrative: that is, with the question of what happens when one of the central cultural forms we have for shaping human sensory data as well as information about the "real world" finds itself in a condition of overstretch. Or more precisely: what happens when much of this data and information is being produced, i.e. recorded and stored, by machines, in cooperation with humans, which has been the case since the beginning of the twentieth century, but which is being fully acknowledged only since the beginning of the twenty-first century. Photography, the cinema, television, and the Internet are all hybrids in this respect: gathering more sense-data than humans can make sense of, and that narrative can contain, i.e. articulate, "linearize" or "authorize." Second, what kind of roles of spectatorship, of participation, of witnessing are afforded by the display and access of this data, especially in an environment which is common, public and collective (like the cinema), but also "dynamic," discrete and "interactive" (like the Internet), that is, which allows for feedback loops, change in real time, and is thus potentially both endless and shapeless.

Narratives are ways of organizing not only space and time, most commonly in a linear, consecutive fashion: they also, through the linguistic and stylistic resources known as "narration," provide for a coherent point of reception or mode of address: what used to be referred to as a "subject-position," or "reader-address." Narratives, in other words are about time, space and subject, or the "here," the "now" and the "me."

My essay starts from the notion that linear temporality (based as it is, in the case of narrative, on our primary experience of time as an irreversible arrow, tending towards closure: and in this respect "death" and "the happy ending" are one and the same thing) is only one axis on which to construct such a sequence and for making connections of continuity, contiguity, of plotting a trajectory and providing closure. It follows that if time is only one of the axes on which to string data and access it, then stories with a beginning, middle and end are only one such cultural form. In the era of simultaneity, ubiquity and placeless places, other cultural forms are conceivable and do indeed exist. Computer games, as just mentioned, are often cited as the competitors for the hegemony of narratives, and so-called spatial stories or spatial narratives increasingly gain attention even outside gamer communities.

Henry Jenkins, for instance, thinks of both narratives and games as "spatial stories." He argues that "spatial stories can evoke pre-existing narrative associations; they may embed narrative information within their *mise en scène*, or provide resources for emergent narratives" (2004), yet they do not have to take the form of classical narratives. He can even claim that

> anyone who doubts that Tolstoy might have achieved his true calling as a game designer, should reread the final segment of *War and Peace* where he works through how a series of alternative choices might have reversed the outcome of Napoleon's Russian campaign. The passage is dead weight in the context of a novel, yet it outlines ideas, which could be easily communicated in a god game like *Civilization*. (2004)

My concern is less to turn Tolstoy or Dickens into game designers before their time (interesting though this may be), but more to see what spatial stories the sites of the Web 2.0 social networks—MySpace, Facebook, Flickr, YouTube—might be able to tell, once a user decides to engage with their dynamic architecture, sets up a few ground rules for him/herself (both narratives and games need rules), and then lets him/herself be taken to different sites, spaces and places, not by the logic of an individual character's aims, obstacles, helpers and opponents (to cite the story formula of Vladimir Propp and many other narratologists), but by the workings of contiguity, combinatory and chance. In other words, neither the causal chain of action and reaction, nor the temporal succession of locales determines the direction or trajectory of the journey, but key-words or tags, tag-clouds or clusters of such key-words, embedded links, user's comments, and of course, one's own "free" associations. There is a long tradition of generating such chains and concatenations in literature, going back to some of the very first narratives we call novels, such as Cervantes' *Don Quixote*, or Lawrence Sterne's *Tristram Shandy*, all the way to films like Luis Buñuel's *The Phantom of Liberty* and Todd Solondz' *Palindromes*.

constructive instability

Thus, when I opted for YouTube as the site of my experiment in scripted spaces, I still very much had the cinema in mind. Not only is YouTube closest to the cinema, in that it shows visual segments extracted from different media (cinema, television, performances, home movies, advertisements, camcorder sessions, pop-concerts), but also because YouTube suggests the illusion—like its owners, Google—of a kind of totality, a full universe: if you cannot find it on Google, many people now seem to think, it either doesn't exist, or is not worth knowing or having, and so increasingly (and equally surprisingly) with YouTube: when recently I needed for a lecture but could not get hold of *A Corner in Wheat* by D.W. Griffith in the video library, a quick check on YouTube reassured me that I would be able to show my scene directly from the web.

Most of us are well aware of the dangers of relying on such a monopoly of information, but we also know, from our frequent, if shamefaced use of *Wikipedia*, how seductive it is to take as reliable fact what has been written, rewritten, amended, deleted and once more rewritten by many hands in a single Wiki-entry. Yet along with millions of others, I accept the convenience such ready-to-use knowledge affords, and willy-nilly align myself with the implied consequences of a potentially momentous development: the creeping fusion of mind, "man" and machine. This, in turn, we tend to take for granted as part of the overall collapse of the nature/culture divide, and more specifically, as part of the so-called post-human condition, which "configures human beings so that they can be seamlessly articulated with intelligent machines" (Abbas). In the post-human, there are no essential differences or absolute demarcations between bodily existence and computer simulation, between cybernetic mechanisms and biological organisms, between robots running on programs and humans pursuing goals or quests. In the words of N. Katherine Hayles, a prominent representative of the post-human view: "What is happening, is the development of distributed cognitive environments in which humans and computers interact in hundreds of ways daily, often unobtrusively" (1999).

One could object that the post-human position too readily subscribes to the more or less *smooth alignment* between man and machine, bios and techné, and thus operates with an adaptationist model of evolution: which according to some eminent recent studies of evolutionary biology (by Francisco Varela, Thomas Metzinger, but also including Antonio Damasio and Daniel Dennett), is much too large an assumption to make confidently,[1] since it would seem that human beings are more likely to remain constitutively un-adapted.

On the other hand, it is true that even if one rejects the full implications of the post-human position, one is well-advised to reflect on the definitions of "culture" and "nature," both of which stand under the sign of techné, but of a techné which needs itself to be refigured around the notion of "art" and "artifice," all of them now practices situated between "design," "engineering" and "programming." This raises an interesting prospect and may even hold out a promise: as "life" becomes more "artificial" by being both engineered and programmable, the possibility arises that "art" (or culture as we normally understand it) has to become more life-like (by emulating processes of reproduction, replication, random generation, mutation, chance and contingency), in order to remain "art," that is, "human," in the sense of "un-adapted" and sensitive to "failure" (which in this context would be another word for finitude, that is the certainty of death, or closure).

Similarly in the sphere of knowledge production and knowledge dissemination: if the principles of "art" and "life" collapse, coalesce or con- verge around replication and repetition, self-regulation and feedback, aggregation and clustering, what kind of art or knowledge, what kind of "convergence culture" can make its home on the Internet? In order to test this question I conducted an experiment: not only of how "art," "knowl- edge" and "life" implicate each other on the web, but of what "narratives" YouTube might tell, when certain of the parameters listed above are set as limits. Accepting, for the sake of the argument, the post-human "human- machine symbiosis" as fact, I aligned myself with the logic of the auto- generated web-links, and their embedded information. At the same time, I imagine myself a Web 2.0-flâneur, mingling with the anonymous crowd in the manner of the metropolitan flâneur made famous by Charles Baudelaire and Walter Benjamin, before being revived by the Paris Situationists and their urban *dérives*. I also fall back on an old-fashioned avant-garde technique popular among the Surrealists—automatic writing—allegedly derived from Freud's psychoanalytic free association. A specific version of the technique—*Cadavres exquis* (Exquisite corpses)—involved a daisy chain of participants, continuing a drawing or a piece of writing without knowing more than a fragment of the previous contribution. Children know the game as "Chinese whispers," and in the way I use it, it easily combines with another popular game: "six degrees of separation" (or its movie-fan version: "six degrees of Kevin Bacon," a parlour version of that part of chaos theory also known as "small world syndrome").

To give some indication of the results of the experiment, I shall introduce the concept of *constructive instability*. This, too, I take ready-made off the shelf, as it were. Its engineering provenance has been overlaid by a neo-con political usage, for instance, by Condoleezza Rice about the Lebanon–Israel war in the summer of 2006: she called the deaths among the civilian population and the resulting chaos in Lebanon and Israel "constructive instability." What interests me about constructive instability is not the implicit cynicism of Rice or Donald Rumsfeld ("shit happens"), but the idea that "instability" and even "failure" have a place in the narratives of adaptive, dynamic or emergent situations. One of the points to make about self-regulatory systems is an obvious one: they involve risk and imponderability. As, among others, the "Internet guru" Jaron Lanier, in his attack on Wikipedia as "digital Maoism," has pointed out, there is real concern about the kind of agency and extent of control individuals and collectives are handing over, when "intelligent systems" run so much of everyday life, in the area of medicine, the government, or—especially—on the financial markets and in the conduct of modern warfare. Information systems such as we have them are considerably more fallible than is usually realized, as can be seen from electricity power-station failures, the gridlock chaos that ensues when the traffic lights are down, or the knock-on effects that come from a local disturbance in the international air-traffic systems. Of course, one could argue that these are not self-regulatory phenomena, but hierarchized and top-down, while the Internet was conceived and built precisely in order to minimize the domino-effects typical of linear forms of communication or command-and-control. It is indeed due to the general success of this package distribution system that we feel so over-confident in the workings of all complex systems and circuits.

Mindful therefore of the fragility and fallibility of both human beings and of machines, I found it advisable to factor in the structural value of "failure": not as a negative feature that needs to be eliminated, but as the very point where potential failure can be seen to become productive. A specific example of such productivity, or rather where potential failure is a special feature, is the USA's advanced fighter planes such as the X-29, designed in such an aerodynamically unstable fashion that not only could they not be piloted by humans alone (which to a lesser extent is already the case of many commercial transatlantic airliners or jumbo jets): they would be extremely dangerous at most sub-sonic aircraft speeds:

> The advantage gained was manoeuvrability. While an ordinary fighter with swept-back wings requires energy to change course, the X-29 [with wings tipped forward] would simply "fall" in the direction indicated. Although this particular plane was never produced, aircraft designers are well aware of the trade-off between stability and manoeuvrability. Fighter planes today are, by design, very close to being unstable, while passenger planes are designed for stability. (Vorhees)

A similar example could be given from the financial markets, where the more advanced trading instruments, such as futures and derivatives, are also inherently unstable: how dangerously so can been seen from some spectacular "crashes" in recent times. One conclusion of my experiment, in other words, was that the principle of instability and volatility, and indeed, fallibility should be built into this human-machine system right from the start: not as a design fault, but specially engineered as a calculated risk, but also a design advantage.

performed failure: narratives of collapse

I now want to report where the idea of constructive instability or performed failure took me in a more circumscribed field of application—film- and media-studies. I focus on the transfers or convergences these disciplines may have with each other in respect to narrative, especially on the Internet, when placed against the familiar horizon of globalization, where classical or modernist terms like progress, medium specificity, the anxiety of influence or the autonomy of style seem increasingly inappropriate, but where the post-modern vocabulary of appropriation, pastiche also have little traction, while the notions of "resistance," "critique," "opposition" no longer mobilize a viable response other than a generalized condition of crisis and criticality.

I understand the term "constructive instability" first in its most literal form, namely as the property of an artefact, constructed and built for the purpose of drawing maximal use from the processes engendered when it collapses or self-destructs. My focus of attention for this new field of force centred on constructive instability as a systemically precarious equilibrium on the Internet, were—as mentioned—the social networking and user-generated content websites, where the monopoly of information (as controlled by Google) is constantly modified and amplified by the users' own sense of what is important, useful, amusing or of what simply exists: modified, in other words, by a thoroughly pragmatic (Richard Rorty tested-and-approved, I am tempted to say) understanding of what is "true" and what is "real." In the case of YouTube, the material or content still rarely originates on the web, but consists of clips from movies, performances, television and personal camcorders. In my experiment, for instance, using the appropriate tags, links and comments, turned up video material from contexts as diverse as the cinema's beginnings in chronophotography and flip-books, gallery shows of avant-garde artists and high-end advertising, children's television, maths classes, as well as game shows and telethons.

Utilizing what I understand to be the underlying algorithmic structure and feedback dynamics of these "open socials" or "social graphs" i.e., the combination of search terms—the *tag clouds*—with the cluster mechanisms and sort algorithms of the YouTube site, I began, a few months ago, to follow the semantic trail of the terms *collapse, instability, chain reaction,* etc., to see where it would take me. Eventually, I decided to make my starting point a two-minute British advertisement. In 2003 it had "made history" not only because its fame and success proved the power of the Internet as a "window of attention" for advertisers, but also because its production values—it cost around six million dollars to produce—put it squarely in the league of Hollywood blockbusters. It also demonstrated the ambivalence of the idea of *collapse,* when understood as a bipolar principle of destruction and creation, with moments in-between: of transition, of balance, of interlinked concatenations, or—to use a favourite term of urbanists and sociologists, but also of ecologists and climatologists—of *tipping points* (Gladwell).

the honda cog

The advertisement is for the Honda Accord car, and is generally known as the "Honda Cog." It generated—besides enormous amounts of Internet traffic—serious coverage in the press, with articles in the *Guardian,* the *Independent* and on the BBC. In short, it had a substantial cross-over effect into the traditional media as well, and became, in fact, an "urban legend." Such is its reputation and recognition factor that it spawned a Monty Python-esque parody, called the "Human Cog," by two promoters of the UK directory assistance service called 118.com.

Looking at the original advertisement more closely, it is clear that the setting connotes a gallery space: white walls, wooden parquet floor, no windows, controlled light-sources. It also alludes in a playful, but unmistakeable fashion to the work of several canonical artists of the twentieth century, notably in the field of sculpture and installation: Alberto Giacometti, Alexander Calder, Jean Tinguely, Carl André. The "floor," as opposed to the wall, has become the main display area; it combines pop art resistance to easel painting with the ecological conceptualism of land art.

It also seems very fitting that a Japanese car maker should have commissioned this ad, for it was Japan that first showed Europe and the US how to make cars with robots, how to reduce costs by just-in-time delivery: in short, it was Japanese auto firms that pioneered several of the principles we now lump together under the term "post-Fordism," but which, on this analysis, could just as well be called "Toyota-ism" (or "Honda-ism"). What we see, then, is the ironic *mise en scène* of a meta-mechanic assembly line which says "look: no hands! Pure magic" or (as the Honda slogan has it) "the power of dreams" (alluding to the oneiric life of objects so beloved by the surrealists). The director, a Frenchman *bien sûr,* Antoine Bardou-Jacquet, is a well-known creative artist of high concept ads and music videos, working in both France and Britain.[2]

The links on YouTube around the "Honda Cog" quickly lead to an extract from a "making-of" video, which gives some glimpses of the immense effort that went into the production of such an effortless and yet inevitable concatenations of collapsing moments and obedient parts. The "making-of" video—which, by a nice coincidence, has as its motto Soichiro Honda's famous "Success is 99% Failure"—ends up celebrating in the language of cinema our fascination with the engineering marvels that are contemporary automobiles, but it also mimics the generic features of a nature documentary, about the patience it takes to train animals (here: car parts), in order for them to perform for humans.

Back to the "Honda Cog": besides the allusions to Japan and post-Fordism, there is the voice at the end, intoning the tag line: "isn't it nice when things just work." I associated it immediately with Sean Connery and James Bond, and so did the users of YouTube. Very soon I discovered tags that led from the Honda Accord to the Aston Martin DB 5, Bond's famous car. The link immediately connected the "life" of the parts of the Honda Accord to the Aston Martin's gadgets, and especially those fabulous demonstrations given at the modifications workshop in the belly of the MI5 headquarters, by the immortal engineer-inventor Q, played by Desmond Llewelyn, notably in *Goldfinger* (1964). Another link brought me to a French mash-up of this scene, which gives it a quite different sub-text and cultural atmosphere: references are now to Christopher Lambert, Bob Marley, the Rastafarians, Californian beach culture and air lift suspension, Rizzla cigarette paper, rolled joints, all played out against intense homophobic/homo-erotic banter between Q and Bond.[3]

The gruff boffin-engineer from MI5 who "never jokes about his work," but visibly delights in his playful as well as lethal modifications, immediately associates one obvious father also of the Honda Cog—Rube Goldberg (1883–1970). The name stands for a kind of machine that does simple or humble tasks (like sneezing into a handkerchief) in an especially complicated, ingenious or roundabout way, utilizing common principles of traction and transmission, but in a manner that makes them meta-mechanic (reminiscent of both Marcel Duchamp and Charles Chaplin).

Apart from the voice, it is the words that hold another key to the ad's cultural layers. For, besides Bond and automotive gadgets, "isn't it nice when things just work?" cannot but evoke—for a British listener, at least—one of the most famous party-political campaigns ever. "Labour isn't working" was the 1979-slogan that brought Margaret Thatcher to power and made advertising chic and hip, thanks to Charles Saatchi (head of the company that devised the poster, and for whom Antoine Bardou-Jacquot has also worked), who in turn "made" "Young British Artists" chic and hip, and to this day is one of the most influential collectors of modern and contemporary art: precisely the sort of art the "Honda Cog" gently mocks as well as generously celebrates.

However, the words of the "Honda Cog" nod-and-wink not only at the knowing cognoscenti (whether of James Bond films, Charles Saatchi or of political campaigns) but also anticipate possible legal problems (which did indeed arise), by acknowledging (not so obliquely) where the makers had "appropriated" the idea for the ad from: not a London gallery, nor a billboard, but from the Kassel documenta of 1987. There, one of the most popular art-pieces was a half-hour video, entitled "Der Lauf der Dinge" literally "the course of things" generally translated as "The Way Things Go," but I think better rendered (exploiting the possibility of the bi-linguistic slippage from "Lauf" to "Life"), as "The Life of Things." Its authors are two Swiss artists, Peter Fischli and David Weis, who have been working together since the early 1970s. This videotape was their international breakthrough.

There are many descriptions of this video on the Internet. One reads:

> Fischli and Weiss' 1987 film, Der Lauf der Dinge follows the
> domino effect of a series of simple objects such as string,
> garbage bags, soap, Styrofoam cups, rubber tires, plastic
> pails, balloons, and mattresses; when combined with fire,
> air (gas), water and gravity, these objects form a hypnotic
> chain of kinetic energy that disturbs the viewer with its
> chaotic potential.[4]

On the (on-line) sleeve of the DVD one finds more hyperbolic endorsements, but also more potential YouTube tags: "ingeniously choreographed—A Duchampian extravaganza!" (*New York Times*); "This masterpiece would have made Picasso envious" (*Flash Art*); "A Rube Goldberg drawing come to life" (*Chicago Tribune*); "An Epic tour de force. . . a gleeful send-up of the Laws of Thermodynamics!" (*Art in America*).

The rough, para-industrial set-up, the processes put in motion as well as the materials used inevitably recall many of the key elements of modern sculpture, conceptual art and other avant-garde practices, notably but not only from the post-World War II period: the concern for balance and suspension (Suprematism and Constructivism), assemblage art (from the late 1940s), kinetic art (from the 1950s and 1960s), trash objects, garbage and recycled materials (from New Realism and Pop), ready-mades and small wasted energies made useful (Marcel Duchamp), and finally, the energies inherent in apparently inert matter from the work of Carl Andre, not forgetting the macho-engineering skills of Richard Serra and the action paintings—here duly automated and pre-programmed—of Jackson Pollock.

The connections between the "Honda Cog" and "Der Lauf der Dinge" (just as the ironic allusions to their respective predecessors in art, cinema and popular culture) are, of course, the very stuff of cultural history

159

in both its modernist and post-modernist variants. The echoes and allusions can be accommodated within the traditional parameters just this side of plagiarism: of "homage," "remediation," "pastiche" and "appropriation." The saturation with puns and arcane references to inter-media phenomena is furthermore the trademark of the smart ad, as pioneered and made global by among others, Saatchi & Saatchi in Britain since the 1970s and 1980s. It is by many seen as part of the problem of the cultural collapse of distinctions, rather than as part of the (democratizing) solution or rescue of high culture, even though this type of advertising has been widely adopted not only for cars and other commodities, but is now a staple promotional tool also for museums and other traditional temples of high culture. Yet the point to make in the present context is that the majority of these cultural references, genealogies and associations were suggested to me not by critical essays, but by the YouTube tags and user comments themselves: in other words, by a different, much "flatter" mode of linkage and hierarchy, in which the (admittedly still mainly verbal) pop-cultural, topical, taste-driven or art-historical knowledge base of the users and uploaders is cross-hatched with a good deal of contingency and chance, while nonetheless seeming to form part of a discernable design, a "narrative": a totality-in-the-making, however amorphous or blob-like it may appear in its early stages of formation.

If I were to draw some preliminary conclusions from my experiment so far, I would highlight the following points: first, the "Honda Cog," while serendipitous in its media-effects (no one anticipated quite what an Internet phenomenon it would be), is very traditional in the ideology of its creation: in the "making of" video one recognizes all the clichés of commercial filmmaking (money and labour invested equals aesthetic value and authenticity) as well as of auteurism (the artist's vision is paramount, he is a driven and relentless perfectionist: success—the perfect take—finally rewards his perseverance).[5]

Second, and as a counter-argument, one can observe also a new frame of reference at work: that of *the test, or test-run*[6] as the paradigm situated quite precisely between Deleuze's "control society" and the concern, already voiced, with the post-human. In the "Honda Cog" it manifests itself in the take, the re-take, here amplified and exaggerated to become its own parody: it took 605 takes to "get it right," eloquently illustrating the "99 percent failure" rule. Likewise, the lab conditions, the stress tests of man and machine are frequently mentioned, humbly put in the service of perfection, excellence and self-improvement, which is to say, in the service of that ever-elusive, dogged-by-failure, performativity. As if to respond to this challenge, there is now a "making of" video also for "Der Lauf der Dinge," specially compiled by Fischli and Weiss for their major Tate Modern retrospective that opened in October 2006. It, too, concentrates on the endless trials, the recalcitrance and resistance of the materials, emphasizing performativity now in the mode "performance of failure" as a goal in itself, rather than any vulgarly asserted "vision thing" (as with the "Honda Cog").

A third point, worth highlighting because it brings the "Honda Cog" and "Der Lauf der Dinge" not only in line with each other, but aligns them with major issues in film studies and film theory, is that both are the work of bona fide filmmakers. I already highlighted this in my comments on the "Honda Cog," and its proximity to the Hollywood blockbuster, but it is worth pointing out that "Der Lauf der Dinge" only exists as a film/video-tape: it is not the filmic record of a performance of machinic self-destruction, such as Tingeley staged them in New York in the 1960s, or the Fluxus Happenings of Wolf Vorstell and the Vienna Actionists, but an event staged specifically for the camera. The *mise en scène* in each case is that of an auteur-director, who decides exactly where to place the camera, when to move it, how to frame and reframe each action and its (con-)sequence. A half-century of film theory comes alive in these mini-films with maxi-budgets, around the "long take" and "montage," and the implication of opting for "staging in depth" or "cutting in the camera." While some "invisible edits" are discernable, long take classic continuity editing is the preferred choice in both pieces, as calculated in many ways as Orson Welles' *Touch of Evil* (1958) opening tracking shot (famously pastiched in Robert Altman's *The Player*, 1992) or the bravura zoom in Michael Snow's *Wavelength* (1967).

Finally, in both works, one notes a studied anachronism, a retrospective temporal deferral at work. This has two aspects: one concerns their respective artistic technique, the other their (meta-) physics. Regarding technique, the "Honda Cog" team are proud to certify in the "making of" video (indeed it is the condition of their success) that they engineered this extraordinary concatenation "for real" and not with the aid of digital effects, which in the aesthetic they are committed to would have amounted to "cheating." And yet, by 2003 digital effects had already become the norm in advertising, so that their decision is a deliberate self-restriction such as one knows it from minimalism or concept art at the highpoint of Modernism. Likewise, Fischli and Weiss produced their tape at around the time when artists were seriously considering their response to the new media technologies of video compositing and digital editing. Their work is clearly a manifesto in favour of materiality and indexicality, an ironic middle finger stuck in the face of the digital to come, and taking their stand in the heated debate about the loss of indexicality in the post-photographic age.

The other studied anachronism concerns the physics used in both works, and the way they figure causality. Neither *Roadrunner* gravity-defying antics here, nor the oneiric dream logic of a Salvador Dalí or Hans Richter film sequence. Causality in these films operates at the familiar middle-level and within human proportions. Rooted in Newtonian physics, the makers celebrate a visible, tangible world, fast disappearing into invisibility at both ends of the scale (at the macro-astronomic as well as at the micro-sub-atomic level), but also insisting on a linear causality vanishing in the media in which one now encounters their work: the Internet and YouTube are, precisely, non-linear and rhizomatic. The "old physics" on display are in the case of the "Honda Cog" highly stylized and deliberately tweaked for humorous effect, while in "Der Lauf der Dinge" the concatenation of build-ups and disasters has also a more sombre, cosmic dimension, as if one were invited to be once more present at the moment of the "Big Bang," i.e. the birth of our own physical universe.

around the world in eighty clicks

Fischli and Weiss have as their motto: *Am schönsten ist das Gleichgewicht, kurz bevor's zusammenbricht* (balance is most beautiful at the point of imminent collapse). While clearly applying to their work as a whole,[7] this aesthetics of the tipping point also encapsulates the main challenge that my experiment with tagging and user-generated links on YouTube poses. For at this juncture in my test, the question arose: where would this semantic knot or node around "constructive instability" and the performativity of failure take me, once I had chosen the "Honda Cog" and "Der Lauf der Dinge" as my epicentres, once "collapse," "concatenation" and "chain reactions" became my search criteria, and once YouTube's tag-clouds defined my self-imposed constraints? One answer was: nowhere at all; a second one: all around the world; and a third answer would be: into the problems of narratology, against a horizon of a "stupid God."

Nowhere at all: following the YouTube tags puts one on a cusp, precariously balanced and perilously poised over an abyss: of hundreds, if not thousands of similar or even the same videos, commented on and cross-referenced to yet more of the same and the similar, plunging one on a serendipitous descent into chaos. In Foucault's epistemic terms, the Internet is "pre-modern" in its regime of representation: resemblance rules, but unlike the Great Chain of Being rising to God, this concatenation extracts the terrible price that everything begins to look like everything else, precipitating a Fall into the Hell of eternal in-difference and infinite repetition.

All over the world: searching the "Honda Cog" and "The Way Things Go" on the Internet and YouTube started off several other chain reactions, which opened up wholly unexpected avenues, in a wonderful efflorescence of rhizomatic profusion, beckoning in all directions and sending one on a most wonderful journey of discovery, more stupendous than Faust and Mephisto on their Magic Carpet in F.W. Murnau's *Faust*, and more recursive, reflexive and self-referential than the Marx Brothers' *Duck Soup* or Buñuel's *The Phantom of Liberty*. But it also took me to many different "real" places: to Cairo in Egypt and Ohio in the US, to Groningen in the

Netherlands and Yokohama in Japan, to Manhattan and to Hamburg, to Purdue, Indiana and to a science lab in Utrecht, to teenagers in Germany and an artist in a New York loft, to a gallery in Tokyo and a television studio in Paris. Not all of these journeys or forking paths can be retraced here, so for convenience's sake, I have sorted and bundled some of them into clusters, and allowed the clusters to become small "cluster-bombs," ignited and radiating outwards from the "Honda Cog" and "Der Lauf der Dinge."[8]

cluster and forking path "rube goldberg"

That the tags from Fischli and Weiss should quickly bring one to Rube Goldberg was to be expected. But little did I suspect that "out there," the idea of building such elaborate mechanical contraptions serving a very simple purpose, has an enormous following, and that several countries, including Germany and the US, hold annual Rube Goldberg conventions, while trials, test-runs and rehearsals of their (usually imperfect) functioning take place in high-school workshops or in large public halls, but are most often videoed in the proverbial Dad's garage in New England, or on the little brother's bedroom floor in a Cairo apartment. With the camcorder always at the ready, geniuses of little more than eight or ten years of age, try out how to fill a cup of coke from a bottle catapulted by a mousetrap snapping tight, or show us how to use the vibrations of the ringer-setting on their mobile phone to set off a chain reaction that switches on the radio. At a major Rube Goldberg convention organized by Purdue University among engineering graduates from all over the US, the task was to squeeze fresh orange juice using a minimum of twelve separate mechanical, self-propelling steps.

A different kind of task preoccupies an obsessively ludic New York artist by the name of Tim Fort, whose website is appropriately named "www.lunatim.com" and who spends his time devising Rube Goldberg hybrids, which turn out to be little allegories of the cinema itself. His homage to the beginnings of cinema (chronophotography, galloping horses, *Fred Ott's Sneeze*), once more evoke the celluloid strip, and its transport by and through machine devices, unseen by the spectator, but here made visible in their mechanic simplicity. Fort himself calls his works "kinetic art movement devices, using an extended repertoire of impulse transmission techniques and the magic of montage," and this originary idea of cinema as pure mechanical movement, hovers, like a fantasmagoric ghost, over many of the Internet's Rube Goldberg meta-mechanical contraptions: so much so that their clustered presence on YouTube makes of the site something like the cinema's reverential funeral parlour, as much as it is—in its Japanese versions at least—an electronic pachinko parlour.

cluster and forking path "pythagoras switch"

From the Rube Goldberg connection it was but "one degree of separation" that led—"laterally" but also by the simple addition of an adjective in one of the user comments—in an apparently quite different direction. The unlikely combination "Japanese Rube Goldberg" landed me among a cluster of videos from a Tokyo-based educational television programme, collectively known as *pitagora suicchi*. This is the Japanese pronunciation of "Pythagoras Switch," and is aimed at children. It shows simple, but ingenious combinations of everyday objects (tea-kettles, books, pencils, rubber bands, steel tape measures, chinaware spoons) aligned in such a way as to allow one or several small balls (or coloured marbles) to travel in a circuitous but steady downward motion. Subjecting the ball to the laws of gravity (Newtonian, for sure), the objects create intricate obstacles, which interrupt but cannot finally stop the ball's trajectory across balancing mechanism of suspension, reversal, dispersion, and through levers, switches and gates that open up unexpected detours, provide surprising side-effects and cause delightful distractions. The journeys always end with a tiny flourish, a point of recursiveness and self-referentiality. Signalled by the moment when the ball falls into a receptacle or hits a mini-gong, the flip confirms the identity of the show and plays a maddeningly addictive jingle. A Pythagoras Switch is a minimalist exercise in creating closure out of indeterminacy, miraculously conjoining the pleasures of free play with the strict rules of physics.

Why is it called Pythagoras Switch? Nobody seems to know, and on the NHK website the makers merely hint at "the Eureka-experience" that children are supposed to have, thanks to a sort of category switch: "'Pythagoras Switch' wants to help kids have that moment of A-HA! We want to raise thinking about thinking, to flip that epiphany switch in every child." Granted that these short performances do indeed flip a switch, I nevertheless tend to think of the name "Pythagoras" as a misnomer and even a parapraxis, a *failed performance*: namely, not only is "Eureka, [I have found (it)]" usually attributed to Archimedes (and not Pythagoras), but it should be called the Archimedean switch also for another reason. After all, the principle of *pitagora suicchi* resembles the famous fulcrum associated with Archimedes' name: the single point of equipoise that he said could lift the universe from its hinges. But the fact that it is called Pythagoras leads one in yet other no less intriguing directions: to geometry and to Euclidean solids, as well as to the so-called Pseudo-Pythagoreans, the first important Gnostics of the ancient world, who survived right into the Middle Ages and beyond, and whose main analysis of the universe was in terms of the magic of numbers and the mysteries of mathematics. Pythagoras would have been a fitting grandfather of the power of algorithms, and thus the appropriate patron saint not so much for the

Pythagoras Switch and instead for the sort- and cluster-algorithms of YouTube that made me discover *pitagora suicchi* in the first place, right next to Rube Goldberg.

cluster and forking path "domino day" and celebrity TV

If the Pythagoras Switch is minimalist and haiku-like, in its elegant economy and delicate epiphanies, a close cousin, by contrast, is all on the side of excess, the incremental and of the nearly "getting out of hand": I am referring to that other major Japanese pastime, having to do with knock-on effects, namely "Domino toppling." Here, too, Japanese television is in the forefront, since it appears to stage regular domino telethons, such as the one I happened to hit upon with another mouse-click, and which featured the entire inventory of Dewi Sukarno, a notoriously rich and flamboyant society-lady and television personality (who models herself on Imelda Marcos, not least by owning racks and racks of shoes). All her belongings—fur coats, shoes, jewellery, books, furniture, etc.—are lined up so as to topple and fall on each other in a descending cascade of conspicuous consumption and commodity fetishism from the top floor of her villa to the basement and out to the swimming pool.[9]

Another of these televised Japanese shows on YouTube features a more high-tech contraption, where the steel ball's trajectory is only one phase, releasing other mechanical agents and setting off further reactions, including small explosions in the manner of Fischli and Weiss, but also gravity-defying underwater action in goldfish bowls. The show is commented on by experts, who fire up and encourage the performing parts, as if they are players in a competitive sports event, like a sack race or a steeple-chase, and one of the videos in particular combines the conceptual grace of *pitagora suicchi* with the rambunctiousness of Sumo-wrestling, while serving a typically Rube Goldberg purpose, namely to make a simple task—in this case to prepare a bowl of Ramen noodles with an egg on top—very complicated and intricate indeed. Once again, it is worth noting the aesthetic that oscillates between the cinematic and the televisual: while the Pythagoras Switch programme prefers long takes, with a camera that pans and reframes rather than cuts, the Japanese Rube Goldberg contest and the Domino telethon, by contrast, favour the typical action replays of televised sports events, but with their spoken commentary they are also reminiscent of the "benshi" tradition of silent cinema, and they even re-invent the action overlap from the very first Edwin Porter films.

The domino toppling contests also brought home another lesson of globalization: "don't follow the flag, follow the tag." Just as commodities, trade and labour no longer "respect" the boundaries of the nation state, so the tags "chain reaction" or "domino telethon" easily cross borders and even continents. The world of domino toppling, for instance, also has an annual championship, the "Domino Day," which made the Netherlands a mere click away from Tokyo. For it seems that for several years now (in alternation with the South Koreans), the Dutch have been world champions and holders of the Guinness record for toppling the largest number of dominoes in one go: 4, 079 381 million of them, to be exact, at the 2006 world championship, held on November 27, 2006 in Groningen, on the theme of "Music in Motion" designed by the Weijers Brothers Domino Production Company and televised by Endemol. As the dominoes fell, they formed an ever-changing kaleidoscope of images that fitted the year's theme. Music, magnitudes and motion were all in the service of an "image," comparable to the formations one sees at the opening ceremonies of Olympic Games or to the flag-waving girls in North Korea, whose assembled multitudes make up a gigantic portrait of their Dear Leader.

between epiphany and entropy

Perhaps it is fitting to interrupt this "Tour of the YouTube World" with an image, and one of totalitarian domination. While multitudes (of dominoes or of young women) forming a recognizable likeness highlight the coercive, normative power of such software as operates the Internet at the level of the algorithms, of the codes and protocols—mostly hidden from view and in any case incomprehensible to the ordinary user—the idea of an "image" reminds us of the fact that in the man-machine symbiosis, two very different kinds of system are expected to communicate with each other. For this "image" is nothing but the filter, membrane or user-friendly face—the "interface," in short—between stupid but infinitely patient (and performative) machines, running on programmes relayed to gates and switches (electric-electronic dominoes, one might say), and intelligent but increasingly impatient (as well as accident-prone) humans, requiring visual representations that give a sense of recognition and self-presence, relayed through words, sound and above all: images.

The concept of the interface at this juncture raises more issues than can be tackled here, but it allows me to return to the question I started with, namely the place of *narrative* as interface between data and user. As the logic of the time–space continuum, i.e. the diegesis is transformed into clusters of multiply interrelated and virally proliferating semantic links (the "fabula" or "story"), narrational authority, i.e. the (uneven) distribution of information, and the order or sequence in which it is accessed (the "syuzet" or "plot") seems to pass from "narrator" to "narratee," from storyteller to user. Yet since the user depends on the "machine" to generate the access-points, by way of sort-algorithms and tag-clouds (whose internal logic generally escapes him/her), a new "authority" interposes itself, both "stupid" like chance and "all-knowing" like God. How can one describe the effects of this encounter?

166

Fischli and Weiss see the encounter in both ethical and aesthetic categories. That they are aware of the problem of who or what is in control and of who or what has agency and responsibility is shown by their remarks on "Der Lauf der Dinge." By fully implicating "the things" themselves, they comment meta-critically on the dilemma that agency for the human-machine symbiosis poses:

> Naturally, this tape is also concerned with the problem of guilt and innocence. An object must be blamed for not proceeding further, and also for proceeding further. "An unambiguously CORRECT result of experiments exists; this is obtained when it works, when this construction collapses. Then again, there is the BEAUTIFUL which ranks above the CORRECT; this is obtained when it's a close shave or the construction collapses exactly the way we want it to—slowly and intricately, that is, a beautiful collapse. The aesthetic layer on top of a function is like the butter on a sandwich—rather thin and smooth. The wrong result is obtained when things get going of their own accord, and the wrong result is obtained when they don't get going at all. The CORRECT range (which in terms of moral theology might also be called GOOD) is, in our view, incredibly narrow. Similarly, GOOD and EVIL are often very close, for example when the candle on the swing sets fire to the detonating fuse. Because they are nice and childish, the candle and the swing tend towards the good, whereas the detonating fuse is evil because you don't need it for harmless things. On the other hand, every object in our installation is good if it functions, because it then liberates its successor, gives it the chance of development. (Fischli and Weiss)

In the context of narrative, it suggests that the "worlds" which open up as a consequence of following the semantic trail of "The Honda Cog" and "Der Lauf der Dinge" both have a creator-narrator (multiple, anonymous, but nonetheless singular-in-plurality) and do not have one (to the extent that they are self-generated). By bringing together various individuals, their activities, skills and obsessions in very different locations, they can be called "scripted spaces" (since their coming to my attention is at least in part "scripted" or "programmed"), but they are neither directly comparable to the classic novel (even if one were to apply Jenkins' generous re-interpretation of *War and Peace*), nor do they resemble a video game like *Grand Theft Auto* or a virtual world like *Second Life*. Yet what one encounters is nonetheless a story-world of sorts, rich in human interest, detail and characters, full of humour and wisdom: in the genre of what one could call *the digital picaresque*.

YouTube, as indicated, is a user-generated content site, with a high degree of automation, where nonetheless a certain structured contingency obtains, as suggested by the semantically quite coherent clusters, which I was able to extract via the tags attached to the videos. My "Travels with YouTube" led to a series of forking path narratives, where the multiplicity of strands made up for some weak plotting and meandering storylines, which together nonetheless make out of exquisite corpses a lively clutch of shaggy dog stories, reminiscent of Jan Potocki's *Manuscript Found in Saragossa*, Borges' *Garden of Forking Paths*, or Buñuel's *The Milky Way*.[10] This creates the paradox alluded to above: the structured contingency is, on the one hand, strongly informed and shaped by mathematics, via the site's programming architecture and design, based on its search and sort algorithms. On the other hand, the chaos of human creativity, eccentricity and self-importance prevails. My clusters around "collapse" were only small islands of sense carved out of a sea of boiling magma made up of human self-presentation and self-performance, the trials and errors of the collective "me," which is YouTube. But who is to say that this *performative persistence to be, to be present and to be perceived* does not mimic certain forms of narrative self-reference, create a cast of believable characters, and even generates a particular mode of narrative address?

Narrative self-reference: The rhizomatic branching or viral contagion propagating in all directions, while non-hierarchical and "flat" or "lateral" in its linkage, nonetheless seems to produce a surprisingly high degree of self-reflexivity and auto-referentiality, no doubt due to the effects of "positive feedback": the demonstrations of chain reaction, mechanical concatenation, Pythagoras switches and falling dominoes are performative also in the sense that they either enact their own conditions of possibility or remediate a previous stage of their own mediality, as nostalgic or ironic pastiche and repetition. For instance, via the Pythagoras Switch another meta-dimension emerged, which brought one of the core mechanisms of YouTube into view. One of the creators of the Pythagoras Switch series is the video artist Sato Masahiko, one of whose installations, called "Bubble Sort" I was linked to, obviously filmed illegally in a gallery space and uploaded onto YouTube. The piece, which shows a line of people waiting, re-arranging themselves in fast-forward motion, according to size, completely baffled me, until its tags led to several other videos, also having to do with sorting. Masahiko's video, it transpires, visualizes a popular sorting algorithm, called indeed "bubblesort," explained on YouTube by tens of videos, all manually "remediating" or graphically "interfacing" the different sorting algorithms (insertion sort, selection sort, shell sorts, etc.): apparently a favourite pastime for first year computer science students.[11]

The cast of characters, as we saw, included some well-known names, such as "Rube Goldberg," "Pythagoras," "James Bond," "Dewi Sukarno"; others become known because they "sign" their work: Antoine Bourdou-Jacques,

Fischli and Weiss, Tim Fort, Sato Masahiko, the Wijers Brothers; many more merely present themselves to the camera in low-res home-made videos. Thanks to all of them, however, the YouTube ways of knowing and travelling are ludic and reflexive, educational and participatory, empowering and humbling, in short: marking an unusually soft dividing line between creative design and hard-core engineering, storytelling and role playing, singularity and repetition.

To put this in the terms of another discourse, more germane to the post-human: it is to find oneself in the presence of strange organisms, pulsing, moving and mutating, depending on the tags one enters or encounters, as YouTube sorts, filters and aggregates the choices I am not even aware of making. That they cluster themselves semantically (instead of letting a more Gestaltist organization—an "image"—determine their shape) is partly another concession to the "human interface," but partly also because of special heuristic value: it is where the cultural noise of verbal language encounters the information of the mathematical program, providing the constructive instability of performed failure, and throwing the grit of human creativity and dirt of human unpredictability into the machinery of perfect human-machine adaptation.

Mode of address. With the traditional a-symmetry of the single point of origin (the author, the narrator) addressing a potentially infinite number of readers or viewer already deconstructed by Roland Barthes' "writerly text" and many other narratologists since, the multiple authorship of the YouTube tales should not in itself present the biggest problem. Whether, when accessing YouTube, I behave more like a user than a reader/viewer (with all the attendant problems of the relation between "narrative" and "game") is also not my main concern. Rather, the mode of address I am trying to focus on is the "empty space" of enunciation, classically conceived, but now refigured by the specific subject-effects of the YouTube user/viewer: On the one hand, a site like YouTube is inherently addictive, as one video drags one along to another and another and another. Yet after an hour or so, one realizes how precariously balanced and delicately poised one is, between the joy of discovering the unexpected, the marvellous and occasionally even the miraculous, and the rapid descent into an equally palpable anxiety, staring into the void of an unimaginable number of videos, with their proliferation of images, their banality or obscenity in sounds and commentary. Right next to the euphoria and the epiphany, then, is the heat-death of meaning, the ennui of repetition and of endless distraction: in short, the relentless progress of entropy begins to suck out and drain away all life. "Epiphany" and "entropy," one might say, is what defines the "subject-effect" of YouTube, encapsulated in the recursiveness of its own tagline "broadcast yourself," which to this extent quite accurately describes its specific "mode of address." YouTube's scripted spaces or picaresque narratives are held together not by a coherent diegesis nor by a coherent "subject-position" (whether articulated by a psychoanalytic, cognitivist or pragmatic theory of spectatorship), but by a perpetual oscillation between the "fullness" of reference and recognition and the "emptiness" of repetition and redundancy, the singularity of an encounter and the plurality of the uncountable in which the singular occurs.

Whether there is a better name for this oscillation, I do not know, but it puts me on notice that my experiment would be incomplete and even misleading, if I did not emphasize its central place, and instead gave the impression that it was either possible or responsible to gather my clusters like floral bouquets, or cherry-pick the gems like the "Honda Cog" or "Der Lauf der Dinge" while ignoring or even disavowing the rest. Like the fighter plane with its wings tipped forward, or the high wire acrobat sensing at all times the trembling tightrope underneath her feet, the pleasure of the YouYube tales is narrative in its referential expanse, but kinetic in its visceral response. Epiphany and entropy remind us of our finitude, and—held against the open horizon of our "stupid God," the Web 2.0 feedback loops with their unimaginable and yet palpable magnitudes—they suspend us between infinity and indefiniteness, a state only made bearable and even pleasurable, thanks to constructive instability and the performativity of failure, for as Fischli and Weiss so wisely put it: *am schönsten ist das Gleichgewicht . . .*

notes

1. Keith Ansell Pearson writes that: "A living system resolves its problems not simply by adapting itself through modifying its relationship to its milieu, but rather through a process of self-modification, in which it invents new structures which then serve to mediate and define its rapport with the environment" (147).
2. "Antoine Bardou-Jacquet signed to Partizan Midi Minuit in 2000. He had previously studied graphic design in Paris before setting up his own graphic design company, situated within the same offices as his close friends from Solid (an independent record company that is the centre of the French electronic music scene with such artists as Alex Gopher and Etienne de Crecy)." *Partizan* web-site: http://www.partizanlab.com/partizanlab/commercials/?antoine_bardou_jacquet/biography
3. My special thanks to Fabrice Ziolkowski (Paris) for providing the translation and cultural commentary on the clip.
4. http://www.sfmoma.org/exhibitions/exhib_detail/98_exhib_fischli_weiss.html.
5. "In 2003, he directed the internationally acclaimed and multi award winning Honda 'Cog' commercial for London's Weiden & Kennedy. It is a 2 minute commercial showing Honda parts bumping into each other in a chain reaction. It took months of meticulous planning and trial and error, with a four day shoot at the end. It was shot in two takes and was all done for real. It was a victory for patience and passion! It first caused a stir running throughout the entire commercial break during the Grand Prix and went on to win a Gold Lion at Cannes, Best commercial and Gold at BTAA

and a Gold Pencil at D&AD to name but a few." *Partizan* web-site: http://www.partizanlab.com/partizanlab/commercials/?antoine_bardou_jacquet/biography.

6. For more on the new regime of the test as a paradigm of the control society, see Avital Ronell.

7. As demonstrated, for instance, by their series *Equilibres—Quiet Afternoon* (1984), on show in the Fischli and Weiss "Flowers & Questions" retrospective at the Tate Modern in London (Oct 2006–Jan 2007).

8. A button on the YouTube Screen now allows one to "explode" such clusters around the selected video and see the tag-clouds scatter. My thanks to Pepita Hesselberth (Amsterdam) for drawing my attention to this feature.

9. My special gratitude goes to Aaron Gerow (Yale) for his hints, links and elucidations regarding all things pertaining to Japan in this essay.

10. The link between interactive storytelling and Buñuel has been made before, most systematically by Marsha Kinder.

11. Different types of sorting: insertion sort, selection sort, and shell sorts, but bubble sort is the simplest, if the least efficient—electronic spread-sheets, the computer's first "killer application" (VisiCalc) and the mythical "birth" of Apple computers.

works cited

Abbas, Niran. "The Posthuman View on Virtual Bodies." *CTheory.net*: http://www.ctheory.net/articles.aspx?id=266 (accessed June 1 2008).

Ansell Pearson, Keith. "Bergson and Creative Evolution/Involution: Exposing the Transcendental Illusion of Organismic Life." *The New Bergson*. Ed. John Mullarkey. Manchester: Manchester University Press, 2006. 146–167.

Fischli, P. and Weiss, D (n.d.). *Media Art Net*: http://www.medienkunstnetz.de/works/the-way-of-things/ (accessed June 1 2008).

Gladwell, Malcolm. *The Tipping Point: How Little Things Can Make a Big Difference.* New York: Little Brown, 2000.

Hayles, N. Katherine. An interview/dialogue with Albert Borgmann and N. Katherine Hayles on humans and machines (1999): http://www.press.uchicago.edu/Misc/Chicago/borghayl.html(accessed June 1 2008).

Jenkins, Henry. "Game Design as Narrative Architecture" (2004). http://web.mit.edu/cms/People/henry3/games&narrative.html (accessed June 1 2008).

Kinder, Marsha. "Hotspots, Avatars and Narrative Fields Forever: Buñuel's Legacy for New Digital Media and Interactive Database Narrative." *Film Quarterly* 55.4 (Summer 2002): 2–5.

Lanier, Jaron. "Digital Maoism: The Hazards of the New Online Collectivism" (2006). *Edge*: http://www.edge.org/3rd_culture/lanier06/lanier06_index.html (accessed June 1 2008).

Ronell, Avital. *The Test Drive*. Urbana: University of Illinois Press, 2005.

Vorhees, Burton. "Virtual Stability: A Principle of Complex Systems" (2002). http://necsi.org/events/iccs/2002/Mo14_Vorhees.pdf (accessed June 1 2008).

part two

feminism,

philosophy,

and

queer

theory

reformulating

the symbolic

universe

e i g h t

kill bill and

tarantino's

transcultural

imaginary

s a š a   v o j k o v i ć

circularity of influences: europe–hollywood–asia

The capacity of Hollywood to absorb the influences of other cinemas, to incorporate them into its system, and to turn the familiar into the unfamiliar or vice versa is well known. In the past, Hollywood's exclusive source of inspiration was European film. In some ways it was an even exchange, because while European films influenced American films, European ideas were "Americanized" and re-imported into European cinemas. Even in European auteur cinemas and film movements such as the French New Wave, authorial Otherness is affirmed precisely through mirroring; in these cases, however, the recourse to a Hollywood genre implied its simultaneous subversion.

One of the most pertinent examples is surely Jean-Luc Godard's *Breathless* (*A bout de souffle* 1959), in which the main protagonist, Michel, is literally mirrored in the image of Humphrey Bogart in the film poster of *The Harder They Fall* (Mark Robson 1956). Instead of confirming his status as a gangster of Hollywood calibre, however, Michel will be remembered as a European anti-hero who was betrayed by his American girlfriend. While Godard's film deconstructs ("de-realizes") classical Hollywood style—that is, while it jettisons the principle of continuity editing, breaks the 180 degree rule, or employs the direct address of the camera—Kristin Thompson argues that the neorealist film of Vittorio De Sica, *Bicycle Thieves* (*Ladri di biciclette* 1947), leans on the stylistic strategies of the classical Hollywood (Thompson). Thompson is dovetailing on cognitivist film theory and David Bordwell's definition of narration as an interaction of the viewer and the plot, or *syuzhet*. Through this interaction the viewer constructs the story, or *fabula* (Bordwell *Narration*). Regardless of the fact that the *syuzhet* or the narrational process itself in *The Bicycle Thieves* draws on the principles of the classical Hollywood style, the film's *fabula* alludes to the fictional world that opposes the fictional worlds of the Hollywood films and is conditioned on a completely different cultural imaginary. Therefore, when the circularity of influences is at stake, it is necessary to take into consideration the film's *fabula*, for it is in the film's *fabula* that the cultural imaginaries are incorporated. They regulate the relations between the characters as well as all that is imaginable (or unimaginable) within the film.

In the past, the dominant exchange of influences was between Hollywood and European cinema. Today, with the movement of globalization, increasingly present on the (trans)cultural screen, is the third element which has been inserted into the Euro–American exchange—Asian cinema. There are an increasing number of films in which the circularity of influences depends precisely on their transcultural imaginaries, but in the center of our interest is Tarantino's *Kill Bill* vol.1 (2003) and *Kill Bill* vol.2 (2004). Before the "honkongification"[1] of Hollywood film, Tarantino was one of the first directors who incorporated the influences of that cinema in the most innovative ways, an example of which is his *Reservoir Dogs* (1992). At the time the Western audiences were not familiar with the fact that Tarantino appropriated one of the lines of the *fabula* of Ringo Lam's film *City on Fire* (*Long hu feng zun*, 1987): a secret agent and a cop become friends; the agent saves the gangster's life, and in return the gangster takes his side when the boss of the gang accuses him of betrayal. Scenes such as the one in which Mr. White is holding Mr. Orange in his arms, an interaction inspired by the *City on Fire*, are still extremely rare in contemporary European and Hollywood productions. At stake is the specific representation of masculinity typical of the imaginary of Hong Kong gangster films —the idea of brotherhood and loyalty promoted especially in the Hong Kong films of John Woo. Woo's gangsters are emotional, and they engage in intimate (frequently bodily) contact, yet this kind of relationship between two men is not perceived as homoerotic, does not provoke homophobia, and does not require a dramaturgical disclaimer by inserting a heterosexual relationship (which is almost regularly the case in Hollywood cinema). Hence, at stake is the influence of cultural imaginaries on the questions of genre, style, identity, and the representation of gender. I will discuss psychoanalytic film theory as applied to Tarantino's *Kill Bill* vol.1 and vol.2, and explain why Judith Butler's reconceptualization of Lacan's law of signification is a necessary precondition for an examination of Tarantino's transcultural universe. My central concern is the representation of femininity in a fictional world where the traditional Lacanian Law-of-the-Father does not hold. Following Butler, my endeavor presupposes a reformulation of the Lacanian symbolic to expand and alter the normativity of its terms. If psychoanalysis is to be brought into a productive relation with the emerging changes on the cultural screen we need to explore the possibility of reworking the symbolic universe.

transcultural imaginary and gender: putting pressure on lacan's symbolic order

The French New Wavers insisted on proving that the directors of the classical Hollywood are authors and that in spite of all the imperatives of the Hollywood system, they are more interesting than their French "filmic fathers." Similarly, the directors of New German cinema, such as Wim Wenders or Rainer Werner Fassbinder, did not look for inspiration in their "German fathers" but instead turned to their role models on the other side of the Atlantic—Douglas Sirk, Nicholas Ray, or Samuel Fuller (Elsaesser). Nevertheless, if we consider the fact that Douglas Sirk emigrated from Germany to Hollywood, the circularity of influences is even more evident. In comparable spirit, the most successful Hong Kong director in Hollywood, John Woo, describes the relationship between Hong Kong and Hollywood in the following way, "It is ironic that Hollywood started to imitate Hong Kong films of the late 1980s and 1990s because Hong Kong films (to a certain degree) are imitations of Hollywood films, so Hollywood is imitating Hollywood" (cited in Stokes and Hoover 309). In any case, cinemas are being revitalized through the influences of Others. Through the cinematic texts a new line of communication is opened up that reaffirms the urgency of intersubjective engagement, as well as intercultural and transnational literacy. Accordingly, as I have mentioned, this requires a reworking of Lacanian psychoanalysis.

Speaking of the circularity of influences in relation to the image of femininity, pertinent for the discussion is the French film *Irma Vep* (1996) by Olivier Assayas. In this film the fictional director Rene Vidal (played by the French New Wave icon Jean-Pierre Leaud) who is preparing a re-launch of the Irma Vep character in the remake of the 1916 French film classic *Les Vampires* by Louis Feuillade, decides to engage a Hong Kong actress. This director of the film within a film chose Maggie Cheung on the basis of her performance in a Hong Kong film *The Heroic Trio* (1993) where Cheung joins forces with two women of action—Anita Mui and Michelle Yeoh—and saves the world from a despotic eunuch. According to the vision of the fictional director, this woman of action from the Far East is the ideal replacement for the French actress Musidora who starred in the original version of *The Vampires*. It is the present-day mobility, as it were, that brought this about, for as the story goes, the director has seen *The Heroic Trio* in Morocco in the city of Marrakech.

The type of female character featured in *The Heroic Trio* is interdependent with a certain mode of cultural expression that informs the film's *fabula*. The actions the women from Hong Kong films are able to perform have to do with the connection between the narrative and the rules and norms that regulate what kind of female character is imaginable and conceivable. Speaking generally of Asian films that feature fabulas populated with female heroes, it is possible to argue that these films work contrary to the laws of common sense that govern the social imagination of Western traditions. The viewing pleasure derives from the exhilarating action scenes and the super human skills of the female characters, but at the same time the sense of female empowerment emanates from the fictional worlds/*fabulas* predicated on specific conventions and practices.

In spite of female subordination in daily life, the stories of women warriors remain alive and, remarkably, women play a heroic role to an extent that is without parallel in European or Anglo-American action-adventure films. Apart from Taoism and Confucianism, when it comes to the question of social and cultural formations that regulate what women can do, we also need to consider the third dominant religion in China—Buddhism. Since the way towards transcendence under Buddhism was equally applicable to both men and women, it is not strange that this would emerge in films. Therefore, the fact that women are depicted as skilled fighters is related to the specificities of the genre incorporated into the process of cinematic storytelling, but it is the specific vision of the film, a vision that exceeds the level of the fictional world, that determines what kind of female subject is conceivable and which actions she can perform. The intelligent women fighters, women who are knowing subjects—the types of female characters that can be found for example, in Beijing Opera, martial arts novels, or the traditional Chinese stories of the fantastic and the supernatural—are dependent on the norms that circulate within Chinese cultural heritage.[2] One prototype that has served as a model for many Chinese girls and women who wished to abandon a strictly feminine role and gain access to the political sphere is Hua Mulan (Fa Mulan in Cantonese) the heroine of the Five Dynasties (420–588). A legendary figure, she has remained famous (and even absorbed by Hollywood) because of an anonymous poet who sang her praise in the famous "Song of Mulan."

We will see that, as with the above mentioned films, Tarantino's *Kill Bill* vol.1 and vol.2 put pressure on Lacan's symbolic order. The symbolic, as Butler reminds us, is "the normative dimension of the constitution of the

178

sexed subject within language. It consists in a series of demands ... with the power to materialize subjectivating effects" (106). I am also referring here to Jacques Lacan's notion of the Law-of-the-Father, which governs the symbolic order (Lacan).[3] Lacan's concept of the "Symbolic" was inspired by the writings of the French anthropologist Claude Lévi-Strauss.[4] His ideas are crucial for Lacan's theory of the subject in that he proposes a close connection between the structuring agency of the family and language. The family, as part of a symbolic network, is defined by a set of symbolic relations that always transcend the actual persons; these are cultural positions and need not have a biological/natural connection. Lacan further strengthens the relationship between the Oedipus complex and language through the paternal signifier—which he calls the "Name-of-the-Father."

For Lacan, this is the determining signifier in the history of the subject and the organization of the larger symbolic field. Lacan also introduces the term *phallus* to indicate the cultural privileges and positive values that define male subjectivity within patriarchal society, to which the female subject has no access. Basically, this aspect of Lacan's theory has provoked and continues to provoke feminist criticism. In "Field and Function of Speech and Language," Lacan suggests that, in order to acquire cultural privileges, the male subject mortgages "that pound of flesh," that is, he mortgages the penis for the *phallus*. As feminist critics have argued, Lacanian theory turns the woman into the foreclosed element, as the "constitutive outside" of the Law-of-the-Father, for she lacks that which the male subject renounces to enter the symbolic order.

In Judith Butler's terms the constitutive outside is the unspeakable, the nonnarrativizable. "It means that identity always requires precisely that which it cannot abide" (Butler 188). The emergence of the constitutive outside is predicated on entrance into the symbolic order, but the loss effectuated in the process is structurally emblematized by the feminine. When we consider a non-Western cultural imaginary populated with female warriors, as is the case with Japanese and Hong Kong cinema which have influenced Tarantino's *Kill Bill* vol. 1 and vol. 2, it is clear that the woman warrior cannot be observed as dependent on the paternalistic symbolic order theorized by Lacan. It is not difficult to conclude that Beatrix Kiddo's universe is contingent on an alternative symbolic network based on alternative fabulas and worldviews. While Lacan's concept of the Symbolic urges us to consider Beatrix Kiddo as a cultural position defined by a set of symbolic relations, at the same time, precisely the fact that Beatrix Kiddo is a cultural position makes it difficult to place her into a theoretical framework based on symbolic relations that inform Lacan's psychoanalytic concepts.

Butler is radically opposed to the view that the "constitutive outside" can be delimited through a pre-ideological or prediscursive "law" because insistence on the pre-ideological status of the symbolic law has anti-feminist consequences. Crucial here is Butler's objection to the idea that woman emerges as the "outside" itself, as the "stain" of the symbolic order. Under such conditions, she appears as that which cannot be symbolized and, therefore, she is not available as a political signifier. Paradoxically, woman emerges as the very condition of this prediscursive order. A way, then, to change the status of the woman as the rock upon which the symbolic stumbles, is to work with the notion that what counts as the real, in the sense of unsymbolizable, is always relative to a linguistic domain that authorizes and produces this foreclosure.[5] To explore this potential of Tarantino's *Kill Bill* vol. 1 and vol. 2 to thematize the "outside," we first need to go to Japan and then to China, where the mentors of Beatrix Kiddo reside. They will help us to conceive the terms to start reworking Lacan's symbolic universe.

the woman of action and the division between the sexes: masculine/feminine vs. yin/yang

In *Kill Bill* vol. 1, Tarantino is inspired by the manga story *Lady Snowblood*, which was also made into a feature film directed by Toshiya Fujita in 1973. The film is structured through volumes and chapters. The main character, Oyuki, was born in jail, and her mother passed on to her a mission to take revenge on four people who murdered her father and brother. As with Beatrix Kiddo, she is an expert killer and she has a death list. Tarantino's vol.1 is to a great extent centered on O-Ren Ishii, the head of the Tokyo mafia and the number one person on Kiddo's death list. Beatrix Kiddo is dressed in a Bruce Lee-like outfit, revealing a connection with Hong Kong kung fu films, while O-Ren Ishii wears a kimono, a traditional Japanese costume. Lady Snowblood also wears a kimono, which does not inhibit her performance as a woman of action.

The scene of the final duel between O-Ren Ishii and Beatrix Kiddo is a garden covered with snow, reminding us of the last scene in *Lady Snowblood* (but also one of the scenes where she begins her quest for revenge), in which the main protagonist, Oyuki, has to face the final challenge. Even though, iconically, Oyuki can be compared to O-Ren Ishii (both are Japanese women dressed in kimonos), structurally, Beatrix Kiddo is the one who figures like a Japanese heroine. The question of heritage is quite important: O-Ren Ishii is Japanese-Chinese-American, but she does away with anyone in the Yakuza clan who brings up this issue. In the final show-down between O-Ren Ishii and Beatrix Kiddo, O-Ren Ishii brings up the issue of Kiddo's race, insinuating that a "white girl" can only pretend to be a samurai. When she is struck by Kiddo and is ready to die, she apologizes for that comment. Apart from Beatrix Kiddo, who occasionally appears as the narrator, the highest narrational authority in *Kill Bill* vol. 1 is Hatori Hanzo, the master swordsman from Okinawa who makes a sword for Kiddo. Without his sword it seems unlikely that she could have liquidated a series of enemies, particularly in *Kill Bill* vol. 1. It is thus her mentor from a Japanese cultural imaginary that affects the representation of female subjectivity in the film.

As mentioned above, the types of imaginary solutions that can occur in a given narrative, such as the idea that a woman can be the best fighter, are bound up with the legal sensibility of a concrete socio-cultural imaginary. Within the Chinese and Japanese cultural contexts, alternative structures of signification are at work, and the potential for imagining alternative female characters acquires new dimensions. This presupposes also that the notorious Freudian division between the sexes—active/male versus passive/female—needs to be complemented with the models of signification at work in different cultural imaginaries. For example, the Taoist rule of contraries traceable in the myriad of Hong Kong films infers interdependency rather than the strict separation of masculine and feminine forces.

I am also referring to the "body of Tao," the Taoist priority given to the human body over social and cultural systems. The inevitable pair of complementaries is yin and yang—the Taoist principle of equal exchange between activity and passivity. Yin and yang are the two fundamental phases of Tao's action; they serve to designate cold and hot, moon and sun, soft and hard, feminine and masculine, death and life. Their complementary opposition exists in everything, and their alternation is the first law of Chinese cosmology: when yin reaches its apex, it changes into yang, and vice versa. We can trace this tradition in Beijing Opera, which, as mentioned earlier, had such a profound influence on the martial arts and swordplay genre of Hong Kong cinema. Traditionally, the "masculinization" of female fighters in Hong Kong cinema is not perceived as a problem, and it does not bring the character's femininity into question. Their masculinity does not presuppose the loss of femininity, for their character entails duality, two in one, as is typically the case in Beijing Opera. This type of female character is called *wudan*, and it designates a cross-dressing woman of action who maintains her feminine appeal.

If we go back to the 1960s, to King Hu's *A Touch of Zen* (1969), which can be taken as exemplary of a trend of Hong Kong action heroines, we will find that the woman is active and a skilled fighter, while the man, her unwed husband and the father of her child, on many occasions acts as an observer and supports her cause. In this film, a government officer who has come to arrest the woman interrupts this idyllic situation. The man, completely ignorant of her extraordinary fighting skills, makes an attempt to defend her. The woman steps forward ready to defend herself and reaches for her dagger. He is absolutely stunned when he realizes that the woman with whom he has just spent the night is an expert fighter. *A Touch of Zen* was produced in 1969 and screened at the Cannes film festival in 1971, two years before Laura Mulvey's seminal article "Visual Pleasure and Narrative Cinema" was written, and four years before it was published in the journal *Screen*. Let us recall that the article takes as its starting point the way film reflects socially established interpretation of sexual difference that controls images, erotic ways of looking and spectacle. Especially relevant is Mulvey's argument that an active/passive heterosexual division of labor controls the narrative structure of classical Hollywood films.

There is a split between spectacle and narrative, which supports the man's role as the active one who advances the story, making things happen. In the meantime, Mulvey has revised her views but she still relies on Freud's ideas (albeit in a critical manner) when the active solution for the crisis of femininity is concerned. For Freud, as Mulvey reminds us,

> femininity is complicated by the fact that it emerges out of a crucial period of parallel development between the sexes; a period he sees as masculine, or phallic, for both boys and girls. The terms he uses to conceive of femininity are the same as those he has mapped out for the male, causing certain problems of language and boundaries to expression. These problems reflect very accurately, the actual position of women in patriarchal society. (30)

In relation to Mulvey's discussion let us additionally recall two paths Freud saw as the possible resolutions of the crisis of femininity:

> Even for narcissistic women, whose attitude towards men remains cool, there is a road which leads to complete object love. In the child which they bear, a part of their own body confronts them like an extraneous object, to which, starting out from their narcissism, they can give complete object-love. There are other women, again, who do not have to wait for a child in order to take a step in development from narcissism to object love. Before puberty they feel masculine and develop some way along masculine lines; after this trend has been cut short on their reaching female maturity, they still retain the capacity of longing for masculine ideal—an ideal which is in fact a survival of the boyish nature that they themselves once possessed. (Freud 82–84)

182

As Kaja Silverman contends, putting a man in the place of her ego-ideal would be the active solution to the crisis of femininity (Silverman). In other words, unlike the women who position themselves as love objects and seek access to self-love through another person's love for them, these women seek to embody the man who represents their narcissistic ideal. Speaking of mainstream cinema, this option in principle involves action-heroines in the service of patriarchy. These are the action-heroines who can perform "masculine" tasks: they are physically strong and display high combat skills, they can act as leaders, and maintain or restore the law and order of patriarchy.[6] Most importantly, they are inserted into the Oedipal trajectory, implying that they are initiated into the father's universe.[7]

Traditionally, in the context of feminist film theory, discussions on gender in films are informed by psychoanalytic concepts, implying also that the specific structuring of the narratives has been theorized in terms of the Oedipalization of the subject. According to the psychoanalytic scenario, the son's "destiny" is to take the father's place. In the new Hollywood this process is principally no longer at work, but the father and the son nevertheless remain the two central protagonists of the symbolic universe; instead of internalizing the authority of the father, the son has to recreate this authority (see Vojković). The thematizing of paternal authority can be brought to bear on Jacques Lacan's notion of the Law-of-the-Father. It is precisely this authority that is being reconceptualized in Tarantino's *Kill Bill*.

beatrix kiddo and the space of exile

While the male characters can easily engage in an intersubjective exchange, this is not readily the case when female characters are concerned. In keeping with the woman's mythological role as a monster, or in Lacanian terms, the object of plenitude, the female characters often end up stuck in-between the subjective exchange of the male characters. This space can also be theorized as the space of exile and in this context it will be considered in positive terms.[8] In *Kill Bill* vol. 2 we learn about Kiddo's mentor, or perhaps, we should say *shi fu,* a term from Hong Kong cinema. A *shi fu* (Romanized Mandarin) or *si fu* (in Cantonese) is a person who possesses spiritual and practical skills, acts as a teacher and mentor in a relationship with (usually a male) student. In principle, a si fu can function as a father figure, that is, he enjoys the highest authority. In terms of the medium of film, we have encountered si fu characters in kung fu films. Tarantino's film *Kill Bill* vol. 2 proves, however, that the character of the traditional mentor from the Hong Kong imaginary can be resurrected in a Hollywood film. But it is not only a question of hommage, referentiality, or recycling: for, a si fu who discloses secret knowledge to the main female character, Beatrix Kiddo, the monk Pai Mei has a key position in the narrative structure of the film.

In the place of exile, with Pai Mei as her mentor, Beatrix Kiddo will redefine herself, as did the heroine from *A Touch of Zen/Hsia nu/Hap lui*, for example, when she retreated to the Buddhist temple in King Hu's 1969 masterpiece. Hidden away in the mountains, she was taught swordplay skills by Buddhist monks. The fabulas of these films echo the structures of meaning on the extradiegetic level. An example from literature is Maxine Hong Kingston's novel *The Woman Warrior: Memoirs of a Girlhood Among Ghosts*, which tells of a young woman who goes away to learn kung fu, and then returns as a general, riding at the head of an army of men to defend her village from a monstrous horde. When Beatrix Kiddo completes her training, first with Hatori Hanzo and then with Pai Mei, just as Ayuki, she can take revenge.

Let us recapitulate the *fabula* of *Kill Bill* vol. 2: Beatrix Kiddo, known as the Bride as well as Black Mamba, is a member of Bill's Viper Squad, a group of professional killers. When she gets pregnant with Bill's child she decides to start a new life far away from Bill and his vipers. She disappears without any explanation, adopts a new identity (Arlene Plympton), and finds a suitable fiancée—a modest owner of a record shop. In spite of her efforts to start a new life, Bill is on her trail, and with the help of his poisonous squad, executes a massacre in the church on her wedding day. The Bride miraculously survives Bill's sado-masochistic attack of jealousy, but she spends the next four years in a coma. When she regains consciousness, she sets out on a search for the snakes. In the first part, *Kill Bill* vol. 1, she sets the score straight with Vernita Green and O-Ren Ishii, and in *Kill Bill* vol. 2 she goes after Bud, Elle Driver, and finally Bill the Snake Charmer.

What makes the revenge possible, gives Beatrix Kiddo super-human strength, and conditions the successful achievement of a practically irrational goal, are fighting techniques and strategies that originated in the Far East. In the first film, before facing O-Ren Ishii, Kiddo first visits the phenomenal master Hattori Hanzo who crafts for her an incredibly sharp sword. "Incredibly," of course, from the perspective of the Western imaginary. With the help of this lethal samurai instrument, the blonde, white-skinned female warrior manages to overpower an unimaginable number of Yakuzas; in the end she scalps their untouchable female boss, O-Ren Ishii. In that sense, the film's *fabula* draws its logic from the transcultural imaginary, which in the first place implies that a character such as Beatrix Kiddo would be unthinkable without her Oriental si fus. Clearly, Tarantino's fantasy about such a character is conditioned by his own (not only) Oriental role models, and surely, this could not be achieved without the help and guidance of Yuen Woo Ping, possibly the most famous si fu and advisor for the martial arts as far as the filmic medium is concerned.

Beatrix Kiddo's first si fu/mentor/"father," who turned her into Black Mamba and who ultimately became her lover, is Bill. He is the only one who addresses her by her last name—Kiddo—which in some ways confirms his patronizing attitude, because for him she is a "little girl," a "kid," which is what the word is partly implying. Since in Tarantino's authorial universe one meaning serves only to propel new and conflictual allusions, "kiddo" points to both a female and a male child. Through the connection fe/male kid new connections open up; one example is the connection with the Hong Kong film *Swordsman 2/Ching Siu-tung* (Stanley Tong, 1991), where the name of the hero's female helper is translated as Kiddo. It is not strange that a name is used that negates the gender differences, because in the concrete film the action is set in the far-away past, at a time when women, especially those who had knowledge of the martial arts, dressed as men. Tarantino's Hollywood Kiddo reminds us, then, of the Hong Kong Kiddo, who reminds us of the Chinese traditional "pretty girl"/"warrior" character that stems from Beijing Opera. The reinvention of femininity and masculinity through the action genre involved cases such as men being turned into a spectacle as well as women becoming both masculinized and *musculinized*.[9] In contrast to the Hollywood examples, the women warriors in Hong Kong action films cannot be described as *musculinized*, for their bodies are generally not muscled and man-like even when they have a masculine appearance.

Regardless of Tarantino's semiotic games, displacements, and subversions, Bill as the true patriarch represents the authority and law, and Kiddo, even though she is a grown woman, figures as a little girl. This is underscored in a short flashback: a teacher is calling out the girls' names in a classroom but when she calls out Beatrix Kiddo, instead of a little girl, the adult Kiddo responds. In order to change the power relations and to get her revenge, Kiddo must draw on the secret knowledge she has received from her Chinese si fu, Pai Mei.

forging the law-of-beatrix kiddo, reworking the symbolic order

In Beatrix's flashback, Bill narrates an anecdote about Pai Mei from the year 1033, which means that this is a person outside of time, because how else could Pai Mei be Beatrix's contemporary? The construction of truth, that is, of a lie about Beatrix's apprenticeship with Pai Mei becomes extremely transparent. This is in any case a reason for Beatrix Kiddo to become intertwined with the history of Hong Kong cinema, whereas Pai Mei is inserted into Hollywood's present. In Tarantino's *Kill Bill* Pai Mei acquires a new meaning; he is the character who taught Kiddo how to break a wooden board with the tips of her fingers, and even more importantly, he teaches her the five-point-palm exploding heart technique.

If a Hong Kong woman was tied up, shoved into a coffin and buried six feet under, broke her way out with the help of Shaolin kung fu, Western viewers would perhaps find that bizarre but they would not expect a narrative justification, that is, a flashback that explains how this person acquired such a skill. The case is reversed when a Hollywood imaginary is at stake; Beatrix's return from the dead would not only be as convincing without the flashback with Pai Mei, but going back to the past discloses another part of her personality expressed through the fanatical commitment and loyalty to the tradition and authority personified by Pai Mei. We encounter this kind of commitment in the Hong Kong films produced by the Shaw brothers starring the magnificent Gordon Liu Chia-hui. It is interesting, in fact, that Tarantino chose the type of character that Pai Mei is, and that he engaged Gordon Liu to play the part. According to some

185

legends, Pai Mei, also known as White Brow, is an extremely negative character, whom we meet in several Hong Kong films, such as *Shaolin Executioners* (Lau Kar-leung, 1977) and the *Fist of White Lotus* (Lo Lieh, 1980). Pai Mei entered the history of Hong Kong cinema as a traitor, as a Shaolin monk who took the side of the Manchurian perpetrators. With the fall of the Ming Dynasty in the seventeenth century, Manchuria conquered China and established the Ching Dynasty, which caused numerous rebellions and riots. The Manchurian government was continuously introducing repressive measures and, amongst other things, wanted to ban the teachings of Shaolin, fearing that the martial arts from the ancient monastery would spread among the Chinese population.

The role of the monk Pai Mei who betrayed his Shaolin brothers in the Shaw brothers' production was played by Lo Lieh, while Gordon Liu played the rebel. Apart from this, in the film *The 36th Chamber of Shaolin* (Lau Kar-leung, 1978), Liu played a Shaolin monk named San Ta who wants to learn the martial arts in order to fight against the forces of the intruders. Therefore, in one schizophrenic move, Tarantino connects two completely opposite characters—a rebel and a traitor—one who wants to spread martial arts skills throughout the world, and the one who is helping to destroy the source of the martial arts teachings. Tarantino's decision to resort to the condemned and discarded Pai Mei (who sits alone on top of the hill) instead of choosing one of the famed heroes is surprising at first, but if we think about which one of the celebrated heroes would be willing to disclose the secret knowledge to the characters of a Hollywood film, his decision seems quite wise. It is logical that Pai Mei, the ancient traitor, the one who collaborated with the intruders who conquered China, is the mentor of Bill's professional killers.

Tarantino usually offers a new chance to cult actors; in this case, the cult persona is a negative character who is given another chance.[10] Regardless of how contradictory, evil, excessive, or "flat" Pai Mei is as a character, he ultimately personifies the highest narrational authority in the film. With the help of his "explosion of the heart technique" Kiddo will forever free herself from her charismatic si fu Bill and finally accomplish that which she had planned four years earlier, before Bill caught up with her. In Tarantino's transcultural imaginary, Pai Mei makes possible the complete emancipation of Beatrix Kiddo, and she will start a new life with her daughter. In return, through the interaction with the blonde female warrior, Pai Mei as a character is drastically redefined—the despised monk of the Shaw brothers' productions became the si fu of a Hollywood film.

woman's position on a transcultural screen

Stories and imaginings are bound up with a law that is rejoined to other cultural formations of human life such as religion, the division of labor, or history (Geertz). I would add here that the characters' vision is bound up with a worldview that exceeds the fictional world of the film, and that it is dependent on critical and philosophical concerns of the outer world. More specifically, this vision can be related to the level of the *fabula*. Clearly, the *fabula* of *Kill Bill* vol.1 and vol. 2 offers an image of femininity that challenges the Lacanian symbolic universe where the Law-of-the-Father is at work. What this means is that the symbolic universe governed by the Law-of-the-Father should be seen as just one possibility and not as a norm, because there are various alternative signifiers and alternative universes. Judith Butler's reconceptualization of Lacan's law of signification underscores the fact that this law is not predetermined or fixed (Butler). What interests Butler is the move from the signifier as an always incomplete promise to return to the real, to the political signifier, hence to that point where phantasmatic investments can occur. In that sense, a political signifier acquires its power to define the political field through a two-way process, that is, through creating and sustaining its constituency. The signifier is thus capable of structuring and constituting the political field, of introducing new concerns and new subject positions. "Woman," according to Butler, can be taken as category, as a signifier, as a site of new articulations. Even though this term alludes to a false unity, an all-inclusiveness, the initial suspension of difference is the condition for the production of future signifiers:

> It is necessary to learn a double movement: to invoke the category and, hence, provisionally to institute an identity and at the same time to open the category as a site of permanent political contest. That the term is questionable does not mean that we ought not to use it, but neither does the necessity to use it mean that we ought not perpetually interrogate the exclusions by which it proceeds, and to do this precisely in order to learn how to live the contingency of the political signifier in a culture of democratic contestation. (Butler 222)

Hence, Butler is advocating the necessity of acknowledging the universal term, ideology, as a site which is open to contest, but she is also insisting on the possibility of subverting the universal term through repetition. According to Butler, what one takes as a political signifier is itself a settling of prior signifiers. A political signifier implicitly cites the prior instances of itself, drawing on the phantasmatic promise of those prior signifiers. Repetition can have a subversive function because it presupposes a return. Butler argues for a site of political contestation which can be understood as a space of analysis where "woman" as a prescriptive model for female subjectivity becomes open for re-negotiation. This presupposes that woman's status as a "stain" of the symbolic needs to be considered in terms of a temporary linguistic unity.

At stake is not only the possibility of investing the space of the excluded (from the Lacanian symbolic ordered by the Law-of-the-Father) with meaning, at stake is the possibility of conceiving an altogether separate symbolic order, or even multiple symbolic orders. As a subject, Beatrix Kiddo is dependent on her position within Tarantino's transcultural imaginary, implying her position in the *fabula*/the symbolic universe.[11] It is this (trans)cultural position that defines her as a subject on the (trans)cultural *screen.*[12] New universes can come into being to the extent that alternative signifiers are enabled to compete with the paternal signifier. Tarantino's Beatrix Kiddo engages our capacity to envision a different kind of (especially) female existence, and it is an occasion for alternative subjectivities to come into being. When regarded within this alternative normative injunction, the space of exile (the constitutive outside, the real) reserved for female characters, offers the possibility for renegotiating and redefining female subjectivity. The recourse to the space of exile in relation to female characters is not completely new. The potential solution for the "discursive exile" is announced in the *Star Wars* trilogy, for example. (Although *Star Wars* thematizes the space outside the galactic empire, far away from Earth, the structuring of the narrative is not dependent on the structuring of female subjectivity.) Quite similar to the *fabula* of *Star Wars*, the father of Princess Yuki Akizuki in Akira Kurosawa's *Hidden Fortress* (1958) was defeated, and she is herself hunted by the ruler of the expanding Yamana Country. The Princess must flee to Hayakawa Country where she will have the protection of Lord Hayakawa until a situation arises for the House of Akizuki to be restored. The journey is circular: Akizuki Country borders on Hayakawa Country and Yamana Country, but because Akizuki Country was defeated by Yamana Country, the border between Akizuki Country and Hayakawa Country is much more difficult to cross than the border from Yamana Country to Hayakawa Country. Therefore, to reach the safe territory, the Princess must cross the territory of the enemy. Paradoxically enough then, the Princess departs from Hayakawa Country to arrive at Hayakawa Country.

Princess Leia's brief period of leadership in the history of the universe inspired by Kurosawa's Yuki Akizuki, clearly points to that territory of exile, somewhere between Hayakawa and Hayakawa, Okinawa or ancient China, in a universe far, far away, a universe that does not have a referent in reality. Nevertheless, conceptualizing this type of universe is the precondition for the production of new cultural forms of sexuality that will not, as Butler puts it, evaporate under the prohibitive force of the symbolic. At stake is not only the structuring of the imaginary which on occasion contests the symbolic, at stake is a reformulation and proliferation of the symbolic itself.

notes

1. This is David Bordwell's term that he puts forward in his *Planet Hong Kong* (19).

2. Speaking of legendary Beijing Opera stereotypes where a female character is made to be both a pretty heroine and a military hero, the most famous one is certainly Hua Mulan (Fa Mulan in Cantonese pronunciation). In *The Legends of China* series presented at the Hong Kong Cultural Center there was a magnificent opera *The Ladies of the Great Yang Family*, based on a heroic story of twelve women warriors of the Song Dynasty, all of whom are skilled in martial arts, and the head of the family is the grand-mother. For the examples of women warriors in martial arts novels, see for example Jin Yong's (Louis Cha) *Deer and the Cauldron* and *Fox Volant of the Snowy Mountain*. See also *Classical Chinese Tales of the Supernatural and the Fantastic* edited by Karl Kao, in particular the story "Li Chi, the Serpent Slayer."

3. In terms of Lacan's methodological distinction between the psychic fields, a brief definition is as follows: while the Imaginary designates the relation between the ego and its images, the Symbolic produces the subject through language and realizes its closed order by the Law, that is, the Law-of-the-Father. The third field Lacan introduces is the Real. The Real forms the residue of all articulation which escapes the mirror of the Imaginary as well as the grids of the Symbolic. It is neither Symbolic nor Imaginary, and it can be understood as a foreclosed element. It stands for that which is lacking in the symbolic order. See Laplanche and Pontalis.

4. In brief, Lévi-Strauss has suggested that the family is the agency by means of which an entire symbolic network can be elaborated. In *Elementary Structures of Kinship*, Lévi-Strauss argues that the rules of kinship and marriage (incest taboo) create the social state by "reshaping biological relationships and natural sentiments, forcing them into structures implying them as well as others, and compelling them to rise above their original characteristics" (490). Lévi-Strauss ultimately emphasizes the importance of language in securing that all the members of a group inhabit the same psychic territory.

5. The woman as the stumbling block of the symbolic recalls Naomi Schor's discussion on *skandalon* in *Breaking the Chain: Feminism, Theory and French Realist Fiction*. *Skandalon* "*is the detail* whose contour breaks the smooth surface of the text" (84).

6. In *Spectacular Bodies*, Yvonne Tasker offers an account of the history of the action heroine. Tasker describes the action cinema of the 1980s as a "muscular cinema." Taking into consideration films such as *Red Sonja* (1985), *The Long Kiss Goodnight* (1996), *Strange Days* (1995), *Speed* (1994), *Twister* (1996), *Terminator 2* (1992), and *Blue Steel* (1990), for example, Tasker adds that "masculinity" is not limited to the male body. She addresses the emergence of a muscular female heroine and the problems these figures pose for binary conceptions of gendered identity. For further implications of Linda Hamilton's muscular body in *Terminator 2*, see also "New Hollywood's New Women: Murder in Mind—Sarah and Margie," in Neale and Smith, and Sharon Willis' "Combative Femininity: *Thelma and Louise* and *Terminator 2*," in her *High Contrast*. In *Working Girls*, Tasker looks at female roles in other genres, and she establishes an important connection between the representation of women and their status as social agents. This issue is particularly relevant for the *Alien* series. Sigourney Weaver, who also plays the leading role in the films, produced the last two films of the series.

7. While the film *Thelma and Louise* (1991) demonstrates the impossibility of escaping the laws of patriarchy, films such as *Blue Steel*, *Silence of the Lambs* (1991) and *GI Jane* (1997) radicalize the extent to which women are constrained to appropriate both musculinity and masculinity. In *GI Jane*, the female character is trying to prove that women belong in the military. Frustrated by her seargent's derogatory treatment, she exclaims, "Suck my dick!" In *The Long Kiss Goodnight*, faced with a complete crisis, the main female character utters the same line.

8. This notion that women are "extraterritorial" is inspired by a number of texts by feminist critics and philosophers: Luce Irigaray, "Women's Exile, Ideology and Consciousness"; Sarah Kofman, "Ex: The Woman's Enigma," Julia Kristeva "Women's Time."

9. See Susan Jeffords, *Hard Bodies*, and *Remasculinization of America*.

10. An example is the globally popular actor from the 1970s—John Travolta—who achieved cult status with his disco dancing in *Saturday Night Fever* (1977). Travolta was re-launched to stardom via Tarantino's *Pulp Fiction* (1994). Similarly, the biggest African American female star from the early 1970s, Pam Grier, played the leading role in Tarantino's *Jackie Brown* (1997). Perhaps most pertinently for the discussion at stake, Tarantino's recycling of the image of David Carradine, the star of the 1970s TV series *Kung Fu*, is definitely an important piece of intertextual information, in particular for the viewers growing up in Britain and the US. As Warren Buckland, the editor of this volume informed me, his generation knows Carradine as the star of this TV series, and it was the essential viewing for his generation.

11. This is the argument I elaborated in *Subjectivity in the New Hollywood Cinema*.

12. Kaja Silverman introduced the term "cultural screen" in her *The Threshold of the Visible World*.

works cited

Bordwell, David. *Narration in the Fiction Film*. London: Routledge, 1985.

———. *Planet Hong Kong: Popular Cinema and the Art of Entertainment*. Cambridge, Mass.: Harvard University Press, 2000.

Butler, Judith. *Bodies That Matter: On the Discursive Limits of Sex*. New York: Routledge, 1993.

Elsaesser, Thomas. *New German Cinema: A History*. Basingstoke: Macmillan Press, 1989.

Falkenberg, Pamela. "Hollywood and the Art Cinema as a Bipolar Modeling System: *A Bout de souffle* and *Breathless*." *Wide Angle* VII.3 (1985): 44–53.

Freud, Sigmund. *On Metapsychology: The Theory of Psychoanalysis*. Trans. James Strachey. London: Penguin, 1991.

Geertz, Clifford. *Local Knowledge: Further Essays in Interpretive Anthropology*. New York: Basic Books, 1983.

Hong Kingston, Maxine. *The Woman Warrior: Memoirs of a Girlhood Among Ghosts*. London: Picador, 1977.

Irigaray, Luce. "Women's Exile." Trans. Couze Venn. *Ideology and Consciousness* 1 (1977): 62–76.

Jeffords, Susan. *The Remasculinization of America: Gender and the Vietnam War*. Bloomington: Indiana University Press, 1989.

———. *Hard Bodies: Hollywood Masculinity in the Reagan Era*. New Brunswick/New Jersey: Rutgers UP, 1996.

Kao, Karl S. Y. (ed.). *Classical Chinese Tales of the Supernatural and the Fantastic: Selection from the Third to the Tenth Century (Chinese Literature in Translation)*. Bloomington: Indiana University Press, 1985.

Kofman, Sarah. "Ex: The Woman's Enigma." *Enclitic* 4.2 (Fall 1980.): 17–28.

Kristeva, Julia. "Women's Time." *The Kristeva Reader*. Ed. Toril Moi. New York: Columbia University Press, 1986.

Lacan, Jacques. *Écrits: A Selection*. Trans. Alan Sheridan. New York, London: W. W. Norton & Company, 1977.

Laplanche, J., and J.-B. Pontalis. *The Language of Psycho-Analysis*. Trans. Donald Nicholson Smith. New York: Norton, 1973.

Lévi-Strauss, Claude. *The Elementary Structures of Kinship*. Trans. James Harle Bell, John Richard von Sturmer, Rodney Needham. Boston: Beacon Press, 1969.

Mulvey, Laura. *Visual and Other Pleasures*. Bloomington: Indiana University Press, 1989.

Neale, Steve and Smith, Murray eds. *Contemporary Hollywood Cinema*. London: Routledge, 1998.

Schor, Naomi. *Breaking the Chain: Feminism, Theory, and French Realist Fiction*. New York: Columbia University Press, 1985.

Silverman, Kaja. *The Threshold of the Visible World*. New York/London: Routledge, 1996.

Stokes, Lisa, and Michael Hoover. *City on Fire: Hong Kong Cinema*. New York: Verso, 1999.

Tasker, Yvonne. *Spectacular Bodies: Gender, Genre and the Action Cinema*. London: Routledge, 1993.

———. *Working Girls: Gender and Sexuality in Popular Cinema*. London: Routledge, 1998.

Thompson, Kristin. *Breaking the Glass Armor: Neoformalist film Analysis*. Princeton: Princeton University Press, 1988.

Vojković, Saša. *Subjectivity in the New Hollywood Cinema: Fathers, Sons and Other Ghosts*. Amsterdam: ASCA Press, 2001.

Willis, Sharon. "Combative Femininity: *Thelma and Louise* and *Terminator 2*." *High Contrast: Race and Gender in Contemporary Hollywood Film*. Durham: Duke University Press, 1997.

(broke)

back to the

mainstream

queer

theory and

queer cinemas

today

h a r r y   m .   b e n s h o f f

Movies with lesbian, gay, bisexual, or transgendered (LGBT) characters have been produced in unprecedented numbers since the late 1980s. After decades of invisibility and/or connotative stereotyping (enforced by the Hollywood Production Code and the film industry's more far-reaching and long-lasting heterosexism), the last twenty years have seen the rise of a vigorous gay and lesbian independent cinema, including the so-called New Queer Cinema. Television has given us mainstreamed queers-next-door like "Ellen" (1994–1998) and "Will & Grace" (1998–2006), while quasi-independent Oscar-winning films like *Boys Don't Cry* (1999), *The Hours* (2002), *Far From Heaven* (2002), and *Capote* (2005) play to ever-widening audiences. Even recent mainstream Hollywood comedies firmly aimed at heterosexual consumers such as *Talladega Nights* (2006) and *I Now Pronounce You Chuck and Larry* (2007) have included not-wholly derogatory gay subplots and characters. Importantly, this rise in the number of LGBT images has been accompanied by the development of queer theory, both a broad approach to restructuring the ways we think about human sexuality as well as a more focused critical method that allows us to make better sense of the cultural artifacts that represent and construct contemporary sexualities.

Yet, what does all this signify about our current understandings of (homo)sexuality and the American film industry? Does the mainstreaming of gay and lesbian culture and concerns necessarily mean its commodification and depoliticization? Several queer critics have suggested as much: that the new images of "nice gays"—overwhelmingly white, asexual, and removed from the queer community—have worked to create a new demonization of "bad queers"—people who have the kinds of sex and sexual politics that clash with white picket fences (Walters; Warner). That thesis is probably accurate up to a point, dependent as it is on the notion of mainstreaming vis-à-vis culturally pervasive media institutions such as Hollywood and network television that tend to cater to and replicate dominant ideologies. However, such mainstreaming is an important development in the history of queer representation because it affords not just a *quantitative* difference in queer representation (i.e. more and more images), but also a *qualitative* difference: the greater number of images being produced also allows for a greater diversity and complexity of images. Such diversity more accurately reflects the actual demographics of Western queer communities, and challenges the use of stereotypes and other marginalizing tactics that work to contain and control any minority group (Dyer, *The Matter of Images*). Furthermore, continuing innovations in film distribution (such as Hollywood's development of art house boutique subsidiaries, straight-to-DVD sales and rentals, satellite and cable television channels, web-based technologies) also allows for a broader-than-ever spectrum of queer images to be distributed to audiences of all kinds.

This boom in LGBT media mirrors the tremendous gains that lesbian, gay, bisexual, and transgendered people in Western nations have made in most areas of real life. Before and during the early years of the AIDS crisis (1981–1985), Western culture was often hostile to anyone who dared to question dominant notions of gender and sexuality. Doctors and psychiatrists considered homosexuality a disease, the courts considered it a crime, and most religions condemned it as a sin. Homosexuality was a nasty little secret used to blackmail and blackball. Homosexuals were expected to stay in the closet, hiding their sexual orientation from friends and families. There were no civil rights protections for LGBT people, and certainly no discussions of gay marriage (Chauncey; Weeks; D'Emilio). Today, however, openly LGBT people are a much more common sight in America. While homophobia and heterosexism still persist, the closet door is not as firmly latched as it once was. Doctors, psychiatrists, and educators now declare homophobia—not homosexuality—to be a social and psychological disease. In 2003, any and all state laws criminalizing consenting sexual behaviors between adults were struck down by the United States Supreme Court.

And although many fundamentalist religions still condemn homosexual behavior, they profess to love homosexuals themselves. More importantly, many mainstream denominations are beginning to welcome homosexuals into their congregations and even into their clergy. The debate for gay marriage, which most LGBT people could not have even imagined taking place twenty years ago—has moved to center stage.

Yet, visibility is not the same thing as equality (Walters). Homophobes can laugh at "Will & Grace" and still gay-bash, just as mainstream politicians—even those who allegedly support equal rights for LGBT people—still balk at the idea of same-sex marriage. Nonetheless, I would argue that visibility—both onscreen and in real life—is a necessary component of the fight for equality and the passing of civil rights laws. After decades of invisibility and marginalization, the coming out of LGBT people dispels myths, challenges perceptions, and changes the culture's understanding of (homo)sexuality in general. The one-note cinematic stereotypes of past decades—swishy white male interior designers or mannish prison matrons—have been joined by a wide range of multifarious queer types, distinguished by individualizing traits of race, gender region, class, ability, age, body type, etc. (It should be noted at the outset that this increasing divergence of queer types on screen is still limited by the structures of white patriarchal capitalism; queer women and people of color are not represented in these texts as regularly as are white gay men.) Still, at this moment in American history, one can find films like *Latter Days* (2003, about gay Mormon teenagers), *Saving Face* (2004, about an Asian American lesbian surgeon in New York City), *Brother to Brother* (2004, about queers in the Harlem Renaissance), *Quinceañera* (2006, about a gay cholo in Los Angeles), and *Brokeback Mountain* (2005, about a pair of ruggedly masculine queer cowboys in the recent American west). As discussed below, the unprecedented number and diversity of queer images in Western film is due to a host of interrelated factors, including developments in the industrial structure of American filmmaking, political and social activism in the streets and polling places, and the development of queer theory, a set of ideas that challenges us to rethink what it is we think we know about human sexualities.

queer theory, queer film theory

Queer theory emerged from and now transects multiple academic discourses, including film and television studies, literature, history, sociology, philosophy, anthropology—in short any discipline that deals in any way with human sexualities and how they impact upon history, culture, and identity. Even more broadly, queer theory critiques "normalising [sic] ways of knowing and of being that may not always initially be evident as sex-specific" (Sullivan vi). It can and does draw upon previous lesbian and gay history and theory (Hocquenghem; Wittig), as well as the disciplines of cultural studies, reception theory, and psychoanalysis. Perhaps most closely, queer theory is informed by many of the poststructuralist and postmodern ideas that shape third wave feminism, postcolonial theory, and other ways of thinking about the politics, practice, and production of social identity. Like much of that thinking, queer theory postulates that human sexuality is not an essentialized or biological given, but is rather a fluid construct that is shaped by the various discourses within which it is spoken. As such, Michel Foucault's *The History of Sexuality* is an important foundational text of queer theory. In it, Foucault suggests that sexuality is not repressed by dominant culture, but is in fact actively constructed by dominant culture through various ways of institutionalized speaking, such as those of the medical establishment (sexuality as healthy or diseased), the law (sexuality as criminal or legal), and the church (sexuality as sinful or more rarely holy). Expanding on Foucault's premises, historians and sociologists now regularly practice a sort of queer archeology—reconstructing and/or exploring diverse human sexualities as determined by place, time, and institution.

The work of feminist philosopher Judith Butler has also been foundational to queer theory. Her concepts about the performativity of gender and sexuality—i.e. that gendered and sexualized identities are produced through actions, that identities do not exist prior to actions but rather are produced by them—also insist on the fluidity and social construction of human sexualities (Butler). In a slightly different register, literary scholar Eve Kosofsky Sedgwick's work on homosocial desire queered Western literature and its myriad patriarchal contexts (Sedgwick, *Between Men*). Sedgwick has also explored numerous paradoxes in Western culture's understanding of human sexuality, and shown how the closet functions to regulate the hetero–homo binary that structures much of Western thinking (Sedgwick, *Epistemology*).

In broad terms, queer theory insists that there is a general overlap between all forms of human sexuality—and that all forms of sexuality are shaped by the words, actions, and images we use to describe them. As such, one of its central goals is to continually deconstruct and complicate Western culture's illusory straight–gay binary. As queer historians have noted, the terms heterosexuality and homosexuality were coined in the late nineteenth century, although their original meanings were somewhat different than today: both connoted a state of disease (Katz). By the middle of the twentieth century, however, heterosexuality and homosexuality had become fairly synonymous with the more colloquial terms straight and gay. This binary continues to dominate contemporary thinking about human sexuality (and is used to classify types of people and not just behaviors), even as scientists and historians have argued for decades that there is a huge gray area between these seemingly essentialized poles. In truth, millions of unique, multifarious human sexualities are denied or made invisible by the straight–gay binary. For example, both heterosexual and homosexual couples can and do engage in anal eroticism; however, within heterosexist thinking, anal intercourse is often associated with gay men, and often branded disgusting, profane, or bestial. The fact that—in terms of sheer numbers—there are probably more heterosexuals than homosexuals practicing anal sex is hidden by the straight–gay binary, which tends to suggest an understanding of human sexuality strictly divided between "normal" heterosexuals and "deviant" homosexuals. Use of the term queer exposes the inadequacy of the straight–gay binary, as well as the gendered and sexualized hierarchies it creates and supports.

Queer theory, then, examines the social construction of all human sexualities (not just LGBT ones), in order to deconstruct the ideologies and institutions of heteronormativity, a broad social structure that claims that "married-straight-white-man-on-top-of-woman-sex-for-procreation-only" is the only normal and desirable sexuality. Queer, then, becomes an umbrella term that can be used to describe most—if not all—human sexualities. But describing something as queer is only the starting point for the exegete, for one of the goals of queer criticism is to illuminate the specific and unique discourses and institutions that impact upon and ultimately construct the shape and experience of any human sexuality. While most popular culture, including Hollywood movies, contribute to simplistic understandings of gender and sexuality as either-or binaries, queer theory allows us to dissect those images and begin to analyze them for the ways in which they maintain (or more rarely critique) the various hierarchical meanings of gender and sexuality.

Queer theory began to be applied to film studies in the late 1980s and 1990s, as influential essays appeared in a series of special journal issues and edited anthologies (de Lauretis; Bad Object-Choices; Fuss; Gever; Creekmur). Queer theory has been applied to film studies in various ways, complicating the "spot the gay" type of "positive or negative" image analysis that preceded it, an approach perhaps best exemplified by Vito Russo's book *The Celluloid Closet: Homosexuality in the Movies*. Russo's exhaustive catalog of what his title refers to as "homosexual[s] in the movies" should in fact be considered queers, for the images all vary a great deal and were produced under different industrial and social conditions. Thus one of queer film criticism's basic tasks is to complicate what we even mean by homosexual, or heterosexual, or transvestite—something that Russo never addresses.

Queer film theory has also been applied to auteur studies of classical Hollywood directors like James Whale, George Cukor, and Dorothy Arzner (Mayne; Doty, *Making Things*). It has been used to explore the work made by AIDS video collectives and contemporary LGBT filmmakers (Gever). Other critics have used it to explore the queerness of mass culture and its reception (Doty, *Making Things*), while still others employ psychoanalysis and poststructuralism to unwind the queer aspects of classical Hollywood syntax (Hanson; Miller in Fuss). Some queer film critics argue that some cinematic *forms* are themselves best understood as queer—film genres like the horror film, the musical, film noir, and the animated film all construct unreal worlds in which queer forces can and do run amuck (Benshoff; Farmer; Griffin; Dyer). Most recently, queer film theorists are joining with third wave feminists and social historians to queer the monolithic notion of cinematic heterosexuality (Katz; Dixon).

Historically, queer theory developed in the academic world alongside queer activism in the street, and the first wave of work inspired by queer theory—both critical as well as creative—was infused with fury and vigor. For activists fighting against governmental inaction and bigotry toward AIDS, queer was used to designate a necessary "community of difference," inclusive of a broad variety of sexual *identities* and *behaviors* (Duggan). People fighting AIDS and institutionalized homophobia in the late 1980s represented a highly diverse population (even though mainstream media tended to reduce that population to the image of the sad, white man dying with AIDS). That historically specific queer community included the usual denizens of bourgeois gay or lesbian ghettos, but also bisexuals, cross-dressers, transgendered people, disabled people, people of color, straight people, leather queens, drag kings, and so on—anyone who resisted Western culture's dominant structures of gender and sexuality. Queer communities (both then and now) cross borders of class, race, gender, and region as well as sexuality, uniting very different people in a shared cause. As with their use of the word queer itself (reclaiming and reinvesting a previously pejorative term with new meanings), the first wave of queer activists and theorists meant to be provocative and unruly. So were many of the era's LGBT filmmakers, who began to produce work directly informed by queer theory, work that collectively became quickly known as the New Queer Cinema.

new queer (and not so queer) cinemas

New Queer Cinema describes an independent filmmaking practice located in and around North America and Western Europe circa the early 1990s (Aaron). These films and videos used queer theory as structuring principles and were more overtly political than many of the lesbian and gay independent features that had come before them. Indeed, many New Queer filmmakers had been involved in AIDS activist groups, video collectives, and/or had studied contemporary cultural theory at colleges and universities. First identified at LGBT film festivals, New Queer Cinema found critical acclaim and commercial success in art house theaters. Its films and videos openly challenged notions of taste, form, and ideology, as well as race, class, gender, and sexuality. New Queer Cinema style has sometimes been dubbed "Homo Pomo" because the films partake of postmodern styles and ideas (as does queer theory itself). They tend to focus on permeable formal boundaries, the crossing of styles and genres, and almost always emphasize social constructionist models of identity. Some of the first films and filmmakers of this movement were *Tongues Untied* (Marlon Riggs, 1989), *Looking for Langston* (Isaac Julien, 1989), *Paris is Burning* (Jennie Livingston, 1990), *Edward II* (Derek Jarman, 1991), *Poison* (Todd Haynes, 1991), *Swoon* (Tom Kalin, 1991), *The Living End* (Gregg Araki, 1991), *My Own Private Idaho* (Gus van Sant, 1991), *Zero Patience* (John Greyson, 1993), *Go Fish* (Rose Troche, 1995), and *The Watermelon Woman* (Cheryl Dunye, 1995).

Unruly and transgressive, New Queer Cinema simultaneously draws on minimalism and excess, appropriation and pastiche, the mixing of Hollywood and avant-garde styles, and even the mix of fictional and documentary style. *The Living End* and *My Own Private Idaho* reappropriate the Hollywood buddy/road movie for HIV positive queers and teenage hustlers, while *Zero Patience* is a ghost story musical about AIDS. *Poison* is made up of three interwoven stories told in three different cinematic styles, specifically to call attention to how queerness is usually figured within different cinematic genres. Similarly, *Go Fish* punctuates its straightforward lesbian romance with experimental sequences, again calling attention to how media languages or discourses shape the form and content of the sexualities they represent.

Many New Queer films also challenge master narratives like history. *Edward II* and *Swoon* are deliberately anachronistic, asking the viewer to think about the nature of history—and how it is often told from the position of those in power. Works like *Looking for Langston* and *The Watermelon Woman* also examine the ways and means (or lack thereof) that allowed for the existence and representation of queer African Americans in the early part of the twentieth century. The more straightforward ethnographic documentary *Paris is Burning* is an exemplary queer case study of poor queers of color in New York City in the 1980s and how they fashioned their own unique underground culture. Similarly, *Tongues Untied* focuses on various aspects of being black and gay in northern California during that same era. Drawing together poetry, dance, personal reminiscences, historical and found footage, and even playful fictitious vignettes, *Tongues Untied*—like most New Queer films and videos—explores and questions not just social identity—but also the cinematic styles used to represent them.

New Queer Cinema was not always applauded by LGBT audiences, many of whom were concerned with New Queer Cinema's alleged "negative" images. Some of the films do recycle (in order to question) old stereotypes such as the queer psycho-killer (*Swoon*, *Poison*, *The Living End*), and many LGBT filmgoers found the films to be dry, unpleasant, and theoretically pretentious. After all, American movie audiences, whether straight or gay, are still weaned on and often still desire Hollywood-style movies with happy endings. Those types of movies are also now being made by lesbian and gay independent filmmakers. For example, *The Incredibly True Adventure of Two Girls in Love* (1995), *The Broken Hearts Club* (2000), and *Eating Out* (2004) draw upon the conventions of Hollywood narrative form and the genre of the romantic comedy, but insert lesbian and gay lovers into previously heterosexual roles. The production of such unchallenging films (compared to New Queer Cinema), has led some critics to decry the state of contemporary LGBT independent cinema, seeing more radical New Queer impulses as dead or dying. However, recent films like *Hedwig and the Angry Inch* (2001) and *Tarnation* (2003), as well as quasi-independent Hollywood films like *Monster* (2003) or *Brokeback Mountain* seem to suggest that queer cinema (as opposed to lesbian or gay cinema) continues to thrive.

LGBT and queer independent filmmaking, serving more or less queer niche markets, is often facilitated by new distribution channels such as direct-to-home DVD sales and rentals. Specialized mail-order video companies such as TLA, Wolfe Video, and Culture Q Connection have been marketing to the queer community for many years now, and they are also moving into film production, funding projects that they then release through their mail-order catalogues. And with the advent of the Internet and websites like PlanetOut/PopcornQ and YouTube, all types of queer shorts, videos, and features are increasingly being advertised and/or distributed to consumers through such private venues. However, while LGBT independent filmmaking may be thriving, it rarely generates much revenue for its financial backers when it gets ghettoized as a gay or lesbian film. For example, the highest grossing gay-identified independent films of 2003 were *Camp* (from IFC Films) and *Mambo Italiano* (from Samuel Goldwyn Films), and each only grossed between $1–2 million at the art house box office (Goodridge 13). Compared to the hundreds of millions of dollars a Hollywood film like *Philadelphia* (1993) or *The Birdcage* (1996) can earn, such revenues are almost negligible. Thus, more and more independent films with queer content are being pitched and distributed as auteur-based art house pictures, rather than specifically LGBT films. With bigger stars and budgets than the usual queer independent film, by the start of the twenty-first century, these films were emerging as Hollywood's latest attempt to market queer themes to ever-wider audiences.

The rise of New Queer Cinema did not go unnoticed by Hollywood, and they briefly tried (unsuccessfully) to market a few films that explored more open parameters of sexuality, such as *Three of Hearts* (1993) and *Threesome* (1994). However, most queers in 1990s mainstream Hollywood films were supporting characters—neighbors, best friends, family members—who were regularly denied both queer community and a political point of view (Walters). Even the few films to focus centrally on LGBT characters were regularly constructed according to dominant Hollywood formulas, genres, and stereotypes. For example, *Philadelphia* follows the traditional social problem film format, centering on a nice, desexualized, bourgeois white gay man played by Tom Hanks, one of the most non-threatening known-to-be heterosexual actors in Hollywood. As its critics pointed out, *Philadelphia* failed to dramatize the queer community's activist response to the AIDS crisis, centering instead on tearful family melodrama. Hollywood revisited old drag queen stereotypes in comedies like *The Birdcage* and *To Wong Foo, Thanks for Everything, Julie Newmar* (1997), and more straight actors played gay in a handful of comedies like *In & Out* (1997). Emulating "Will & Grace," and broadening its potential audience base, Hollywood then created a few gay man–straight woman buddy films such as *My Best Friend's Wedding* (1997) and *The Object of My Affection* (1998). Similarly, *Bound* (1996) was an attempt to draw in both lesbian spectators as well as heterosexual male audiences titil-lated by the film's butch-femme aesthetic.

Perhaps the most interesting development in recent queer filmmaking is its increasing validation by critical and professional institutions such as the Golden Globes and the Academy of Motion Pictures Arts and Sciences. During the 1980s, queer work began to be honored by the Academy: *The Times of Harvey Milk* (1984) and *Common Threads: Stories from the Quilt* (1989) each won an Oscar for Best Documentary Feature. However, by the 1990s and into the new millennium, queer films were garnering an unprecedented number of Oscar nominations and wins. The Oscar attention—and the wider distribution that usually accompanies it—is due in part to the ways these films are now being produced and distributed. As is well known, during the 1990s and 2000s, almost all of the major Hollywood studios acquired various independent companies (Miramax was acquired by Disney, New Line Cinema was absorbed into Time/Warner), or else they established their own vaguely separate "independent" distribution outlets such as Sony Pictures Classics, Fox Searchlight, and Warner Independent Pictures. And while the creation of these quasi-independent boutique sub-sidiaries has been decried by many critics for supposedly narrowing the playing field for "truly" independent film production and distribution, the evidence suggests that this new production and marketing strategy has been successful in bringing queer concerns to wider audiences. As "inde-pendent" cinema these films play at festivals where they garner good reviews and multiple awards. But as films also backed by major Hollywood studios, they can then be distributed via a platforming release pattern to larger, more mainstream audiences in American multiplexes. Instead of being niche marketed to small urban LGBT audiences, the films are mar-keted as prestige pictures that just happen to have queer content.

Among the films that have followed this pattern of production and dis-tribution are *The Crying Game* (1992, Miramax), *Gods and Monsters* (1998, Lion's Gate/Universal), *American Beauty* (1999, DreamWorks), *Boys Don't Cry* (1999, Fox Searchlight), *Far From Heaven* (2002, Focus Features/Universal), *The Hours* (2002, a co-production between Miramax and Paramount), *Monster* (2003, Newmarket/Columbia TriStar Home Entertainment), *Brokeback Mountain*

(2005, Focus Features/Universal), *Capote* (2005, Sony Pictures Classics), *Notes on a Scandal* (2006, Fox Searchlight) and *Infamous* (2006, Warner Independent Pictures). Some of these films were made by former New Queer filmmakers and most are queer in form as well as content, emphasizing the social and historical discourses that shape the queer lives they depict. *Gods and Monsters*, for example (which won an Oscar for Best Adapted Screenplay) is an imaginative queer historiography of classical Hollywood filmmaker James Whale, played in the film by gay actor Sir Ian McKellen (who was also nominated for an Oscar). Queerly stylized, the film flips back and forth in time, between memory and the present, between "reality" and the bizarre worlds depicted in James Whale's horror films, exploring the nature of Whale's homosexuality and how it impacted upon his life and work.

Boys Don't Cry (which won a Best Actress Oscar for Hilary Swank) is based on the true story of Brandon Teena, a female-to-male pre-operative transsexual who was brutally raped and murdered. Directed by Kimberly Pierce, the film complicates issues of gender and sexuality and emphasizes how class and regionality doom Brandon to become a target of queer-phobic violence. *American Beauty* (which swept the Oscars and won for Best Picture) thematizes sexual repression: the brutality and violence of the film's retired Marine (Chris Cooper) is shown to be the result of his repressed homosexual desires. *Far From Heaven*, written, directed, and produced by New Queer filmmakers Todd Haynes and Christine Vachon, is a gloss on the form and content of the classical Hollywood melodrama. As with the best of Haynes's films, *Far From Heaven* is a comment on cinematic style as much as it is a queer exploration of race, class, gender, and sexuality. Stephen Daldry's *The Hours* is another queer take on the cinematic melodrama and was honored with nine Oscar nominations (and one win, for Nicole Kidman's Best Actress turn as Virginia Woolf). Based on Michael Cunningham's Pulitzer prize-winning novel of the same name, *The Hours* intercuts three different but thematically related stories, each focusing on a single day in the life of three different women living in different times and places. What emerges is a historicized look at the possible lives and relationships available to queer women across one hundred years of Western history.

brokeback mountain: queer not gay

Probably the most-well known example of this recent crop of films is Ang Lee's *Brokeback Mountain*, yet another quasi-independent award-winning and widely distributed queer film. *Brokeback Mountain* was misunderstood by most popular discourses as a "gay cowboy movie." Yet neither Ennis Del Mar (Heath Ledger) nor Jack Twist (Jake Gyllenhaal) claims a gay, queer, or otherwise homosexual identity. ("You know I ain't queer," says Ennis. "Me neither," replies Jack). In fact, aside from their occasional sex together, both Ennis and Jack are quite publicly and obviously heterosexual through-out most of the film. *Brokeback Mountain*—like its central characters—is thus not gay in the narrow, "identity-politics" sense, but it is quite queer in the broader theoretical sense, making strange the social institutions of a par-ticular place and time in order to dissect the multiple discourses—includ-ing those of gender, class, and region—that produce complex and distinct human sexualities. And in so doing, *Brokeback Mountain* sounds a strident cri-tique of compulsory heterosexuality and its denial and oppression of homosexual desire. Instead of being a "gay film" that was not "gay enough"—as many gay audiences complained—*Brokeback Mountain* is better understood as a film that uses the tools and methods of queer theory to critique the dominant institutions and subject positions created within white, Western, heteronormative discourses.

Brokeback Mountain caused a pop culture panic because it forthrightly pos-ited that one of the most iconic images of heterosexual masculinity—the American Cowboy—may have had and might still have homosexual desires. A similar film about two women in love such as the western-themed *Desert Hearts* (1985) would not have caused such consternation, nor would a film about two "queer eye" interior decorators in New York City (Mendelsohn). But by placing male homosexual desire into the American heartland and specifically into its iconographic masculine subject, *Brokeback Mountain* blurs the borders between straight and gay, between homosocial and homosexual. It upsets the institutions of heteronormative patriarchy not so much because it is a "gay cowboy movie," but because it looks so much like a *straight* cowboy movie. Thus it was dismissively labeled "THE gay cowboy movie" to particularize it, to let everyone know that it was indeed very different from all the other Westerns that it so closely resem-bles both in terms of its *mise en scène* as well as its thematic concerns: civiliza-tion versus the wilderness, conformity versus freedom, and ultimately the preference for male bonding over heterosexual romance. As such, *Brokeback Mountain* literally queers the uber-butch generic space of the Hollywood Western, something the many jokes, cartoons, and comedy sketches that circulated during the film's release nervously attempted to contain through humor and disavowal. Like the tag-line "gay cowboy movie," each was designed to figure *Brokeback Mountain* as a deviant Other, to situate it as an anomaly, and not something central to the dominant mythologies of the American West and its traditional cowboy masculinity.

The author of *Brokeback Mountain*, Annie Proulx, also disowned the "gay cowboy" label as simplistic and naïve when it was first attached to her short story. Proulx was out to do something more than create a simple tragic love story; instead she wrote something that might be classified as queer historiography. Indeed, in common with much theoretically queer think-ing, she sees herself as a "geographic determinist," writing about how "regional landscapes, climate, and topography dictate local cultural traditions and kinds of work." Thus, she specifies that Jack and Ennis were "a couple of home-grown country kids, opinions and self-knowledge shaped by the world around them, finding themselves in emotional waters of increasing depth" (Proulx, 130). Far from identifying them as gay (or even as cowboys), Proulx writes that Jack and Ennis "were clearly homophobic themselves, especially the Ennis character. Both wanted to be cowboys, be part of the Great Western Myth, but it didn't work out that way" (130). For Proulx, her story was one of "destructive rural homophobia," not gay cowboys. Director Ang Lee approached the film in a similar fashion, seeing Jack and Ennis as extensions of their environments. Lee's intense focus on period and generic detail underscores the many ways that place and time shape the film's characters and the choices they make. Arguably one of the film's most significant aesthetic achievements is its creation of an almost palpable feeling of place and time, the dominant ideological apparatuses and structures of feeling that marked the recent American West, both real and mythic.

The film's dual focus—queer male love story and critique of Western heteronormativity—played out in interesting ways across the film's production, marketing, distribution, and reception. Its life as a film began when gay independent producer James Schamus, who had been involved with several seminal New Queer films of the early 1990s, optioned Annie Proulx's short story. No one in Hollywood wanted to bankroll the project because of its homosexual content, and in the seven years it took to get the film made, the script became known throughout Hollywood as one of the greatest unproduce-able screenplays ever written. It was actually a fluke of corporate restructuring that allowed the film to find financing. Schamus's independent production company (Good Machine) was bought by Universal Pictures in June of 2002 and merged into a new Universal subsidiary named Focus Features; as the new co-president of Focus Features, Schamus was then able to green light his own project.

As an urban independent art house film, *Brokeback Mountain* could afford to be understood as queer love story. But as a mainstream, multiplex, suburban release, it had to downplay those aspects, framing itself instead as more of a universal love story, a weepie, a western, and/or (perhaps most importantly as it won multiple awards and glowing reviews) as a *prestige* picture. Significantly, the film had at least two different ad campaigns. The ads aimed at heterosexual consumers "practically de-gayed the film—showing Jake Gyllenhaal cooing over his newborn son held by his picture-perfect wife." On the other hand, the film's publicists sent gay newspapers blue *Brokeback Mountain* bandanas, which according to the decades-old Gay Hanky Code, represent anal sex, "worn on the left for tops; worn on the right for bottoms" (Kusner 37). And while the film was obviously meaningful to urban and rural gay men, recent reception studies have also demonstrated its tremendous appeal to heterosexual women in the American heartland (Groth). The film seems to speak to anyone and everyone who has ever questioned the dominant structures of gender and sexuality under which we live.

Brokeback Mountain's critique of heteronormativity necessarily borders on a critique of patriarchal masculinity and compulsory heterosexuality; many theorists have argued that homophobia and heteronormative masculinity are in fact deeply imbricated with one another. As Calvin Thomas expresses it in *Straight with a Twist: Queer Theory and the Subject of Heterosexuality*:

> The terror of being mistaken for a queer dominates the straight mind because this terror *constitutes* the straight mind; it is precisely that culturally produced and reinforced horror of/fascination with abjected homosexuality that produces and maintains "the straight mind" as such, governing not so much specific sexual practices between men and women (after all, these things happen) as the *institution* (arguably antisexual) of heteronormativity itself. (98–99)

Nowhere in the story or film of *Brokeback Mountain* is this formulation more apparent than in the character of Ennis Del Mar, a man who maintains his own "straight mind" out of abject terror. As his back-story reveals, nine-year-old Ennis was taken by his father to view the mutilated body of a murdered gay man, in what was meant to be an object lesson as to how violent masculinity justifiably punishes queers. The lesson was so successful that even as an adult Ennis fears that he and Jack will be murdered if their relationship is ever discovered. As he ages, Ennis grows increasingly paranoid, imagining that people in town are staring at him, singling him out because they somehow know of his sexual relationship with Jack. Ennis is literally "scared straight"—he defines himself as heterosexual less because of his sexual desire and more because he has been terrorized into accepting it as the normative identity.

The idea that institutionalized heterosexuality traps men and women into narrowly-defined social roles derived from their biological sex has been a central tenet of feminist and queer theories for decades. As one theorist puts it, "Performing straightness entails rigid self-discipline. It is a state of monotony, repetition, and predictability" (Dixon 8). Those adjectives clearly describe the characters in *Brokeback Mountain*, rural uneducated people living on the extreme margins of second wave feminism. All of them lead lives circumscribed by white, heteronormative, patriarchal capitalism. The women especially derive their identities solely from their location within heterosexual relations—as wife, girlfriend, daughter, or mother. Commentators who complained that the film ignores the plight of the men's spouses seemed to miss this point: the film is not treating its female characters in a sexist manner, it is dramatizing how Midwestern American culture of the 1960s–1970s was itself a limiting and sexist structure (Floyd). Similarly, Jack and Ennis unthinkingly follow careers outlined for them by the tenets of traditional heteronormative patriarchal capitalism. Ennis is especially resigned to his place in this social structure, even though on some level he realizes it is destroying him. As he ruefully tells Jack at one point, "If you can't fix it … you gotta stand it." His stoicism—a conditioned part of his traditional masculinity—is in this case an attribute that works to further confine him within his limited and nearly loveless existence.

Furthermore, heterosexuality in *Brokeback Mountain* is not the cornerstone of "family values"—in fact every heterosexual family unit in the film is disordered in significant ways: neurotic, distant, and ultimately hostile to its own members. Ennis and Alma work hard at their version of heterosexuality—they produce two children but their marriage is empty and unbalanced because of his other desires. Their heterosexual life together is a vision of domestic hell, complete with sick and crying babies, and cramped and dingy apartments. Repeated scenes show both Ennis and Alma and fleeing from their apartment—he to the woods with Jack and she to her job at the grocery store. Heterosexual desire was also responsible for tearing apart what was left of the young Ennis's family. After his mother and father were killed in a car accident, Ennis was raised by his sister and brother, both of whom abandoned him when they acted upon their own desires and married others, leaving Ennis alone with no economic or familial resources. Jack's own brutal and dysfunctional parents are revealed during the film's climactic moments. Earlier, Jack had told Ennis that his father never taught him anything or supported any of his efforts, and in effect drove Jack away from home. When this bad father is finally revealed onscreen, he is surly and silent and as cold and remote as the stark off-white farm house in which he lives. Jack's marriage to Lureen perhaps looks better than any of the others, but he tells Ennis that it could be conducted over the phone equally as effectively. Importantly, Lureen's father never hides his contempt for Jack, and Jack believes that L. D. would actually pay him to leave Lureen.

The Thanksgiving dinner scene at Lureen and Jack's home is especially effective in delineating the various dis-eases of Western heteronormativity. In it, Jack and his father-in-law L. D. jockey for masculine superiority while their wives sit by silently. As Jack begins to carve the turkey (traditionally the duty of the "man of the house"), L. D. grabs the utensils from Jack with the snide admonition that the "Stud Duck'll do the carvin' round here." In order to keep the peace, Jack defers to him, while Lureen suggests that she will have to turn off the televized football game if her son doesn't eat his dinner. Agreeing with Lureen, and out of respect to her efforts in preparing the meal, Jack shuts off the TV. L. D.—one of the film's most obvious symbols of traditional patriarchal attitudes—stops carving the turkey, crosses the room and turns the TV back on, admonishing that "You want your boy to grow up to be a man, don't ya? Boys should watch football." Now more agitated,

Jack again rises and shuts off the TV. As L. D. once again makes his way towards the TV set to turn it back on, Jack finally bellows at him, "You sit down you old son of a bitch. This is *my* house, *my* child, and you are *my* guest. Now you sit down before I knock your ignorant ass into next week." Cutaway shots reveal that Lureen and her mother have remained silent throughout this exchange, although Lureen's slight smile indicates her approval of Jack asserting his dominance through traditional patriarchal means. In this one scene, *Brokeback Mountain* suggests that even so-called "normal-looking" heterosexual families are far from ideal, but are instead filled with rarely spoken tensions, rivalries, and the barely contained threat of physical violence.

Even though Ennis and Jack are queer by reason of their shared homosexual relationship, most of their behaviors and attitudes are still derived from heteronormative patriarchal assumptions about competition and violence. As one theorist of heterosexuality has expressed it, "dominant culture's most repetitive message to men is that it is infinitely preferable for them to compete with each other viciously, to batter each other violently, even to murder each other brutally, than it is for them to fuck each other passionately" (Thomas 98). Thus, Ennis, who is much more invested in a traditional model of masculinity than is Jack, is especially prone to violent outbursts that serve to express what he will not or cannot say with words. Even their first sexual coupling verges on rape, not same-sex desire, yet another moment in the film that belies the moniker "gay cowboy film." Indeed, at least one gay critic found their intimacies to be "the kind of sex that a person who's neither gay nor a cowboy imagines gay cowboys must have" (Carpenter 13). Another way to decode the scene might be to say that it depicts homosexual sex between two heterosexual men.

In fact, not knowing anything about gay culture and its sexual mores—or in the case of Jack not admitting to such knowledges—Ennis and Jack mostly express their desires through discourses of heteronormative homosociality. We see them physically rough-housing, wrestling, punching, and teasing one another, but they barely speak of desire or love, let alone tenderness and intimacy. And although they may appear on the surface to treat one another as equals, they repeatedly fall back into heterosexist assumptions about the nature of relationships—i.e. that real relationships are composed of one dominant partner and one submissive partner. Sexually, Ennis seems to be the active, dominant top in the relationship. In broader terms, Ennis's silence, aloofness, and ability to dictate the terms of their relationship also help construct him as the dominant half of the relationship. Conversely, Jack's character is marked by attributes thought to be more feminine: he is more likely to voice his feelings and desires, and is willing to accept—however grudgingly—most of the limits Ennis places upon their relationship.

Representing sex between men was a significant hurdle the film had to overcome in order to reach wider audiences. The fact that sexual intercourse between Ennis and Jack is depicted in the film only once—and almost as rape—is perhaps an indication of how the film panders to straight sensibilities. Queer theorist Thomas Yingling has argued that

> anal pleasure is the single most interdicted of those pleasures open to male bodies in our culture—and, I argue, is also the "thing" still that defines homosexuality. If the Phallus is the fetish, and masculinity the reified identity it signifies, the single most unthinkable event for the masculine is anal penetration *as pleasure.* (192–3)

Thus, if and when heteronormative patriarchy imagines anal penetration between men, it is almost always figured as a violent rape that demeans and degrades one's masculine status. Images of pleasurable anal intercourse between men (or between men and women) are almost non-existent in mainstream media. Although one can infer that Jack and Ennis's off-screen sexuality includes willful and pleasurable anal intercourse, the film itself shies away from it.

In the end, the debate about whether or not *Brokeback Mountain* was "gay enough" or whether it pandered too much to straight sensibilities is ultimately reductive. As I have been arguing, the film engages with straight sensibilities in order to critique them. It destabilizes patriarchal heteronormativity, queerly teasing out the interrelated connections between homosexuality, heterosexuality, and male homosociality. In this respect, the scene between Jack and the ranch foreman outside the Childress social club is highly significant, and it encapsulates much of the film's subversive effect. In it, the ranch foreman invites Jack to a "cabin down on a lake" to "drink a little whiskey, fish some, get away, ya know?" The epistemological uncertainty of this brief exchange is highly disruptive of patriarchal hetero normative discourses and knowledges: is the invitation strictly homosocial, or is it a not-so-thinly-veiled homosexual proposition? Of course, different audiences can read this scene in different ways—just as they did the film as a whole. Yet this one moment, as does the entire film, suggests the intimate contiguity of male homosocial and male homosexual desire. After all, what "normal" straight guy doesn't long to get away from his wife and kids and spend a few days camping in the woods with his best buddy?

(broke) back to the mainstream?

Queer theory can also illuminate texts that are seemingly more hetero normative, such as the mainstream hits *Talladega Nights: The Ballad of Ricky Bobby* (2006) and *I Now Pronounce You Chuck and Larry* (2007). Both films are major studio Hollywood comedies aimed at young heterosexual males in multiplexes across the globe—and both (somewhat remarkably) feature gay characters and thematize gay marriage and/or domestic partner rights.

Talladega Nights satirizes the homosocial world of Nascar racing, centering on the heterosexual buddy racecar team of Ricky Bobby (Will Ferrell) and Cal Naughton, Jr. (John C. Reilly); hilarity ensues when they are challenged by Jean Girard, a gay French racecar driver (Sacha Baron Cohen). *I Now Pronounce You Chuck and Larry* is a sort of liberal *Black Like Me* (1964) social message comedy about two straight firemen (Adam Sandler and Kevin James) pretending to be gay in order to receive domestic partner benefits. Both films employ gay and lesbian actors (Jane Lynch, Richard Chamberlain, Lance Bass) and feature gay male supporting characters drawn with many stereotypical touches. For example, Jean Girard is not just the "villain" of *Talladega Nights*, but he is also highly cultured, talks "funny," and is married to the rather swishy Gregory (Andy Richter). *Chuck and Larry*'s gay male supporting characters include Kevin "Butterfly" McDonough (Nick Swardson)—the name says it all—and Fred Duncan (Ving Rhames), a hyper-macho African American fireman who is inspired to come out of the closet when he thinks that Chuck and Larry have done the same.

Yet, as does *Brokeback Mountain*, both *Chuck and Larry* and *Talladega Nights* expose the slippery slope between male homosexual and male homosocial desire. However, unlike *Brokeback Mountain*, these more mainstream films use that situation for comedic ends, arguably disavowing that queer slippage with laughter. As Alex Doty has put it,

> comedy is fundamentally queer since it encourages rule-breaking, risk-taking, inversions, and perversions in the face of straight patriarchal norms. Although you could argue that most comic gender and sexuality rule-breaking is ultimately contained or recuperated by traditional narrative closure (as it attempts to restore the straight status quo), or through the genre's "its just a joke" escape hatch, the fact remains that queerness is the source of many comic pleasures for audiences of all sexual identities. (*Flaming Classics* 81)

Both *Chuck and Larry* and *Talladega Nights* do end with the formation of heterosexual couples, even as they also allow for a few homosexual ones. The films insist that being gay is not all that different from being straight, especially if being gay means you can still be macho and desirous of a wedding. More outré queer sexualities (ironically embodied by the promiscuous and group-sex-loving Chuck) must ultimately be contained within heteronormative, monogamous, and implicitly procreative unions.

More queerly however, *Chuck and Larry* repeatedly draws direct comparisons between heterosexual homosocial love and homosexual love. When Chuck and Larry are outed as gay, their fellow firemen shun them, fearing that Chuck's homosocial "grab-assing" in the past may in fact have been homosexual. At a costume party, Chuck is attracted to the sexy butt of a

Playboy bunny, only to discover real-life homosocial buddy David Spade in a cameo appearance. When Larry first proposes his scheme, Chuck responds with the cliché "I *love* you but I'm not *in love* with you," and both men confess their (homosocial) love for the other during a climactic courtroom scene in which everyone else thinks they are declaring their homosexual love. For Larry, homosocial bonds are more trustworthy and true than heterosexual ones, which is why he asks his buddy Chuck to marry him instead of a woman. Although both men are (for the most part) firmly situated as heterosexual—Larry has a dead wife and two kids while Chuck describes himself as a heterosexual "whore"—there is one comic moment that suggests they have had three-way sex with Larry's surly maid Teresa. Also intriguing is the way that Chuck and Larry's put downs of one another reveal an obsession with homosexual acts. There is much talk of "ass beatings," being a "dick," "baton swallowing" and even having a pole inserted into one's anus that would turn one into a human "lollipop."

Director Denis Dugan invokes a great deal of (hetero)sexism, racism, and general xenophobia as he attempts to keep *Chuck and Larry* anchored within the dominant structures of traditional white patriarchal heterosexuality. The rough-and-tumble macho world of heterosexual firemen is constructed through hand-held camerawork and thrilling montage sequences. More disturbing is the film's sexist and racist baseline. The script constructs Chuck as a lothario who sleeps with multiple beautiful women; they fall into his bed even after he demeans them in public in front of his approving and adoring buddies. Formally, both Chuck and the film itself repeatedly objectify women's butts and breasts in slow motion subjective shots. And aside from its gratuitous Latina-bitch and stupid-stoner stereotypes, the film's wedding chapel planner (Rob Schneider) is one of the most embarrassing Orientalist stereotypes since Mickey Rooney played Mr. Yunioshi in *Breakfast at Tiffany's* (1961). While the film may be deliberately constructing white heterosexual masculinity as something in need of modification (just as Chuck is eventually domesticated by Larry and his kids), it also seems to justify and even celebrate its own (hetero)sexism and racism.

Yet all of this is wrapped up in the film's "liberal" message of respect and tolerance, and its endorsement of gay marriage (or at least gay partnerships). In liberal Hollywood fashion, all the bigoted firemen soon realize they were being "thickheaded," and come to support Chuck and Larry who are nonetheless good firemen, even if they are gay. At the end of the film, "real gays" Butterfly and Fireman Fred get married while Chuck and Larry are resituated as heterosexuals who have learned many valuable lessons by pretending to be gay. Even Larry comes to accept his musical-theatre-loving, Easy-Bake-Oven-cooking son. And although the film has referenced Cher, George Michael, and *Brokeback Mountain* as the markers of actual homosexuality, the film ends with both gay and straight characters

209

dancing to George Michael's "Freedom" and Freddy Mercury's "You're My Best Friend." While the film was felt by many audiences to be offensive—for its racism, its sexism, its very premise that pokes fun at a real civil rights issue—the film nonetheless makes available to its viewers (who probably wouldn't be caught dead at a screening of *Brokeback Mountain*) a liberal critique of homophobia. And for the queer exegete, the film seems to exemplify the pathological relations of white patriarchal capitalism.

Talladega Nights works in similar fashion. Although it is less interested in promoting a (however conflicted) "gay positive" message, *Talladega Nights* arguably satirizes and/or queers its white lower middle class homosocial racecar drivers as much or more than Chuck and Larry's firemen. As with Chuck and Larry, Ricky and Cal mean more to one another than any woman can. In fact, Ricky's first wife is even triangulated between the men when she dumps the losing Ricky for Cal. Yet Cal is so desirous of his relationship with Ricky that he cannot understand why they cannot still be friends, even though he is now living in Ricky's house and having sex with his wife. In other moments that destabilize heteronormativity, Cal (who is sort of the female half to Ricky's more dominant top) reveals that he has posed nude and "spread his butt cheeks" for a porno spread under the name Mike Honcho. (*Honcho* is a well known gay porno magazine.) At the end of one sequence, as Ricky passes out from pain and too much "gayness" in the room, he even blurts out "Cal, I love you!"

Homosexual and homosocial impulses coexist and blur together in Jean Girard, who can seemingly play on both teams—macho racecar driver and gay husband. Girard's interest in racing is a sort of homosocial game he enjoys playing with Ricky, not a defining masculine identity. Girard would rather be teaching Komodo dragons to perform *Hamlet*, and he wants Ricky to beat him fairly in a race so that he can retire. Girard repeatedly brings queerness into his homosocial relationship with Ricky. When they walk together holding hands as friends/enemies, Girard announces that he has an erection, deliberately panicking Ricky. At another point, he taunts Ricky by asking for a kiss as a sign of his humility in the face of Girard's superior racing skills. Ultimately, after a climactic slow-motion race to the finish line, scored to Pat Benatar's love song "We Belong [Together]," Ricky does manage to beat Girard, and kisses him in an extended lip lock. As in Chuck and Larry, the film ends with all heterosexual and homosexual couples united, although Jean Girard and Gregory disappear from the film's final scenes. Narrative closure re-stabilizes traditional heteronormativity, even as it has been satirically undermined for the preceding 90 minutes.

conclusion

Queer theory provides contemporary film critics with the tools to tease apart and examine cinematic representations of sexuality. Whether independent, mainstream, or something queerly in between, recent American films have begun to feature new and queer ideas about human sexuality; queer theory provides us with the ways and means to understand them. It allows us to see *Brokeback Mountain* as something so much more than just a "gay cowboy movie," or *Talladega Nights* as more than just a film with a funny homosexual stereotype. Instead of forthrightly dismissing something like *I Now Pronounce You Chuck and Larry* as simplistic and homophobic, queer theory can be used to reveal its more complex ideological landscape, one that seemingly endorses sexism and racism even as it pleads for the acceptance of (male) homosexuals into its patriarchal milieu. Arguably, Chuck and Larry "celebrates" macho homosexual love as just another version of patriarchal homosocial love, a negotiation that still maintains the hegemony of white patriarchal capitalism.

Ultimately, queer theory rejects all either-or binaries, whether they be those used to classify sexualities or those simplistically used to judge cultural artifacts as progressive or reactionary. Over the last twenty years, queer theory has been instrumental in changing the cinematic landscape—not just from a production standpoint (New Queer Cinema and its more recent incarnations) but also from a reception standpoint. In examining and exposing the connections between cinematic discourses of gender, sexuality, race, class region, etc., queer film theory implicitly examines and exposes how those structures work in the real world as well. By challenging all of these ideological assumptions in new ways, queer theory continues (and continues to expand) the rich critical projects of previous generations. Like the Marxist, feminist, and LGBT film theorists who came before, queer theorists are committed to changing the cinematic landscape—and by extension the social, cultural, and political landscapes—into ones that are truly more egalitarian.

works cited

Aaron, Michele, ed. *New Queer Cinema: A Critical Reader*. Edinburgh: Edinburgh University Press, 2004.

Bad Object-Choices, ed. *How Do I Look? Queer Film and Video*. Seattle: Bay Press, 1991.

Benshoff, Harry M. *Monsters in the Closet: Homosexuality and the Horror Film*. Manchester and New York: Manchester University Press, 1997.

Butler, Judith. *Gender Trouble: Feminism and the Subversion of Identity*. New York: Routledge, 1990.

Carpenter, Dale. "The Other Side of the *Mountain*." *TXT Newsmagazine*, 23 December 2005: 13.

Chauncey, George. *Gay New York: Gender, Urban Culture and the Making of the Gay Male World 1890–1940*. New York: BasicBooks, 1994.

Creekmur, Corey and Alexander Doty, eds. *Out in Culture: Gay, Lesbian, and Queer Essays on Popular Culture*. Durham, NC: Duke University Press, 1995.

de Lauretis, Teresa ed. "Queer Theory: Lesbian and Gay Sexualities." Special volume of *differences* 3:2 (1991).

D'Emilio, John, and Estelle B. Freedman. *Intimate Matters: A History of Sexuality in America*. New York: Harper & Row, 1988.

Dixon, Wheeler Winston. *Straight: Constructions of Heterosexuality in the Cinema*. New York: State University of New York Press, 2003.

Doty, Alexander. *Flaming Classics: Queering the Film Canon*. New York: Routledge, 2000.

———. *Making Things Perfectly Queer: Interpreting Mass Culture*. Minneapolis: University of Minnesota Press, 1993.

Duggan, Lisa. "Making It Perfectly Queer." In *Sex Wars: Sexual Dissent and Political Culture*, ed. Lisa Duggan and Nan D. Hunter. New York: Routledge, 1995, 155–172.

Dyer, Richard. *The Culture of Queers*. New York: Routledge, 2002.

———. *The Matter of Images: Essays on Representation*, Second Edition. New York: Routledge, 2002 (1993).

Farmer, Brett. *Spectacular Passions: Cinema, Fantasy, Gay Male Spectatorships*. Durham, NC: Duke University Press, 2000.

Floyd, Jacquielynn. "*Brokeback* Ignores Plight of Spouses." *Dallas Morning News* 20 January 2006: 1–2B.

Foucault, Michel. *The History of Sexuality, Vol. 1: An Introduction*. Trans. Robert Hurley. New York: Vintage Books, 1990 (1977).

Fuss, Diana, ed. *Inside/out: Lesbian Theories, Gay Theories*. New York: Routledge, 1991.

Gever, Martha, with John Greyson and Pratibha Parmar, eds. *Queer Looks: Perspectives on Lesbian and Gay Visibility*. New York: Routledge, 1993.

Goodridge, Mike. "Gay and Lesbian Films: Coming Out Soon." *Screen International* 2 July 2004, 12–14.

Griffin, Sean. *Tinker Belles and Evil Queens. The Walt Disney Company From the Inside Out*. New York: New York University Press, 2000.

Groth, Lyndsey. "On *Brokeback Mountain*: Why Chicks Go For This Gay Male Flick." Unpublished paper.

Hanson, Ellis, ed. *Out Takes: Essays on Queer Theory and Film*. Durham, NC: Duke University Press, 1999.

Hocquenghem, Guy. *Homosexual Desire*. Daniella Dangoor, trans., Durham, NC: Duke University Press, 1993 (1978).

Katz, Jonathan Ned. *The Invention of Heterosexuality*. New York: Dutton, 1995.

Kusner, Daniel A. "Marketing *Brokeback*." *Dallas Voice* 23 December 2005: 37.

Mayne, Judith. *Directed by Dorothy Arzner*. Bloomington: Indiana University Press, 1994.

Mendelsohn, Daniel. "An Affair to Remember." *The New York Review* 23 February 2006: 12–13.

Proulx, Annie. *Brokeback Mountain: Story to Screenplay*. New York, Scribner, 2006.

Russo, Vito. *The Celluloid Closet: Homosexuality in the Movies*. Revised Edition, New York: Harper & Row, Publishers, 1987 (1981).

Sedgwick, Eve Kosofsky. *Between Men: English Literature and Male Homosocial Desire*. New York: Columbia University Press, 1985.

———. *The Epistemology of the Closet*. Berkeley: University of California Press, 1990.

Sullivan, Nikki. *A Critical Introduction to Queer Theory*. New York: New York University Press, 2003.

Thomas, Calvin. *Straight with a Twist: Queer Theory and the Subject of Heterosexuality*. Chicago: University of Illinois Press, 2000.

Walters, Suzanna Danuta. *All The Rage: The Story of Gay Visibility in America*. Chicago: University of Chicago Press, 2001.

Warner, Michael. *The Trouble With Normal: Sex, Politics and the Ethics of Queer Life.* Cambridge, MA: Harvard University Press, 1999.

Weeks, Jeffrey. *Sexuality and Its Discontents.* London: Routledge, 1989.

Wittig, Monique. *The Straight Mind and Other Essays.* Boston: Beacon Press, 1992.

Yingling, Thomas E. "Homosexuality and the Uncanny: What's Fishy in Lacan." *The Gay '90s: Disciplinary and Interdisciplinary Formations in Queer Studies.* Ed. Thomas Foster, Carol Siegel and Ellen E. Berry. New York: New York University Press, 1997.

demystifying
deleuze

french

philosophy

meets

contemporary

u.s. cinema*

d a v i d   m a r t i n - j o n e s

During the 1980s, French philosopher Gilles Deleuze wrote two books on cinema, *Cinema 1: The Movement-Image* (1983), and *Cinema 2: The Time-Image* (1985). For some scholars working in Anglo-American film studies, Deleuze's works appear to be throwbacks to the "bad old days" of the 1970s and early 1980s, when high theory dominated the field. Deleuze's at time dense and complicated texts are often criticized for being impenetrable, too focused on auteur cinema, and only applicable to European art films. By contrast, this chapter unpacks Deleuze's film philosophy to demonstrate its usefulness for analyzing contemporary US cinema, both in its mainstream and alternative, independent forms.

Firstly, the Hollywood rom-com *Fifty First Dates* (2004) is examined, to provide an understanding of the route into mainstream films offered by Deleuze's philosophy. *Fifty First Dates* falls somewhere in between Deleuze's categories of the movement-image and the time-image. When analysed in relation to these categories it provides valuable insights into both the

---

* Thanks to Philip Drake for his invaluable help with my initial research into the Hollywood rom-com.

development of the incredibly popular genre of the rom-com, and its ability to negotiate issues pertinent to contemporary US society. In the second half of the chapter, the very different idea of "minor cinema" is examined. The concept of minor cinema is typically used to discuss films from Africa, South America, or peripheral European countries. Here, however, it is applied to Gregg Araki's *The Doom Generation* (1995) to illustrate how Deleuze's philosophy offers a new approach to the analysis of alternative US cinema. In both instances, the advantages of using Deleuze's philosophy is that it retains the "engaged interventionist analysis" (Collins et al. 3) of film theory in the 1970s and 1980s, but is still applicable to these US movies of the 1990s and 2000s.

deleuze's images

Deleuze's philosophical project is complex and sophisticated, and for the purposes of this discussion it is not necessary to understand its every detail. Rather I will explore the broad distinction Deleuze draws between movement-image and time-image. Deleuze's discussion of the movement-image in *Cinema 1* initially draws on a number of European film movements, before concluding with a discussion of the movement-image in Hollywood. Thus the epitome of the movement-image is found in Hollywood's classical narrative form, that which Deleuze calls the "action-image" (*Cinema 1* 141). The movement-image, and in particular the action-image, is characterized by the unbroken sensory-motor continuity of its protagonists. In other words, in the movement-image characters are able to act in order to influence their situation, usually to their advantage. Accordingly, the time of the narrative is edited around the actions of the protagonist. As all moviegoers know, in mainstream films, events taking place in days, weeks, months or even years are compressed in this way. No matter how many different locations a film visits, continuity is created by the actions of characters whose stories we follow. Therefore, in the movement-image we see an indirect image of time, of time subordinate to movement. Moreover, in the movement-image time is predominantly linear, with the outcome of the narrative (the bad guy dies, the world is saved, the couple get together) coherent with the logic of the narrative world. Because we are following the story of a particular protagonist or protagonists, the time span of their story is also the time span of the film. Therefore, in order for the film to finish, the narrative requires the characters to resolve whatever crises they face. This inevitability Deleuze described as the movement from situation, through action, to changed situation (SAS'). This formula relies entirely on the protagonist's unbroken sensory-motor continuity, their ability to act decisively in whatever situations they may find themselves in.

In contrast to the movement-image there is the time-image. Most typically found in European art films (for instance in the works of *auteurs* such as Jean-Luc Godard, Alain Resnais, Federico Fellini, Michelangelo Antonioni,

Andrei Tarkovsky or Theo Angelopoulos), the time-image is characterized by a disruption of the protagonist's sensory-motor continuity. Unable to physically react to events in order to influence their situation, protagonists in the time-image begin to wander without a definite sense of purpose or goal. Indeed, it is not unusual for the time-image's seers to move virtually within time. Hence in *Cinema 2* Deleuze broadly differentiated between the protagonists of these two types of cinemas as the "doers" of the movement-image, and the "seers" of the time-image (2). In the time-image, then, we see a direct image of time, of time's virtual movement, rather than the indirect view of time (time spatialized by character movement) seen in the movement-image.

This direct image of time usually takes one of two forms. In the films of Antonioni or Angelopoulos the time-image emerges in the extended long take. For instance, the camera may linger over landscapes, without a moving character to guide the viewer's gaze. This ensures that the passing of time is experienced in its own right. In the films of Fellini or Resnais by contrast, disruptive movements occur within time, often when a character slips into reminiscence about the past. Here memory plays a key role as we witness a character's virtual movement within time. In these instances, editing becomes discontinuous, and does not provide a logical progression of events, as disconnected spaces pass before our eyes without the agency of a character to provide us with a linear temporal focus. These spaces may be from different periods in time (past, present, future), and—as is the case in films from *L'année dernière à Marienbad* (1961) to *Eternal Sunshine of the Spotless Mind* (2004)—the viewer may or may not be able to reconstruct this time-line easily. Accordingly, in the time-image, time is often labyrinthine and there is a greater sense of the malleability of historical "truth." As characters slip through time there is the possibility that revisiting the past can change or falsify it, even if only by enabling the reconsideration of a previous memory. Alternatively, events in the present can shed new light on the past, making previous events, or memories of them, suddenly seem "untrue." In the time-image, then, there is far less of an expectation that events in the narrative world will be entirely coherent than there is in the movement-image. Moreover, as the protagonist's sensory-motor continuity has been disrupted, and they are no longer able to act decisively in order to influence their situation, the resolution of the narrative trajectory SAS' may either be subject to a prolonged suspension, or even indefinitely postponed.

For the purposes of this discussion, these definitions of Deleuze's image categories are painted with very broad strokes. In fact, Deleuze's philosophical approach to cinema is so fascinating because it maps together an unusual number of different types of cinema under the heading of the movement-image, including not only classical Hollywood, but also French Impressionist, German Expressionist and Soviet montage filmmaking. Indeed, in *Cinema 2* Deleuze expanded his discussion of the time-image beyond the European new waves, to incorporate filmmakers from countries as far afield as Senegal and Brazil. Even so, reading the two cinema books it becomes clear that Deleuze conceived of the movement-image as a "classical" foil to the seemingly more innovative, "modern" cinemas of the post-war era (essentially the various New Waves), in which the time-image emerged. In the 1990s and 2000s, however, mainstream cinemas around the world have begun to produce films that are, broadly speaking, hybrids of Deleuze's two image categories. As has been noted elsewhere, more often than not these are movement-images which have incorporated aspects of the time-image (Pisters; Martin-Jones, *Deleuze, Cinema*). Thus, as I will now demonstrate by examining *Fifty First Dates*, the status of the contemporary Hollywood movement-image is in need of reconsideration, to enable a broader understanding of the way it constructs narrative time, and the ends to which it does so.

deleuze and the rom-com: fifty first dates (2004)

Fifty First Dates is set in Hawaii, and is the story of Henry Roth (Adam Sandler) a young veterinarian specializing in marine wildlife and seducing young female holidaymakers. Although afraid of commitment, he is also growing bored of his playboy lifestyle, and hopes to sail to Bristol Bay, Alaska, to study walruses. When his recently repaired yacht breaks apart during a test run, Henry runs into Lucy Whitmore (Drew Barrymore) in a local diner. Lucy has a short-term memory loss condition brought on by an automobile accident. As a result she cannot remember the recent past and wakes up every day thinking it is the morning of the day of the accident. As each new day is wiped clean by a good night's sleep, Henry is required to seduce her anew every morning. With the support of Lucy's father, Marlin (Blake Clark) and younger brother, Doug (Sean Astin), Henry hits on a plan to enable Lucy to live a meaningful life, and "remember" her ongoing relationship with him. He video records their relationship, splicing together this footage with factual news reports of significant events she has missed since the accident, and leaves her a tape to watch each morning. The videotape repeatedly restores her memories since the accident, their romance blooms, and the end of the film sees Henry, Lucy, their two children, and grandfather Marlin on Henry's restored boat, all together in Alaska.

Fifty First Dates is a romantic-comedy. Historically one of the most popular genres in US cinema, the rom-com actually dates back several centuries to pre-cinematic origins in the European Renaissance (Evans and Deleyto 3). In *Creating the Couple* (1993), Virginia Wright Wexman charts the development of the genre, noting that its contemporary manifestation upholds "the validation of romance as a key to individual identity" (13). In other words, the fulfilment of romantic love in the rom-com is the goal towards

217

which all people strive in order to become complete. However, the genre is also noted for perpetually stalling the process through which the couple comes together, keeping them apart for as long as possible in order to maintain audience interest in their potential union (Neale and Krutnik 136–48). Seen in a Deleuzian light, in classics of the genre such as *It Happened One Night* (1934) and *Bringing Up Baby* (1938), the forestalling of the romantic union relies upon the temporary suspension of the protagonist's ability to turn perception into meaningful action. In *It Happened One Night* the recently unemployed Peter Warne (Clark Gable) and the independently minded heiress Ellie Andrews (Claudette Colbert) take a diversionary road trip, throughout which their lack of control over their movements reflects the loss of direction from which each of their lives suffers. Similarly, in *Bringing Up Baby*, David Huxley (Cary Grant) is forever being distracted from his objective (the recovery of the brontosaurus bone and his imminent marriage) by the impetuous Susan Vance (Katharine Hepburn). Here again the narrative's progress towards resolution is effectively one long circuitous detour, during which David is drawn into a series of increasingly humorous comedic situations over which he is unable to assert any kind of authority through his own actions. In both instances, sensory-motor continuity is disrupted, or temporarily suspended for the majority of the film. In purely formal terms, then, there is a large degree of narrative suspension between the initial situation and the eventual, changed situation (S-S'), which enables the creation of comedic spectacle. In this sense these movement-images begin to display qualities normally found in the time-image, as their characters suffer a degree of suspension to their sensory-motor continuity that begins to verge on that of the wandering "seers" of the time-image.

To a large degree the same is true of *Fifty First Dates*. In an early scene, Henry, testing out his newly repaired yacht the *Sea Serpent*, momentarily loses control when the mast breaks, swings across the deck and knocks the ship's wheel overboard. Due to this set back Henry winds up having breakfast in the same diner as Lucy. As the narrative then proceeds to chart Henry's various attempts to seduce Lucy with each new day, we witness the sustained sensory-motor disruption of the rom-com. Unable to captain his own ship and take off for Alaska, Henry is caught in a moment of sensory-motor discontinuity. Each day he is forced to invent new and amusing ways of attracting Lucy's attention, and yet each night he returns to square one. However, in *Fifty First Dates*, the obstacles that we expect to find in the path of a couple on their way to romantic fulfilment are also self-consciously toyed with through the introduction of Lucy's unusual memory condition. For this reason *Fifty First Dates* takes a step closer to the time-image than its predecessors, enabling Deleuze's approach to cinema (with its focus on memory and time) to become a particularly useful tool for analysing the film. Time, for Lucy at least, is shown to be labyrinthine.

Each day her life is literally reinvented, rendering the events of the previous day "untrue." Lucy's state of mind leaves her unable to extend perception into action (to restore her sensory-motor continuity), as she remains trapped repeating the same day in perpetuity. Thus the entire course of the film, from Henry's initial attempts to sail away, to the culmination of this desire in the final moments in Alaska, provides the diversionary narrative we expect of the rom-com's particular form of the movement-image, but is also a suspended moment in time which verges on the time-image. The narrative of *Fifty First Dates* is caught somewhere in between movement- and time-image, in a suspended moment where, for the most part, characters' actions are unable to change a situation for the better as they would in the movement-image, yet without their being as entirely incapacitated as characters in the time-image.

Ultimately the narrative arc of *Fifty First Dates* tends towards resolution, as is typical of the movement-image. After all, its protagonists are eventually able to overcome their situation through decisive action. Henry, giving up his playboy lifestyle for Lucy, becomes an effective ship's captain. Lucy for her part has the continuity of her life restored to her, and becomes a mother. However, along the way *Fifty First Dates* derives much of its comedy, and indeed, romantic suspense, from the extended pause it creates between its characters' desires and their ability to fulfil them. Put another way, using Deleuze's terms it is possible to see how aspects of the time-image invade the movement-image in *Fifty First Dates*, rendering far more literal than usual the process of sensory-motor disruption that has been a generic characteristic of rom-coms since *It Happened One Night* and *Bringing up Baby*. To return to Wright Wexman's quote, in the rom-com "the validation of romance as a key to individual identity," ensures that the characters are only able to find fulfilment through romantic involvement with another. In *Fifty First Dates*, together with this restoration of identity, comes the resolution of the film into the movement-image. In the interim, time is effectively suspended until both characters can be "cured" of their respective shortcomings by romantic love. Thus, for the duration of the film, time is distended as the time-image momentarily takes control, only for the movement-image to reinsert itself with the narrative's resolution.

So far this application of Deleuze's work to the rom-com has demonstrated both its usefulness for examining US popular genre films, and indeed, one of the drawbacks of Deleuze's conclusions. As this brief analysis of *Fifty First Dates* demonstrates, the time-image does not just exist in European art cinemas that construct narratives different to those of Hollywood. Rather, the time-image exists as part of a dynamic interplay with the movement-image, an interplay that to some extent has always been a part of certain classical Hollywood genres, like the rom-com. Moreover, in addition to this understanding of how time is constructed in *Fifty First Dates*, Deleuze's image categories can also help us to understand how the temporally interrupted narrative malaise through which Henry and Lucy wander is deployed to negotiate national identity.

deleuze and history

From Steve Neale and Frank Krutnik in 1990 to Celestino Deleyto in 2003, the cinematic rom-com has been examined as a genre that, whilst thematically consistent, has emerged in a number of different guises in response to changing social conditions in the twentieth and twenty-first centuries. This process is most obvious in such turbulent historical moments as the 1930s—when screwball comedies like *It Happened One Night* combined romance and comedy to examine class and economic inequalities thrown into the public eye by the depression—or the so called "nervous" and neo-conservative romances of the 1970s and 1980s, as they respectively negotiated increasing divorce rates and burgeoning female economic independence. To begin with, then, we need to understand a little more about why *Fifty First Dates* chooses to explore memory reconstruction in the wake of a physical trauma, during the early years of the twenty-first century.

One way of analysing *Fifty First Dates* is to position it within a broader trend of US films that attempt to make sense of events following 9/11. Not least of these was the Adam Sandler comedy *Anger Management* (2003), which explored the emotional torment of its protagonist Dave Buznik (Sandler) in the context of post 9/11 New York where the inhabitants struggled to express their pent-up rage and frustration. Admittedly, one might be forgiven for immediately thinking that, unlike the New York based *Anger Management*, a feel good rom-com set in Hawaii has very little to do with 9/11. Yet, although *Fifty First Dates* does not explicitly mention 9/11, as Philip John Davies and Paul Wells note in *American Film and Politics from Reagan to Bush Jr* (2000), it is not unusual for a Hollywood film to provide a very oblique, or disguised discussion of contemporary events, smuggling politics in under the cover of an otherwise innocent looking plot (7–9). As a concrete example of this process, let us briefly consider *Fifty First Dates*'s most obvious predecessor, *Groundhog Day* (1993).

Another extremely popular rom-com (although with a greater emphasis on the "com" than the "rom"), the narrative of *Groundhog Day* undoubtedly influenced *Fifty First Dates*. *Groundhog Day*'s story concerns cynical weatherman Phil Connors (Bill Murray) who becomes magically trapped in Punxsutawney, a small American town reminiscent of Bedford Falls in Frank Capra's *It's a Wonderful Life* (1946). Connors is doomed to repeatedly live out the same day in Punxsutawney until he can reconsider his selfish life, reconstruct his masculinity, and win the love of female colleague Rita (Andie MacDowell). In this way *Groundhog Day* creates the same sense of temporal hiatus evident in *Fifty First Dates*, again taking to its temporal limits the genre's technique of stalling the inevitable moment of narrative and romantic resolution.

In 1995, analyzing *Groundhog Day* alongside *Falling Down* (1993), Jude Davies argued that:

> Produced after the 1992 Los Angeles riots, they leave intact, and add strength to, a white patriarchal discourse of crisis itself. Both *Falling Down* and *Groundhog Day* take the moment of crisis for granted, and narrativize male responses to a historical moment. As a result, the construction of crisis itself is rarely presented in either film as something that can be contested. (229)

Like *Fifty First Dates*, at first glance *Groundhog Day* does not seem to have anything meaningful to say about contemporary political events. Yet, Davies notes, its saccharine small town setting is prefigured by a passing reference to "continued gang warfare in California" (224) and the increased presence of sex and violence in the media. The former social problem is explicitly noted by Connors during his opening weather forecast. For Davies, then, the story of Connors' redemption in Punxsutawney is posited by the film as "some sort of resolution of these social and cultural problems" (225). Although apparently divorced from harsh social realities, *Groundhog Day* obliquely engages with them, in spite of its utopian setting. In fact, *Groundhog Day*'s escape into a fantasy of the US's small town past facilitates an examination of possible cultural solutions to a perceived national crisis whilst conveniently sidestepping the "economic considerations" (227) and class concerns that actually accompany issues such as urban gang warfare. Thus the crisis is reconfigured as that of the lost authority of normative white masculinity in the 1990s, and Connors' reconstruction as a more sensitive "New Man" is offered as the solution. Something extremely similar occurs in *Fifty First Dates*, where contemporary events are again referenced in passing, and seemingly unconnected events in Hawaii offered as a solution to these problems.

When Henry first plays Lucy his homemade videotape he contextualizes their personal romantic narrative through a brief montage of major historical events (major at least from a US perspective) that she has missed since her accident. These include everything from Snoop Doggy Dogg briefly giving up weed to Arnold Schwarzenegger's election as Governor of California. Noticeably the second of these images is a shot of the statue of Saddam Hussein in Firdos Square, Baghdad, being hauled down by the US military in April 2003. There are two significant points to note about this image. Firstly this is an iconic image that very briefly encapsulates the US military's involvement in Iraq after 9/11. Secondly, it is not an image of 9/11, which for the US was the most important political event of the 2000s. We must presume, therefore, that Lucy, like the nation, has no difficulty remembering this particular traumatic event. In *Fifty First Dates*, the moment of national crisis of 9/11 is left unspoken and unseen, even though the aftermath of the crisis is evident in the fall of the statue of Saddam Hussein. Thus, like *Falling Down* and *Groundhog Day*, *Fifty First Dates* also "takes the moment of crisis for granted," and like *Groundhog Day*, focuses instead on creating a comedic and romantic response to it, set in a utopian context. This time, however, rather than a fantasy of small town life in the US, the utopian context is Hawaii. It is therefore possible to consider *Fifty First Dates* as an attempt to obliquely engage with the crisis following 9/11, with Lucy's personal trauma standing in for the nation's trauma in the wake of the national crisis.

In the videotape, major historical events that followed 9/11 are evoked to illustrate that the nation has moved on since the crisis. Lucy, however, remains lost in the past until Henry arrives. Through the visual medium of the videotape he is able to construct, almost in the manner of a newsreel, her personal narrative in the wake of both her personal crisis and 9/11. If we return to Deleuze's image categories at this point their usefulness for interpreting this situation is again apparent. It is noticeable that Lucy's two states of being are rendered using the two different images. Stalled in the past and physically unable to move on, Lucy lives a perpetual time-image. Like Connors in *Groundhog Day*, she is doomed to live one day repeatedly, although unlike Connors she is unaware that she is trapped in this way, and needs Henry's assistance to free herself. Forever unable to act in order to resolve her own personal narrative, she inhabits a prolonged moment of sensory-motor suspension like the incapacitated seer of the time-image. Only through the continuous narrative constructed by the movement-image (the videotape's narrative of events after her accident) is Lucy's narrative restored to her. The time-image is used, then, to illustrate how a nation's day to day life in the wake of a crisis like 9/11 must be rejuvenated, or else, like Lucy, the nation will face an eternity in sensory-motor limbo. This return to decisive action necessitates a conscious will to repair the nation, and thereby ensure the consistency of identity needed to act. Rather than waking every new day and forgetting there is a crisis—as the Hawaiian setting suggests, the equivalent of a state of perpetual vacation— *Fifty First Dates* advocates the need to be constantly reminded of events since 9/11, as only this narrative of progression can provide a platform on which the nation can rebuild.

Through the videotape *Fifty First Dates* also obliquely points to the need for continued watchfulness over the way the immediate past is remembered and reconstructed. The linear narrative of the tape specifically posits the movement-image—the dominant form of US cinema—as the ultimate form in which the truth of the past can be retained and the nation saved from the malaise of inaction illustrated by the time-image. This emphasis on cinema's ability to record an "accurate" account of history is further emphasised in the film by the privileging of the home video over Lucy's notebooks, which she symbolically burns when she breaks up with Henry, deliberately erasing her memories of him from her past. Despite their absence, she is unable to forget the memory of Henry, and ultimately returns to a visual record of her lover by obsessively painting his image as it emerges to haunt her dreams. Ultimately the video replaces the journal in the film's conclusion, demonstrating its supposedly greater accuracy as an informed historical record of the past.

The legitimacy of the movement-image as the only real cure for this malaise is further reiterated by the presence of a videotape of *The Sixth Sense* (1999), which Lucy has bought for her father's birthday. *The Sixth Sense* is a ghost story about a child psychologist, Dr Malcolm Crowe (Bruce Willis) who, not realizing he is dead, haunts a supernaturally gifted child medium, Cole Sear (Haley Joel Osment). When Cole is visited by a ghost of a young girl, Crowe and Cole together uncover the truth about her murder at the hands of her mother. This murder was recorded on videotape, the playing of which at her funeral brings justice to bear on the murderous mother and saves the remaining little sister from a similar fate. It also enables Crowe to come to terms with his own demise, and Cole to grow into his role as, as it were, "ghost psychologist." Thus, in *The Sixth Sense* a videotape restores continuity to the past (by solving the mystery surrounding the little girl's murder) just as Lucy's personal videotape does in *Fifty First Dates*. Whilst Lucy's daily memory of a different meeting with Henry evokes the discontinuous experience of time typical of a time-image, not to mention its ability to constantly falsify the past, the video Henry creates for her—like the video in *The Sixth Sense*—returns continuity to her life, restoring her memories by creating the linear narrative of the movement-image.

Thus, for a nation seeking to understand events in the wake of 9/11, reference to the traumatic reality of the contemporary crisis is nearly entirely absent from *Fifty First Dates*. Yet as in *Groundhog Day*, this enables a seemingly unconnected examination of apparently culturally necessary factors—in this case the need to formulate a coherent national narrative stemming from a crisis in the recent past—using visual media like the movies, in order to facilitate the nation's return to action seen in the war in Iraq.

There are several other ways in which *Fifty First Dates*'s construction of a model of time suggestive of the time-image enhances this reading of the film. These include the unproductive malaise represented in Henry's playboy lifestyle, his constant failure to get his yacht back on the water, and the continual repetition of one lazy Sunday morning breakfast in Hawaii. This sense of Henry's bachelorhood existing outside of a meaningfully linear time (the time of the movement-image) is conflated with Lucy's condition, suggesting that both their lives are an unnatural, or unhealthy state that needs to be "cured" by romance. This understanding of the film resonates with the broader concerns of many contemporary rom-coms, which,

Diane Negra has noted, express "an increasing interest in the single man" as though he were a social problem in need of a solution. Negra's observations are drawn from the early twenty-first century context in which anxiety surrounds the usefulness of men in contemporary society (and the need to recuperate their productivity within a heterosexual couple), as seen in films like *Failure to Launch* (2006). Hence, from a Deleuzian perspective, the interrupted wandering of protagonists caught in the sensory-motor interruption of the time-image is rendered an unnatural or unhealthy state of being when it is conflated with Henry's bachelorhood and Lucy's memory loss. It is the movement-image, whether videotape or the rom-com more generally, that offers a meaningful solution to this contemporary social issue.

In conclusion, *Fifty First Dates* is a self-conscious work of fantasy (the song which accompanies the end is Somewhere Over the Rainbow from *The Wizard of Oz* 1939) in which the interplay between movement-image and time-image operates to create an Hawaiian holiday in which a most unlikely romance can blossom, only for normality to be restored and the characters "cured" by the return of the movement-image. At the same time, however, it obliquely engages with the perceived need for the US nation to return to action after 9/11, and the integral role that the movies can play in this process. These two uses of a temporal model typical of the time-image, both to construct the necessary narrative malaise for the prolonged narrative suspension typical of the rom-com and to obliquely consider a moment of national crisis, are inextricably linked in *Fifty First Dates*. Much as romance is the "key to individual identity" in the rom-com, so too is it the guarantor of the nation's return to normality. For this reason, the film's generic return of the movement-image to prominence in its conclusion—after its extended, comic exploration of the malaise of the time-image—enables both the couple and the nation to attain fulfilment. Deleuze's ideas, then, are apparently useful for analysing mainstream genre movies, in particular because they enable us to unlock layers of meaning in films like *Fifty First Dates* which may otherwise be passed over by more traditional approaches to Hollywood films. This was the case, for instance, in Tamar Jeffers McDonald's recent book, *Romantic Comedy: Boy Meets Girl Meets Genre* (2007), which was unable to get to grips with this particular film, dismissing it with the briefest of passing comments as "rather unconvincing" due to its inability to conform to the same parameters as the majority of recent urban based rom-coms (89). By contrast, as I have shown, there is a great deal to be said of *Fifty First Dates* if we examine it through a Deleuzian filter.

minor u.s. cinema

By now we have seen how Deleuze's notion of the movement-image from *Cinema 1* enhances our understanding of the way time and memory function in mainstream US cinema. As a contrast, I now turn to the concept of minor cinema, an idea that developed out of Deleuze's work on the time-image in *Cinema 2*.

Towards the end of *Cinema 2*, Deleuze introduced the term, "modern political cinema" (218) to describe the works of filmmakers from countries like Turkey, Egypt, Brazil, Quebec (Canada) and Senegal in Africa. Often these were marginalized filmmakers—such as Yilmaz Güney, Youssef Chahine, Glauber Rocha, Pierre Perrault and Ousmane Sembene—who were either globally marginal, or who produced films outside of the mainstream production and distribution centres. Modern political cinema was concerned with the fact that, as Deleuze put it, "*the people are missing*" (216). By this he meant that, in contrast to Soviet montage, classical Hollywood and other such classical cinemas, in modern political cinema there was no existing, coherent concept of "the people." Often this was because modern political cinema was created in situations where the identity of the people was contested, such as in countries ruled by military dictatorships, or in emergent post-colonial countries. These filmmakers, then, were attempting to imagine, or create a concept of the people that could be politically effective in revolutionizing, rebuilding or reshaping a country.

For anyone familiar with Deleuze's previous works, modern political cinema is immediately reminiscent of a previous idea that he developed with his long time friend and collaborator, Félix Guattari. In a book they co-wrote on Franz Kafka, *Kafka: Towards a Minor Literature* (1975), Deleuze and Guattari outlined a concept which they called a minor literature. A minor literature was written using a dominant language, but this language was (mis)used in such a way that it began to speak in a different voice, to stutter, stammer or wail. Kafka was their preferred example because he was a Czechoslovakian Jew who lived in Prague during the time of the Austro-Hungarian Empire. For Deleuze and Guattari, Kafka took the dominant imperial language (German) and, in his distinctive literature, pronounced it in a very minor way. A minor language, then, is not necessarily minor in the sense of minority. Rather, it should be understood as minor in a musical sense. A minor work takes a dominant language, and plays it in a minor key, making it sound altogether different, and potentially challenging its established and accepted meanings. Deleuze's concept of modern political cinema owes a great deal to this notion of the minor. Accordingly, David Rodowick, the first film studies scholar to write a book dedicated to Deleuze, *Gilles Deleuze's Time Machine* (1997), used a Deleuzian analysis to describe certain works by Senegalese filmmaker Ousmane Sembene—whose cinema is dedicated to exploring and questioning the changing face of post-colonial Africa—as works of "minor cinema" (153). Thus, modern political, or minor cinema is potentially subversive, and has the ability to challenge accepted norms, especially as they are propagated in mainstream cinemas.

For Deleuze there were three ways of identifying this subversive mode of cinema. The first was the aforementioned attempt to imagine or create a vision of "the people" that might function as a future basis on which to manufacture a sustainable identity for a community or nation. The second was the blurring or blending of spaces created in these cinemas, which reflected the erasure of established divisions between public and private spaces. Such a blurring of public and private typically occurs when a minority people come under the surveillance of a majority. Characters in works of minor cinema often inhabit the margins of society, and their private actions (forever under scrutiny by the surveillance of the centre) cannot help but have public ramifications. Third and finally, minor cinema self-consciously plays with the possible identities that might emerge in a people yet to come, either by refusing to specifically fix on one preferred hero or character type, and indeed, by exploring the artistic process through which fictional identities are created. This latter practice, although at times making for a rather stylized aesthetic (as though replaying normative images but in ironic quotation marks), asks the audience to question the way in which identities, and particularly negative stereotypes, are constructed in mainstream films.

For film theory, minor cinema's most obvious advantage is that it offers a way of understanding subversive or critical political cinemas. In this respect it may initially seem similar to the idea of "third cinema," a broadly defined term which has been used to refer to a number of revolutionary and post-colonial cinema that emerged in the 1960s, in particular in parts of South America and Africa (Espinosa; Solanas and Gettino; Gabriel; Pines and Willeman). Indeed, one director very often discussed in terms of third cinema is Ousmane Sembene. In brief, third cinema is an intellectually—as opposed to emotionally—engaging mode of filmmaking. It is considered distinct from the escapist spectacles of first cinema (e.g. Hollywood) and the nostalgic emphasis on the past of second cinema (the national-industrial, often state sponsored model). Instead third cinema directly engages, in a combative manner, with present day issues of relevance to the people of the nation. In order to do so effectively, third cinema actively seeks out various alternative sources of funding, producing cinema in a low budget, artisanal way, such that meaning is not pre-determined by the ideological agendas of the film's backers.

Minor cinema shares third cinema's concern over the manner in which dominant forms of cinema represent political issues, and construct identities. However, the most crucial difference between the two ideas is that minor cinema does not place as much emphasis on an artisanal mode of production as third cinema does. Partly as a consequence of this, the term minor cinema can also be applied to any number of cinemas outside of revolutionary, post-colonial or third world situations. For instance, Deleuze begins his discussion of modern political cinema with an exploration of

French filmmakers like Alain Resnais, Jean Rouch and Jean-Marie Straub. Perhaps due to this greater degree of applicability, Deleuze's work on minor cinema is currently the most widely applied of his ideas in film studies. Examples include not only Rodowick's work on African cinema, but also women's cinema as minor cinema (Butler), diasporic and exilic filmmaking in a number of first world contexts (Marks; Naficy), and small cinemas in, amongst other locations, Quebec (Marshall), Denmark (Hjort) and Scotland (Martin-Jones, *Orphans*).

Even so, the idea of a minor US cinema may seem a little contradictory, as it is often in tacit opposition to the global dominance of Hollywood that the notion of a minor cinema is evoked. Yet independent US cinema in general does offer the potential to be minor, especially (if you will forgive the pun) in relation to the Hollywood majors. For instance, in *Cinema 2* Deleuze briefly mentions African-American indie cinema of the 1970s, with passing reference to filmmakers Charles Burnett, Robert Gardner, Haile Gerima, and Charles Lane (220). Alternatively consider Butler's exploration of the role of memory in relation to diasporic identities in Julie Dash's contemporary US indie, *Daughters of the Dust* (1993) (112–15). It is noticeable that in both instances the racial aspect of these US films ensures that they play the major voice of US cinema in a minor way. As I will now demonstrate through an analysis of a work of New Queer Cinema, *The Doom Generation*, a cinematic examination of sexuality can also open the way for a minor US cinema.

the doom generation (1995)

The Doom Generation is an irreverently funny road movie, set in California, about three teenaged slackers, Amy Blue (Rose McGowan), Jordan White (James Duval) and Xavier Red (Jonathan Schaech). Amy and Jordan are a couple until Xavier comes along and they begin to explore their sexual potential as a threesome. They embark on a murder spree after Xavier accidentally kills a Korean Quickie Mart proprietor, and are pursued by the FBI and a number of Amy's ex-lovers. The film's violent ending depicts the rape of Amy on a US flag (including penetration by a statue of the Virgin Mary) by a thug with a huge Swastika painted on his chest. This shocking event takes place to the sound of the US national anthem. It is shortly followed by the castration of Jordan, and then a bloodbath as Amy kills the rapist and his companions. The final shot is of Amy and Xavier driving away together.

The Doom Generation was Araki's fifth feature film. It was made on a budget of $1m, most of which came from French sources (Macnab 38). In many respects it develops themes explored in *The Living End* (1992), an earlier low budget road movie ($22 700) about two gay men with AIDS (King; Mills). Although Araki ironically subtitles *The Doom Generation* "A Heterosexual

Movie by Gregg Araki," it is in actual fact an exploration of how hetero-sexual norms can be challenged by minor sexual practices. This is unsurprising, as director Gregg Araki belongs to a film movement that emerged in the early 1990s, known as New Queer Cinema (Davis), a movement distinctive in its questioning of the politics of representing sexual identity. Indeed, this use of the road movie to explore different identities is not unusual either. In his contribution to *The Road Movie Book* (1997), Bennet Schaber used Deleuze's concept of the minor to note how American road movies since WWII have explored the possibilities of creating a people yet to come. Schaber shows how, in contrast to pre-war road movies like *It Happened One Night*, *The Wizard of Oz*, or *The Grapes of Wrath* (1940) where the people already exist, post-war road movies since *Easy Rider* (1969) have gone in search of a missing people, putting together random assemblages of characters to explore how a people of the future might develop. Road movies in the 1990s in particular have often used the motif of limitless travel to explore potential ways of reconsidering established identities. Similarly, although a genre film, *The Doom Generation* clearly conforms to the three characteristics of minor cinema.

Firstly *The Doom Generation*'s three teenaged loser protagonists create a bizarre assemblage that questions standard norms of behaviour, suggesting a new model for a people yet to come. When Amy and Jordan are joined by the explosive Xavier the norm of the heterosexual couple suddenly begins to stutter, their sexual relationship becoming a ménage a trois. This is not only rendered in the film's enthusiastic emphasis on their sexual behaviour (on several occasions when two people are fucking the third will be watching and masturbating, and the film's penultimate scene begins with a threesome), but also in the framing of the characters.

In mainstream Hollywood cinema it is usual to see a "two-shot" of two characters talking within a single frame. Usually this consists of two people facing each other on either side of the screen, creating a symmetrical compositional balance. Very often the coupling will be a man and a woman. In *The Doom Generation* Araki causes this convention to stutter, and in doing so questions heterosexual norms. Soon after Amy and Xavier first meet they are framed in this conventional way, talking heatedly outside Amy's car. Jordan's head then humorously appears in the bottom of the frame, as he—getting out of the car—inserts himself in between them. The comically dopey Jordan disturbs the accepted symmetry of the shot, as Araki uses a stuttered or queered shot composition to foreground and question established ways of representing heterosexual norms. Furthermore, on more than one occasion when the three are shot together in the same frame Amy will leave the discussion, and the convention two-shot will reconsolidate around the two male characters. This has the effect of further queering the two-shot convention, the homosexual undertones of such conversations between male characters in, for instance, buddy movies,

228

suddenly coming to the fore as Jordan and Xavier continue to discuss sex without Amy being present. Ultimately the film climaxes with an actual threesome, the physical manifestation of this alternative sexuality fulfilling the potential offered by the alternative framing offered throughout the film. The threesome is predominantly filmed from one camera angle, with the three characters' faces uncomfortably crammed into a single shot, again deliberately queering the construction of the two-shot.

Fulfilling the first criteria of a work of minor cinema, then, *The Doom Generation* points to a different possibility for sexuality, suggesting that a people could exist in the future that are not necessarily contained by the standard norm of the heterosexual couple. Despite this, however, the film somewhat pessimistically ends with a nihilistic renunciation of this potential. The three characters—symbolically named Red, White and Blue to represent a potentially new US national identity—are beaten, raped, and in Jordan's case murdered, on a US flag, to the sounds of the national anthem. The Nazi thugs demonstrate how the USA's right wing establishment represses such alternative potential, using violence if necessary. In addition to the symbols of the nation (flag and anthem) the statue of the Virgin Mary used to abuse Amy resonates with the film's tongue-in-cheek questioning of established religion in the US, and its role in normalizing sexual identity into the heterosexual couple. This resonates with slogans seen throughout the film ("Welcome to Hell," "Pray for Your Soul," "Prepare for the Apocalypse"), which—along with the recurring gag that everything the three outlaws buy costs $6.66—comment on the climate of religious fear that abounded in the USA in the 1990s, as it was left reeling from the AIDS epidemic.

Thus, even though Amy is ultimately victorious in her battle with the thugs, the final image is of a shell-shocked Amy and Xavier driving away in the car. As the radio begins to play the national anthem Amy switches it off. The film ends, then, with the union of a heterosexual couple much as you might expect of a mainstream Hollywood film. Here however, the preceding events and the upsetting tone of the finale demonstrate how far from a happy ending this is for Amy and Xavier. The ending posits several open questions, the two most obvious being, what future is there for alternative sexualities in this national environment, and how can alternative identities in the US create a people yet to come?

The second criteria for a work of minor cinema is also met. In the perpetual movement of their travels the characters find that there is no difference between the personal and the political. Denied a home beyond their garbage-strewn car, the characters are orphans on a journey with no end. Xavier's parents are both dead, Amy's abusive father is dead and her heroin addict mother converted to Scientology, whilst Jordan's parents live in Seattle and his only attempt to communicate with them via telephone is cut off by the answering machine. These homeless characters inhabit a hinterland of motels, Quickie Marts, charity shops, and roads strewn with the wrecks of other cars. Living in a perpetually public space their actions are always political. For instance, not having enough money to pay in a Quickie Mart leads to the murder of the proprietor, which in turn leads to a news report and a national man hunt by the FBI. Moreover, every purchase they make is shown through a security camera, emphasizing the way their lives are monitored at all times. Finally their sexual ambiguity leads to the violence of the film's finale, as their temporary warehouse shelter is invaded by the public forces of the state representatives, the brutal Nazi thugs.

Fulfiling the third criteria of a work of minor cinema, Araki's self-conscious cinematic style is used to insert the film into a dialogue between filmmaker, fictional story and audience in order to force a consideration of the way normative queer stereotypes are constructed in the media. As numerous critics have noted, Araki's films stand out from the mainstream due to his incorporation of aspects of the *avant-garde* (Chang, 53; Moran, 19–20; Mills, 308–13; Hart, 33; King, 83 and 235–6). As opposed to the transparency of form adopted by Hollywood, the *avant-garde* foregrounds the fictional status of the film, asking the viewer to think about how the world is "normally" represented to them by film. In *The Doom Generation* the Hollywood product is played in a minor key due to the insertion of an excessive queer aesthetics—like that of Kenneth Anger or John Waters— and a European *avant-garde* sensibility which Araki clearly owes to Jean-Luc Godard. As James M. Moran notes, "Godard … is perhaps the figure most representative of Araki's conception of the independent who can work within the institution of cinema in order to change it" (20). As the above critics have discussed in depth, there are countless ways in which this is achieved in the film, through the use of expressionistic shadows, unusually bright colours, garish motel room sets and so on.

The effect of this stylistic experimentation is the foregrounding of the film's discourse on sexual identities, which places it in stylistic quotation marks. Throughout its narrative *The Doom Generation* refuses to fix its characters as either types or counter-types. Both Xavier and Jordan are extremely ambiguous males for "A Heterosexual Road Movie." Jordan debunks established representations of the dominant male, as he is sexually dominated by Amy. Xavier on the other hand demonstrates an almost *über*-heterosexuality. Moreover, the erotically charged conversations between these two men suggest blatant homosexual desire, ensuring that their sexualities are constantly ambiguous, constantly transforming. Indeed, Amy, although conforming to the role of vamp or *femme fatale*, is perpetually undermined in this by the army of ex-lovers they bump into at every stop. The names by which they address her multiply (Sunshine, Kitten, Brandy), their cuteness undermining any legitimacy she might possibly have as a *femme fatale*, and their proliferation pointing to the potential for continuous identity transformation.

Perhaps the most obvious example of this use of foregrounded style in order to question established types is the dressing of Xavier in the second-hand clothes of a cowboy. This icon of the American West is here queered when it is reduced to an ironic dress code inhabited by the sexually poly-morphous Xavier. Xavier is a man whose sexual experimentation stops at nothing. He even enjoys eating his own semen. In this respect, then, he is very different from the John Wayne figure we might expect to find wearing a cowboy's clothes. Part of his outfit consists of a kitsch novelty belt buckle depicting two pistols in holsters, bracketing an image of a cowboy on a bucking stead. Whenever the buckle is wiggled, the horse bucks its rider. In a moment of blatant homosexual desire, Jordan requests permission to wiggle the buckle, then does so as he and Xavier look at each other and laugh. The image of bucking cowboy attached to Xavier's groin is ren-dered—twice—in close-up. In this way, as a work of minor cinema, *The Doom Generation* presents such stereotypes (sexual, and in the US case, national) in quotation marks, asking us to reconsider their normal, and normative uses. This unusual rendering of established norms of identity takes place in a film shot as though in stylistic quotation marks (witness its elaborate, expressionistic *mise-en-scène*, etc), thereby doubly questioning the dominant norms of identity representation in Hollywood cinema.

In conclusion, as these two very different examples illustrate, there is much to be gained from using Deleuze's work to examine contemporary US movies. From mainstream rom-coms to independent works of New Queer Cinema, Deleuze's theories offer various interesting and useful ways of demystifying the movies.

works cited

Butler, Alison. *Women's Cinema: The Contested Screen*. London: Wallflower, 2002.
Chang, Chris. "Absorbing Alternative." *Film Comment* 30:5 (1994): 47–53.
Collins, Jim, Hilary Radner and Ava Preacher Gardner. "Introduction." *Film Theory Goes to the Movies*. Eds. Jim Collins, Hilary Radner and Ava Preacher. New York: AFI/Routledge, 1993. 1–7.
Davies, Jude. "Gender, ethnicity and cultural crisis in *Falling Down* and *Groundhog Day*." *Screen* 36.3 (1995): 214–232.
Davies, Philip John and Paul Wells. "Introduction." *American Film and Politics from Reagan to Bush Jr*. Eds. Philip John Davies and Paul Wells. Manchester: Manchester University Press, 2000. 3–12.
Davis, Glyn. "Camp and Queer and the New Queer Director: Case Study—Gregg Araki." *New Queer Cinema: A Critical Reader*. Ed. Michele Aaron. Edinburgh: Edinburgh University Press, 2004. 53–67.
Deleuze, Gilles. *Cinema 1: The Movement-Image*. London: The Athlone Press (1983) 1986.
———, *Cinema 2: The Time-Image*. London: Athlone (1985) 1989.
Deleuze, Gilles and Félix Guattari. *Kafka: Towards a Minor Literature*. Minneapolis: University of Minnesota Press [1975] 1986.

Deleyto, Celstino. "Between Friends: Love and Friendship in Contemporary Hollywood Romantic Comedy." *Screen*, 44.2 (2003): 167–182.

Espinosa, Julio Garcia. "For an Imperfect Cinema." *Film Theory An Anthology*. Ed. Robert Stam and Toby Miller. Oxford: Blackwell (1969) 2000. 287–297.

Evans, Peter William and Celestino Deleyto. "Introduction: Surviving Love." *Terms of Endearment: Hollywood Romantic Comedy of the 1980s and 1990s*. Eds. Peter William Evans and Celestino Deleyto, Edinburgh: Edinburgh University Press, 1998. 1–14.

Gabriel, Teshome H. *Third Cinema in the Third World: The Aesthetics of Liberation*. Michigan: Ann Arbor, 1979.

Hart, Kylo-Patrick R. "Auteur/Bricoleur/Provocateur: Gregg Araki and Postpunk Style in *The Doom Generation*." *Journal of Film and Video* 55.1 (2003): 30–40.

Hjort, Mette, *Small Nation: Global Cinema*. Minneapolis: University of Minnesota Press, 2005.

Jeffers McDonald, Tamar. *Romantic Comedy: Boy Meets Girl Meets Genre*. London: Wallflower, 2007.

King, Geoff, *American Independent Cinema*. London: I.B. Taurus, 2005.

Macnab, Geoffrey. "The Doom Generation." *Sight and Sound* 6.6 (1996): 37–8.

Marks, Laura U. *The Skin of the Film: Intercultural Cinema, Embodiment and the Senses*. Durham and London: Duke University Press, 2000.

Marshall, Bill. *Quebec National Cinema*. Montreal: McGill-Queen's University Press, 2001.

Martin-Jones, David. "*Orphans*, a work of minor cinema from post-devolutionary Scotland." *Journal of British Cinema and Television* 1.2 (2004): 226–241.

——, *Deleuze, Cinema and National Identity*. Edinburgh: Edinburgh University Press, 2006.

Mills, Katie. "Revitalizing the Road Movie." *The Road Movie Book*. Eds. Steven Cohan and Ina Rae Hark. London: Routledge, 1997. 307–329.

Moran, James M. "Gregg Araki: Guerilla Filmmaker for a Queer Generation." *Film Quarterly*, 50:1 (1996): 18–26.

Naficy, Hamid. *An Accented Cinema: Exilic and Diasporic Filmmaking*. Princeton: Princeton University Press, 2001.

Neale, Steve and Frank Krutnik. *Popular Film and Television Comedy*. London: Routledge, 1990.

Negra, Diane. "Where the Boys Are: Postfeminism and the New Single Man." *Flow*, 4.3. April 14 2006: http://flowtv.org/?p=223 (accessed February 28 2008).

Pines, Jim and Paul Willeman, eds. *Questions of Third Cinema*. London: British Film Institute, 1991.

Pisters, Patricia. *The Matrix of Visual Culture: Working With Deleuze in Film Theory* California: Stanford University Press, 2003.

Rodowick, D.N. *Gilles Deleuze's Time Machine*. Durham and London: Duke University Press, 1997.

Schaber, Bennet. "'Hitler Can't Keep 'Em That Long': The Road, The People." *The Road Movie Book*. Eds. Steven Cohan and Ina Rae Hark. London: Routledge, 1997. 17–44.

Solanas, Fernando and Octavio Gettino. "Towards a Third Cinema." *Movies and Methods*. Ed. Bill Nichols. Berkeley: University of California Press (1969) 1976. 44–64.

Wexman, Virginia Wright. *Creating the Couple: Love, Marriage and Hollywood Performance*. Princeton: Princeton University Press, 1993.

rethinking affects, narration, fantasy, and realism

trauma,

pleasure, and

emotion

in the viewing

of *titanic*

a cognitive approach

c a r l   p l a n t i n g a

And what could be more romantic, in the dark and heart-wrenching sense of the word, than Titanic, with its stories of men and women torn from each other en masse by a cruel twist of fate, of widows scanning the faces of the few male survivors for the husbands and lovers, of the terrible loss and grief of the morning after . . . of so many hearts broken. (James Cameron vi)

trauma and the popularity of *titanic*

What could be more *romantic* than stories of men and women torn from each other by death? What could be more wistfully beautiful than freezing and drowning in the cold North Atlantic Ocean? One initially wants to ask James Cameron, director of the blockbuster *Titanic* (1997), what he could possibly have been thinking when he wrote the words quoted above. When one considers it for a moment, it is surprising that such a story would provide audiences pleasure at all. Yet Cameron understands something of what it takes to powerfully and pleasurably move an audience. And there is something about *Titanic* that attracted mass audiences, despite, or perhaps because of, its horrific subject matter.

Cameron describes the story of the *Titanic* as a "canvas offering the full spectral range of human emotion," and writes that his aim in making *Titanic* was to "convey the emotion of that night [of the ship's sinking] rather than the fact of it" (vi, ix). But this also is questionable. Among the emotions of "that night" were terror, grief, fear, and an overwhelming sadness. Only a sadist would want to recreate that for an audience. My basic assumption here is that the viewing of a film, even a film about a horrific event, must offer audiences a pleasurable or otherwise rewarding experience, not one, for example, of sheer terror and grief.

In this essay I will show that cognitive film theory can help identify the affective appeals that *Titanic* offers and relate those to the audience pleasures derived in its viewing. I describe and examine this fascinating paradox about the popularity of *Titanic*. In its popularity, at least as measured by its box office take, *Titanic* is one of the most successful films of all time on the international market, and in domestic theatrical receipts it runs second only to *Gone with the Wind* (1939) when the numbers are adjusted for inflation (*Box Office Mojo*). Unlike *Gone with the Wind*, however, the appeal of *Titanic* extended around the world, with roughly two-thirds of its box office revenues being generated outside of the United States.

Yet the film represents traumatic events and evokes negative, and what are conventionally thought to be unpleasant, emotions. Given this, how did it attain the popularity it enjoys? What strategies does it use to manage and transform the horrific into the pleasing and uplifting? *Titanic* is the quintessentially successful example of popular art. Perhaps in addressing what might be called "the paradox of negative emotion" in *Titanic*, we can learn something about the psychological appeal of much popular art that elicits negative emotions.

cognitive theory and affect in the movies

Early cognitive film theory concentrated on the interaction between spectator and film text in two registers: filmic perception and narrative comprehension. To take perception first, cognitive theory asked how spectators make sense of moving images and offered hypotheses rooted in the findings of cognitive science and philosophy. How is it that spectators see a two-dimensional visual array as a three-dimensional world of space and depth? If screened film consists of the projection of 24 still frames per second, why does the spectator invariably see this as a moving image? This study of perception was accompanied by examinations of narrative comprehension that explore the mental activities the spectator undertakes to make sense of story and character (Anderson; Bordwell, *Narration*; Branigan).

What I am particularly interested in with regard to *Titanic* is not perception and narrative comprehension per se, but more centrally the affective and emotional responses generated by the film, and what a "cognitive-perceptual" theory can show us about that. One cannot seriously examine emotional effect without considering perception and narrative comprehension. Yet this essay will focus on *Titanic* in relation to the affects and emotions it elicits in audiences, or more precisely, those that it is intended to elicit, as gauged by the structuring of the film's narration.

First I offer a word about a cognitive-perceptual theory of emotion (Plantinga, *Moved and Affected*). Cognitive theorists argue that emotions are not shapeless feelings but rather structured mental states, differentiated and defined by a particular kind of relationship between a person and a situation, and accompanied by physiological and neurological changes, feelings (subjective impressions), and action tendencies (flight in the case of fear, expulsion or distancing in the case of disgust, to cite two examples). For the purposes of this essay, we can characterize an emotion as a "concern based construal" (Roberts). An emotion arises when the subject appraises or perceives an event or situation in relation to her or his concerns. I call this a construal. The conjunction of particular kinds of construals and concerns defines the emotion. One common construal in jealousy is that one's lover is focusing her/his amorous attentions on another. The concern in jealously is the maintenance of the lover's exclusive amorous attentions. To take another example, fear arises when one construes a situation or object as threatening to one's safety or the safety of one's associates. The concern is for survival and/or the maintenance of health and happiness.

When the spectator views a film, she not only has emotions, strictly considered, but also various other sorts of responses that we might call "affects." Although the differentiation between emotions and affects is fraught with difficulties, we might simplify issues by associating affects with non-cognitive or "primitive" feeling states such as moods, affective mimicry and contagion (by which affect is "caught" by or transferred to a viewer), autonomic responses, etc. Emotions, then, have a stronger cognitive component and typically take an "object," that is, they are a response to particular event(s) or state(s) of affairs. The line between emotion and affect is not always clear; scholars disagree about whether to call surprise or startle, for example, affects or emotions. To recognize this lack of clarity in some cases is not to question the legitimacy of the categories, however. The recognition of the fuzzy boundaries between emotion and affect does not affect the recognition that there exist prototypical and clearly differentiated examples of both categories.

A fundamental tenet of cognitive film theory is a basic assumption of what I call a "conditional realism" in spectator response. The "realism" in this equation stems from the following: the spectator has emotions and affects in response to narrative events in a film that suggest that she perceives and responds to a fictional world in some of the same ways she would perceive and respond to the actual world. This isn't really a controversial or remarkable claim, as the consideration of a few examples will make clear. The curiosity and anticipation of the spectator about narrative events function in similar ways to the curiosity and anticipation the spectator has about actual events. Just as traveling to another country might elicit fascination in the tourist, so might being introduced to the exterior contours and inner workings of the magnificent ship in *Titanic* elicit fascination in the spectator. The qualities of character that elicit our admiration for a friend or public figure might also elicit admiration for a filmic character such as Jack or young Rose in *Titanic*. Similar events might elicit compassion or pity for a real person or for a character; just as we might have pity on someone who dies of exposure or loses a loved one, so we have pity for Jack and Rose (for dying and for losing a loved one, respectively). The spectator's default assumption is that film characters have psychologies similar to those we attribute to actual people, and we respond to film characters using a "person schema," as though they were in some sense real (Bordwell, *Making Meaning* 151–57).

I call this a conditional realism because it is subject to qualifications. The first qualification is the spectator's recognition of fictionality. Barring a serious mental disorder, viewers understand that what they experience is a fiction and not the actual world. Thus although structural similarities exist between fear responses to fictional and actual events, the fear responses to fictional events are characterized by an essential and additional element—an audience awareness of the imaginary nature of the events. The remarkable realism of the film medium may set in motion the affective and emotional processes of spectators, yet those will be modified by the background "set" that includes the basic assumption that they view a fiction.

The second qualification to this conditional realism of response is the spectator's recognition of mediation. Viewers understand or perceive, if only at an implicit or non-conscious level, that the narrative is a mediated construct. Thus they may be willing to experience unpleasant or negative emotions (such as pity or sadness) because, knowing that the film is a product of mainstream Hollywood, they expect that a happy ending or some other fortuitous outcome will provide emotional compensation for the unpleasant affect experienced during sections of the narrative. Many spectators have implicit understandings of narrative and genre conventions, and will chafe at the romantic comedy that omits the expected unification of the romantic couple, or the melodrama that fails to provide sufficient and expected admiration for the pitied protagonist, or the Western that neglects to offer the requisite violent confrontation at the film's end. Thus the responses elicited by a narrative film are realistic in the sense that they mimic real-world responses, but are conditioned and altered by the spectator's implicit knowledge of the institutional nature of the movies and other institutions of fiction (Smith, "Film Spectatorship").

The attempt to understand or predict the nature of mass spectator response based on textual characteristics is of necessity somewhat speculative. Of course, audience members vary in response in relation to personal and contextual differences. One might limit one's speculations about response to an ideal spectator, as much of Screen theory has done. The spectator of Screen theory is an ideal spectator because it is literally an *idea* and not a person. The spectator is conceived of as a hypothetical entity, a "position," "role," or "space" constructed by the text. Yet such theories invariably describe the functions of films in psychological terms, claiming, for example, that in the "film viewer" a "state of regression is produced" and "a situation of belief is constructed" (Stam et al. 147). Screen theory at times argues that the spectator is not a flesh and blood person, but then describes spectatorship in ways that apply to human beings and not to abstract entities. In his introduction to film theory, Robert Stam implicitly recognizes this problem when he distinguishes between the "spectator" and the "actual spectator" (Stam 231). Yet this only invites further terminological confusion. And it gets us no further in understanding when, and under what conditions, actual spectators occupy the "role of the spectator" (Prince).

Another alternative to the attempt to determine a hypothesized mass response is to abandon the project altogether in favor of the empirical investigation of the actual historical responses of individuals. This can be achieved by looking to personal reports and diaries, film reviews, movie chat sites on the web, or with post-viewing questionnaires and surveys. One might even wire the spectator to devices that gauge galvanic skin response or changes in pulse, for example. All of this might be very useful, but still limited to relatively few subjects. The scholar of popular film is also interested in mass responses, that is, in the means by which films manipulate audience emotions on a grand scale. Audience response is ultimately determined by a combination of "conditioners," that is, contextual and individually idiosyncratic factors, and "elicitors, or the features of the text and its evocation of affect through structure and style" (Feagin 24–31). The more similar the social and psychological make-up of the audience, the more important elicitors become in the evocation of mass response. Moreover, it is not outrageous to assume that some films have the capacity to elicit similar responses in diverse audiences.

Although audiences will respond to films in various ways, we can rightly assume that certain basic elements of response will be similar for audience members who allow themselves to experience a sympathetic viewing. That is, spectators who "give in" to the text and who do not maintain a wholly distanced or oppositional stance will tend to have some shared responses.

Perhaps audience members have different capacities for empathizing with characters, or experience fear or pity in varying degrees or under somewhat different conditions. Yet emotions are not free-floating and random; emotions are structured states caused by similar circumstances. If emotions are concern based construals, as I have argued, and if Hollywood films offer narratives which presume basic, easily comprehended concerns and textually-inscribe pre-focused construals (Carroll, "Film, Emotion"), then audience members will tend to share similar responses. When Jack dies in the cold North Atlantic Ocean, for example, only the most oppositional spectator will laugh at this rather than pity him. When the *Titanic* sinks and the passengers scream with terror, few audience members will feel jealousy or pride rather than the usual suspense, fear, and sadness.

For the purposes of gauging mass response, then, I will assume what could be called "cooperative spectators." These are viewers who hold a largely positive stance toward the film in the viewing and thus respond in large part in congruence with the film's intended affective trajectory. These spectators represent a significant percentage of the film's overall audience. We might expect that this percentage will differ depending on the particular film, audience, and viewing conditions. For some especially popular films, we might expect that the percentage of cooperative spectators will be quite high.

direct and sympathetic appeals in *titanic*

What sort of emotions does *Titanic* elicit for the cooperative spectator? To answer this question, it would benefit us to consider four basic types of emotions that films elicit: (1) direct, (2) sympathetic/antipathetic, (3) artifact, and (4) meta (Plantinga, *Moved and Affected*). Direct emotions are responses to the narrative and its unfolding; I call these emotions "direct" because their object is the narrative and its progression and they are not necessarily bound by a concern about any particular character. Characteristic direct emotions include curiosity, suspense, anticipation, surprise, and startle. Sympathetic and antipathetic emotions, on the other hand, take as their object the concerns, goals, and well-being of film characters. Examples of sympathetic emotions are compassion, pity, admiration, and happiness, and antipathetic emotions would include anger, disdain, and socio-moral disgust (Plantinga, "Disgusted"). Artifact emotions such as admiration, fascination, amusement, disdain, and impatience are directed at the film as an artifact. The fourth kind, meta-emotions, such as pride, guilt, shame, and disdain are aimed at the spectator's own responses or the responses of other viewers. It is important to note that emotional responses in relation to films can be mixed; I can experience more than one at a time. Thus, for example, I may simultaneously experience the sympathetic emotion of pity and embarrassment—a meta-emotion—that the film made me teary-eyed. Emotions may also interact with each other in intriguing ways, creating synergy and amplifying effect, in other cases interfering with each other, and in yet other cases creating an aesthetically and psychologically interesting friction.

The blockbuster film often attempts to provide attractions for diverse audiences. Thus the pleasurable emotions generated by *Titanic* are varied, including all four of the types just mentioned. When a film becomes an "Event," as *Titanic* did, the emotional responses of many audiences will include artifact emotions, as the status of the film as "horrendously expensive," "the most successful movie ever made," "the film everyone is seeing," or as the "consummate example of bad taste in popular art," all generate responses that take the film itself as their object. The film's publicity campaign is essential in creating the buzz that generates this sort of response. When a film attains the status of *Titanic*, more of the audience engages in the sort of activities that generate meta-emotions as well, as audiences compare their reactions with others, wonder why they liked it while others did not, etc.

Yet it is the direct and sympathetic emotions that I am most interested in here. To enter this discussion, first note that scholars have identified *Titanic* as a film that offers a melodramatic story mixed with elements of the disaster film. Moreover, *Titanic* is an example of an important trend in American action/adventure films: the self-conscious appeal to female audiences (Krämer; Bernstein). In general terms, this is partly accomplished through the use of female protagonists such as Sigourney Weaver's Ripley in *Alien* (1979) and Linda Hamilton's Sarah in *The Terminator* (1984) and *Terminator 2: Judgment Day* (1991). *Titanic* is Rose's story, and we see "young" Rose (Kate Winslett) engaging in many of the exuberant behaviors of the traditional action hero: running through corridors, jumping from lifeboats, swinging axes, and saving her lover Jack (Leonardo DiCaprio) from drowning when he is handcuffed to a water pipe below decks as the ship sinks. At one point, she even spits.

Titanic enjoyed popularity in part due to its combination of love story and disaster scenarios, since these scenarios lead to both sympathetic/antipathetic and direct emotions. Take the direct emotions first. The subject of the sinking of the *Titanic* itself is of strong intrinsic interest apart from the interest in the fates of Rose and Jack and Cal. The historically accurate modeling of the ship, the precise attention to the details of its sinking, and the riveting cinematic representation of the disaster has direct appeal to audiences who may well presume that this is, moreover, a relatively accurate reenactment of an actual historical event, at least in many of its technical details. Independent of the fictional characters, many viewers are curious about, interested in, shocked, and fascinated by the unfolding story of the sinking of this mammoth ship. Thus Cameron manages to acquaint the spectator with the ship's geography and inner workings, including the bridge, the boiler room, the engine room (in which the camera is placed directly before the gigantic whirling pistons), and the cargo hold. Moreover, those interested in scientific expeditions and exploration will be enthralled by the frame story, in which, as expedition leader Brock Lovett (Bill Paxton) views the sunken *Titanic* from his submersible, 2-and-one-half miles (3.8 km) beneath the surface, through 9-inch thick windows. Those familiar with James Cameron's experience with deep sea exploration will be more likely to put confidence in the film to get the technological details right. The film initially and throughout its duration appeals to curiosity about the design of the *Titanic*, an interest in the contemporary expedition to the sunken *Titanic*, nostalgia for the past, and anticipation of and fascination with the details of its sinking. These are direct emotions; that is, they do not fundamentally depend on a sympathetic engagement with characters.

Hollywood films, however, depend on the evocation of spectator allegiances with favored characters and the generation of strong sympathetic (and antipathetic) emotions (Smith, *Engaging*), and *Titanic* does not fail to satisfy in that regard. Although the narrative takes care to elicit direct emotions, it also quickly attempts to generate the sympathetic and antipathetic emotions of melodrama, introducing the audience to Jack Dawson, the wandering artist and free spirit, and Rose DeWitt Bukater, the ingénue trapped in an engagement to a man she does not love, the wealthy and arrogant Cal Hockley (Billy Zane). The romance between Jack and Rose develops quickly, and eventually Rose strongly desires the love of Jack, desires that she escape her repressive family and fiancé, and later desires that both Jack and herself escape death as the *Titanic* sinks. The viewer's emotional responses are directed by alignment with and reaction to Rose's desires (and to an extent, Jack's), generating the fear, pity, and other responses that I have called sympathetic emotions.

But the spectator's sympathetic responses are not limited to Rose and Jack. James Cameron puts the love story of two individuals within the context of a disaster on a grand scale. Although the spectator grows in allegiance for both Jack and Rose, Cameron consistently relates their plight to that of the other victims and puts Jack's eventual death into the context of the roughly 1500 other passengers who died, and thus amplifies the sympathetic emotions. As Cameron writes, "I wanted the audience to cry for *Titanic*. Which means to cry for the *people* on the ship, which really means to cry for any lost soul in their hour of untimely death" (Cameron). Thus in the film's second half, as the *Titanic* sinks, Jack and Rose's plight is foregrounded, but the narration also carefully highlights the anguish, fear, stoic bravery, and panic of other passengers.

Interspersed between shots of Jack and Rose, the narration intercuts shots of both the dead and the soon-to-be dead. We see Captain Smith as he awaits his fate on the bridge, the water breaking the glass and pouring in. We see the musicians who continue to play, despite the growing certainty of their deaths. Andrews, the architect, awaits his fate in the ballroom. An old couple embraces on their bed, knowing what will soon come. A mother reads with quavering voice to her two children as the frigid water rushes in. We see a low angle shot of a drowned girl from below as she floats suspended in water, her diaphanous nightgown flowing beneath the bright lights of the Grand Staircase's chandelier. After the sinking, the camera displays the hundreds of bodies bobbing on the surface of the frigid North Atlantic. These scenes are designed to evoke pity and sadness, and more powerfully because the predicament of these people is shared and noticed by the favored protagonists, for whom many spectators have formed strong sympathies.

the frame story I: the rhetoric of sincerity

If one dominant narrational stance in Hollywood is irony, *Titanic* might be called a melodrama of absolute sincerity. That is, it invites the audience to respond with seriousness to the plight of its characters, and without the "knowing" reflexivity that marks the ironic stance. The film is set during a contemporary scientific expedition to find the sunken ship, and more specifically, to discover a valuable diamond, "The Heart of the Ocean," that is thought to have gone down with the ship. The expedition leader, Brock Lovett (Bill Paxton), seems to be something of a modern-day pirate, his primary intention being to find that diamond. The expedition salvages a safe in which the explorers believe "The Heart of the Ocean" lies. Upon opening the safe, however, they discover no diamond, but do find the drawing of a nude, reclining woman, a drawing that is broadcast on the television news. Cut to Rose Dawson Calvert (Gloria Stewart), an old woman at a potter's wheel who sees and recognizes this picture. "I am the woman in this picture," she tells them. Since all who know about the diamond are thought to be either dead or on the expedition, Lovett invites "Old" Rose to the ship, where she relates her story. The story of the sinking of *Titanic* and Jack and Rose's brief and tragic love affair is narrated by Rose in flashback, framed by the story of her having been flown to the expedition ship.

The frame story fulfills a central function in the emotional appeal of *Titanic*. While much has been made of attempts of Hollywood to attract females to the action/adventure elements of the film, it is just as important to prepare males, traditionally thought to avoid sentiment in movies, for the romance and melodrama. The frame story begins by presenting the expedition and its crew as cool, objective, and cynical, and by implying that this is a moral lapse on their part. As his submersible descends toward the deck of the sunken *Titanic*, Brock Lovett carries with him a video camera and records voice-over for the video he is making: "Seeing her coming out of the darkness like a ghost ship, still gets me every time." As he continues, Lewis Bodine (Lewis Abernathy), his snickering assistant, laughs, "You are so full of shit, boss." After Lovett switches off his camera, he says, "All right, . . . enough of this bullshit." Lovett is in it for the money. Upon the group discovering the safe, Brock says "It's payday, boys."

While Lovett and Bodine are jaded and mercenary, the narration takes a different perspective once the expedition explores the wreck of the *Titanic*. As the submersibles glide over the surface of the sunken ship, the soundtrack features the barely audible sounds of yelling voices, as though the wreck were haunted by those who perished in its 1912 sinking. As the minisub enters the interior of the wreck, its camera lingers on various reminders of human loss: a tattered boot, spectacles, the face of a doll. The expedition may be peopled by detached observers whose motivation is the search for treasure, but the film's narration reminds the spectator of the human meaning of the wreck of the *Titanic*.

Cynicism and crass lack of emotional involvement is represented primarily in the figure of Bodine, and then secondly, in Brock Lovett. After Rose Calvert telephones the expedition, Bodine is the one who is deeply suspicious of her motives. Bodine shows Rose a computer simulation of the sinking of the ship, narrating the sinking in flippant and insensitive terms, saying that at one point "her ass is sticking up in the air," and "that's a big ass—20 to 30,000 tons." After he finishes he looks at his spectators, "Pretty cool, huh?" Rose calls this his "forensic analysis," but says that her experience of it was "somewhat different." They ask Rose to tell her story, and she does. "*Titanic* was called the 'ship of dreams'," she says, "and it was—it really was," adding that to her, at least initially, "it was a slave ship, bringing me back to America in chains."

This frame story prepares the audience to reject the dominant trope of irony for one of sincerity and sentiment—by making irony and cynicism unattractive (Davis and Womack). In fact, the ironic, cynical perspective— most clearly exemplified by overstuffed Bodine—is shown within the world of the film to be morally reprehensible. Thus *Titanic* embraces a rhetoric of sincerity, a rhetoric designed to prepare viewers for the melodrama of romance and loss and death that is to come. The frame story functions in part to disarm the skeptical spectator who might otherwise respond with a reflexive disdain, and psychologically prepares the viewer for the sympathetic emotions yet to come.

melodrama and romantic tragi-comedy: the love story

A given film may elicit varied and complex emotions, but the dominant emotions it evokes and its emotional tone correspond with genre conventions. *Titanic* combines romantic and family melodrama with a disaster narrative. Its most important generic structuring, however, is its uses of the conventions of melodrama, albeit a "sublime" melodrama set not in the antechambers of private rooms but more often in the public space of a great ship set against the vast expanses of sea and stars. The term "melodrama" is elusive. Its etymology suggests a play (*drama*) accompanied by music (*melos*), the music used to guide and boost the drama's elicitation of emotion. Today we use the term as a genre category referring to films, novels, or plays that feature scenarios having to do with family relationships, romance, forced marriages, separation from loved ones, etc. *Melodrama* has also been traditionally associated with exaggerated demarcations of good and evil, leading to the elicitation of clear sympathies and antipathies on the spectator's part.

Melodramas are thought to elicit strong sympathetic emotions, especially mixtures of pity, admiration, and elevation (of which more will be said below), often accompanied by tears. We pity the protagonist for her tribulations, but admire her for her virtuous behavior in the midst of trouble (Carroll, "Film, Emotion" 35–8). It isn't just any sort of admiration that melodrama elicits. We can admire persons for many reasons including their accomplishments, talents, good looks, or even their taste in footwear. Melodramas elicit admiration of a particular kind, what psychologist Jonathan Haidt calls "elevation." This emotion, Haidt writes, is the opposite of social disgust. The objects of elevation are human acts of moral beauty or virtue; thus we might see elevation as narrower in scope than admiration broadly considered. This admixture of pity and elevation makes problematic the claims by some theorists that melodrama functions psychologically as a form of masochism (Williams), for the suffering of the protagonist and the emotions that elicits are coupled with the strongly positive emotion of elevation it brings to the spectator. One might even argue, as I do below, that the strength of negative emotions such as pity and fear contribute to the power of positive and pleasurable emotions that the film ultimately evokes by its end. *Titanic*, like most melodramas, elicits tears but also elation.

Titanic fits the category "melodrama" exceedingly well. It evokes both pity for the plight of Rose and Jack and the other passengers of the *Titanic*, plus admiration for Rose and especially for Jack, and elevation for the virtuous selflessness Jack shows in saving Rose's life, and eventually sacrificing his own. As Rose says, Jack saved her in every way possible. Jack becomes an object of pity for his death and an object of elevation for his qualities as Rose's savior. *Titanic* also exhibits the exaggerated dichotomy between good and evil often characteristic of melodrama. We can see this in the depiction of Jack's rival, the villainous Cal Hockley, who although good looking and rich (qualities that the film implies are important only to moral philistines), has nothing but foul qualities in the remainder. A good villain is essential for the elicitation of simple and unproblematic emotions in such a melodrama.

Rooted in degrees of allegiance for various characters (Smith, *Engaging*), the spectator develops sympathies and antipathies that generate the concerns that in part make up emotional response. The spectator's sympathetic emotions are elicited in relation to his or her concerns or desires for the well-being of the protagonist, and it is the villain who countermands these desires. If the spectator desires that Rose escape the oppression of her family and class, it is Cal Hockley who plans to oppress her. If the spectator desires that Rose and Jack unite in romantic union, it is Cal who opposes this. If the spectator desires that Rose and Jack escape death, it is Cal who wishes Jack, and perhaps also Rose, dead. Yet the maintenance of verisimilitude demands a believable villain, and if the spectator can't have that, the villain should at least be fascinating, as is Hannibal Lecter (Anthony Hopkins) in *The Silence of the Lambs* (1991) or Nurse Ratched (Louise Fletcher) in *One Flew Over the Cuckoo's Nest* (1975). The depiction of Cal Hockley tends toward stereotype, and risks distancing the viewer and eliciting disdain, an artifact emotion, for the broad strokes with which he is depicted.

Titanic is not merely an example of a mainstream Hollywood blockbuster, or of an American version of melodrama melded with a disaster film. We might also describe the film as an instance of a universal narrative structure, what Patrick Colm Hogan calls "romantic tragic-comedy." If a narrative is the expression of a concern-based construal, as I have argued, then mainstream narratives will tend to be accessible and somewhat familiar to diverse audiences. Hogan claims that human appraisals of and responses to innumerable phenomena are "guided and organized by a limited number of standard narrative structures" (5). Two prominent structures of narrative worldwide are what he calls the "romantic tragi-comedy" and the "heroic tragi-comedy," deriving, respectively, from prototypes for personal and social happiness. Romantic tragi-comedies take as their subject romantic union, while heroic tragi-comedies embody narratives of social/political power, including material prosperity. The most common plot structure cross-culturally, Hogan claims, is almost certainly romantic tragi-comedy.

One is struck by the nearly perfect correspondence between the story of *Titanic* and the archetypal romantic tragic-comedy. Romantic tragi-comedies revolve around the union, separation, and eventual reunion of lovers, and typically involve a rival as well. Usually the lovers cannot be united due to some conflict between their love and the social structure, often represented by parental disapproval. Most importantly for my purposes, the separation of the lovers often involves death or the imagery of death. In the end, however, the lovers are reunited, although perhaps only in the afterlife. As Hogan writes,

> sometimes the lovers die and are reunited only in death; sometimes there is a rumor of death or an apparent death; sometimes there is a death and resurrection; sometimes

> there is a reunion in a divine world that suggests death;
> sometimes there is a near death; sometimes there is exten-
> sive imagistic and metaphorical reference to death. (102)

Hogan claims that the romantic tragi-comedy is an "absolute universal," that is, a narrative structure that occurs in all cultures. But that is not the main issue here (although I suspect that Hogan *is* right on this). This arche-typal structure occurs with great frequency in diverse narratives and mines a vein of common and deeply-felt human concerns. Thus the following brief analysis of *Titanic* will have application not only to the melodrama and to classical Hollywood cinema, but more broadly to the archetype of romantic tragi-comedy that is common in many films of diverse genres.

mixed and attenuated emotions

From the standpoint of spectator emotion, a most intriguing fact about *Titanic* in relation to its popularity is that it is a narrative in which Jack Dawson, a most sympathetic protagonist and the representative of exuber-ance, vitality, and perhaps the Life Force itself, dies along with 1500 other passengers. Jack freezes to death, and when Rose releases his dead hand from her grip, we see his body in a high angle shot as it descends silently into the blue ocean, gradually disappearing into the deep, his arm stretched out above him as though he bids farewell. Typically when people suffer the irrevocable loss of someone dear to them, it becomes a life-altering event that elicits grief. We might expect that Rose will experience grief, as will many of the survivors in the film. Her grim face and the melancholy strains of the film's theme song, "My Heart Will Go On," suggest so. But what does the spectator experience? Does the sympathetic spectator also experi-ence grief in relation to Jack's death and that of the other *Titanic* victims?

I suspect that for many spectators, the emotions are mixed, consisting of something like sadness mixed with the pity and elevation characteristic of melodrama. Sadness is milder in its effects than grief. Like grief, sadness results from the loss or unavailability of someone or something that one holds dear (Roberts 234–40). But while we might experience sadness over a cancelled vacation or the theft of a favorite bicycle, it would not seem right to respond to these losses with grief. We typically reserve grief for the loss of a person (or perhaps an animal) who we hold particularly dear. Given the spectator's understanding of the conventional nature of film viewing and *Titanic*'s status as fiction, most viewers' responses could hardly be char-acterized as grief. The experience of sadness, to whatever degree it is milder in its cognitive and physiological effects, may still resemble the "feeling tone" of grief in central respects.

Why would millions of spectators subject themselves to sadness and pity? Assuming, for a moment, that a film's popularity depends in part on its ability to offer a pleasurable affective experience, how can a film like *Titanic* take a scenario of heartbreaking loss, separation, and death, and turn it into something that attracts one of the largest movie audiences of all time? I would give a two-part answer to this question. First, the narration of *Titanic* encourages a construal that both takes the unpleasant edge off of the deaths and also mixes such responses with conventionally pleasurable responses. The second part of my answer, to be described in the next section, is that *Titanic* contextualizes the deaths into a broader narrative that offers affective rewards for the viewer.

First, how does the narration soften the impact of Jack's death and those of the other 1500? The familiar concept of foreshadowing is important here. Foreshadowing is often discussed but its purposes and effects are often left unexplored. It has many functions but among the most important is its use in softening the emotional impact of a negative event. The story of Jack and the ship's sinking is Rose's story; it is she who literally tells the story to the crew of the expedition ship. Since we learn early on that she has survived, but that Jack is no longer alive and there is no record of his existence, the spectator will strongly suspect that Jack will not survive the sinking of the *Titanic* as Rose's story unfolds. Foreshadowing is sometimes used to create suspense, but more often it is used to allow the spectator time to process the possibility of a negative outcome, to soften the blow when it occurs. (Note how rare it is that the death of a major character will occur without advance warning, as it does in Hitchcock's *Psycho*, in which Marion Crane is surprisingly murdered just as she decides to return the money she has stolen.) Foreshadowing colors the spectator's construal of the event, eliminating surprise in favor of a sense of fate or inevitability that facilitates coping. If the spectator expects that Jack will die, his eventual death will elicit sadness but not shock.

The spectator's construal of narrative events is often influenced by extra-filmic scenarios prevalent in culture, some of which have an affective force that strikes the spectator through association. Filmmakers draw from well-known scenarios to tap into their pre-existing emotional power. On the explicit level, the screenwriters disavow institutional Christianity by associating it with the duplicity and stuffy arrogance of Rose's family and their ilk. At one point Jack invades and then treats lightly a religious service at which the participants appeal to God for, among other things, safety for those at sea. The implication is that these prayers will be ineffective, and that at any rate, Jack has little use for them. Yet in spite of the film's explicit disavowal of religion, the figure of Jack is clearly used as a sacrificial figure, and his story borrows from scenarios of heroic self-sacrifice and especially the Christ story. It may be a cliché to refer to Jack as a kind of Christ figure, but upon a few moments' reflection, such an analogy between the one who saves Rose "in every possible way" and Jesus Christ is difficult to deny.

Jack's self-abnegating behavior toward Rose becomes apparent from the very beginning, as he selflessly takes as his primary interest her need for a fulfilled life and escape from oppression. He prevents Rose from committing suicide and shows her how to live again. As the ship sinks, Jack engineers Rose's survival once more, putting them both on the ship's stern in a position to emerge from the ship's downward draft, then finding a floating headboard on which Rose can escape the freezing water. (It is important to note that Rose is also instrumental in saving Jack's life when he is handcuffed to a pipe on a lower deck; the saving goes both ways.) As Jack freezes to death, he tells Rose that winning the ticket that allowed him to embark on the *Titanic* was "the best thing that ever happened to me" because it "brought me to you." Jack may be dying, but his love for Rose is so deep that it trumps the importance of his own death. Jack's interest then turns to Rose's future life, and he insists that she promise that she'll survive and "never let go," and predicts that she'll make lots of babies and die an old woman warm in bed. She promises to survive, which the spectator is later led to believe provides her the strength to retrieve a whistle from a frozen body and effect her own rescue. Jack's love is, in fact, a perfect love.

Many spectators will construe Jack's death, then, in light of heroic stories of self-sacrifice such as Christian narrative (which was clearly shown to have emotional power for contemporary audiences with Mel Gibson's *The Passion of the Christ*). Just as we construe the deaths of soldiers in terms of serving one's country, thus granting their deaths a meaning that renders them less biting, *Titanic* manipulates the spectator's construal of Jack's death as one which saves Rose. Jack's death is not meaningless; it does not result from foolishness, false bravado, or stupidity. It is a good death, a sacrificial death with meaning.

Her life saved, Rose has been able to pursue her longstanding interest in the arts; the first shot of old Rose shows her working a potter's wheel. Old Rose's daughter accompanies her to the expedition ship; she has had at least one child. Just before Rose's vision of transcendence, the camera tracks by the photographs on her nightstand, providing an understanding that Rose's life has been fortunate indeed. In those photographs she is shown pursuing the kinds of activities that make life worth living, according to the film's resolutely bourgeois ideology: riding horses, flying airplanes, making pottery, and traveling to exotic parts of the globe. Jack died so that Rose might live. Jack's death also has meaning within the political ideology of contemporary American politics, hearkening to the feminist and civil rights movements. Jack rescued Rose from oppression and died for Rose's freedom. Her life, a woman's life, takes on ultimate value, unconstrained by social oppression that would threaten her freedom and self-determination. As the rescue ship, the *Carpathian*, arrives in New York, we see young Rose look up as she floats beneath the statue of liberty, towering above her.

frame story II: transcendence and elation

So far I have demonstrated that *Titanic* is able to take the edge off the negative emotions it elicits through foreshadowing and by putting Jack's death into the context of heroic self-sacrifice. In its last episodes, *Titanic* does much more than that. It offers a quasi-religious ritual of commemoration and celebration that not only leads to *relief* from strong negative emotions, but *converts* these into pleasurable emotions that depend for their strength on prior arousal. What is converted are not the emotions per se but the physiological residue of the painful emotions, which through emotional "spillover" increases the strength of the positive emotions at the film's end.

How does this process work? First, the narrative of *Titanic*, for the sympathetic spectator at least, takes this mixture of pleasure and pain of which I have spoken, and in gradual fashion, increases the pleasure and decreases the pain through a ritual of commemoration that marks the end of the film. The commemoration occurs in a kind of impromptu funeral ritual, as old Rose takes the invaluable blue diamond, "The Heart of the Ocean," and drops it into the ocean, where it descends into the deep much like Jack's body did earlier in the film. (The diamond has come to signify, in the film, Jack's life and also the love of Rose and Jack.)

A funeral service functions to celebrate the lives of the dead, offer solace to the living, and facilitate the grieving process, and this scene, similarly, works to memorialize both Jack and the "Great Love" of Rose and Jack. The usual Hollywood narrative is "hyper-coherent," that is, it compresses stories by leaving out the extraneous bits and including only those that are most salient and dramatic. In a similar fashion, the conventions of Hollywood narrative call for the experience of emotions in rapid succession, which audiences find to be pleasurable and which may arguably be therapeutic. This ritualistic scene serves some of the functions that actual memorial rituals serve, but condensed and perfected by the careful deliberation of the filmmaker. It does so by demonstrating the importance and effectiveness of Jack's sacrifice, thus assuring the spectator that it had a purpose; Rose has led a happy and fulfilled life. It also lays Jack to rest, so to speak, and by having old Rose drop the stone into the deep, releases the spectator from further need to pity, as though the memorial act absolves one of serious further concern and symbolically restores a sense of order. The dropping of Jack's memorial stone into the ocean becomes a kind of sacrifice-in-kind, its value mirroring the value of Jack's life, just as the high angle shot of the stone descending into the ocean mirrors the earlier shot of Jack's body descending into the deep.

But the scene also elicits the emotions of elevation and admiration, for Rose's action is not only a ritual commemoration of Jack's life, but is also morally virtuous in that she recognizes that The Heart of the Ocean is valuable not for its monetary worth, but primarily because it represents the life of the sacrificial hero, and through him, the lives of those who perished when the *Titanic* sank. As a kind of memorial stone, it belongs deep in the ocean, where Jack had vanished years before, and Rose is admired for realizing this and acting on it, despite the stone's great monetary value. (The filmmakers also suggest elements of the sublime here, carefully showing the infinite number of stars above Rose and the infinitude of space in relation to the vast depths of the dark expanse of ocean. Thus Jack's memorial is given a cosmic significance.)

Near the end of the narrative comes what might be called a scene of transcendence, which adds hope and elation to the mixture of relief, admiration, and elevation that the commemoration scene elicits. After Rose drops the diamond into the sea, the scene dissolves to old Rose's cabin on the research ship, where old Rose lies in bed. The shot dissolves to a tracking shot with a rapid approach to the sunken *Titanic* deep beneath the ocean's surface, as though Rose's soul or mind is approaching the ship. As the camera tracks deeper toward the sunken ship, the ship becomes the new *Titanic* once more, the corroded surfaces turning polished and gleaming and the dark of the ocean becoming light. The camera tracks into the ship, and there is the Grand Staircase, gleaming, new, brilliantly lit, with many of the people we know to have died now alive and welcoming Rose. Finally, we see Jack, standing above on the landing. He turns to look downward, extending his hand to welcome young Rose (who we now see in the frame), and they kiss passionately as the other *Titanic* passengers smile and applaud. The camera has been tracking elegantly throughout, and it now moves beyond the embracing couple above them to the source of light, where it dissolves to a bright and undifferentiated white-bliss.

The scene is polyvalent. Whether the spectator sees this scene as a wish, a dream, or a vision of heaven, however, it not only celebrates and commemorates their "Great Love," but expresses a hope for or perhaps a belief in the transcendence of love, a hope that love can survive death, loss, and separation. The film offers the hope or wish or dream of a connection with loved ones who have died. In this it is similar to several other films that offer a vague hope in transcendence, including *Ghost* (1990), *Always* (1989), and perhaps, one could argue, *The Sixth Sense* (1999). The success of this scene in *Titanic* depends on its lack of clear reality status. That is, that the scene is interpretable in so many ways makes it more likely that it will be effective for a diversity of audiences, as in fact it seems to have been.

The sadness, fear, and pity characteristic of the earlier scenes are transformed, for many audiences, into positive emotions—elevation, admiration, hope, and exhilaration—through a ritual commemoration of Jack (and all he stands for) and an affirmation of transcendence. In what sense are the negative emotions *converted* into positive emotions, rather than merely *replacing* them? The emotions have a marked physiological component, such that the physiological effects of preceding emotions can transfer to the experience of later emotions, because physiological effects recede slowly. Thus the "Excitation Transfer Theory" would postulate that the spectator's response to a later scene can be affected by the residual physiological effects of an earlier scene (Zillman, "Excitation Transfer" and "Transfer of Excitation"). Thus if strong negative emotions are accompanied by physiological arousal, this arousal may contribute to the strength of later positive emotions and lead to the experience of elation.

Another reason for claiming the conversion or transformation rather than the mere replacement of emotions is that the concern based construals that constitute the positive emotions at the film's end incorporate what has come before. That is, the construals that lead to admiration, relief, and exhilaration take into account the terrifying and piteous events that have come before. In both physiological and cognitive terms, then, prior emotions are not merely replaced but are incorporated into later cognitive and emotional responses. There is a sense in which the positive construals at the film's end take into account the alarming negative construals that precede them. The positive emotions gain strength from the negative emotions that were endured earlier, and the fact that they have been incorporated and transformed brings not only elation but relief.

In sum, for many spectators the overall affective experience is pleasurable despite the painful negative emotions that are elicited near the film's climactic point. This is true because, as I have shown, (1) at the point of the film's most traumatic moments, painful affect is both attenuated in its effect *and* is mixed with pleasurable affect, and (2) through the scenes of commemoration and transcendence, negative emotions are gradually converted into positive emotions, such that by the film's end, the overall experience for many spectators is intensely pleasurable.

the power of *titanic*

The question of how this relates to the ideological effect of *Titanic* and its function as a therapeutic narrative for the masses is an interesting one. Emotions are not merely feelings, but also ways of construing the world. Emotions are firmly bound up with ideas, ways of seeing, and ways of valuing. This is in part why emotions have a powerful rhetorical force in persuasion (Plantinga, "Disgusted"). This topic will have to be dealt with elsewhere, however. In this chapter the subject has been the emotional power of *Titanic* as embodied in its textual strategies for eliciting emotion.

As I mentioned above, the tremendous popularity of *Titanic* no doubt arises from a complex of factors, both textual and contextual. Some of these have not been accounted for in this chapter. Yet no account of the film's box office success can be sufficient without identifying the central affects and emotions it elicits and other pleasures *Titanic* offers in its viewing, and this I attempted to do here. The textual power of a movie for audiences can be conceived along two axes: widespread and intense engagement (Carroll, *Theorizing* 78–93). Widespread engagement refers to the accessibility of a film, which I will here consider in its affective component. An affectively accessible film elicits strong and simple emotions that appeal to the masses, and also offers varied affective pleasures in an attempt to appeal to audience diversity. We have seen that *Titanic* is not only a clear and simple example of a common narrative archetype—the romantic tragic-comedy—but also mixes the popular genres of melodrama and the disaster film. Thus it offers a full spectrum of direct and sympathetic emotions for diverse audiences. I also demonstrated that the film attempts to prepare audiences for the sympathetic emotions it elicits through textual strategies I call its "rhetoric of sincerity."

Intense engagement refers to the ability of a movie to elicit rapt attention and strong emotional and affective responses. In this regard I have asked why, given its terrifying and sad subject matter, *Titanic* was not in fact too intense for mass audiences. My answer to this question is two-fold. First, through various textual strategies *Titanic* not only attenuates the negative emotions, but also offers positive emotions mixed with the negative even during the most potentially disturbing scenes. Second, my claim is that since the affective experience of a film is temporal, many audiences are willing to experience negative emotions if the expectation is that such emotions will be transformed into positive emotions by the film's end. Thus *Titanic*, though it elicits fear, sadness, and pity, gradually transforms these emotions into relief, elevation, admiration, and elation. Further, I argued that the emotional strength of the ending depends to an extent on the power of the earlier negative emotions to generate physiological responses that carry over and thus strengthen the eventual positive responses *Titanic* generated for millions of viewers.

works cited

Anderson, Joseph D. *The Reality of Illusion: An Ecological Approach to Cognitive Film Theory*. Carbondale: Southern Illinois University Press, 1996.

Bernstein, Mathew. "'Floating Triumphantly': The American Critics on *Titanic*." *Titanic: Anatomy of a Blockbuster*. Eds Sandler and Studlar, 1999. 14–28.

Bordwell, David. *Narration in the Fiction Film*. Madison: University of Wisconsin Press, 1985.

———. *Making Meaning: Inference and Rhetoric in the Interpretation of Cinema*. Cambridge, MA.: Harvard University Press, 1989.

Box Office Mojo. 29 Mar. 2007. 30 Mar. 2007 <www.boxofficemojo.com/alltime/>.

Branigan, Foreword *Narrative Comprehension and Film*. London and New York: Routledge, 1992.

Cameron, James. "Foreword," *James Cameron's Titanic*. New York: Harper Perennial, 1997.

Carroll, Noël. *Theorizing the Moving Image*. Cambridge: Cambridge University Press, 1996.

———. "Film, Emotion, and Genre." *Passionate Views: Film, Cognition, and Emotion.* Eds Carl Plantinga and Greg M. Smith. Baltimore: Johns Hopkins University Press, 1999. 21–47.

Davis, Todd F. and Kenneth Womack. "Narrating the Ship of Dreams: The Ethics of Sentimentality in James Cameron's *Titanic.*" *Journal of Popular Film and Television,* 29.1 (Spring 2001): 42–48.

Feagin, Susan. *Reading with Feeling: The Aesthetics of Appreciation.* Ithaca: Cornell University Press, 1996.

Haidt, Jonathan. "The Positive Emotion of Elevation." *Prevention and Treatment* 3.3 (March 2000). www.journals.apa.org/prevention/volume3/pre0030003c. html. (Accessed September 2, 2004.)

Hogan, Patrick Colm. *The Mind and its Stories: Narrative Universals and Human Emotion.* Cambridge: Cambridge University Press, 2003.

Krämer, Peter. "Women First: *Titanic,* Action-Adventure Films, and Hollywood's Female Audience." *Titanic: Anatomy of a Blockbuster.* Eds Sandler and Studlar, 1999. 108–31.

Plantinga, Carl. "Disgusted at the Movies." *Film Studies: An International Review.* 8 (Summer 2006): 81–92.

———. *Moved and Affected: American Film and the Spectator's Experience.* Berkeley: University of California Press, 2009.

Prince, Stephen. "Psychoanalytic Film Theory and the Case of the Missing Spectator." *Post-Theory: Reconstructing Film Studies.* Eds David Bordwell and Noël Carroll. Madison: University of Wisconsin Press, 1996. 71–87.

Roberts, Robert C. *Emotions: An Essay in Aid of Moral Psychology.* Cambridge: Cambridge University Press, 2003.

Sandler, Kevin S., and Gaylyn Studlar (eds). *Titanic: Anatomy of a Blockbuster.* New Brunswick: Rutgers University Press, 1999.

Smith, Murray. *Engaging Characters: Fiction, Emotion, and the Cinema.* Oxford: Clarendon Press, 1995.

———. "Film Spectatorship and the Institution of Fiction." *Journal of Aesthetics and Art Criticism* 53.2 (Spring 1995): 113–27.

Stam, Robert. *Film Theory: An Introduction.* London: Blackwell, 2000.

Stam, Robert, Robert Burgoyne, and Sandy Flitterman-Lewis. *New Vocabularies in Film Semiotics: Structuralism, Post-Structuralism and Beyond.* New York: Routledge, 1992.

Williams, Linda. "Film Bodies: Gender, Genre, and Excess." *Film Theory and Criticism: Introductory Readings.* 5th edition. Eds Leo Braudy and Marshall Cohen. New York: Oxford University Press. 701–715.

Zillman, Dolf. "Excitation Transfer in Communication-Mediated Aggressive Behavior." *Journal of Experimental Social Psychology* 7 (1971): 419–434.

———. "Transfer of Excitation in Emotional Behavior." *Social Psychology: A Sourcebook.* Eds J.T. Capacioppo and R.E. Petty. New York: Guildford Press, 1983. 215–240.

mementos of contemporary american cinema

twelve

identifying and responding to the unreliable narrator in the movie theater

volker ferenz

In episode 41 of the second season of the original *Star Trek* television series, first aired in 1967, Captain Kirk shows us once again just how clever he is. *The Enterprise* has been hijacked by androids. Their strength is overwhelming, yet they have one fatal flaw: they can only think in a strictly logical manner. To them, a statement must speak for itself and must be unequivocally either true or false. Kirk then tells the androids that Commander Spock always lies. Thus, every time Spock opens his mouth the androids are profoundly confused. No matter what Spock says and how sensible this may sound to them, they tend not to believe a word he says. And so the crew of *The Enterprise* learns to defeat the androids by behaving irrationally and illogically, which results in the leader of the androids having an electronic nervous breakdown.

What Commander Spock represents to the androids—and what the lying Cretan constitutes for philosophers—the unreliable narrator is for those interested in narrative theory. Although there has been disagreement in film narrative theory about what exactly unreliable narration in the cinema refers to, there is also more and more evidence that the concept of unreliable narration ought to be reserved for "realist" films in the classical Hollywood cinema tradition that feature so-called pseudo-diegetic narrators (that is, character-narrators who "take over" their films) who then turn out to be unreliable guides to the fictional world, as is the case in films like *The Usual Suspects* (Bryan Singer, 1995), *Fight Club* (David Fincher, 1999) and *Memento* (Christopher Nolan, 2000). In these cases, character-narrators are so inscribed in "their" films as to appear not only a creation of the films but also, first and foremost, their creators. Only in such instances will viewers attribute textual incongruities and referential difficulties to a character-narrator whom we treat like one of us and who can be given sufficient authority over their narrative and thus the blame for their unreliable reporting, interpreting or evaluating. When facing textual and referential problems in storytelling situations other than that, we already have an adequate set of recuperation strategies at hand in order to resolve such difficulties, and concepts like the art film, the uncanny or the genre of the fantasy film will lead to more satisfactory readings.

In this essay, I will be explaining why only under this specific set of circumstances viewers usually resort to the interpretive strategy of unreliable narration. My initial focus will therefore be one of cognitive narrative theory. In a second step, however, I will also be looking at the question as to what emotional and cognitive responses unreliable narratives may call forth in film viewers.[1] Are there any emotional and cognitive responses that unreliable narratives may be said to be prone to elicit? Although theoretically suspect, is there some kind of "package deal" that can be agreed upon when talking about the cognitive-emotional responses to unreliable filmic narration? So far, theorists have tended to deliver exclusive accounts of this question, claiming that unreliable narration elicits merely one particular response or, as more "rhetoric-oriented" writers would put it, serves only one dominant function. Consider the following three remarks regarding this matter:

> What precisely is the domain of unreliability? It is the discourse, that is, the view of what happens or what the existents are like, not the personality of the narrator. (Chatman, *Story and Discourse* 234)

> the purpose, it seems to me, of unreliable narration, is to foreground certain elements of the narrator's psychology. . . (Wall 21)

> The whole point of the strategy of unreliable narration is that we cannot gain access to the work until we have discarded the lazy assumptions and preconceptions about narrative which we have derived from other works, and on which we tend inertly to rely in making sense of new ones.

258

> The assumption that we can always believe what "I" says is
> especially hard to renounce, not only because the only
> obvious alternative to it seems to be that the narrative is
> simply nonsense, but also because our instinctive identifi-
> cation with "I" makes it necessary for us to doubt the reli-
> ability of our own perceptions and judgements before we
> can doubt the narrator's. Unreliable narration undermines
> the reader's *suffisance* along with the narrator's authority,
> and the sense of disorientation it induces is so extreme that
> one is hardly surprised that *Detour* is one of the few movies
> which have dared to make use of it. (Britton 178)

While Seymour Chatman foregrounds the function of highlighting the discourse at the expense of the character-narrator's psychology in the context of Vladimir Nabokov's novel *Lolita* (1955), Kathleen Wall does the exact opposite in an introductory part to her analysis of Kazuo Ishiguro's novel *The Remains of the Day* (1989) and Andrew Britton, in his discussion of the *film noir Detour* (Edgar Ulmer, 1945), focuses on the viewers questioning their largely contextual frames of reference they bring along to the cinema. Although, at first sight, these results seem rather contradictory, I believe that they are not necessarily so. On the contrary, upon closer inspection these statements seem to be supplementing each other when we take into account that, while superficially discussing the primary cognitive-emotional response to unreliable narration, Chatman, Wall and Britton seem to be answering different aspects of one and the same issue. Chatman concentrates on the novel *Lolita* as a *production*, highlighting Nabokov's mastery of the craft. Wall pays particular attention to the character construction within Ishiguro's *text* by stating that the reader's attention is redirected to the character-narrator's mindset. And Britton focuses on the impression unreliable filmic narration can leave in the process of our *reception* of a particular film. In short, an exclusive account of the cognitive-emotional responses to unreliable narration isolating only one particular response appears to be a rather limited answer to a highly complex question. Instead of trying to ascertain what *the cognitive-emotional response* to unreliable narration is, we had better ask what the often-interconnected *main responses* to unreliable narration can be.[2]

What I have in mind, thus, is not to provide an exclusive package deal simply because the "same form or formal pattern can always serve as means to different effects, and vice versa" (Yacobi, "Package Deals" 223), yet a package deal of sorts which is flexible and dynamic enough to account for the various cognitive-emotional responses which are easily elicited by unreliable filmic narratives. These responses which often complement one another rather than preside over each other are as follows: firstly, and referring to Murray Smith's seminal work *Engaging Characters* on fictional characters as our entry points into fiction, unreliable narrators are engaging characters of a special kind as they require the viewer to engage with them in an often-exhaustive and sometimes-exhausting way; secondly, unreliable filmic narratives frequently "exhibit" highly satirical elements about the time and age they are set in; and thirdly, films such as *Memento* invite us to think about the modern discourse of epistemological scepticism because they playfully stage the epistemic limitations experienced by their respective character-narrators, which is, I would like to argue, facilitated by the strategy of unreliable narration. Any one of these responses alone demands the viewer to be highly alert and active, yet it is the inextricable connection of these responses that makes unreliable narration such a rich theme and situates it at the interface of aesthetics and ethics as well as description and interpretation.[3] Because unreliable narration often elicits several complex cognitive-emotional responses at the same time, it potentially possesses a very activating, or maybe, one might argue, unsettling quality.

identifying unreliable narration in the cinema

In film narrative theory, the concept of the unreliable narrator is increasingly being treated with a little disrespect.[4] In fact, it has become something of a mixed bag, which is largely due to an unfortunate unawareness of several key texts in narrative theory displayed by a number of writers. Initially, some scholars allowed for two classes of unreliable narrators in film: unreliable character-narrators who appear to be the source of what we see and hear and then turn out to be unreliable with regard to the facts of the fictional world, and unreliable voice-over narrators whose subjective interpretations of particular scenes are instantaneously undermined by the image-track which provides the "correct" reading of such scenes (Chatman, *Story and Discourse* 235–37; Chatman, *Coming to Terms* 136; Burgoyne 8). Other writers have sought to widen the scope of unreliable filmic narration by examining instances of unreliable narration in films without a personalized narrator. In this respect, unreliable narration has been approached as a kind of narration that leads the viewer to draw incorrect inferences (Bordwell 83; Buckland; Currie; Wilson 39–44). Again others have interpreted the narratological category of the unreliable narrator in a rather journalistic fashion by ultimately equating narratorial unreliability with the aesthetics of the "second surrealism" of the European art film of the 1960s (Koebner; Meder) or merging it with the notion of the uncanny (Liptay; Thompson). As it stands today, the term is as popular and imprecise as ever.[5]

In literary narrative theory, no such profound confusion exists. Although there has been disagreement over which position best meets its explication, the participants in the debate have always shared a common vision of the concept of the unreliable narrator. Whether writing within a more rhetorical and ethical tradition and adhering to the notion of the implied author (Booth; Chatman, *Coming to Terms*; Olson; Phelan; Rimmon-Kenan) or approaching the topic from a more cognitive angle emphasizing the role of the reader (Fludernik, "Defining"; Jahn; Nünning, "Unreliable"; Zerweck), most scholars usually envisage the unreliable narrator as a character-narrator "whose rendering of the story and/or commentary on it the reader has reasons to suspect" (Rimmon-Kenan 100).[6] In unreliable narration, thus, readers sense a discrepancy between the character-narrator's version of the story events and the events as they "truly" are or have been. This discrepancy is consequently ascribed to the character-narrator who is then described or judged as unreliable. Unreliable narration is therefore a case of dramatic irony. Due to certain textual signals that allow the recipient to read between the lines, s/he gains some additional knowledge of the character-narrator's reliability and begins to call the character-narrator's statements into question. Whether the character-narrator's unreliability is of a factual, epistemological or ideological nature, s/he eventually becomes the "butt of irony."[7]

It is this significant discrepancy between the overall agreement in literary narrative theory and the vagueness dominating film narrative theory on the issue of the unreliable narrator which provides the point of departure for the present chapter. Although overlooked for more than a decade, Seymour Chatman has already warned against an inflationary use of the concept. Buried in a footnote in his seminal *Coming to Terms*, Chatman argues that we

> must be precise in our use of the term "unreliable narration."
> It is a meaningful concept only when it refers to the actual
> and overt misrepresentation or distortion of story "facts," by
> a narrator's guile, naiveté, or whatever. (225, note 21)

Is it sensible, as Chatman does, to reserve the concept of unreliable narration merely for strongly personalized narrators? In other words, what is the scope of unreliable filmic narration?

Let us turn directly to a type of narrator which is quite rare in the cinema, the "pseudo-diegetic narrator." First captured by Gerard Genette (236–7), the pseudo-diegetic narrative has been defined as follows: "A second-degree narrative . . . brought up to the level of the primary narrative and taken in charge by its narrator" (Prince, 78). David Alan Black has taken up the cue and applied this category of the pseudo-diegetic narrator to film narrative theory. As Black (22) puts it: "The story-within-a-story, in other words, becomes the story. One generation of quotation marks is excised; everything beyond is shifted by one level." Black then refers to *Double Indemnity* (Billy Wilder, 1944) as one of the more prominent examples of pseudo-diegesis in film, and indeed the films commonly associated with the term *film noir* seem to feature some of cinema's most famous pseudo-diegetic narrators.

In these films, the primary narrative level gives way to the embedded narrator who takes over the function of the principal storyteller.

Note how differently the effect of pseudo-diegesis can be achieved. First, the most common way to do this is to have a character tell another character her or his story, as is the case in a film such as *The Usual Suspects* in which Verbal Kynt, apparently a low-profile criminal, talks to an officer about his involvement in the drug deal that led to the film's initial climax. We frequently return to the primary level, and there is no chance of mistaking pseudo-diegesis for primary action. Second, other films, such as *Fight Club*, go a step further in reducing the metadiegetic way station. *Fight Club* opens *in medias res* with their respective main characters in a highly troubled condition. They then take over their narratives, and the film returns to the framing action only at the very end. As Mieke Bal states:

> Often the primary fabula is hardly more than the occasion for a perceptible, character-bound narrator to narrate a story. The primary fabula may, for instance, be presented as a situation in which the necessary change cannot be made, because . . . then the embedded narrative follows. (54)

Third, a film such as *Spider* (David Cronenberg, 2002)—to borrow from a non-North American title—is more elusive since there is no clear demarcation of exactly when the film's narration switches from the impersonal rendering of the story to the personal mode of its main character. Very often, the protagonist literally walks inside his memories about his childhood, and (imagined) past and (factual) present merge into one. This is a technique used quite frequently in the European art film. Several diegetic levels flow into one image- and soundtrack. The crucial difference to the European art film is that finally those levels can be easily separated out, and the confusion between them can then be attributed to the protagonist.

A brief look at how the set-up of a pseudo-diegetic narrative can look in a film shall suffice at this point. The opening shots of the film *Fight Club* show how in no more than a minute and in fewer than a dozen shots a film can convincingly establish a pseudo-diegetic narrative. After the logo of the distribution company (20th Century Fox), the logo of the production company (Regency) and the title sequence, the film opens with a close-up shot of the face of the character that begins speaking in the voice-over after only a few seconds. The image-track then seems to follow his thinking. When he pictures several vans full of explosives in the underground parking lots of the surrounding buildings, the camera follows suit. From then on, the character-narrator sets the pace in the voice-over, and the image-track follows straight after. After only one minute, the film leaves the framing action behind and flashes back to several months earlier when the narrator finds his earlier self in a support group for men with testicular cancer. Therefore, little more than a minute of discourse time passes, and the story time covers already little less than a year. Writing on the 1946 *film noir The Locket*, Branigan (*Point of View,* 32) sums up the narrative principle at work in *Fight Club*:

> While time in one sense is marked as discontinuous, it is also
> marked as continuous in another sense; namely, discontin-
> uous as to narrative space . . . but continuous as to charac-
> ter. . . More specifically, the time of character memory will
> now justify the telling of the story.

Included the logos of distribution company and production company and the title sequence, we have taken several steps down in the hierarchy of narrative levels in a rather short space of discourse time, from the level of the financial backers and the creative team (historical author) to the workings of an extradiegetic narrative instance (cinematic narrator) that presents some fictional characters (character), one of which then takes over the narration (pseudo-diegetic narrator) and tells us about his current plight (external focalization), invites us to share what he experienced earlier (internal focal-ization surface) and even reveals some of his dreams and hallucinations to us (internal focalization depth). After that, the narrative as a whole doesn't leave the last three domains. Thus, what is being forcefully set in place here is a pseudo-diegetic storytelling situation which resembles that of homodi-egetic narration in literature with its characteristic distinction between nar-rating-I (the voice-over) and experiencing-I (the image-track). Subjective devices throughout the entire film then render it a character-narration, and we have good grounds for ascribing textual peculiarities and referential abnormalities to the character-narrator apparently in charge of the film.

The ways in which pseudo-diegesis can be achieved are numerous, and in these cases the character-narrator in question is so inscribed in the film as to seem the generator of not only images and sounds but also *mise en scène*, fram-ing, editing, etc. In other words, some films create the sense of character-narration so strongly that the viewer accepts the pseudo-diegetic narrator as if s/he were not only a creation but, first and foremost, a creator. An often-voiced objection to the idea of the "first-person film" has been film's lack of the personal pronoun. Due to its technical nature and, narratologically speaking, rather impersonal codes and conventions, film does not have an equivalent to the literary homodiegetic narrator. This is certainly the case. However, one should not ignore the fact that several films, some of which have been mentioned above, feature pseudo-diegetic narrators who appear to be in charge of the images we see and the sounds we hear. In these cases, images and sounds can be clearly attributed to a character, even if the film as a structural whole sooner or later gives way to the unlimited powers of the cinematic narrator.

David Alan Black has summed up the tension created by character-narrators taking over a narration or a large part thereof:

The tension of attribution generated by a scene's invocation by a character on the one hand, and its dramatic fruition by the film's primary agency on the other, can be characterized now as a struggle between two narrators at two levels; or, similarly, as an ambiguity as to the level on which the narrated sequence itself belongs. Is . . . the narrational territory [that] of the invoking narrator or of the intrinsic, extradiegetic narrator? (22)

Black describes the mechanism at work in film sequences that can in some way be attributed to a character-narrator as an unfair struggle between two narrators at two different levels: the always diegetic personal narrator and the always extradiegetic impersonal narrator. The logics of the cinematic narrator and the conventions and traditions of classical narration have it that this external narrative agency is granted total authority and freedom, and can at any moment supersede a character's invoked discourse. It is common knowledge now that character-subjectivity in film is sooner or later embedded in the doings of the cinematic narrator, and that very few fiction films have tried to maintain character-subjectivity throughout. However, one should not take the stance that sustained character-subjectivity in the cinema is an impossibility, an argument still widely prevalent today. A more moderate stance that acknowledges cinema's inherent dual agency, yet grants the possibility of pseudo-diegesis is far more desirable. As Edward Branigan (*Narrative Comprehension* 101) argues:

Characters, of course, may become storytellers or dreamers by recounting events to someone. These events may even be dramatized visually for the spectator as in a character flashback or dream sequence. In both these cases, however, the character has a new and *different* function in the text at another level, no longer as an actor who defines, and is defined by, a causal chain, but as a diegetic narrator (i.e., a narrator limited by the laws of the story world) who is now recounting a story within a story: he or she as an actor in a past event becomes the *object* of his or her narration in the present.

As Branigan indicates, in cinematic pseudo-diegetic narration we will almost inevitably find the literary distinction of narrating-I and experiencing-I. In fact, what we witness is a proximity to the literary homodiegetic narrator. As Brian McFarlane has shown in his analysis of David Lean's adaptation of *Great Expectations*, although the notion of "first-person film" appears to be misleading, we still observe a near closeness to the novel's basic narrative situation:

What Lean's film offers, then, is not a first-person narration as the novel does, but an enunciatory strategy which

> goes a long way towards ensuring parallelism between
> Pip's and the audience's knowledge. This constitutes not a
> transfer . . . but an adaptation in terms of what the screen
> can, in its classical fictional mode, approximate in this
> respect. (127)

Techniques such as the voice-over, subjective camera, the main character's near omnipresence, the composition of screen space, and also the
musical score, all contribute to the sense that the film appears to be generated by its protagonist.

Hence, only in the case of the cinematic pseudo-narrator does the
term unreliable narrator stand on a sound narratological basis. Because
in pseudo-diegetic narration we deal with a character-narrator who can
be given a voice, a body and sufficient authority over her/his narrative, it
is only in this case that we can resolve referential difficulties and textual
incongruities according to the perspectival principle as elaborated by
Tamar Yacobi. In these instances, "the inferred source of the tensions and
hence the mechanism of their reconciliation takes on a perspectival
form: the form of a limited figure who observes (narrates, experiences,
evaluates) the represented world" ("Fictional Reliability" 118). This is the
case in such films as *The Usual Suspects*, *Fight Club* and *Memento*—and let me
also refer to other contemporary but not strictly North American films
American Psycho (Mary Harron, 1999), *Spider*, *The End of the Affair* (Neil Jordan,
1999) and *The Machinist* (Brad Anderson, 2004). It is not the case in films
such as *Badlands* (Terrence Malick, 1973) because the film's voice-over narrator at no time assumes the role of the principal storyteller. It is also not
the case in a film like *Barry Lyndon* (Stanley Kubrick, 1975), because the
heterodiegetic voice-over narrator usually lacks both personality and
involvement in story matters. Nor is it the case in such diverse films as
Jacob's Ladder (Adrian Lyne, 1990), *The Sixth Sense* (M. Night Shyamalan,
1999) or *Secret Window* (David Koepp, 2004), because we may well attribute
inconsistencies to some strong supernatural forces or horror conventions at work in these films. However, once we face a pseudo-diegetic
narrator in the form of a clearly identifiable character who relates her/his
own story, we deal with a strongly personalized kind of narrator whom
we can make the scapegoat for the contradictions in her/his unreliable
narrating.

265

unreliable narratives on the screen: emotional roller coasters in the audience

After explaining under what specific circumstances viewers usually identify
an unreliable narrator in the cinema, it is worthwhile to inspect the cognitive-
emotional responses these narrators often elicit in the film viewer. This is

because unreliable narratives can be said to "happen" on the borderline of the mainstream and the art film and thus call forth "unusual" responses. First of all, because unreliable narratives inevitably create psychologically rich situations—we are spatiotemporally aligned to a character-narrator who gives us access to their thoughts, subjective imagery charges the cinema with an air of intimacy, the revelation of their unreliability brings about a mixed bag of feelings—they usually engage the viewer in a host of largely emotional ways. I therefore would like to claim that unreliable narratives are prone to be received as emotional roller coasters, because viewers have to inspect their feelings for a particular character-narrator time and again or may in certain cases even form "perverse allegiances," as that character-narrator often isn't straight with us or even morally suspect.[8] This kind of response to unreliable narrators demands the viewer to actively engage with the film in question because of its potential to evoke "fringes of sympathy" for morally highly suspect character-narrators.

In unreliable filmic narration, we are invited to share a character-narrator's perspective to a very large extent, and because we treat that narrator like one of us, we grant her or him the liberty to speak rather positively about her- or himself. As a consequence, it shouldn't come as a surprise that particular character-narrators choose to characterize themselves in worthy terms, thus eliciting positive feelings for themselves. It is a common tendency in unreliable filmic narration, hence, that many unreliable narrators, who might not even be consciously aware of their shortcomings, present themselves as victims or underdogs. But because in unreliable filmic narration there always potentially exists another discourse above the one offered by the character-narrator, our sympathetic feelings for that character-narrator hinge to a large part on how and when we find out about both the fact and the extent of her or his unreliability. Once viewers detect the unreliability of a certain character-narrator, they are then likely to apply their cognitive schemata to find out what "really" happened in the story world in order to resolve the character-narrator's limited, distorted or false perspective and construct the "right" version of the story world. Consequently, once we discover a character-narrator's unreliability, we are likely to withdraw some of our sympathetic feelings for her or him. Just as the colloquial use of the adjective "unreliable" is negatively burdened in real life, the usage of the term unreliable narrator continues to be somewhat tainted, as it implies an inability or unwillingness to be "honest" and tell the "truth" about the story world. And even though, in constructivist terms, this might be considered just natural or normal or whatever, against much of our Western folk model of psychology this remains to be regarded "deviant."

Just consider the highly charged response to the 1999 film, *Fight Club*, where the character-narrator's unreliability is merely alluded to intermittently in the film and exposed only towards the end. Because the clues and signals pointing to narratorial unreliability are dropped rather sparsely in the form of well-hidden Easter eggs, the viewer is not necessarily poised to question the character-narrator's mimetic authority, his judgements or his characterizations of other characters. The viewer knows the character-narrator to be irrational and even amoral, but because s/he will not find out about his unreliability until the end of the film, much of what we see and hear goes unchallenged and is reassessed only in retrospect. In such a case, viewers are likely to grant the character-narrator more narrative authority because the guideline goes that he is "reliable" until he's shown to be "unreliable." What this kind of postponing the revelation of narratorial unreliability until the very end facilitates, then, is that viewers are likely to gain a deeper understanding of the reasons of the character-narrator's being unreliable. We might not feel sympathy with him thanks to his questionable moral values and his brutal excesses, but we may understand his motivations and we might even agree with him that he is to a certain extent victimized himself by contemporary society, his business company or whatever. It is this very fact which may draw us closer to the main character; if *Fight Club* had been rendered in the impersonal mode, this sort of engagement would have been virtually impossible, as the depiction of the main character would have been likely to be more pathetic than it already is in the personal mode.

This form of engagement with an unreliable character-narrator takes an even sharper turn in the film *American Psycho*. Other than in films such as *Fight Club* or *Memento*, in *American Psycho* no significant signs concerning the character-narrator's unreliability are dropped during most of the film. Patrick Bateman (Christian Bale) might be an "unreliable person," but that he also might be an unreliable narrator we find out only close to the film's ending. Throughout, we are aligned to Bateman, and our allegiance with him is one of complete antipathy. Occasional moments of sympathy for him may occur, when, for instance, he scolds a business associate for making anti-Semitic remarks. Also, sporadic moments of pity for Bateman may arise when we learn that he obtained his job on Wall Street only due to his father's owning the company. Other than that, however, Bateman is a classical anti-hero for displaying such abundance in attributes that make us dislike him. Concerning the events of the fictional world, however, the viewer is in this case presented with a rather consistent account of the story world, yet we have to realize towards the end that the character-narrator might be mad and that everything up until then might have been figments of his mind. We either accept the possibility that carnivorous cash machines exist or we ascribe this to the character-narrator's narrating activity. Most viewers will entertain the second notion and will have to admit that none of what we have seen so far might have been "true." This sudden and surprising discovery of the character-narrator's madness makes *American Psycho* an extreme case in our engagement with the film's main character. The discovery of the character-narrator's probable unreliability will not automatically lead the viewer to condemn or stigmatize the character-narrator as psychologically insane; rather, s/he is likely to bear in mind that we were given a long and at times rather impartial insight into the world of thought of a mentally ill person. This kind of character engagement seems to be limited to unreliable narratives: had the character-narrator's madness been revealed earlier in the film, we would have felt repelled far earlier.

These different ways of our engagement with unreliable character-narrators are distinguished by (1) when and (2) how the fact and extent of their unreliability is revealed to the spectator and (3) how character-narrators respond to their unreliability. (1) Unreliable narratives may reveal both the fact and the extent of narratorial unreliability early in the film, they may disclose slowly the fact and only at the end the extent of the character-narrator's unreliability and they may unveil only the fact but not the extent of unreliability. (2) The revelation of their unreliability may be initiated by the unreliable narrators themselves as part of their characters' developments or a higher narrative level may instigate it. And (3) unreliable narrators may act on or indulge in their shortcomings. Generally speaking, the earlier unreliability is revealed, the more it seems initiated by a character's development and the more unreliable narrators act on it and seek to correct their "shortcomings," the more pleased viewers will be. (1) and (2) chiefly depend on our drive to establish character coherence, aesthetic coherence and narrative coherence. These processes thus largely happen on the level of reading, understanding and making sense of films. (3) takes into account that many viewers favour more "realist" frameworks and like to see the "relativism" embodied by many unreliable narrators either rejected or at least acknowledged, a point that I will turn to later in this chapter. This process therefore occurs largely on a level of interpretation and evaluation.

Because many viewers are likely to be offended in some way by the character-narrators' discourses in films such as *Fight Club*, *American Psycho* and *Memento*, it is unsurprising that unreliable narratives often lay bare the viewers' predispositions. In his analysis of Nabokov's novel *Lolita*, James Phelan makes some pertinent points regarding this idea. The debate around the unreliable narrative *Lolita*, writes Phelan (2005 102), is "ultimately about the ethics of reading and about the relation between aesthetic and ethics." What Phelan writes with respect to the novel *Lolita*, I would like to set in the context of the film *Fight Club*. Defenders of the film usually make two key ethical assumptions. First, a film's treatment of its topic is more important than the topic itself and some individual aspects of its treatment; that is, we need to see the character-narrator's discourse of *Fight Club* in the wider context of contemporary society and its inherent areas of difficulty. Second, we ought to be open to the possibility of reform; hence, several critics have taken up the opportunity of discussing *Fight Club* as a coming-of-age story. As Phelan succinctly puts it, "both of these assumptions entail the principle that aesthetics and ethics are inextricably intertwined, though they tend to give pride of place to aesthetics" (102). Those objecting to the film usually make two oppositional ethical assumptions. First, the very act of representing certain sensitive topics, such as the explicit violence in *Fight Club* or being solely aligned to the doings of a potentially insane serial killer in *American Psycho*, is ethically suspect, for the reason that some topics and aspects of their aesthetic treatments are so offensive as to seriously impair any larger project undertaken by the filmmakers. Second, giving credence to the perpetrator in a film like *American Psycho* puts the emphasis in the wrong place. Again, aesthetics and ethics are interconnected, but pride of place is this time given to ethics.

It would appear that unreliable narratives elicit several largely emotional responses that are more intense than many other narrative films rendered in the impersonal mode do. First, "understanding a character is in itself pleasurable, not least when the complexity of the narrative film is rooted in the development of the character" (Tan 191). Yet because both the fact and the extent of a character-narrator's unreliability will often cause spectators to re-inspect, postpone, change, etc., their understanding of that character-narrator, this process can become the source of emotional frustration. Generally speaking, the earlier we detect a character-narrator's unreliability and we can "nail down" a character onto certain personality traits and hence establish character coherence, the more pleased we will be. If this is not possible, many viewers will be emotionally frustrated and—an objection often voiced in the reception of unreliable narratives—feel disappointed or even cheated. However, when we finally understand a character to be unreliable and have been eventually able to establish character coherence, we will find cognitive and emotional pleasure by having unearthed the figure in the carpet. As a result, by having made sense of the character and thus having been able to establish aesthetic and narrative coherence as well, spectators will then feel to have taken charge of the film as a whole. Second, even more exhaustive and complex in our engagement with unreliable character-narrators is the fact that often we have to emotionally position ourselves again and again. And third, though this may be frustrating as well, under certain circumstances this can also become a pleasurable activity, namely, when we consciously engage in "perverse allegiances" and derive a degree of pleasure from sympathizing with a character whose norms and values we would find despicable in real life. Thus, unreliable narratives in film are certainly emotional roller coasters, and for those spectators ready to postpone moral judgement they provide a risk-free opportunity to inspect the schemata we use in making sense, understanding, judging, evaluating, etc., screen characters and therefore, by implication, real people as well.

same time, same place, same coffee: unreliable narration in film and its satirical tendencies

When surveying the unreliable filmic narratives touched upon so far, one of their salient common features is that they have often been interpreted in terms of satire. As a rule, a filmic satire is perceived to be a mode of filmmaking that exposes the failings of individuals, institutions or societies to ridicule and scorn. Its tone may vary from tolerant amusement to bitter indignation, and it can range from being formal and direct (in which case the filmmaker addresses the audiences more or less "directly") to informal and indirect (in which case the satirical elements are merely "indirectly" displayed but not explicitly pointed out by the filmmaker). Unreliable filmic narration, I would like to contend, is prone to be recuperated in terms of indirect satire because it uses, per definition, the means of structural or dramatic irony, as unreliable narration involves a contrast between a character-narrator's view of the fictional world and a contrary state of affairs, which viewers can sooner or later grasp. Consequently, this contrast between the character-narrator's perspective and the viewer's grasp on the story world creates a gap that may allow for occasional relief in the form of indirect satire. Sometimes these two differing views or stances couldn't be more different, making the character-narrator and his ethical or ideological stance the object of satire.

But there is more to it than that. Not only the unreliable narrator but also the fictional world depicted in an unreliable narrative may be subjected to satire. Because the viewer is solely aligned to an unreliable character-narrator, who habitually exhibits a somewhat deviant or erratic behaviour and whose capacities may be quite limited, it is the viewer who is likely to notice the laughable or ridiculous elements of the depicted fictional world. Hence, very frequently in unreliable filmic narration, satirical elements are merely alluded to in the discourse of an unreliable narrator, and it falls to the viewer to imply another level of meaning "above" that discourse. While viewers will continue to ascribe the film's oddities to the respective unreliable character-narrator, some of these oddities will lead viewers to arrive at another level of meaning in the film as a whole. To express it in terms of the aesthetic paradox: while we treat a narrative film as if it depicted reality and therefore, in a first step, we blame the character-narrator, who appears to be in charge of the film, for its inconsistencies, we know too well that the narrative strategy of unreliable narration is often— yet not necessarily always—an intentional act ascribable to a filmmaker or, more appropriately, a creative team.

On the basis of her or his foreknowledge and already existing frames of reference, it is the viewer who, in a highly active act of naturalization, questions and, if need be, overrules the unreliable character-narrator's stance. We then arrive at an important theoretical issue, and the question is whether unreliable narration ought to be described as a means of reconfirming the viewer's world picture or as a means of challenging the viewers' ethical and moral values. As one writer, slightly ironically, states:

> The naturalization of the text through the dissolution of the hermeneutic tension created by the inconsistencies of an unreliable narrative constitutes a kind of closure which privileges the reader's horizon over that of the narrator and allows the recipient ultimately to sink back into his armchair there to spend a nice and cosy evening with the ideas of his reconfirmed world picture. In new historicist terms, this would turn unreliable narration into an instrument of containment only and would ignore its subversive potential. (Antor, 358)

By evoking satire through a clash between an unreliable character-narrator's discourse and our grasping their unreliability and the "true" state of affairs, viewers will often rush to reconfirm their already existing frames of reference. Antor sarcastically describes this mechanism as

> this yearning for consistency and harmony, for a well-patterned world that can clearly, accurately, and reliably be represented by the frames and schemata of our world models . . . a reflex of our need for orientation, our will to understand and thus control and domesticate the world we live in order to be able to feel safe in it. (358)

But is this really a contradiction? I believe there is no need for sarcasm in theorizing unreliable narration as both potentially subversive (being confronted with the often-unsettling discourse of an unreliable narrator) as well as potentially affirmative (being able to dismiss the unreliable character-narrator as, well, unreliable). However, I believe that, firstly, in our Western cultural context and, secondly and more importantly, within the tradition of the classical Hollywood cinema, unreliable filmic narration still possesses a transforming quality, because it confronts the viewer with an unreliable view of certain affairs and thus encourages the spectator to take an ethical position. In the case of the satirical elements of unreliable narratives, this means that unreliably narrated films may display the negative effects of societal problems which are indirectly criticized. These satirical elements in turn can be either played down or pointed out by the individual viewer, but they surely demand the viewer to take an ethical stance and to rather consciously apply her or his frames of reference.

I would like to demonstrate this point with reference to the film *Fight Club* and some of the critical reactions to it. First published in the *Chicago Sun-Times*, one review exemplifies the somewhat paradoxical effect of unreliable filmic narration of being potentially subversive by displaying severely satirical elements while at the same time allowing for the critic to dismiss

271

these satirical elements as mere figments of an unreliable narrator, thus reaching a kind of closure by eventually reconfirming an already existing world picture. After branding the film "the most cheerfully fascist big-star movie since *Death Wish*," film critic Roger Ebert goes on to observe that *Fight Club* has at its core a "depressed loner filled up to here with angst. He describes his world in dialogue of sardonic social satire. His life and job are driving him crazy," which leads him into the arms of a character called Tyler Durden, "a shadowy, charismatic figure, able to inspire a legion of men in big cities to descend into the secret cellars of a Fight Club and beat one another up." The fairly arbitrary move of branding *Fight Club* a fascist vehicle while describing it as a satire culminates in the following speculation:

> Of course, *Fight Club* itself does not advocate Durden's philosophy. It is a warning against it, I guess; one critic I like says it makes "a telling point about the bestial nature of man and what can happen when the numbing effects of day-to-day drudgery cause people to go a little crazy." I think it's the numbing effect of movies like this that cause people to go a little crazy. (Ebert)

Clearly, the critic feels forced to take an ethical stance in the face of having watched a screening of *Fight Club*. What is more important here, however, is the critic's conscious choice not to interpret and evaluate the film as a satire, after admitting that this possibility clearly exists. But he does not, and instead he makes a most radical U-turn. After accurately observing that *Fight Club* can easily be read as a satire on contemporary society, he at least weakens, if not effectively contradicts, his initial statement that the film is a cheerful fascist vehicle.

This unwillingness to consequently interpret *Fight Club* as a social satire is in no way limited to a few right-wing commentators. In a similar fashion, there has been a tendency with some politically left-leaning reviewers and academics to lament *Fight Club*'s regressive tendencies or lack of solution of any kind for the crisis its character-narrator faces. Henry Giroux, for instance, laments the film's alleged conflation of the issue of emasculation and the notion of consumerism which, in Giroux's view, had better treated separately: "If Jack [the film's character-narrator] represents the crisis of capitalism repackaged as the crisis of a domesticated masculinity, Tyler represents the redemption of masculinity repackaged as the promise of violence in the interests of social and political anarchy" (Giroux, 34). Thus it comes as no surprise that Giroux finds that "*Fight Club* has nothing substantive to say about the structural violence of unemployment, job insecurity, cuts in public spending, and the destruction of institutions capable of defending social provisions and the public good" (33).

What these commentators don't seem to be willing to acknowledge, one may well argue, is the extent to which *Fight Club* sets out to satirize not only its character-narrator and the society he lives in but also the solutions he comes up with to overcome his identity crisis. *Fight Club*'s character-narrator (Edward Norton) might be clever at times, he might generate some spectatorial sympathy and he might be said to represent a sense of alienation, but he is also very pathetic in his struggle, highly hysterical in dealing with other people and extremely laughable in his admiration for his *alter ego* Tyler. To the same extent, his *alter ego* (Brad Pitt) is also subjected to satire in that he neither represents a positive nor negative alternative to the character-narrator's fundamental problems. Tyler himself "builds a bridge from the anti-materialist rhetoric of the 1960s [. . .] into the kind of paramilitary dream project that Ayn Rand might have admired" (Maslin 14). In short, he has a bit of Janis Joplin about himself, cites a few phrases of Ayn Rand and seems to know one or two things about Nietzsche, but— just as the nameless character-narrator—Tyler is a patchwork of attitudes and phrases, which he does not seem to be able to fully control. He is most certainly not a credible solution to the character-narrator's predicament. Furthermore, just as the helpless character-narrator and his pathetic *alter ego* are subjected to ridicule in the film, so is the society that produces individuals like the character-narrator. Everywhere the character-narrator goes, we can find satirical elements that escape his horizon. In his open-plan office, when he stands at a photocopier, we see several employees making copies in the exact same manner whilst sipping their Starbucks coffee in the exact same manner. Also, when we see the character-narrator sitting at his work desk, he in his pastel-coloured suit perfectly blends in with his pastel-coloured office furniture. Or, when his superior approaches him with a file, the character-narrator reduces him to his tie by reading the day of the week from the colour of his tie. All this may be usual for the character-narrator himself, but it is at the same time ridiculous for the viewer. These inference invitations to read *Fight Club* as a social satire continue when the character-narrator decides to visit self-help groups in which, for the most part, an American flag looms well-lit in the darkened background. And it is this abundance in inference invitations that allows the viewer to interpret *Fight Club* as a social satire.

Similar instances of satire can be attributed to most of the other unreliable filmic narratives in film. From *American Psycho* to *The Usual Suspects*, the evidence for the claim that unreliable narration often seems to "exhibit" elements of satire is overwhelming. This suggests that unreliable narration facilitates the bringing about of satirical elements, and theoretically this claim can be underpinned with recourse to the notion of dramatic irony. While we hear and see what the unreliable narrators say and do, we may resolve certain textual difficulties such as the stereotypical depiction of other characters on a higher level of satire. Because we have defined the unreliable narrator as a pseudo-diegetic character-narrator who can be said to be, to a certain extent, in the driving seat of the narration, s/he can distort, manipulate or limit the viewers' access to the story world. And because viewers bring with them their frames of reference and knowledge about the world, they know that the characters crowding the self-help groups in *Fight Club* or the Wall Street Yuppies in *American Psycho* are not entirely realistic depictions. By having an unreliable narrator giving a somewhat shrewd perspective onto the story world, the filmmaker can remain in the background and deliver indirect satires of certain characters, particular institutions or contemporary society, and it is the viewer who has to conduct the critique of the *status quo* when the unreliable narrator is incapable and the filmmaker unwilling to do so. We can therefore now assert that satire is often a side effect of the narrative strategy of unreliable narration.

the usual unreliable narrators and their main offence: epistemological scepticism

Because unreliable narratives present us with character-narrators who either cannot or do not want to tell what "really happened" in the story world, they tend to have as one of their major themes the question as to whether "objective truth" is easily accessible. By having this question at their thematic cores, unreliable narratives can be said to be rather old-fashioned by standing in the tradition of literary modernism, since postmodernism would deem such a question to be rather naïve and ultimately beside the point. The upshot of unreliable narration is that we are always referred back to a subject from whose perspective we experience the constraints imposed onto her or him, a point that is overlooked in much postmodernist criticism.

Yet epistemological scepticism has many forms, and in unreliable narratives we often face only one or two aspects of this rather complex issue. In *Memento,* for instance, the central issue of epistemological scepticism with its roots in radical constructivism is staged by the film as a whole. *Memento*'s main character, Leonard (Guy Pearce), can be regarded as a textbook case of psychological constructivism. Within the fictional world, the existence of an outer reality is denied at no point, yet most of what we get to know in this film is what the autopoietic human being makes of it. Furthermore, Leonard actively constructs his memories according to his situation and his needs in the here-and-now, just as he chooses to ignore certain facts about his past. Similarly, his continuous voice-over mirrors what constructivists call the endless autobiographical dialogue we hold with ourselves. And although a "realist" view of objectivity is alluded to several times during the film when, for instance, Teddy (Joe Pantoliano) tells Leonard that his wife wasn't diabetic, implying that Leonard himself accidentally killed her (which viewers are invited more than once to conclude for themselves), that view is quickly rejected by the main character. This is manifest in the two images that pass through Leonard's head at that point: one shows him injecting his wife with a dose of insulin, the other shows him pinching his wife's thigh. In a rather playful manner, we are here given not only two versions of, presumably, the same event, but also asked to make a choice between two oppositional philosophical concepts; that is, between a more realist view of objectivity (him injecting his wife with a dose of insulin) and a radical constructivist view (him pinching his wife's thigh because he doesn't want the former version to be true). Is objectivity accessible, or is it obfuscated, distorted and finally perverted by the autopoietic organism? With the benefit of hindsight, many viewers are likely to choose the former version of the event while the fictional character Leonard embraces the latter. The epistemological scepticism *Memento* stages is, then, of a very fundamental nature in that inductive reasoning is shown to be an end in its own right.

Concerning the notion of personal identity, Mary Litch (85) has argued that *Memento*'s Leonard seems to be highlighting some of the difficulties of more realist identity models. Indeed, there seems to be an overarching theme that we could call an examination of the notion of personal identity. For one, notice the textual evidence for such a claim. At the beginning of the film, shortly before Leonard kills Teddy, the following brief conversation takes place:

TEDDY: You don't even know who you are.
LEONARD: I'm Leonard Shelby. I'm from San Francisco, and I'm . . .
TEDDY: That's who you *were*, you don't know who you *are*.

Almost the exact same conversation resurfaces two more times, once in the middle—what several screenwriting teachers would call the slow-paced and understated mid-point of the film where the film's central themes are reflected—and then again at the end. In addition to that, Leonard's comments on his condition sound at times like common sense when he, for instance, talks about the unreliability of everybody's memory capacities. Moreover, the ultimate revelation that Leonard cannot be said to be physically ill because he is in fact capable of making new memories and manipulating old memories, puts his alleged condition into another, broader context. Teddy's ironic comment upon this is pertinent here: "So you lie to yourself to be happy. *There's nothing wrong with that. We all do it!*"

Therefore, Leonard seems to embody a radical example of what has been named narrative identity. The work in this emerging field of psychology focuses on

> questions of how individuals seek to make meaning of
> their lives, both how they understand themselves as unique
> individuals and as social beings who are multiply defined
> by life stage, gender, ethnicity, class, and culture. At the

core of these efforts at self-understanding is the role of narrative memory and life story construction. (Singer 438)

In the course of this research, it has become apparent that autobiographical memory is always in part construction and not so much reconstitution.
A compelling account of autobiographical memory thus demands a model
of the self and a recognition of "how personality processes interact with
cognitive processes to create a goal-based hierarchy of autobiographical
knowledge. This autobiographical knowledge is expressed through narrative memories that give accounts of the individual's goal pursuits, obstacles, and outcomes" (Singer 441). It would seem that *Memento*'s Leonard fits
into this model. He shapes his memories according to his current goals. In
order to lead a meaningful life, he lives in a permanent state of self-denial
and, in his plight, rather bullies himself into remembering that someone
else killed his wife. According to narrative identity researchers, this would
be, in his circumstances, understandable. That he willingly turns himself
into a serial killer can be said to be the unfortunate and, certainly, ironical
side effect of this continuous process that "yields a life story schema that
provides causal, temporal, and thematic coherence to an overall sense of
identity" (Singer 438). Thus, Leonard's unreliable narration appears to
mirror the possibility that this process of forming a somewhat stable personal identity might be—in extreme cases—a ticking time bomb.

What is remarkable in this context is the struggle of two philosophical
models embodied by Leonard. On the one hand, he demonstrates on a
sophisticated level that he is fully aware of constructivist premises (the
unreliability of memories, the constructed nature of ideas, the turning
subjective habits into "objective truths," etc.) and that personal identity
can be largely seen as a subjective meaning-making activity. On the other
hand, he subscribes to a simplistic form of realism and fixed model of personal identity, as evidenced by his conversations with Teddy. It is certainly
no coincidence that the aforementioned conversation takes place at three
significant points in the film (the beginning, the middle, the end). Equally,
when Leonard convinces himself in the film's epilogue that the outside
world doesn't disappear when you close your eyes, when he says that he
knows what it feels like when he grabs an ashtray and what it sounds
like when he knocks on wood, he eventually embraces a crude realism.
For him, because (a) in such an objective and mind-independent world
somebody else killed his wife (a subjective interpretation), his goal of (b)
revenging her death is just (it is a self-righteous concept). Therefore, (c) it
is okay for him to hunt down that mysterious John G. (a subjectively
understandable form of justice). However, the assumption that some
junkie killed his wife has already been shown to be untrue, and thus this
whole line of reasoning collapses. On the level of the film's story, Leonard's
line of reasoning is but an excuse of sorts to remain a serial killer. On the

level of interpretation, it is a pity for his victims that he preaches constructivism yet practises realism.

It appears that unreliable narration in film is "predestined" to stage this struggle between constructivism and realism on the one hand, and between the model of narrative identity and a more fixed understanding of personal identity on the other hand. The interesting thing about *Memento* is that a more constructivist epistemology is presented as a sensible way of understanding the main character, yet that it may easily lead to the erosion of personal responsibility. Leonard time and again describes himself as a victim of external circumstances and that his "just" mission is merely a wheel in some system of thinking he cannot wholly control. What he lacks is a reflective distance that would enable him to observe the causes of his suppression as though from the outside. Such distance would render the possibilities of freedom even more real for him, his options would increase, and he would assume responsibility for his decisions and for exploiting or disregarding opportunities. Leonard therefore has to opt for a deterministic and bleak view of constructivism; otherwise he would face the uncomfortable and tragic facts of his having become a serial killer. Presenting himself as a small wheel in the big machine of constructivism that cannot be controlled gives him the excuse of sidestepping the issues of personal responsibility and guilt. On the level of interpretation, thus, one is led to think that a philosophical realism of sorts, where we discover features of objective reality rather than construct them, is preferable in the real world.

In *The Usual Suspects*, another aspect in the context of epistemological scepticism is brought into the spotlight, and that is the unreliability of eye-witness testimony. In this film, an apparent small time crook called Roger "Verbal" Kint (Kevin Spacey) is interrogated by the ambitious US customs detective Dave Kujan (Chazz Palminteri) about the heist seen in the initial sequence. According to Kint, a mysterious and phantom-like half-German, half-Turkish super villain is behind it all, yet Kujan believes his archenemy, the ex-cop Keaton, to be the mastermind. Several reasons make the viewers trust Kint's version of the events, no matter how far-fetched and comic-like they may seem: first, they appear to be in accordance with the seemingly impersonal initial sequence in which Keaton is shown to be shot by a shadowy figure; second, Kint's story is presented in nine long flashbacks which all seem coherent and trustworthy, as only few markers render them as subjective accounts of what happened; third, Kujan's alternative version is shown in only one fast-paced sequence dominated by his aggressive voice-over; fourth, the mild-mannered and boyish character qualities of Kint attract more sympathies than the hard-boiled and cynical US customs detective Kujan. Hence, the audience has good grounds for laying its trust with the criminal.

But it shouldn't. Another thread in the film's plot continually shows a survivor of the night before. After initially only being able to mumble the words "Keyser Soze"—which is, of course, another reason for believing Kint's version of the story—a severely wounded Hungarian skipper starts describing Keyser Soze to an illustrator, who finishes his illustration just after Kint has left the police building close to the film's ending. It shows no Keaton and no phantom, but instead it shows none other than Kint himself, or at least a person with features resembling that of Kint. At this point, one might argue that *The Usual Suspects* has left the rules of fair play behind, as the initial sequence contains a POV shot which we were able to ascribe to Kint. However, as it turns out at the end, this shot couldn't have been a POV shot at all because Kint couldn't have been in two places at the same time, witnessing the killing of Keaton from a removed vantage point and committing the killing of Keaton. Hence, we are asked to entertain the idea that even this allegedly impersonal initial sequence was in fact not impersonal at all. Therefore, a profound uncertainty concerning the imagery's truth is raised, and we are likely to ascribe *this* to the filmmakers and not to the film's character-narrator, Kint. It is not that the camera has made itself the accomplice of a criminal, it is that the personal mode hasn't been personal in the first place. Even though, retrospectively, one could point out the breaking of fundamental narrative conventions, one might as well admit that this concern is secondary to the film. In breaking both the conventions of fair play and the viewing contract, *The Usual Suspects* might not play straight despite posing realist throughout, but the film certainly remains an entertaining play with the viewers' expectations.

It is highly intriguing to notice how the notion of epistemological scepticism and those who represent it is dealt with in the fictional worlds of the unreliable filmic narratives themselves. For one, almost all of the unreliable narrators discussed so far are in some form associated with mental institutions or prisons. *Memento*'s unreliable narrator, Leonard, was at some point transferred to a mental institution and has since escaped. Both narrators of *Fight Club* and *American Psycho* would surely benefit from psychiatric help. Kint, the character-narrator of much of the film *The Usual Suspects*, only just escapes imprisonment. Trevor Reznik, the character-narrator of *The Machinist*, hands himself in to the police at the end of the film. And also those characters usually associated with unreliable filmic narration, such as the murderer in *Stage Fright* (Alfred Hitchcock, 1950) or every single one of the characters in *Rashomon* (Akira Kurosawa, 1950), face an intra-diegetic form of persecution.

Without being an apologist for any of these characters, one can say that most of them are discriminated against right from the start by being situated in traditional discourses of mental health, justice and, most importantly, epistemology. Within these traditional discourses, the epistemological scepticism embodied by character-narrators such as *Memento*'s Leonard are deemed unacceptable, as they would throw the traditional notion of truth into turmoil. While any one of the characters just cited is in some form guilty of certain misdoings ranging from spying to multiple homicides, it seems that they are, above all, guilty of exposing the shaky foundations of a more realist notion of truth. By facing intra-diegetic prosecution from the very beginning of their narratives, a form of poetic justice is installed which, to use a post-structuralist catchphrase, "always already" situates them and judges them negatively. Note in this context that in many unreliable narratives the actual acts of crime are regularly neglected to such an extent as to appear side issues, with the focus centred upon the unreliable narrators' deviant forms of epistemological scepticism. Hence, the textual evidence strongly suggests that the character-narrators of such films as *The Usual Suspects*, *Memento* or *American Psycho* are wanted for laying bare the foundations of realism just as much as they are pursued for being criminals. Their main offence appears to be their epistemological scepticism.

A closer look at the films reveals this. In *The Usual Suspects*, for example, the cynical US customs detective Kujan snarls at the unreliable narrator Kint several times as he mythologizes Keyser Soze. What he dislikes most about Kint's narrative is not so much the multiple murders and robberies he should be interested in pursuing, but the presentation of the run-up to the initial heist in the form of some folksy fairy tale. At times, Kujan attentively listens to Kint, he even appears to be entertained by what Kint narrates, but he is quick to reject all this as a silly myth for hard-boiled criminals. Kujan almost fanatically insists on his realist epistemology, which excludes myths and folk tales from the investigation. Similarly, in *Fight Club*, it is ironically the suicidal Marla who laments the mental instability of the film's unreliable narrator. "You have deep emotional problems," she observes but completely ignores all of his other excesses. He might be handsome and "spectacular in bed," yet his "serious emotional issues" make her reject him. In the same manner, the unreliable narrator of *The End of the Affair* is looked down upon by the priest and Sarah for being obsessed with his highly subjective and narrow epistemology. All of his other shortcomings—his jealousy, his bigotry and his violent temper—are easily forgiven by the other characters, but it is his epistemological scepticism and, in this case, his stubborn denial of the existence of God that the other characters persistently seek to correct. Hence, and to put it provocatively, most unreliable narrators in film would be forgiven the worst deeds by their intra-diegetic counterparts if only they let go of their epistemological scepticism to instead embrace a more realist framework.

This again can be backed up by reference to the films. For instance, in *Fight Club*'s concluding sequence, Marla is poised to forgive the character-narrator his bad behaviour when she finds him devastated after having shot himself and successfully battled with his imaginary Other. Eventually, he admits to Marla that "you have met me in a strange period of my life," indicating that this period is now done and dusted. Despite his former abusive behaviour and the mayhem he has caused, Marla might look stunned, yet she doesn't reject his hand, indicating her willingness to deal with him now after his "healing." Along the same lines, in *The Usual Suspects*, Kujan might not have caught the phantom Keyser Soze, but he shows signs of vindication in that his form of investigation is reinforced at the end of the film. He has never trusted Kint's myths about the shadowy Keyser Soze, and although his own assumptions have been proven false, his epistemology has been vindicated.

Thus, those films in which unreliable narrators are converted from an epistemological scepticism of any kind to embracing a more realist framework usually end on a positive note, leaving the impression that this struggle is central to their narrative. And in those films in which such a successful conversion does not occur, as in *American Psycho* or *Memento*, we deal with open endings that extend the process of narrative comprehension over the film's credits. In either case, a more realist framework is presented as being more desirable or superior, as the relativism embodied by the unreliable character-narrators is in some way presented as being dangerous. Within the aesthetic "realism" of mainstream Hollywood cinema, the epistemological "relativism" exhibited by most unreliable character-narrators usually doesn't pay off.

conclusions

I have tried to explain how film viewers usually identify and respond to unreliable narratives in the cinema. Especially my account of the main cognitive and emotional responses is by no means to be understood as an exclusive account. Rather, I have tried to propose a dynamic and flexible model that takes into account some of the major responses repeatedly elicited by films considered under the heading of unreliable narration. Due to the nature of unreliable narration, we are presented with a character-narrator who either obfuscates, distorts or perverts the facts of the fictional world, opening a Pandora's Box of multifaceted questions and intense debates concerning epistemology. Any one of these responses is at times complex enough to cope with, but very often in unreliable narratives, all of these responses happen at the same time, making unreliable narration such a rich and diverse narrative strategy to explore.

Thus, there is a fundamental richness and ambiguity about unreliable narration. Unreliable narratives will make their viewers—willingly or not—check their conventional frames of reference concerning film, other persons and themselves. Therefore, it would appear that the character-narrator's behaviour in the penultimate sequence of the film *Memento* turns out to be a pointed illustration of the most common viewing strategy of unreliable narratives in the cinema. When confronted with some supposedly uncomfortable facts and a view of the world he doesn't want to believe in, Leonard writes down the note "Don't believe his lies" on the back of the photo of Teddy, whom he believes to be an "unreliable narrator." Leonard then asks himself whether he lies to himself to be happy, before rushing to confirm his world-view and version of reality by thinking to himself: "In your case, Teddy, yes I will."

This short sequence exemplifies *in nuce* the most common viewing strategy and interpretation of unreliable narration in the cinema. First, viewers will quickly blame some unreliable narrator for textual and referential inconsistencies that threaten their view of the world and patterns of thinking ("Don't believe his lies"). In a second phase, however, we may come to doubt the very concept of "reliability" and "truth." Like Leonard, we may ask ourselves whether the notion of "truth" is actually that sound a concept, or whether that concept is merely an illusion we like to believe in in order to make sense of the world ("Do I lie to myself to be happy?"). Leonard essentially represents a radically pragmatic version of "truth." In this view, "truth" is what works for the individual, and "false" is ultimately only what kills her or him. Again, this is a thought which the character of Leonard eerily personifies. When we remember that he is on a mission to find and kill the murderer of his wife, and that is, as we find out, himself, then the "objective truth" must be "subjectively false" for Leonard—because it would literally kill him. Of course, we don't have to question the common notion of "truth," and as I hope to have shown with recourse to several reactions to unreliable narratives in film, many viewers will interrupt their interpretation and will rush to confirm their already existing realist norms and values—thus doing what the, maybe not unintentionally, *un*reliable narrator Leonard does ("In your case, Teddy, yes I will"). Hence, only viewers who have a relativist tendency will engage in an optional third phase of interpretation, a phase that Britton (178) describes as questioning "the reliability of our own perceptions and judgements" before we can question the character-narrator's perceptions and judgements. This last phase of interpretation is an additional phase only and very much depends on the particular viewer's folk psychological vanity and how much s/he wants to believe in or challenge her or his—more or less—rational, autonomous, centred, stable and realist notion of her or his self.

The fundamental ambiguity of unreliable narration is that it allows us to both apply *and* challenge our drive to coherence in making sense of films, the world and ourselves simultaneously. Of course, any narrative film can elicit such a response, yet via the intermediating function of an unreliable narrator this cognitive response appears intensified. Unreliable narratives make us reflect on the habituated beliefs and automatized schemata we hold and which make us often jump to conclusions, interpretations and evaluations. Therefore, unreliable narratives eventually throw us back on our own presuppositonal framework and ourselves. Thus, it seems to me that unreliable narration turns out to be a powerful metaphor for the human condition. It would appear that those unreliable narrators in film who show less of a factual but more of an interpretive or evaluative unreliability are not necessarily perceived as deviant. On the contrary, in our Western context, overbearing subjectivity and hence a degree of unreliability are accepted as normality and reality in certain, often unpopular, lines of thought. According to these schools of thought, complete reliability would seem an impossibility. Hence, maybe those down-to-earth cognitive film theorists who liken humans to "animals in general" and describe them as mere "organisms" emphasize quite rightly the drive for coherence as our train impulse when reading, understanding and interpreting the world. Maybe we are not so much after "truth," but more after what appears coherent, meaningful and sensible to us.

notes

1. On a theoretical note, and as will be obvious by now, I do not believe that the film viewer's relationship to a scene in a movie is like an infant's experience witnessing the primal scene or that viewers identify not with screen characters but instead with the omniscient "point of view" of the camera. The belief that film spectators are "passive" receivers and that any given film "railroads" them into "identifying" with the "ideology" of that film remains hugely popular in much of current writing in the field of film studies, yet this belief is as problematic and, eventually, self-defeating as it is popular. On the contrary, throughout my essay I shall be assuming that comprehension of narrative films is essentially a matter of inference, driven by the viewer's primarily psychological strive for coherence and meaningfulness "as the key driving force in the reception process" (Persson 22). In this framework, cinematic discourse acts as triggers or cues for different kinds of cognitive-emotional reactions. The viewer therefore actively makes use of a wide set of various schemata in order to establish, for example, character coherence and narrative coherence. The case of the unreliable narrator, I shall argue, provides an overwhelming piece of evidence that film viewers infer on the basis of their already existing knowledge rather than decode what they are given. It is not that a particular unreliable character-narrator or a film as a whole fools us; on the contrary, we sometimes fool ourselves because we fill in gaps all-too readily and tend to jump to conclusions because of our psychological disposition. It is for this reason that I prefer to speak of emotional and cognitive responses which particular films "elicit" rather than speak of aesthetic functions that certain films "exhibit."

2. See Bläss, who discusses similar "functions" of unreliable narration in literary texts.
3. See Nünning ("Reconceptualizing") for an elaboration on this thought.
4. See Ferenz, for a discussion of the conditions of unreliable filmic narration.
5. See Helbig's (*Camera Doesn't Lie*) collection of articles which perfectly illustrates the variety of understandings of the term.
6. Booth's original definition went like this: "I have called a narrator reliable when he speaks for or acts in accordance with the norms of the work

(which is to say the implied author's norms), unreliable when he does not" (158–9). But since several writers found the norms of the implied author "notoriously difficult to arrive at" (Rimmon-Kenan 101), or were generally unhappy with the concept of the implied author (Nünning, "Deconstructing"), there has been an intense debate about how to approach the topic in general.

7. See Olson, Nünning ("Reconceptualizing") and especially Fludernik ("Unreliability") who all survey recent works on the unreliable narrator in literary narrative theory. Although both Olson and Fludernik leave open whether third-person narrators can also be appropriately called unreliable, neither denies that it is predominantly first-person narrators that are deemed to be prototypical unreliable narrators. See Phelan and Martin and Fludernik ("Defining") on the different types of narratorial unreliability.

8. "Perverse allegiances" means that in certain cases we may derive a degree of pleasure from sympathizing with a character whom we would find despicable in real life. See Smith ("Gangsters") for an account on this matter.

works cited

Antor, H. "Unreliable Narration and the (Dis-)orientation in the Postmodern Gothic Novel: Reflections on Patrick McGrath's *The Grotesque* (1989)." *Erzählen und Erzähltheorie im 20. Jahrhundert: Festschrift für Wilhelm Füger zum 65. Geburtstag*. Ed. J. Helbig, Winter, Heidelberg (2001): 357–82.

Bal, M. *Narratology: Introduction to the Theory of Narrative*. 2nd edition. Toronto: University of Toronto Press, 1997.

Black, D.A. "Genette and Film: Narrative Level in the Fiction Cinema." *Wide Angle* 8.3–4 (1986): 19–26.

Bläss, R. "Satire, Sympathie und Skeptizismus: Funktionen unzuverlässigen Erzählens." *Was stimmt denn jetzt? Unzuverlässiges Erzählen in Literatur und Film*. Eds. F. Liptay and Y. Wolf. München: edition text + kritik, 2005. 188–203.

Booth, W.C. *The Rhetoric of Fiction*. Chicago: University of Chicago Press, 1961.

Bordwell, D. *Narration in the Fiction Film*. London: Routledge, 1985.

Branigan, E. *Point of View in the Cinema: A Theory of Narration and Subjectivity in Classical Film*. Berlin: Mouton Publishers, 1984.

———. *Narrative Comprehension and Film*. New York: Routledge, 1992.

Britton, A. "Detour." *The Movie Book of Film Noir*. Ed. I. Cameron. London: Studio Vista, 1994. 174–82.

Buckland, W. "Relevance and Cognition: Towards a Pragmatics of Unreliable Filmic Narration." *Towards a Pragmatics of the Audiovisual*, volume 2. Ed. E. J. Müller. Münster: Nodus, 1995. 55–66.

Burgoyne, R. "The Cinematic Narrator: The Logic and Pragmatics of Impersonal Narration." *Journal of Film and Video* 42.1 (1990): 3–16.

Chatman, S. *Story and Discourse: Narrative in Fiction and Film*. Ithaca: Cornell University Press, 1978.

———. *Coming to Terms: The Rhetoric of Narrative in Fiction and Film*. Ithaca: Cornell University Press, 1990.

Currie, G. "Unreliability Refigured: Narrative in Literature and Film." *Journal of Aesthetics and Art Criticism* 53.1 (1995): 19–29.

Ebert, R. "*Fight Club.*" *Chicago Sun-Times*, 15 October (1999). Available at: http://rogerebert.suntimes.com/apps/pbcs.dll/article?AID=/19991015/REVIEWS/910150302/1023&template=printart (accessed 30 June 2006).

283

Ferenz, V. "Fight Clubs, American Psychos and Mementos: The Scope of Unreliable Narration in Film." *New Review of Film and Television Studies* 3.2 (2005): 133–59.

Fludernik, M. "Defining (In)sanity: The Narrator of *The Yellow Wallpaper* and the Question of Unreliability." *Grenzüberschreitungen: Narratologie im Kontext. Transcending boundaries: narratology in context.* Eds. W. Grünzweig and A. Solbach. Tübingen: Narr, 1999. 75–95.

———. "Unreliability vs. Discordance: Kritische Betrachtungen zum Literaturwissenschaftlichen Konzept der Erzählerischen Unzuverässigkeit." *Was stimmt denn jetzt? Unzuverlässiges Erzählen in Literatur und Film.* Eds. F. Liptay and Y. Wolf. München: edition text+kritik, 2005. 39–59.

Genette, G. *Narrative Discourse: An Essay in Method.* Trans. Jane E. Lewin. Ithaca: Cornell University Press, 1980.

Giroux, H. "Brutalised Bodies and Emasculated Politics: *Fight Club*, Consumerism, and Masculine Violence." *Third Text* 53 (2001): 31–41.

Helbig, J., ed. *Camera Doesn't Lie. Spielarten Erzählerischer Unzuverlässigkeit im Film.* Trier: WVT, 2006.

Jahn, M. "*Package Deals*, Exklusionen, Randzonen: das Phänomen der Unverläßlichkeit in den Erzählsituationen." *Unreliable Narration: Studien zur Theorie und Praxis Unglaubwürdigen Erzählens in der Englischsprachigen Erzählliteratur* Ed. A. Nünning. Trier: Wissenschaftlicher Verlag, 1998. 81–106.

Koebner, T. "Was stimmt denn jetzt? Unzuverlässiges Erzählen im Film." *Was stimmt denn jetzt? Unzuverlässiges Erzählen in Literatur und Film.* Eds. F. Liptay and Y. Wolf. München: edition text+kritik. 2005. 19–38.

Liptay, F. "Auf Abwegen, oder wohin führen die Erzählstraßen in den *road movies* von David Lynch." *Was stimmt denn jetzt? Unzuverlässiges Erzählen in Literatur und Film.* Eds. F. Liptay and Y. Wolf. München: edition text+kritik, 2005. 307–23.

Liptay, F. and Y. Wolf. (eds) *Was stimmt denn jetzt? Unzuverlässiges Erzählen in Literatur und Film.* München: edition text+kritik, 2005.

Litch, M. *Philosophy Through Film.* New York: Routledge, 2002.

McFarlane, B. *Novel to Film: An Introduction to the Theory of Adaptation.* Oxford: Clarendon Press, 1996.

Maslin, J. "Such a Very Long Way from Duvets to Danger." *The New York Times,* Section E, 15 October, 1999: 14.

Meder, T. "Erzählungen mit Schwarzen Löchern." *Was stimmt denn jetzt? Unzuverlässiges Erzählen in Literatur und Film.* Eds. F. Liptay, and Y. Wolf. München: edition text+kritik, 2005. 175–87.

Nünning, A. "Deconstructing and Reconceptualizing the *Implied Author*: The Resurrection of an Anthropomorphized Passepartout or the Obituary of a Critical Phantom?" *Anglistik* 8 (1997): 95–116.

———. "Unreliable, Compared to What? Towards a Cognitive Theory of Unreliable Narration: Prolegomena and Hypotheses." *Grenzüberschreitungen: Narratologie im Kontext. Transcending boundaries: narratology in context.* Eds. W. Grünzweig and A. Solbach. Tübingen: Narr, 1999. 53–73.

———. "Reconceptualizing Unreliable Narration: Synthesizing Cognitive and Rhetorical Strategies." *A Companion to Narrative Theory.* Eds. J. Phelan and P.J. Rabinowitz. Oxford: Blackwell, 2005. 89–107.

Olson, G. "Reconsidering Unreliability: Fallible and Untrustworthy Narrators." *Narrative* 11.1 (2003): 93–109.

Persson, P. *Understanding Cinema: A Psychological Theory of Moving Imagery.* Cambridge: Cambridge University Press, 2003.

Phelan, J. *Living to Tell About It: A Rhetoric and Ethics of Character Narration.* Ithaca: Cornell University Press, 2005.

Phelan, J. and M.P. Martin. "The Lessons of "Weymouth": Homodiegesis, Unreliability, Ethics, and *The Remains of the Day.*" *Narratologies: New Perspectives on Narrative Analysis.* Ed. D. Herman. Columbus: Ohio State University Press, 1999. 88–109.

Prince, Gerald. *A Dictionary of Narratology.* Lincoln: University of Nebraska Press, 1987.

Rimmon-Kenan, S. *Narrative Fiction: Contemporary Poetics.* London: Methuen, 1983.

Singer, J. "Narrative Identity and Meaning Making Across the Adult Lifespan: An Introduction." *Journal of Personality,* 72.3 (2004): 437–59.

Smith, M. *Engaging Characters: Fiction, Emotion, and the Cinema.* Oxford: Clarendon Press, 1995.

Smith, M. "Gangsters, Cannibals, Aesthetes, or Apparently Perverse Allegiances." *Passionate Views: Film, Cognition, and Emotion.* Eds. C. Plantinga and G. Smith. Baltimore: Johns Hopkins University Press, 1999. 217–38.

Tan, E. *Emotion and the Structure of Narrative Film: Film as an Emotion Machine.* Mahwah: Lawrence Erlbaum, 1996.

Thompson, N. "The Unreliable Narrator: Subversive Storytelling in Polish Horror Cinema." *Fear Without Frontiers. Horror Cinema Across the Globe.* Ed. S.J. Schneider. Godalming: FAB Press, 2003. 231–41.

Wall, K. "*The Remains of the Day* and its Challenges to Theories of Unreliable Narration." *Journal of Narrative Technique,* 24.1 (1994). 18–42.

Wilson, G. *Narration in Light: Studies in Cinematic Point of View.* Baltimore: John Hopkins University Press, 1986.

Yacobi, T. "Fictional Reliability as a Communicative Problem." *Poetics Today* 2.2 (1981): 113–26.

——. "Narrative and Normative Patterns: On Interpreting Fiction." *Journal of Literary Studies* 3.2 (1987): 18–41.

——. "Package Deals in Fictional Narrative: The Case of the Narrator's (Un) reliability." *Narrative* 9.2 (2001): 223–29.

Zerweck, B. "Historicizing Unreliable Narration: Unreliability and Cultural Discourse in Narrative Fiction." *Style* 35.1 (2001): 151–78.

fantasy audiences

versus

fantasy audiences

t h i r t e e n

m a r t i n   b a r k e r

> *Adapted from a children's novel by precocious teenager*
> *Christopher Paolini, this cut-and-paste "sword and sorcery"*
> *film [*Eragon*] is a painful reminder of what fantasy cinema*
> *was like before the "Lord of the Rings" trilogy re-wrote the*
> *rules.* (Anon, *Time Out London*, December 13–20, 2006)

An interest in fantasy cinema has long been a pretty minority pursuit, looked upon with a degree of condescension. After all, are not such films, and their audiences, "childlike," simplistic, and not much up to exploring "reality"? The astonishing success of *The Lord of the Rings*—from potential company-buster, to must-see trilogy generating nine Oscars, and a multi-billion dollar global franchise—for a while moved the axis of amusement. This was among the many reasons why in 2003–4 we mounted the largest-to-date attempt to study audience responses to a film. With a research base in twenty countries, and operating in fourteen languages, the international *Lord of the Rings* audience research project set out to explore the meaning and significance of film fantasy in the lives of different kinds of viewers around the world. Oddly, our most important findings may not have been directly about "fantasy" *per se*.[1] But it is what I focus on in this chapter—in the teeth, as it were, of other traditions of talk about fantasy cinema which have long had a tendency to "know in advance" what is involved in embracing this kind of film. Using Peter Jackson's films as my case-study, I want to broach the question: how do people go about being audiences for a film that they regard as "fantasy"?

Up to now, there have been a number of distinctive strands of thinking and research around fictional fantasy. In one chapter I cannot review these anything like as adequately as they may require. Instead, what I want to emphasize about these approaches is the way each embeds within its concepts and theories definite ways of conceiving "the audience," and through these conceptions the cultural roles they variously attribute to fantasy.

popular discourse

Within ordinary discourse, perhaps especially in the UK which has a particularly puritanical and judgemental attitude to fictional forms as a whole, "fantasy" has long been associated in popular talk with cultural weakness. This is very common, and so readily and stereotypically produced. Take as an exemplar a report in the UK's *Radio Times*, originally the BBC's own, now a self-standing listings magazine (Anon.,"Unreality TV"). Trailing the new TV series *Heroes* for UK audiences, the magazine embodied all the tendencies of so much casual commentary on fantasy. It must be noted first that this was not in any sense a condemnatory article. With a wry smile and a dismissive wave, it quite welcomed this fantasy stuff and nonsense with typical expressions such as "escapism" and "wish-fulfilment." This means a break away from all constraining rules; normally required controls are "replaced by flights of fancy, leaps of imagination and a collective suspension of disbelief." Then there's a charge of persistent infantilism ("a society where no-one wants to grow up, or put away childish things"), so if value is to be found in fantasy a special plea has to be entered ("We find ourselves living in a very complicated world right now . . . where there are very few answers that are satisfying"). From these, with ease, flow notions that fantasy audiences must lack critical criteria and judgements. They are at best odd folks ("the quiet girl at the back of the class . . . bearded men with thick glasses"—geeks to the last one of them), so beware the rest of you who might visit such a domain . . . this stuff might be contagious.

This discursive package is amused by fantasy at best, marginalizes it, but always with the possibility of pathologizing it. Fantasy on this account is undisciplined, un-educational, uncontrolled, and unedifying stuff—all negatives. Perhaps it is harmless, in which case it is allowed to be silly fun, but the sooner we get ourselves back to thinking "realistically" the better.

This is a package with a long history, connected with the rise of a separate sphere of popular culture (as Shiach and others have made clear), connected with the rise of formal education within which frequently a distinction is made between "imagination" (creative, structured, focusing, and good) and "fantasy" (all the opposites of these). And while fantasy literature might be redeemed a little by getting the blighters to read, at least, other media including film lack even these educational features. This conception has, too, cast a long and complicated shadow over the various attempts to research and theorize the fantastic, as it emerged in various versions, particularly after the 1960s.

aficionado discourse

The obvious flipside of this suspicious public discourse is the overtly celebratory, to be found in particular in books on the history of the genre. Much as the more common books on horror, or on banned genres, these books seek to recover and catalogue their objects (eg Vale et al.). These are loving books, generous in their inclusiveness, consciously seeking out the neglected, the lost, and the recondite, and not at all afraid of offering insider judgements on the relative worth of the films they bring back. Clute and Grant's vast and comprehensive (1997) *Encyclopedia of Fantasy* is a good example of this kind of work. By no means simply "fan" works (Clute and Grant have a very interesting section on the relevance of Mikhail Bakhtin's work, for instance), they can nonetheless deliver sharp retorts to the "dry" approaches of strictly academic critics. So, for instance, Alec Worley's *Empires of the Imagination* (2005), the most recent such book, which tracks four traditions of fantasy cinema (fairytale, "magic earth," epic, and heroic) across 100 years. Alert to academic commentary, Worley delivers a critical rejoinder to Yvonne Tasker's judgements on the role of myth in heroic epics such as *Conan*. After quoting her on the doubling between seriousness and hilarity, Worley responds:

> What Tasker fails to recognise is that "the intense earnestness of the mock mythologies" is precisely necessary if a secondary world fantasy does not wish to distance its viewers with the irony she implies we must regard them all. Serious films like *Conan the Barbarian*, *Excalibur* and *The Lord of the Rings* are only received with "hilarity" when the viewer intellectually dismisses them. (206)

Thus is an academic corrected by insider knowledge, reminding her that serious fans are always involved in making judgements and comparisons. The price is that Worley himself both projects and, of course, helps to create, a figure of an audience thoroughly bathed in the history of the genre: "we" know and compare across the corpus of such films, such that each new addition can be lovingly (or maybe "hilariously") slotted into an historical array. The audience which visits for a *particular* fantasy will struggle for air in this vast arena.

policing the science fiction (SF) borders

It is worth noting that alongside these rather occasional histories of cinematic fantasy, there exists a more firmly-grounded tradition of studying science fiction film. Closely associated with journals such as *Extrapolation* (founded 1959) and *Science Fiction Studies* (1973), this parallel tradition has from time to time obsessed about boundary maintenance between the two. And this is perhaps the primary reason for mentioning it. Influential writers such as Darko Suvin have offered definitions of SF as "the logic of the possible"—marked by cognitive estrangement, and thus with a radical/critical edge—and of fantasy as the "logic of the impossible," reiterating thus a belittling, escapist image.[2] Others such as S.C. Fredericks were more sympathetic, even seeing the most interesting of it (such as Roger Zelazny's) as questioning the "antithesis of science and magic" (1978). One important and voluminous writer who, perhaps more than any other, has resisted such normative dismissals is J. P. Telotte. His *Science Fiction Film* (2001), borrowing heavily from Tzvetan Todorov's concepts (see below), argues that cinema (rather than literature, Suvin's primary domain) has a special capacity to deal with the "marvellous." This is because cinema has a strong tradition of genre-combination, and in recent years in particular many films have melded the genres of fantasy, science fiction and horror (think *Star Wars* [1977], think *Alien* [1979], think *The Fifth Element* [1997] as just a few). Cinema also, because of its capacity to deploy spectacle, builds a tense line between fascination with the means and the achievement of special effects.

Telotte's account, though, declines to deal with audiences at all, only ending with an optimistic plea that if "we" all examine SF, we may find great use in its address to the world as it might be, could be, or is in danger of being if we don't do something about it. This is a statement of hope, even a manifesto, rather than an analytic position. In other words, his interest is in the possible cultural value and significance of SF as a general phenomenon. There is nothing in here to help us understand how particular communities might select some films for their own meaningful uses, or how a particular film might rise to prominence at a particular cultural moment.

the literary fantastic

Literary work on "the fantastic" has blossomed to become a substantial self-sustaining field—indeed, the main source for thinking about fantasy narratives overall. But at a heavy price. Nurtured by a series of international conferences (29 by 2008) and a journal (*Journal of the Fantastic in the Arts* [founded 1990]), it sprang into prominence in the early 1970s, in particular after the English publication of Todorov's structuralist account. Since then, it has become evident that it is caught between conflicting impulses. On the one hand there is a wish to claim the seriousness of the fantasy tradition, in the face of scepticism from many traditional theorists. But that requires the exclusion of formulaic Fantasy works, to safeguard a "proper" tradition. That of course increases the unease with which ideas of the audience "figure" in this tradition of work: what is the audience doing with fantasy? Why is it worth it? Todorov sought a formal criterion for defining the "fantastic," and found it in the notion of the uncanny—a point of hesitation sustained by narratives which won't permit a decision on whether events are to be explained naturalistically or not. As many critics have noted, his account may have a certain precision, but at the price of having very few exemplars—even stories which resolve themselves one way or the other right at their very end do not really make his canon. But while Todorov's specific criterion may largely have been declined, his notion of seeking some formal defining feature has persisted.

What to my knowledge has not been commented on, perhaps because they are seen as entirely uncontroversial, are his embedded claims about "the audience." These occur almost in passing, for instance when he writes: "We have seen what dangers beset the fantastic on a first level, when the implicit reader judges certain reported events while identifying himself with a character within the narrative" (58). Or again:

> the first-person narrator most readily permits the reader to identify with the character, since we know the pronoun "I" belongs to everyone. Further, in order to facilitate the identification, the narrator will be an "average man," in whom (almost) every reader can identify himself. Thus we enter as directly as possible into the universe of the fantastic. The identification we refer to must not be mistaken for an individual psychological function: it is a mechanism internal to the text, a structural concomitant. Obviously, nothing prevents the actual reader from keeping his distance in relation to the universe of the work. (84)

I cannot forebear commenting on this. Todorov appears here to generate an account of the implied reader wholly innocent of implications for any actual audience members. It is, he insists, a position, rather than a description of a person. Actually, that is not so at all, on at least four grounds:

1. First, his "average man" who appears to bind narrator and reader: the problem is not just the obvious one of the assumed maleness. It is much

more that *real* audiences may become embroiled in books or other fictions precisely because of, and through, their awareness of their *difference* from narrators. Just about all historical fiction has to depend upon our doing this. Todorov rules out such relations by fiat.

2. This "reader" is curiously individualistic, caught if at all in "his" lone world of responding. It is hard to conceive on his account how communities of readers can become other than literary critics.

3. It is interesting that Todorov does not seem to be able to conceive any kind of involvement other than via "identification." He allows anyone to become "distanced," but—as so often happens—can only conceive committed participation as a form of loss of identity. Todorov is not alone in this, of course. It is a default position of many accounts, including Stuart Hall's "encoding-decoding" model. Only rare (and sometimes eccentric—see Nell) critics have taken a different route.

4. That concept of "identification" : aside from the extensive critiques that have now been mounted by myself and others,[3] there is the difficulty that he presumes very *literary* notions of narration, with a "speaker." Only occasionally have cinema scholars claimed to find a formal equivalent to this (see Mark Nash as perhaps the most noted case).

These are not, I would argue, marginal problems. Todorov does need this embedded conception of "the audience," to warrant his formal criterion. Without that, the principle of "hesitation" would be quite empty for no one would be doing it. And at back of his formalist argument is a belief that a particular period (in the nineteenth century) produced cultural tensions likely to accord with such expressive behaviour.

Following Todorov, a series of other literary scholars have paid tribute to his ideas, but offered their own definitional criteria. Rosemary Jackson proposed a political definition, that fantasies either "expel" a desire to alter the way the world is currently organized, or "tell of" it by putting a self-conscious distance between reader and world. Drawing heavily on the peculiar combination of radical politics and psychoanalytic theories gaining popularity at this time, Jackson herself became a point of reference for subsequent work. Her argument, though, depends entirely on their being some simple agreement what shall count as "progressive/subversive" (current debates about religious "extremism" should give pause here). The force of this point can be indicated by comparing her argument with that of Joshua David Bellin whose recent study of cinematic monsters neatly inverts her judgements. Bellin begins by admitting that while *King Kong* is his all-time favourite film, he also sees it as ineliminably racist—and gives many textual and contextual reasons why. He then proceeds to argue that such "fantasy cinema" is the more dangerous because it *activates* current discourses about "race" in particular but in a manner that makes them entertaining *because* they are distanced: "Fantasy films, because of their semantic openness and apparent disconnection from social reality, may permit repugnant social attitudes to operate under a veil of innocence and may thereby lend such attitudes the appearance of the real" (23). For Jackson, distancing is the mechanism of radical critique; for Bellin, the exact opposite. It is very difficult to see how one might ever get beyond the simple oppositeness of such formal deductions of political correctness or incorrectness without some kind of real-world audience test.

Another important contributor, Eric Rabkin, shifted the emphasis from "the uncanny" to the "not-expected" and "astonishment." Seen as a response to emergent rationalism, this is again celebratory. As with Todorov, the formal definition presumes a mode of reader-engagement:

> The fantastic is a quality of astonishment which we feel when the ground rules of a narrative are suddenly made to turn around 180°. We recognise this reversal in the reactions of characters, the statements of narrators, and the implications of structures, all playing on and against our whole experience as people and readers. (41)

It seems almost impertinent to ask who precisely is included in this "we," and what is to be made of those who respond differently. In this model *Alice in Wonderland* is the archetypal fantasy, to which is credited a "serious purpose" (59) which takes it beyond escapism. This need to secure serious intent recurs in his discussion of Alain Robbe-Grillet's *The Erasers* through which he distinguishes mass from "more educated" readers, since for the latter the literary techniques "prevent the reader from suspending disbelief in the narrative world that is merely the subject of that reading experience" (176). Heaven forfend that one should lose oneself in a fantasy narrative.

Kathryn Hume, meanwhile, defined fantasy as "the deliberate departure from the limits of what is usually accepted as real and normal" (xii). At the end of her argument, Hume does appear to show an interest in audiences. In her Chapter 8, she asks: "Why read fantasy? What does a reader gain from non-realistic plots and strange images?" Sadly this is, for her, entirely a theoretical question—there is not a hint of interest in asking actual readers. And the kinds of gain she theorises are entirely general and ahistorical (for instance, satisfying needs for "teleological understanding" [170]).

There are some striking continuities across all these differences. Apart from the lack of interest in actual audiences, there is a persistent will to separate "the fantastic" (approved) from "Fantasy" (dismissable). Partly, surely, because of the embattled status of the study of fantasy within traditionally conservative literature departments, there has been a need to circumscribe a domain of worthy writing. This drive comes to its head in Neil Cornwell's *The Literary Fantastic* (1990). Cornwell feels the need to demarcate "escapist" literature which stresses sensations, emotions, and the shucking off of responsibilities, from the necessary unease and discomfort, and the "continued need for monstrous revelations" (218) which the "real" fantastic offers.

By the 1990s literary work on the fantastic appears to have settled into safe but narrow forms, with the *JFA* publishing almost entirely textual analyses of particular authors or groups of works, each premised on some theoretical fragment. The problem is not simply the lack of interest in reception (my key concern). It is in the overall narrowness of what is covered. It is almost impossible to find any work on: publishing, circulation and display traditions; libraries, collections, archiving and canon-formation; histories of critical thought, shifting genre definitions, reviewing practices and evaluative criteria; and many more. And while several collections claim to address fantasy film as well as literature (see Ruddick, for instance), cinematic fantasies very much play second string to more traditional literary concerns.

psychoanalysis and "phantasy"

There is of course a long tradition of work on film which wants to talk about the role of fantasy—or, more often, phantasy—as a key aspect of all viewing: psychoanalytic film theory. For a time in the 1970s, it could almost seem as if this was co-terminous with film theory, as a whole. Now it constitutes a much more embattled enclave, especially since the rise of explicitly oppositional cognitive film approaches.[4] Because of its sometimes prevalence I cannot ignore psychoanalytic work. But for a number of reasons, I do not spend much time here examining it in detail. The key reason for such a quick excursus is that, with very few exceptions[5] (Walkerdine; Arthurs), while people working in this tradition have been very happy to produce large speculative models of "film spectatorship," they have been embarrassingly unwilling to formulate these in a way that could apply to any particular audiences. And on the few occasions that anything close to a structured application has been made, the problems have been vividly evident (see in particular Stacey).

Psychoanalytic film theory begins, almost without exception, from Jacques Lacan's alterations to Freud's original account concerning the child, its relations in particular with its mother, and processes of repression leading to the formation/separation of ego and unconscious. Lacan's upgrading of the "mirror phase"—a point in a child's development at which s/he founds a sense of self through seeing him/herself as through other people's eyes—offered a ready metaphor for thinking the cinema screen and film spectatorship. Lacan's ideas made their transition to cinema via 1970s *Screen* theory, perhaps most notably via Laura Mulvey's famous (1975) essay, and via a pair of books—Victor Burgin's (1986) edited collection, which frontispieced, manifesto-like, Laplanche and Pontalis' restatement of Lacan's ideas, and James Donald's subsequent (1989) edited application to cinema. One primary motivation here was to recover cultural studies' ability to deal with "identities" (as against categorial explanations by class, "race," gender, etc.), for which, it was believed, psychoanalysis was the only resource. Those who have pursued this Lacanian account of cinema have erected a series of large claims which (for reasons which continually defeat me) insist on seeing cinema as some special ontologically-distinct "institution" doing psychic work that almost nothing else appears to be able to. "In its very form, film necessarily involves recourse to fantasy," writes Todd McGowan (2003), as if this clearly has profound implications. Cinema, apparently, is a medium through which unresolved tensions from childhood gain especial embodiment. Audiences might *think* that in delighting in films they are loving acting, story, humour, cinematography, even beautiful bodies and sumptuous sets. But no, what they are actually doing is regressing in dream-like mode to unresolved issues repressed at the point of emergent subjectivity. In Christian Metz's words: cinema is a "technique of the imaginary" operating on and through "subterranean persistence of the exclusive relation to the mother, desire as a pure effect of lack and endless pursuit, the initial core of the unconscious" (3–4). It is in fact interesting to play with the key word "desire," whose objectless singularity seems to signal something primeval and ineluctable. Substitute other ordinary words—"interest," "curiosity," "wish," "fancy," "fascination"—and the implied motives for participation and their attendant likely consequences alter pretty fundamentally. "Fantasy" in this theory-church is understood as the staging or *mise en scène* of desire (Burgin et al., 2), a place where those unresolvable but ever-active "desires" (always centred around sexual identity) can be played out. And films are that space.

To belong to this church, you have to work hard and accept an awful lot of prior tenets.[6] Once there, the films examined in the name of this approach bear no similarity to those addressed under the banner of "fantasy" in any of the other traditions I have found. Only to a psychoanalytic film theorist could *The Man Who Shot Liberty Valance* or *Suspicion* constitute works of fantasy. Debates in this sphere also tend to be doctrinal, making sense only to converts. This is nicely illustrated by Lapsley and Westlake who comment thus on the debates which followed Laura Mulvey's essay on visual pleasure: "Although by the end of the 1970s psychoanalysis had contributed to a persuasive account of the exchange between film and the male spectator, no comparable account existed for the female spectator" (95). Who precisely do they think has been so persuaded? Only a convert could think that the "male spectator" had been adequately theorised, given not one study of any *actual* male spectators had taken place.

In fact it is probably Metz, one of the earliest (and now heavily criticized) of the psychoanalytical thinkers who comes closest to making concrete proposals for how to consider audience responses. But what we get is a conflicting set of proposals. On the one hand Metz talks much in terms of unified spectatorial positions. He does at one point acknowledge that audiences might decline or refuse an invitation—but his list of reasons why they might do so is very narrowly circumscribed. Then, in a final recognition that actual empirical audiences are not likely to behave as the model suggests, he allows simply that all responses are likely to be completely individuated. This confused account allows everything and nothing and, just as importantly to me, simply does not recognize social and cultural processes.

The central issue is how psychoanalytic theorists go about their business of analysing films. Choosing one essay to exemplify a whole "school"—and not even choosing one of the "classics" (the *Cahiers du Cinéma* collective on *Young Mr Lincoln*, or Stephen Heath on *A Touch of Evil*, or Elizabeth Cowie on *Now, Voyager*[7])—may seem arbitrary. But I have chosen Todd McGowan's analysis of David Lynch's *Lost Highway* because it so overtly addresses the topic of "fantasy," and because in its core strategies it so clearly displays the central tendencies I see elsewhere. McGowan wants to reclaim the film from the "critics and audiences" who have dismissed it as virtually incomprehensible, by proffering a Lacanian reading which finds in it a deep structure of meanings. Typical of so many such works, words like "fantasy" and "desire" become strange dark unities, person-less, object-less, content-less, but ineluctable ("the interrelations of fantasy and desire . . ." [51]; "the enigma of desire . . ." [52]). If McGowan was simply proposing an interpretation which we can choose to adopt or no, then it could stand or fall on its interest (is it fun to read the film this way?) and its scope (how much does it engross in its frame?). It would be, it must be said, a weird allegorical interpretation, requiring characters to be embodiments, *Pilgrim's Progress*-like, of chunky abstractions (Desire, Fantasy, the Law, the Real). But this is not all that he is doing. In an essay that begins by criticising actual audience rejections, "we" crops up 94 times—as some kind of imbricated spectator. "We" do all kinds of things here, from finding images "so bright we close our eyes" (51) to being sure Fred has "sacrificed himself to the Law" (67) but "never being fully and successfully interpellated" because of the film's unique structure (68). Typically, characters become ciphers of psychoanalytic tendencies, the film becomes simultaneously an embodiment of truths about them and about "us," and "our" responses somehow parallel those of preferred characters: "Through the turn to fantasy, both Fred and the spectator escape from the unbearable mystery of desire." The film becomes an embodiment of the truths of Lacanian theory (it "reveals" [69]), almost a lecture via fiction—but with (so he wants to hint) a capacity to probe us, to dredge that which we don't want to, but need to, see in ourselves. By the close, *Lost Highway* has somehow transmuted into a model for all films and for the human psyche as a whole. "Fantasy" in this mode of writing is a shuddering abstraction, films its awesome bearers—audiences its uncomprehending reflections.

This is film theory for converts, in all kinds of ways. I have no interest in denying its adherents their rights to adopt and follow this approach. What concerns me is their hijacking of the word "fantasy," and their deep-rooted but strictly untested imputations about "spectators."

We can see from all the above the way definitions of "the fantastic" are caught up in a version of the loop that Andrew Tudor described, in his much-cited formulation of the definitional problem that infects ideas of genre, generally:

> To take a genre such as the "western," analyse it, and list its principal characteristics, is to beg the question that we must first isolate the body of films which are "westerns." But they can only be isolated on the basis of the "principal characteristics" which can only be discovered from the films themselves after they have been isolated. (cited in Gledhill 95)

Critics in different theoretical modes have their own privileged examples of "fantasy," which hardly count in anyone else's frame of reference. Debate between approaches therefore becomes almost impossible. This loop has been more noticed than overcome, except where genre theorists have moved away from normative definitions towards, for instance, more historical approaches (as for instance Altman, and Neale). But the work of considering their implications for audiences remains undone. And this, I would argue, is the critical test. This is the neglected critical move which film scholars have been unwilling to make, since it is—and I do not pretend otherwise—difficult, and potentially threatening to the easy assertions of textual accounts. The quotation which mast-heads this chapter indicates how readily audiences—professional or amateur—develop their own schemata, histories, and evaluative criteria. My proposal is that with regards to "fantasy" we should tackle it in two ways: by demanding of definitions that they "come clean" as to their claims and implications for audiences; and most importantly by looking at how audiences themselves understand and use the term "fantasy" in the course of their interactions with specific films. In short, I recommend that film theory go to the movies, but take time to notice that there are other people there, doing all kinds of interesting and unexpected things with what they are watching.

One other slowly growing but little-known body of work needs introducing, even though it hardly touches films. This work examines children's general relations with fantasy. In fact this work constitutes virtually all the empirical audience research of fantasy audiences that I have been able to find. Motivated by a determination to preserve children's opportunities to experience fantasy as part of a rich education, these very recent studies reveal the complexity of children's encounters with different kinds of fantasy materials—mostly, but not only, literary.

Nina Mikkelsen's target is those educational approaches which reduce children's encounters with books to a set of fragmented, thence measurable reading skills: telling the difference between fact and fantasy; constructing story-sequences; and reading without pictures, for instance. In place of these, she describes in fascinating detail her work with small groups of children, including her own, showing how they were able to build complex accounts of character, situation, and their own relations to these through encounters with fantasy stories (including *Alexander and the Wind-up Mouse*, *The Hobbit*, and *The Snowman* which of course has no words at all). She shows how they spontaneously work with and develop a whole range of literacy skills which are also human/moral/social skills: from personal/empathetic, to narrative, aesthetic, critical, and socio-cultural. Fantasy, she argues, is a vital resource for them, allowing them to see and think themselves in situations where they can work through tensions and uncertainties in their lives. Far from "passive," they explore characters' characters and choices, assess situations, build accounts across gaps—and even challenge and change endings to stories if by their moral standards they are not "fair." Her words for all this are highly charged: children "co-author" the stories with the books, as they build their accounts—and they can do it better if given space and encouragement. The results are "democratic and egalitarian," and the achievements "celebratory" (108).

There is an important limitation to her work. Mikkelsen is interested in the "burst of literacies" (175) which mark the stage in children's lives when they become self-aware and literate in the broadest sense. This is a point of personal transformation and she is keen that parents, teachers, and others who interact with children should help them to make best use of these resources. But because of this, she is primarily concerned with what we might call the *point of individuation* in children, how they find the imaginative resources to become full humans, "getting their first glimpses" (181) of adult understandings as they go through their own growth processes. This makes sense of her choice to work with small numbers, and to report only on successes. This is research as recommendation, and none the worse for it—but it therefore is a limited model for thinking how adults might use fantasy materials for more culturally-shared purposes. Brilliant as a demonstration of the transformational force that fantasy can have for children, what comes after? Although I don't think she would ever say this, Mikkelsen could be read as suggesting that the essential work of fantasy is done once children have experienced and lived through this individualized liberatory experience. It has "done its work." Now, adulthood, and *real* cultural engagements must beckon.

Something of the same can be said of the study by Maya Götz and her colleagues into children's uses of television. A cross-cultural study between Germany, Israel, South Korea and the USA, this one too sets out to challenge conventional suspicions of fantasy, this time specifically in relation to television. Their focus was on children aged 8–10, and used a mix of methods to explore how children construct make-believe worlds, drawing on combinations of biographical and media experiences:

> Children build upon a wealth of information from a wide range of sources, including their own experience and mediated sources, and freely interweave them to create rich fantasy backdrops for playing out their wishes to act. They wish for acts that are self-empowering: to experience feelings of well-being and thrill; to bond with others; to protect and be protected, to demonstrate their own specialness and independence. (197)

Once again, this is predominantly celebratory. If there is a downside, it is a concern that fantasy materials for *girls* are thinner and more second-hand, and therefore girls have to "invest more energy than boys in altering the media material to meet their needs" (200). As with Mikkelsen, once one gets past the rejection of the popular dismissal of television and celebration of imaginative childhood, it is hard to see what the implications might be for adult make-believe worlds.

The third body of empirical research into fantasy audiences is only now becoming available in English. Arising out of a collaboration across five Baltic Sea countries, this work focuses again on fantasy literature, as part of a wider project on young people's reading (on the broader project, see Kovala and Vainikkala). Using a story by Ursula LeGuin, young people's responses were explored, for evidence of the impact of both individual and cultural factors. In a first report on the project's outcomes, and drawing only on the Finnish responses, Irma Hirsjärvi distinguishes several groups (avid, occasional, and non-readers of fantasy, and SF-readers) and discovers, surprisingly, that being an avid fantasy reader almost seemed to get in the way of understanding this story—a problem not encountered by the SF-readers who

> appeared to read the story metaphorically, i.e., to see it as a speculative mind-game about a fictional society, without trying to find connections to real life. Instead of scrutinizing the story, plot and characters, they seemed to approach it as a philosophical, scientific or sociological dilemma. (Hirsjärvi)

What this suggests is a need to rethink the singular nature of the category "fantasy," and of the skills required for enjoying it.

These few audience studies simply emphasize the size of the gap in our knowledge. The *Lord of the Rings* project was a sustained attempt to begin to fill it. Lasting for 15 months across 2003–4, the project involved three strands of research: a 3-month study of the ways in which the final part of the film trilogy was prepared for in press, magazine, radio, television, and the Internet as well as in marketing, publicity, and merchandising (resulting in the gathering of several thousand prefigurative items); a web questionnaire combining quantitative and qualitative measures (most importantly, a series of paired questions asking people to allocate themselves along various dimensions [for example, how much they had enjoyed the film] and then to say in their own words what this meant)—resulting in just under 25,000 responses from across the world in just over five months; and (in some of the participant countries) follow-up interviews with people who appeared to exemplify patterns that emerged from a preliminary analysis of the questionnaires (in the UK we interviewed 107 people on this basis).

At the heart of the project were three questions: (a) what does film fantasy mean and how does it matter to different audiences across the world?, (b) how was the film's reception in different contexts shaped by its origins as a very English story, celebrating its filming in New Zealand with money and backing from a Hollywood studio?, and (c) how was the film prefigured in different country contexts, and how did this play into the film's overall reception? But I would argue that one of the key strengths of the project was its capacity to generate materials to allow a range of further questions to be asked. Clearly no single research project, however wide-reaching, could simultaneously take on all the challenges posed by my five traditions of theorizing "fantasy." But maybe that is just the point: in refusing to deal with everything at once, in acknowledging that different *kinds* of investigation and evidence may be required, we deliver the sternest response possible.[8] Here, my questions are guided very much by what I would argue is avoided in current theorising about "fantasy," namely: in what aspects of a film—in our case *The Lord of the Rings*—does its "fantasy" nature reside for its audiences? How does this matter to them? And what consequences and implications does this have for their understanding, response, and evaluation of the film?

For purposes of this essay, two components of the questionnaire were critical. One question asked people to choose up to three from a range of twelve options that would best describe the *kind of story* they felt the film to offer: Allegory, Epic, Fairytale, Fantasy, Game-world, Good vs Evil, Myth/Legend, Quest, SFX film, Spiritual Journey, Threatened Homeland, or War Story. (There was an option to answer with a choice of their own, but very few took this.) The other asked people to say in their own words: "Where, and when, is Middle-Earth for you? Is there a place or a time that it particularly makes you think of?" Answers to these questions provided a rich resource for understanding what "fantasy" meant to different audiences for *The Lord of the Rings*.

The first surprising discovery came from our analysis of the overall data. Overall, and unsurprisingly, our research tended to recruit people with overall high levels of pleasure and involvement. But there were more than enough for us to be able to explore which generic understandings

299

Table 13.1 Relations of Kind of World choices with levels of enjoyment and importance

	Enjoy	Import		Enjoy	Import
Allegory	71.0	59.2	Myth/legend	74.7	64.5
Epic	73.8	65.9	Quest	72.0	63.4
Fairytale	64.3	42.9	SFX film	45.3	36.4
Fantasy	66.6	57.6	Spiritual journey	80.3	71.2
Game-world	61.8	41.2	Threatened homeland	71.6	62.5
Good vs Evil	71.2	61.2	War story	65.9	56.1

associated with most pleasure and involvement. So, while "Fantasy" was a common choice to describe the story (9,882 out of 24,739 making it one of their choices—second only behind "Epic" and "Good vs Evil')—when these choices were cross-tabulated with other answers, it was revealed to have a *relatively low* level of association with levels of Enjoyment and Importance of Seeing, as the following Table 13.1 shows.

"Fantasy" ranks seventh in relation to Enjoyment, and eighth in relation to Importance. This becomes even more striking when we isolated those who chose to nominate only "Fantasy." A relatively small number (just 309 in the world set), they have one of the lowest proportions of those nominating Extreme Enjoyment (Fantasy = 57.0 percent as against Spiritual Journey's highest 93.9 percent) and Extreme Importance (Fantasy = 49.8 percent as against Spiritual Journey's 69.2 percent).[9] In our audiences' minds, "Fantasy" as a singular descriptor does not seem to associate with either great pleasure or great value. Yet overall, for those *not* encountering *The Lord of the Rings* in this mode, pleasures and valuations were exceptionally high. So what does our evidence reveal about the contrasts involved here?

One other figure is worth reporting, because it is so nearly unanimous—and so apparently opposite. Within our database, 513 English-speaking respondents used the word "fantastic" to describe their experience of the film. Of these, 510 reported both Extreme Enjoyment, and Maximum Importance of Seeing. This may seem unsurprising, if the word is taken simply to indicate extremity of response. Actually, upon investigation, it appears to have a wider meaning and charge. The following examples capture the typical flavour of these responses:

1. What can I say about this film? It is amazing! One of the things that I find amazing about it is that it deals with so many human issues even though it takes place in a fantasy world. Also all the actors and actresses did fantastic jobs portraying their roles.
2. Well there are not any deeper messages that this movie has projected towards me. In short it was not material that made me wonder about ideas or concepts in general. It was fantastic stuff to watch in terms of visual and sound effects and a nice fantasy.

3. Wow! It was totally mind-blowing. A fantastic end to an epic story.

4. WOW! That was amazing. Legolas was so cool when he brought down the Mumakil single-handed. I liked the relationships and the emotions of the film as well as the action sequences. Pelennor Fields was just how I imagined it to be. Fantastic!!!!!!! I'm going to see it again!!!

5. I thought the film was incredible a fantastic roller-coaster of emotion. The film flowed much better than the first two films and I wasn't ready for it to end.

6. Fantastical magical overwhelming.

7. My emotional response? Wracked with sobs. The ideas and emotions put forth under the guise of a fantastical adventure story were virtually overwhelming and when the movie finished I felt as if a dear friend had passed away satisfied in life but still wise after death.

8. I thought Peter Jackson did a fantastic job interpreting Tolkien work. Yes there were a few scenes that didn't make the theatrical release but given that it was already 3 and 1/2 hours I can see why. I am very eagerly awaiting the extended edition.

9. The only parts that I have problems with are omissions. Despite these ROTK is fantastic and faithful to the spirit of the book. Word is that the Extended Edition is going to be close to 5 hours—that should take care of any of my problems.

10. Aside from disappointment at a few missing scenes I thought it was stupendous. The characters drew you in, they BELIEVED what they were doing, the scenery costumes makeup etc. was fantastic.

A number of themes are evidently at work in these responses. First, the film was loved by many for its sheer sensory, narrative, and emotional overload. It was a complete experience, and one to want more of. This is no small matter in itself, and is one of the sought-after qualities: the frequency with which words such as "mind-blowing," "breath-taking," "awe-inspiring," and "overwhelming" are used is very striking. It seems that a quality that was valued, and that *is* in some senses associated with "fantasy" is straight-forward unrestrained visual, aural, and narrative sumptuousness. An argument can be made that it is this sheer capacity for sensuous excess which is a key quality which is valued by many in contemporary cinema, even if this is contemptuously dismissed as the "blockbuster syndrome" and "FX domination" by many critics.

301

Also particularly striking, because they match broader distinctions we found, are the differences between quotes 2 and 7. For the latter the emotional force of the film *both* couples with ideas it purveys, *and* makes it more than a film—it has become a friend, whose passing is to be regretted.

For the former, because it is perceived as *just* a film, without substantive meanings or ideas, its capacity to move is reduced—it is "nice fantasy" only. For the most enthusiastic, their sense of deep enjoyment and engagement in no way diminishes their capacity to *measure* the film. They can identify the work and roles of director, actors, special effects devisers, and so on. They can note pace, narrative form, cinematography, etc. They can see and acknowledge the limitations of a cinema release. They can love it unconditionally yet be critical of it, simultaneously. They are content to criticize narrative exclusions or alterations, particular pieces of acting, story-realization, the ending. None of these are exempt from complaint, but all are compatible with criticism. Indeed one of the findings of the project was that people were the *more likely to criticize* the more they expressed enjoyment and commitment (see Turnbull in Barker and Mathijs).

What was harder to find, was any association between these kinds of use and commitment to the film and its meanings, and any formal association with the "reality" of Middle-earth. The following answers to our "Where and when is Middle-earth?" question come without any differentiation from all varieties of respondents, whether nominating Fantasy or no:

> Kind of medieval times in this world but forgotten legend.
>
> I think Europe is Middle-earth.
>
> It makes me think of pre-1000 AD Great Britain.
>
> It harkens to Scottish history for me. Otherwise it's just a place and time in Tolkien's imagination.
>
> Tolkien made it because of the lack of a true European fantasy so he paralleled Middle-earth to Europe so it's there.

It is not the notional location of the fantasy world which distinguishes adherents from critics of *The Lord of the Rings*. It is something else. The following *almost exclusively* come from those who nominate "Fantasy" as their Kind of World choice:

> No, this is pure fantasy at its best. Middle-earth is in the mind of anyone who cares go there.
>
> It is a fictitious setting fit for the story. It does not remind me of anything in particular (besides some landscapes which remind me of the US).
>
> It is a construct of the mind.
>
> I don't think Middle-earth exists in our world or belongs as it is to our reality except as a book and a proper fantasy tale. On the other hand it has many characteristics from history of different nations, people and ethnic groups, also geographically.

These responses insist on the fictionality of Middle-earth, its safe distance from us. Meanwhile the following kinds of response are *never* found among those who choose Fantasy, but are found with regularity among those choosing "Spiritual Journey"—the ones with the highest levels of pleasure and commitment to the film:

> Middle-earth for me is when I first read the trilogy—when I was 13.
>
> No, it is not important where and when it is. The spirituality is universal.
>
> Middle-earth is simply another place at this moment in time in this world. Whilst the location may be futuristic, I didn't relate the film to the future.
>
> Not really. I know there are similarities to existing places and existing cultures but it really seems like a different world to me. Or perhaps I do not WANT to think of it as something that was part of our history that is lost. Thinking of it as a separate world helps me bear the pain of realising what we've lost (even though the world and the loss are imagined).
>
> Middle-earth is for me the time that I am living in now. I see mankind and the way we live and think and feel about things from raising children to having and conducting relationships where we live and work and why we do what we do as under threat from what seems a minority who are trying dictate a different lifestyle without giving us the freedom to explore life itself.
>
> Middle-earth is within... it translates to the challenges we face everyday.

What appears to differentiate these last is the *building of a personal relationship to the story-world*. Sometimes a personal life history (when "I" first read the book), sometimes an appeal to a special common humanity ("spirituality within"), sometimes a loose attempt to diagnose the difficulties we face in our shared world.

All this points towards a substantial paradox: the more audience members refer overtly to a category called "fantasy," the more likely they are to mark distance and dissatisfaction with it. Committed viewers of course know that it is, in a strict sense, a fantasy, but that is merely a means to, perhaps an aid to, an uninhibited participation in a project for their world. Consider the density of meanings in this quotation from one questionnaire response:

303

> This is a film for which I had been waiting breathlessly for two years. On the day of the release itself my body felt numb (except for my stomach where a herd of Mumakil were rampaging!). I experienced a mixture of extreme joy that I was going to see *Return* coupled with sadness that the

journey's at an end. . . . Being a fan of LOTR has brought
me into contact with whole communities both in Real Life
and the Internet. It has changed my life. In a time when it
is all too easy to become disillusioned with the world
around us, it was beautiful and uplifting to see how
millions around the world took this tale of honour, love
and duty to their hearts. Through the film I have come
into contact with generous, honourable people who give
me a real hope for the future.

This woman wants to share her passionate involvement. With a teasing
insider-reference (the "herd of Mumakil"), she depicts both the prepara-
tory ("waiting breathlessly," "numb body"), the present ("sadness" that there
is no more), and the long-term ("changed my life") impacts of the story.
She hints at something which this chapter cannot expand, the idea of a
"journey" alongside the events in the trilogy. She also positions herself in
relation to a complex interpretive community, built around her sense not
just of the film's quality but of its moral value to others like her. She is a
type-case of a whole kind of viewer which finds no place in the existing
claims about "fantasy audiences." Yet she is arguably the most important,
because the most moved. My argument is that engaged viewers of a "fantasy film" such as *The Lord of the Rings* are caught within a net of possibilities
and pressures: the pressures of the dismissive discourse which reduces them
to fools (but weakened on this occasion by its success, and the status of its
book-origins); the calls to imaginative freedom not often supported; and of
course all the local circumstances within which they live.

How does this mix of individual and collective forces play out in particular cases? I can do no more than illustrate these too briefly in four ano-
nymized cases, of four of our 107 interviewees. None was interviewed
because s/he had talked about "fantasy," but in all cases it proved to be an
important component.

For Molly, an under-18 female viewer, Tolkien is "the hugest obsession
I've ever had." Introduced to the books by her Dad, she discovered them
again when the films started to come out. She read *Fellowship* and all the rest
immediately after seeing the first film, as did her best friends. They talked
about the stories at all opportunities, saw the films as often as possible, collected merchandise, even generating their own, and joined Internet chat
rooms. Molly measures its international impact by her ability to recognize
other "geeks" by their t-shirt wearing. Although not a devotee, the books
were important as a "source" for the films, and she was irritated at some
of the changes—for instance by the addition of Legolas' killing of the
Mumakil—if they could add that, why couldn't they have kept in such an
important scene as the Scouring? The importance of that scene lay in its portrayal of "home" and trustworthy friends which the Shire offers. The rest is

grand, and enjoyable, but it is just "fantasy." And it was friendship which drove her choice of favourite character: Sam, chosen as the perfect friend. He and the other hobbits are liked because they look at this huge fantasy world and feel all at sea in it—but friendship carries them through. For Molly, the film's "huge fantasy" enables a celebration of pure friendship within an exhilarating *experience of participation* in the film and the huge fantasy it offers.

Ben, an early twenties male, was introduced to the books by his father, providing a sheet-anchor for handling his feelings—things to hold onto in a turbulent world. He loves the *vastness* of the story, and goes for Gimli as he is "cool"—he shouts, he drinks, he uses his axe . . . Ben sets himself a bit apart from other kinds of viewers: the "sad," the "pimply," the "hooligan," the "purist," but still loves watching with them in order to increase the atmosphere. His one demand of the film is that its scale should knock him over. So he invests strongly in the *modernity* of it—he is into the big sound/big screen, he bought a "cool" new DVD sound system to go with getting the DVDs. But this was very definitely a cultural moment for him—he wanted to be able to tell his grandchildren "I saw *LOTR* on the first night." The grandeur of the fantasy outran him, became a *profound* experience which he is still coming to terms with.

For Sylda, a woman in her fifties, it didn't matter who she was with as long as she was with someone whom she could talk to afterwards—it was just good to watch with other people, and have the experience intensified by that. The emphasis in her answers is on the *scale* of the book, the sheer *amount* of characters and events it contains, rather than on any particular narrative organization or direction. So it is OK to have bits left out, as long as in the resultant film you get both emotions and battles. This allows it to be what it is: "escapism," "dreams"—frequently repeated terms. Middle-earth is for her somewhere from whence you can as it were squint at the world sideways, see issues about human nature clarified, simplified. The orcs, for instance, just are perfect personifications of fearful evil—and so they can stand in for the real evils in our world. And it is important to her that in the story the weak can become strong, the underdog *can* win (this is like a religious idea, but she is herself not religious). She makes interesting distinctions in the course of her account—*LOTR* does not count as effects-heavy, whereas *Star Wars* does—it is "genuine fantasy" while *Top Gun* isn't. In a curious way the story's book-source *guarantees* its authenticity for her, entitles her participation.

James (a married man in his forties) first read the books when he was about 12. He is a fantasy reader, more generally, and makes connections to Dungeons & Dragons. The place became big in his imagination, a place he wanted to go to again and again. He is aware from the start of a possible "purist" critical position, but adopts a "lighter" attitude—"as long as it got the key points across" he is content—because that allows him the pleasure of measuring his "very personal" imagination of Tolkien's story-world with "someone else's interpretation," and their "visualization" of it all (a repeated expression). "I'd just been dying to actually see a film version of the book to see what somebody else thought of them." The outcome for him is the "completion" of the experience of the story (and "complete" is another very recurrent term). His many criticisms of the particular version are simply overwhelmed by his love of the *scale* of the story's world, not just its size but its complexity and interwoven stories (he talks of the film keeping the "backbone" of the story). He posits Middle-earth as a wished for reality ("It does remain a fantasy tale and it didn't happen and I'd like to think of it that it did happen," and "You feel that it was once a living place"). It can even replace the inadequacies of our own world ("more interesting than the history we do have"). The principle that binds all these is the commitment to sharing coherent visions (on this, see Barker, 2006).

These abbreviated accounts can only hint at the complex interplays of factors connecting recognitions of "fantasy" with different lived experiences of the film. What is interesting in each case is the coupling of fantasy with hopes and wishes for personal and social futures. Sometimes constrained, but always with a potential for outrunning expectations, the sheer experience of the film could awake new imaginings. Of course, *The Lord of the Rings* was a special case. With a long history as a book trilogy and a committed set of expectant followers, with a widely circulating sense of special cinematic achievement, alongside in many countries discussions around the films' wider significance, it stood apart. And that is exactly the point. The distributed and shared meanings, and the lived responses to any particular fantasy film are a function of many things—not least the embattled status of this much-abused tradition.

notes

1 For the main findings of the project, see Barker and Mathijs.
2 Compare Darko Suvin's 1978 insistence on "what differentiates SF from the 'supernatural genres' or fictional fantasy in the wider sense" with Frederick Pohl's stern statement (1997) that "Above all, science fiction is not, is *positively* not, fantasy."
3 See for instance Smith, and Barker (2005).
4 This is only a partial truth. From the earliest days, querying voices could be heard, although these did not for a time coalesce into an alternative approach. See for instance the astringent comment by Buscombe et al.
5 See Valerie Walkerdine's essay in Donald (ed.); and Jane Arthurs.
6 Each year I teach a class on Ridley Scott's *Alien* (1979) as a means to showing how film analysts work on films. Introducing the psychoanalytic account takes three times as long as any other, because of the amount of prior talk necessary before students can "hear" what is to be said about the film.
7 Cowie's work does deserve a particular mention as one of the most sophisticated of this whole school, and making specific claims about the nature and role of fantasy as "a privileged terrain on which social reality and the

unconscious are engaged in a figuring which intertwines them both" (365). Centered on the manner in which women are represented in films, Cowie comes close at several points to make claims which could in principle be tested. Challenging notions that "identification" has to be with a particular character, she argues rather than we "identify" with the narrational process through which we are able to play out desiring processes "in as much as we are captured by the film's narration" (149). This claim could in principle be operationalized and tested.

8 I am reminded of the "impolite" response by three sociological authors to some of the theoretical largesse that goes under the name of post-modernism—see Woodward, Emmison and Smith.

9 It is worth noting here the much wider discrepancy between importance and enjoyment with the "Spiritual Journey" group, suggesting that pleasures very often outran their expectations—they made an unexpected discovery for themselves in the film that the "Fantasy" group did not, leading to a different characterization of it.

works cited

Altman, Rick. *Film/Genre*. London: British Film Institute, 1999.

Anon. Review of *Eragon*, *Time Out London* (December 13–20, 2006): http://www.timeout.com/film/83511.html (accessed May 2 2008).

Anon. "Unreality TV." *Radio Times* (July 21–27, 2007): 12–16.

Arthurs, Jane. "*Crash*: Beyond the Boundaries of Sense." *Crash Cultures: Modernity, Mediation and the Material*. Eds. Jane Arthurs and Iain Grant. Bristol: Intellect, 2002. 63–78.

Barker, Martin. "*The Lord of the Rings* and 'Identification': A Critical Encounter." *European Journal of Communication*, 20:3 (2005): 353–78.

——. "Envisaging 'Visualisation': Some Lessons from the *Lord of the Rings* Project." *Film/Philosophy— online Journal*. 10:3 (December 2006): 1–25.

Barker, Martin and Ernest Mathijs (eds.). *Watching The Lord of the Rings: Tolkien's World Audiences*. New York: Peter Lang, 2008.

Bellin, Joshua David. *Framing Monsters: Fantasy Film and Social Alienation*. Carbondale: Southern Illinois University Press, 2005.

Burgin, Victor, James Donald and Cora Kaplan (eds.). *Formations of Fantasy*. London: Methuen, 1986.

Buscombe, Edward, Christine Gledhill, Alan Lovell and Christopher Williams. "Statement: Psychoanalysis and Film." *Screen*, 16:4 (1976): 119–30.

Clute, John and John Grant (eds.). *The Encyclopedia of Fantasy*. New York: St Martin's Griffin, 1997.

Cornwell, Neil. *The Literary Fantastic: from Gothic to Postmodernism*. Hemel Hempstead: Harvester Wheatsheaf, 1990.

Cowie, Elizabeth. *Representing the Woman: Psychoanalysis and Cinema*. Minneapolis: University of Minnesota Press, 1997.

Donald, James (ed.). *Fantasy and the Cinema*. London: BFI, 1989.

Editors of *Cahiers du Cinéma*. "*Young Mr Lincoln*: A Collective Text." *Movies and Methods*. Ed. Bill Nichols. Berkeley: University of California Press, 1976. 493–529.

Fredericks, S C. "Problems of Fantasy." *Science Fiction Studies*, 5:1 (1978): 33–44.

Gledhill, Christine. "Genre." *The Cinema Book*. Ed. Pam Cook. London: British Film Institute, 1995.

Götz, Maya, Dafna Lemish, Amy Aidman and Hyesung Moon. *Media and the Make-Believe World of Children: When Harry Potter Meets Pokémon in Disneyland*. Mahwah, NJ: Lawrence Erlbaum, 2005.

Heath, Stephen. "Film and System." *Screen*, part 1, 16:1 (1975): 7–77; part 2, 16:2 (1975): 91–113.

Hirsjärvi, Irma. "Recognising the Fantasy Literature Genre." *Participations: online Journal*, 3:2 (November 2006): http://www.participations.org/volume%203/issue%202%20-%20special/3_02_hirsjarvi.htm (accessed May 2 2008).

Hume, Kathryn. *Fantasy and Mimesis: Responses to Reality in Western Literature*. New York: Methuen, 1984.

Jackson, Rosemary. *Fantasy: the Literature of Subversion*. London: Methuen, 1981.

Kovala, Urpo and Erkki Vainikkala (eds.). *Reading Cultural Difference*. University of Jyväskylä: Research Unit for Contemporary Culture, 2000.

Lapsley, Robert and Michael Westlake. *Film Theory: An Introduction*. Manchester: Manchester University Press, 1988.

McGowan, Todd. "Finding Ourselves on a *Lost Highway*: David Lynch's Lesson in Fantasy." *Cinema Journal* 39:2 (2000): 51–73.

——. "Looking for the Gaze: Lacanian Film Theory and its Vicissitudes." *Cinema Journal*, 42:3 (2003): 27–57.

Metz, Christian. *The Imaginary Signifier: Psychoanalysis and the Cinema*. Trans. Celia Britton. Bloomington: Indiana University Press, 1982.

Mikkelsen, Nina. Powerful Magic: Learning from Children's Responses to Fantasy Literature. New York: Teachers College Press, 2005.

Mulvey, Laura. "Visual Pleasure and Narrative Cinema." *Screen*, 16:3 (1975): 6–18.

Nash, Mark. "*Vampyr* and the Fantastic." *Screen*, 17:3 (1976): 29–67. Reprinted in Mark Nash, *Screen Theory Culture*. Basingstoke: Macmillan, 2008: 28–69.

Neale, Steven. "Melo Talk: On the Meaning and the Use of the Term 'Melodrama' in the American Trade Press." *Velvet Light Trap* (Fall 1993): 66–89.

Nell, Victor. *Lost In A Book: The Psychology of Reading for Pleasure*. New Haven: Yale University Press, 1998.

Pohl, Frederick. "The Study of Science Fiction: A Modest Proposal." *Science Fiction Studies* 24:1 (March 1997) 11–16.

Rabkin, Eric S. *The Fantastic in Literature*. Princeton: Princeton University Press 1976.

Ruddick, Nicholas (ed.). *State of the Fantastic: Studies in the Theory and Practice of Fantastic Literature and Film* (Selected Essays from the Eleventh International Conference on the Fantastic in the Arts, 1990). Westport, Conn: Greenwood Press 1992.

Shiach, Morag. *Discourse on Popular Culture: Class, Gender and History in Cultural Analysis, 1730 to the Present Day*. Stanford: Stanford University Press, 1989.

Smith, Murray. *Engaging Characters: Fiction, Emotion and the Cinema*. Oxford: Clarendon Press, 1995.

Stacey, Jackie. *Star Gazing: Hollywood Cinema and Female Spectatorship*. London: Routledge, 1993.

Suvin, Darko. "On What Is and What Is Not an SF Narration." *Science Fiction Studies* 5:1 (March 1978).

Telotte, J P. *Science Fiction Film*. Cambridge: Cambridge University Press, 2001.

Todorov, Tzvetan. *The Fantastic: A Structural Approach to a Literary Genre*. Ithaca: Cornell University Press, 1975.

Vale, Vivian, Andrea Juno, Jim Morton and Boyd Rice. *Incredibly Strange Films.* San Francisco: Re/Search Publications, 1986.

Walkerdine, Valerie. "Video Replay: Families, Films and Fantasy." *Fantasy and the Cinema.* Ed. James Donald. London: BFI, 1989, 166–99.

Woodward, Ian, Michael Emmison and Philip Smith. "Consumerism, Disorientation and Postmodern Space: a Modest Test of an Immodest Theory." *British Journal of Sociology* 51.2 (2000): 339–54.

Worley, Alec. *Empires of the Imagination: A Critical Survey of Fantasy Cinema from Georges Méliès to The Lord of the Rings.* Jefferson, NC: McFarland & Co, 2005.

"what is

there really

in the world?"

fourteen

forms of theory,

evidence and

truth in *fahrenheit 9/11*

a philosophical and

intuitionist realist approach

ian   aitken

This chapter will shape concepts drawn from a branch of analytical philosophy known as philosophical realism into a model of "intuitionist realism," and apply that model to an analysis of *Fahrenheit 9/11* (Michael Moore, 2004).[1] Some earlier attempts have been made to apply philosophical realism to film studies, most notably in Lovell's *Pictures of Reality* (1980) and Allen and Gomery's *Film History: Theory and Practice* (1985). However, these earlier attempts were part of more inclusive projects (in the case of Lovell, to launch a realist critique of Althuserian Marxism, and, in Allen and Gomery, to develop a general model of realist film history). In addition, these earlier attempts have not been carried forward a great deal into more recent work, and, given this decidedly spare setting, the chapter offered here must be considered as necessarily conditional and exploratory in character.[2]

The perspective on philosophical realism offered here is founded upon three central convictions: (i) that reality exists independently of representation, (ii) that reality and representation can "converge," and (iii) that such convergence can never be unqualified and so the "danger of divergence between thought and reality can never be averted" (Papineau, quoted in Trigg 67). The first of these convictions is fundamental to any realist position, and, while anti-realists might argue that there is no "*reality itself* (whatever *that* might be) but [only] reality-as-we-picture-it" (Rescher 167), or that such a reality is "A world well lost" (Rorty, quoted by Putnam *Human Face* 262), realists believe that "The assumption of a mind-independent reality is essential to the whole of our standard conceptual scheme relating to inquiry and communication" (Rescher, in Trigg 202). The second and third of these convictions, taken together, also appear to imply a requisite degree of conceptual relativism. However, philosophical realist positions contend that, through the institution of various conceptual means, and by dint of viewing realism as a "regulative conception": a realism "of intent," rather than of "definitive truth," correspondence between reality and representation can be theorized, and the compass of conceptual relativism constrained (Rescher, in Trigg 202).

Any philosophical realist attempt to theorize "convergence" between representation and reality must pay considerable attention to the role played by empirical experience, because, realists believe, such experience constitutes our most dependable, though circumlocutory relation, to a reality, both observable and unobservable, which exists outside our conceptual schemes. Philosophical realism holds that "observable entities" are the *effect* of independent, unobservable causal factors, and also the starting point for any analysis of those factors; and it is because such unobservable causal factors *are*, regrettably, unobservable, and also because observable entities *are*, more fortunately, observable, that the latter are so imperative (Devitt 108). From a realist perspective, empirical entities are also important because such entities *may* also be linked to reality, and, if this is the case, may make reality *accessible* (Trigg 200).

A concern with empirical experience is also central to classical empiricist philosophy, which is founded on a belief in the epistemological primacy of experience and the directly observable, and on a conviction that methodological procedures based on inductive analysis can enable interpretations of reality to arise which are comparatively "theory neutral" (Hesse "Duhem, Quine," in Morick 209). However, since at least the 1950s, when a major critique of classical empiricist philosophy emerged within the analytical tradition, most philosophers writing within the framework of that tradition have found themselves to be generally in concurrence with the proposition that there is no such identifiable thing as a "raw fact," and "no rational basis" for a distinction between "fact" and "value" (Putnam *Reason* 127–8). According to such an interpretation there is no possibility of direct admittance to the facts, and no likelihood of developing any "theory neutral language of observation;" because all appropriations of empirical data are already necessarily pre-laden with supposition (Keat and Urry 37). In concurrence with this stance, the critique of classical empiricism, which emerged from the 1950s onwards, in the work of Putnam, Quine, Hesse and others, rejects the idea of the "practical fact" which can be encountered in a direct way (Hesse, in Morick 211); and replaces that idea with the notion of the "theoretical fact," which can only be encountered indirectly, from within the imprisoning framework of a conceptual scheme (Hesse, in Morick 212).

The idea of the "theoretical fact" (Hesse *Revolutions* 86) also implies that, in contrast to orthodox empiricist tenets, empirical evidence cannot provide the fundamental grounds for proving that one theory is qualitatively superior to another, because such evidence is always appropriated by those theories from the outset (Harré 38). This notion is also associated with another of the theoretical models to emerge from the critique of classical empiricism: the "network theory of meaning." According to an extreme version of this theory, appropriation of empirical materials occurs because of the nature of conceptual schemes as intricate "networks" of terms and relations, which can be re-organized in order to preserve the core premises of such schemes in the face of any conceivable evidence (Hesse, in Morick 212). Such an engulfing outcome is also implied by another concept partly derived from the network theory: the "meaning invariance thesis," which contends that it is possible for the same data to be explained in different ways by different theories, and that, as a consequence, "observation language" does not possess meaning *invariant* to its application within different theoretical networks (Hesse, "Duhem, Quine"in Morick 220–1).

According to an extreme version of the network theory, therefore, it appears that conceptual schemes must be considered to enjoy a degree of hegemony and autonomy which renders them free from effective empirical challenge. Such a standpoint concerning the sovereignty of conceptual schemes, and the subsidiary or even nominal status of "facts" in relation to such schemes, will be familiar to scholars of film studies, because comparable "conventionalist" arguments—and concomitant repudiations of "realism"—have generally held sway within the subject area (Lovell 79). However, it is important to understand that the critique of classical empiricism was developed neither as a deconstructive end in itself, nor as prelude to any prospective endorsement of philosophical relativism; but as a necessary foundation upon which new models of rational theory formation, and the role of empirical evidence within such formation, could be elaborated (Hesse, in Morick 227). Such models address the problem of relativism raised by a strong version of the network theory by proposing less extreme versions of that theory, in order to make certain that "the floodgates to conventionalism" are not opened, and that a general "abandonment of empiricism" does not materialise (Hesse, in Morick 212).

One model of rational theory formation which draws upon the network theory, and which attempts to accommodate the empirical in ways consonant with the latter's freshly conceived, but now distinctly moderated epistemological status, is Hilary Putnam's theory of "internal realism." Here, it is not evidence which plays the crucial role in adjudicating between the respective merits of different theories, but sets of rational methodological principles, which Putnam variously refers to as "rational assertability" conditions, "warranted assertability" statements, and "canons and principles of rationality" (Putnam *Many Faces* 34). These principles possess a logical aspect, set limits upon the remit, acceptability and potential array of interpretation, and lead—it is hoped—to optimum outcomes. Although they cannot confer truth value absolutely and specifically, these canons and principles can establish an "explanation space," a circumscribed area within which certain accounts of reality can be argued to be more justified than others on rational "warranted assertability" grounds; and a theory can be said to offer such grounds if it is, amongst other things, more "instrumentally efficacious, coherent, comprehensive and functionally simple" in dealing with the evidence than are competing theories (Putnam quoted in Passmore *Recent Philosophers* 106). Here, the importance of evidence resides not in an ability to verify or falsify theoretical interpretation directly, but in a capacity to establish what is believed to be a trustworthy reservoir of materials, upon which "warranted" rational models can be advantageously assembled.

Putnam's theory of internal realism is premised on the assumption that, within a theoretical network, warranted assertability conditions can be applied to observable cases in a disinterested manner, in order that the network be attuned in relation to the connotations radiating from such cases. However, it may be that a theory employs such conditions in order to interpret observable cases "comprehensively," "coherently" and "efficaciously" in terms of its own a priori understandings, rather than in a spirit of self-adjustment in relation to the empirical; and this suggests (a) that warranted assertability conditions may be insufficient in themselves to guarantee that disinterested qualification occurs, and (b) that the vitality of such a guarantee rests upon the adoption of a predisposition to deploy such conditions in a qualifying manner. Such a predisposition is founded on the mainstay realist conviction that observable cases should, on principle, never be made "comprehensively" subsidiary to theory, because their demi-sovereignty is able to exercise an important curb upon the inherent propensity for theoretical networks to construct unassailable paradigms around themselves.

This chapter has set out to explore conceptual positions drawn from philosophical realism. However, Putnam's relationship to philosophical realism is patchy, and, whilst his early philosophy can be more clearly associated with a philosophical realist stance towards notions of representation and convergence, his later philosophy, which encompasses the theory of internal realism, actually sanctions the salutary "demise" of such a stance (Putnam *Reason* 74), and has been characterized as a form of "anti-realism" (Devitt 7).

313

This anti-realist orientation leads Putnam to develop a theory of internal realism in which the idea of external reality is bracketed out, and "convergence" only refers to the competing claims of rival theories which are "internal" to a particular explanation space (Passmore *Recent Philosophers* 105–7). Here the "best" theory is that which interprets observable cases most effectively in terms of warranted assertability conditions: that which brings about "optimal" *convergence* between such cases and conditions (Putnam *Reason* 52). However, there are a number of problems with this position. First, if warranted assertability conditions are deployed in a "self-interested," rather than "disinterested" manner, this might preclude even "internal" convergence, because the convergence in question would amount to an assimilation of the empirical by warranted assertability conditions. Second, internal convergence might be unrealisable *per se*, because, whilst inferior theories may be rejected, and a degree of convergence thus effected, the eventual alpha theory does not so much bring empirical cases and warranted conditions into convergence, as uses the empirical to consolidate the theoretical network. Here, internal convergence must lead to "paradigm" formation, where theoretical networks take on increasing authority and autonomy (Kuhn xxii). Third, it is possible that a theory which did not deploy warranted assertability principles particularly well could still be nearer to the truth than others that did, because the truth might not conform to the rational character of such principles. Fourth, Putnam appears to endow warranted assertability conditions with an almost transcendent status, higher than that of empirical experience or external reality, and the problem here (aside from the overt idealism involved) is that, in general, life does not appear to conform to such conditions: is not "instrumentally efficacious, coherent, comprehensive and functionally simple;" and so "why ... [should]... we regard these as virtues?" (Passmore *Recent Philosophers* 106). Life, experience—and reality—is made up of the rational and the irrational, reason and the non-cognitive, and this is why philosophical and intuitionist realist positions are premised upon the conviction that an approach which deploys reason (including warranted assertability conditions), experience and intuition in tandem is more likely to converge with the truth than one which enthrones only warranted assertability conditions.

It has been argued here that observable cases should never be entirely appropriated within a theoretical network. However, according to the realist principle of "empirical adequacy," such *misappropriation* is also unlikely to occur, because the intangible complexity which marks such cases contains the latent potential to challenge misappropriation (Devitt 123–7). For a theory to possess "empirical adequacy" that theory must engage with a substantial quantity of diverse empirical materials (Trigg xiv), and such an extensive degree of engagement is important in itself, because it brings theory formation into propitious encounter with materials which are, realists contend, linked tellingly, if indirectly, with a reality existing outside conceptual schemes. However, such engagement also makes it more likely that the generality of conceptual terms and relations within a theoretical network will take on a tendency to evolve and change as a result of such engagement, because, taken as an accumulation, empirical concepts must inevitably contain a far more extensive and nebulous quantity and diversity of terms, connotations and relations than those embedded within the more cognate concepts of a theoretical network (Hesse, in Morick 217). These latter concepts are fashioned by their determinate conceptual and rational nature, whereas empirical concepts are characterized more by both an indeterminate and unsystematic character, *and* by potentially limitless measure (Hesse, in Morick 216). It is this character and measure which endows empirical materials with the ability to challenge conceptual assimilation.

It has been argued here that the network theory of meaning is not a homogenous doctrine, and, whilst, according to a "strong," and, consequently, "relativist," version of that theory, evidence can always be entirely appropriated by a theoretical network; "softer" and, accordingly, more "realist" versions of the network theory, attempt to theorise how, in applicable circumstances, such requisition can be circumvented. However, the notions of empirical adequacy and indeterminate empirical measure also suggest that such misrequisition may not only be fore-stalled, but also completely thwarted, for, where such adequacy and measure are instituted, rational concepts may never be fully sufficient to their plenitude; and this also suggests in turn that, in order to house such plenitude, those concepts must not only be rationally taut, but also requisitely flexible and general. Although theoretical networks *should* be open to the evidence, as a matter of principle, where empirical adequacy applies, such networks may also have little option *but* to be so. As will be argued later, these notions of empirical adequacy, the indeterminate measure of empirical materials, conceptual shortfall, and the potential facility of generalized representation, have implications for understanding *aesthetic* theoretical networks such as *Fahrenheit 9/11.*

In addition to a respect for the semi-sovereign status of observable cases, and a belief in the need to accommodate empirical adequacy through the use of both rationally taut but flexibly general concepts, realist approaches to theory formation are also characterized by a fidelity to the principles of ontological and epistemological depth. A realist theoretical network which possesses epistemological depth will present an account of what Allen and Gomery, quoting Bhaskar, have described as the full range of "*generative mechanisms* that produce the observable event" (Allen and Gomery 15). Such an account must, necessarily, include a range of concepts, from the particular to the abstract, because, according to a realist perspective, external reality is structured in terms of "ontological depth," as a "multi-tiered stratification" (Bhaskar *Possibility* 16). For a theoretical network to be realist, therefore, it must reproduce the framework of ontological depth within its own epistemological perspective.

In contrast to such facsimilication, however, an anti-realist approach to theory formation would circumvent the realist imperative to arrive at epistemological depth by shallowing out such compass. For example, from a realist view-point, the most abstract concepts in a theoretical network are those which refer to fundamental unobservable causal mechanisms. They are the crucial "intransitive objects of scientific theory" (Allen and Gomery 21), and the philosophical "crown" and most important components of any theory (Harré 168). However, avoidance of such concepts is for the most part distinctive of American pragmatist philosophy, and its application to the study of film history in the model of "middle-level" and "piecemeal" theorizing advanced by Bordwell and Carroll (332). A philosophical realist approach to the study of film history, such as that attempted by Allen and Gomery, would, in contrast, reject such exclusion, and exemplify the principle of epistemological depth by embracing the full compass of abstract, intermediary and particular concepts.[3]

Although the deployment of abstract categories within an account founded upon epistemological depth may be appropriate to a philosophical realist approach it is not, however, *sufficient* to such an approach; and what is required, in addition, is that such an account must also "be conceived to be a hypothetical mechanism which might really be responsible for the phenomena to be explained" (Harré 178). A theory *may* possess epistemological depth, but such depth may also be structured primarily in relation to the internal priorities of the theory, rather than an imperative to model that which is external to theory. In the latter case, such "realist" modelling would be described as "analogical." When a realist theoretical network begins to operate it will initially depend upon a conceptual model which has been developed earlier in order to describe and explain observable entities similar to those under current analysis (Harré 178). This model is applied to the new entities under question because it appears to be "analogically similar" to those entities, and because, given the previous success of the model in describing and explaining comparable entities, there are grounds for believing that it will also be able to describe and explain the fresh entities plausibly well. The model is, therefore, not selected at random, but because it possesses "*substantive similarities*" to the phenomena under investigation; and it is this similitude, as opposed to more relativist arbitrariness, that makes analogical models structurally realist (Psillos 140).

However, in addition to possessing an analogical character, a realist model must refrain from explaining the entities under observation in an unconditional way, because, were this to occur, those entities would be divested of their intrinsic complexity. In order to circumvent such an outcome, a realist analogical model must, therefore, contain "negative" and "neutral," as well as "positive" analogies to the observable entities under investigation: there must be respects in which the model is similar (positive analogy) and dissimilar (negative analogy) to those entities, and also respects in which the extent of such similarity and dissimilarity remains undecided (neutral analogy) (Hesse *Models* 8–9). The existence of such negative and neutral "open" areas of explication within a realist theoretical model makes it possible for that model to describe and explain observable entities in a provisional, rather than categorical manner, and also increases the likelihood of both model qualification and convergence.

One final philosophical realist principle to be considered here, and one implied by the realist notions of ontological and epistemological depth, is that of "stratified" explanation (Harré 178). Here, the theoretical model first describes phenomenon and generates a provisional account of causality. After this first "stratum" is established, the model must then describe the causal agents themselves, and produce an account of *their* causality (Harré 179). What occurs, therefore, is "the movement at any one level from knowledge of manifest phenomena to knowledge of the structures which generate them" (Bhaskar *Possibility* 17). This process rolls on in a dialectical manner that encompasses both linear inductive refinement and more lateral reflective generality, as the realist model attempts to relate an increasing preoccupation with empirical and intermediary categories— a preoccupation unavoidably generated by the rolling process of stratification—to the deep abstract categories which make up the centre of the model. Such a process of dialectical relationship formation between abstract, intermediary and empirical categories also implies that a realist theoretical formation must deploy forms of intuitive, as well as rational understanding, an implication supported by the emblematic realist insistence upon the deployment of negative and neutral, as well as positive analogies; and by the realist injunction to establish zones of both rational explication, and areas of more connotative implication. This "intuitionist" aspect of realist theory formation also establishes a link between philosophical realism and the model of "revelatory" and "intuitionist" aesthetic realism which will now be discussed.

Debates concerning the possibility or impossibility of "convergence" are pervasive within analytical philosophy, and associated with a variety of positions (Devitt 123–7). Such debates cannot be considered in a measured manner within the more constrained ambitions of this chapter. However, what *can* be considered, though in a still necessarily epigrammatic way, is the question of how realist notions of convergence and "truthfulness" can be applied within the aesthetic domain. For example, although Putnam's notion of the explanation space is directed at scientific and philosophical, rather than aesthetic enquiry, the circumscribed degree of convergence with "truth" which the notion puts forward also entails that, when applied to questions of aesthetic realism, a similar or even more circumscribed degree of convergence might be all that is attainable. This, in turn, suggests that manifestations of "truthfulness" within the aesthetic domain must be fundamentally tenuous in temper, and, given this, it may be that works of art should not be considered as making lucid "truth claims" about a subject, but, rather, as "offer[ing] a subject" up for debate, or "show[ing] something as" (Beardsley 375).

Here, the work of art shows something as *like* something, rather than *as* something; it "draws attention to" a subject, or puts a subject "up for consideration," instead of making more precise claims. Similarly, the observer of the art object can be considered as searching for something that might be "intellectually illuminating," rather than "true" (Passmore *Serious* 125). Here, the work of art does not so much display truth but "interesting candidates for truth," which the recipient then makes tentative judgements about (Passmore *Serious* 125); and, within this process of expression and reception, the role of the "vision" of the artist, and/or the formal/thematic organization of the work of art, is to provide a broad "perspective" on the subject (Passmore *Serious* 138).

This model of aesthetic expression and reception is primarily "revelatory" and "intuitionist," rather than cognitive and rationalist, and implies that the work of art expresses abstract, intermediary and empirical concepts in a relatively unsystematic manner, *and*, that such concepts are also received by the recipient in a similarly unsystematic manner (Passmore *Serious* 125). This model also suggests that the work of art is not best suited to the representation of either absolutes or particulars, but, rather, intermediary regions of "general experience" which are given particularized form; or particular "things in particular times and places" which are "describe[d] in general terms" (Passmore *Serious* 143). A work of art, such as a documentary film, may *suggest* generalized hypotheses, but, given such generality, and the unsystematic character of aesthetic expression and reception, cannot be charged with *proving* such hypotheses (Beardsley 380). Works of art do not "launch an enquiry" on behalf of the spectator, but call attention to pervasive and noteworthy features of the world (Beardsley 381). All this suggests both a considerable degree of indeterminacy in the representation of the subject, and a substantial degree of inconclusiveness in any intersection with reality which the work of art might attempt to realize. Nevertheless, and as has been argued, such indeterminacy and inconclusiveness remain fully compatible with both intuitionist and revelatory aesthetic realism, and philosophical realism.

fahrenheit 9/11

The realist model of theory and evidence proposed here conceives of aesthetic objects such as documentary films as consisting of a network of theoretical categories which provide both descriptions of the subject as problematic and provisional accounts of causality. However, the initial sections of *Fahrenheit 9/11* do not so much represent the subject of inquiry (the "rigged" 2000 US general election) as problematic but as calamitous. It is not particularly surprising that *Fahrenheit 9/11* begins in such fundamentalist terms, given the film-maker's established reputation as forthright and activist. However, the presence from the outset of such a degree of demonstration makes later qualification and formulation of distinctions more difficult to attain, and also makes the process of knowledge accretion via a process of "stratification," similarly difficult. The presence of such a high degree of certainty-based partiality also means that, from the onset, the film's problematic is not really rendered as a *problematic* at all, if that term is understood as indicating the existence of a configuration of uncertainty, quandary and indistinctness; which, at least initially, can only be accounted for provisionally. What Moore establishes here is more like a *final*, rather than provisional explanation, and this carries the risk that the empirical material employed in the film will be made constitutionally secondary to the film's evolving network of theoretical categories. From the outset then, at least at the level of the film-maker's intentions, *Fahrenheit 9/11* appears to embody the spirit of a "self-interested" anti-realist, rather than "disinterested" realist network. However, and as will be argued later, the impact of those intentions upon the film itself should not be overemphasized.

Fahrenheit 9/11 sets out its initial account using relatively concise units of correlated commentary and visual material. As a picture of the subject of enquiry is elaborated, affirmative statements, which seek to explain in a terse, summarizing manner, are backed-up by empirical images intended to reaffirm the assertions enfolded within those statements. The impact of such perceptible corroboration is forceful, carrying as it does the weight of incontestable authority and veracity (though of course, and as will be argued later, such apparent credence also stems from the fact that the film *leaves out* many gainsaying factors). Neither commentary nor visual material is employed in a particularly protracted manner at this stage of the film, and nor are the explanations offered either coherently phrased, or systematically set out. Instead, the short, interacting units attempt to institute a collage of connotation and evidence which embodies and displays the film's core hypotheses; and the impact of this employment of disparate items of conceptual and visual information, drawn from a wide range of sources, *in conjunction with* the co-affirming relationship which exists between such items in this section of the film, is to imply, in an indicative rather than inclusive manner, that the core hypotheses of *Fahrenheit 9/11* are wholly warranted. Despite the film's ideological disposition, therefore, what appears is an impressionistic rather than unequivocal mobilization of truth claims, and this does conform, to an extent, with a realist model of aesthetic realism. This section of the film could also be said to embody both the realist concept of "empirical adequacy," and a realist use of concepts which contain areas of connotative implication, through the deployment of negative and neutral, as well as positive analogies.

The initial explanatory model put forward in *Fahrenheit 9/11* is structured around three principal conceptual themes: illicit manipulation of the electoral system, institutional impasse, and tragedy. According to the film, powerful figures close to Bush worked to ensure victory. The institutions of the media, Congress and Senate became hopelessly bewildered, and proved incapable of responding to the unfolding events in a manner congruent with their respective mandates. Those events also had particularly tragic consequences for African-American supporters of the Democratic Party, who, the film alleges, were deliberately disenfranchised in order to ensure a Bush victory. At this stage it is this latter theme which is predominant, and the notion that the overthrow of the election has struck some of the poorest citizens of the nation gives the film a poignant and moving force. However, this cogency also masks an underlying problem.

According to a realist network model of meaning, an initial account of any given subject will be necessarily provisional and schematic. However, the preliminary account developed in *Fahrenheit 9/11* does not have the feel of provisionality, but of finality, and, in addition, seems to be mainly motivated by a desire to institute a *select* version of events, rather than by the goal of achieving eventual inclusivity. This reliance upon evidently selective portrayal weakens the film considerably when it attempts to portray the second of the three principal areas referred to above: that of the problems evident within the media, Senate and Congress. Here, disproportionate levels of selectivity over-augment the film's dominant ideology, and lead to a largely unpersuasive embellishment of events. On the other hand, *Fahrenheit 9/11* does appeal to later latent qualification of this initial model, and suggests (by dint of exclusion) a range of auxiliary questions concerning the reasons for the manipulation of the election result. By abridging in a one-dimensional way, therefore, *Fahrenheit 9/11* suggests the subsistence of a more comprehensive causal reality, which the film *may* turn to later, and this, in turn, brings it into closer compliance with a "stratification" model of realist explanation. Here, and not for the last time, a partition appears to open up between the conceptual/ideological and non-conceptual/material structures of *Fahrenheit 9/11*.

Fahrenheit 9/11 begins with a long "prologue." This prologue "explains" the core of the problem using theoretical categories and empirical visual materials which propose relatively unambiguous accounts of causality. The causal theoretical categories projected here consist of: (a) manipulation of the media, particularly by the Fox TV network; (b) a concomitant capitulation to the Fox agenda by the other networks; (c) manipulation of the election result by the Supreme Court; (d) deliberate racial disenfranchisement of the African-American electorate in order to reduce the Democrat vote; (e) manipulation of the vote counting mechanism itself; and (f) either, or both, manipulation of the Congress and Senate, and/or the existence of an institutional seizure within these bodies, demonstrated by the failure of black delegates to mount an effective protest to their alleged disenfranchisement, and by Gore's self-vanquishing obligation, as President of the Senate, to block such protests on procedural grounds.

Although the initial version of causality and depiction of events is refined here, these later accounts are still given without ambiguity, and this lack of doubt concerning causality is reinforced by the film's implication that such a structure of causality is also more or less unique, because one manifestation of that structure, the street protests which erupt during Bush's inauguration ceremony, is also, apparently, exceptional, as the commentary declares. This unequivocal model of causality also gives rise to two further manifestations evident within the final section of the prologue: that of the existence of a siege-like situation, as the new administration faces the nation's wrath; and the notion that nothing can be done to turn the course of the abduction of power.

These representations of the *exceptionality* of the occasion, the *irreparable* divisions which flow from it, and its/their *irreversibility*, further accentuate the fundamentalist position adopted within *Fahrenheit 9/11*, and are also, arguably, generated by one underlying core causal concept: that of the existence of corporate/political misgovernance in America, and the consequences which such misgovernance has for the weakest sections of the country. However, *Fahrenheit 9/11* does not explain *why* such misgovernance exists, or took the form that it did in these instances, or even why it necessarily affects the poor to such an inequitable degree. No underlying cause is established here, and only a vague allusion arises, that such misgovernance is the consequence of some malaise within the body politic. However, if it is *only* such an allusion, and nothing more meaningful, that lies deep in the abstract heart of the theoretical network deployed by *Fahrenheit 9/11*, then that network is neither sufficiently explicit, nor adequately conceptually abstract.

In addition to its deployment of causal explanatory paradigms, the prologue of *Fahrenheit 9/11* also employs an exceptionally extensive range of empirical visual information to describe the manifestations of those paradigms. The broad range of empirical visual materials employed in the prologue of *Fahrenheit 9/11*, includes (a) images of crowds and celebrities prematurely celebrating Gore's likely victory; (b) images of a confident-looking Bush, who, it is implied, appears to have foreknowledge of the fact that his victory has been predetermined in the crucial state of Florida; (c) close-ups of news broadcasters seen both as, alternatively, convinced, then uncertain, of the electoral outcome; (d) images of congressmen and senators; (e) images of black congressmen and women standing forlornly in front of Senate President Gore as he rejects their petitions; and (f) images of an aggrieved crowd pelting Bush's car with eggs.

As argued, the abundance of empirical materials evident here conforms to the realist concept of empirical adequacy, and provides this section of *Fahrenheit 9/11* with a realist model of causality and description incorporating "negative" and "neutral" analogies which, in some cases, seem to undermine the overt positive analogies conveyed by authorial intent and commentary. As with other sections of the prologue, these disparate units of empirical material share a common structural objective to affirm the accompanying verbal commentary. However, a considerable *amount* of such material is present here, and such magnitude holds open the prospect that such material might be difficult to organize in relation to the film's directed ideological substance, and might also work *against* that substance. One possible moment when this occurs concerns the representation of the "rule-bound" debates taking place in Congress. The film characterizes the procedural impasse which occurs as a form of institutional obstruction, or latent jurisprudential bias within the system. However, the wide-ranging sum of visual materials present in these sequences could be read as signifying the existence of an impersonal and unprejudiced framework of historical lineage, which, though manipulated by the Bush camp in this instance, remains of intrinsic advantage. Here, the *sheer assortment and quantity* of empirical visual portrayals succeeds both in undercutting the commentary and authorial intentionality of *Fahrenheit 9/11*, and qualifying the underlying theoretical imperatives of the film.

In addition to these scenes, this kind of unintentional empirical qualification also occurs throughout the final section of the prologue of *Fahrenheit 9/11*, where the film's main thesis: that Bush is a "lame-duck President," largely incompetent, and permanently on holiday, is frequently confounded. The footage here consists of a combination of cinéma vérité-style publicity and stock interview material of Bush on vacation, and, as with other scenes, the complexity of combination favoured here has the effect of disseminating interpretation beyond the parameters of the film's intended address, to suggest other connotations. These include, for example, the notion that Bush is an "average guy" (a connotation promoted by Bush's advisors, and which Moore's approach is unable to undercut); or that Bush is likeable, in control of circumstances, and has his own effective (if unusually relaxed) methods of dealing with the affairs of State. Bush looks unperturbed rather than dim-witted here, and the overall indistinctness of connotation emerging from this section of the film again stems from Moore's chosen technique—one which he is ultimately unable to wholly control—of employing a broad assortment of complex empirical images.

This and other sections of *Fahrenheit 9/11* also consist of two conflicting orientations. The first of these is structured into the substance of the film images themselves, images drawn from promotional materials released by the Bush camp, and organized according to the imperatives of that camp. The second is built upon the editing of these images and the commentary, both of which attempt to undermine the opposing ideological tendency entrenched within the images. However, it is the substance of the images which ultimately triumphs here, resisting the film's conceptual interventions. Once more, the ability of the empirical to evoke difference and antithesis effectively qualifies the initial theoretical model of *Fahrenheit 9/11*, and such equivocation, invoked by largely non-conceptual empirical materials, also corresponds to a realist model of revelatory and intuitionist aesthetic experience.

As mentioned, *Fahrenheit 9/11* begins with a long prologue, which covers the period from Bush's election victory in 2000, to just before the time of the attack on the World Trade Centre, on September 11 2001. After the prologue, the main body of the film commences with a series of images, without commentary, of the Bush team being made up for television appearances. This sequence suggests a relative remoteness from reality, and somewhat synthetic enclosure within the team's sheltered but prevailing milieu. The artificiality of mores evoked in this section of the film is then contrasted with the genuine sense of dreadfulness evoked by the attack on the twin towers, an attack portrayed first, by a black screen with off-screen sounds of the explosions, then the agonized faces of spectators looking upward towards the smoke-filled sky. The mood now changes from the earlier atmosphere of artificial self-indulgence to one of tragedy, as *Fahrenheit 9/11* attempts to invoke the magnitude of the attack and its consequence.

This sequence of *Fahrenheit 9/11* also appears to share a number of structural similarities with the first part of the prologue. At the thematic level, the same sense of gradually unfolding tragedy appears palpable, though a contrast can still be found between the depictions of premeditated misgovernance and pounding down of the black poor in the prologue, and the more heightened portrayals of preening marionettes and world-changing events in the later section. Both sections also appear to have an African-American focus, as the locus for the most intense expression of emotion in the later section is that of a young Black woman, gazing in horror at those throwing themselves to their deaths from the towers. At the level of theory formation, and, as in the prologue, this section of *Fahrenheit 9/11* also offers up similarly problematic and provisional representations for later explanation. A degree of ambivalence is evident here, which, as in the prologue, is established by empirical materials, rather than language and concepts.

The relationship of contrast perceptible between the two sequences set at the beginning of the main division of the film (those of the Bush team preparing for television appearances, and the attack on the twin towers) also exemplifies the characteristic approach adopted within the remainder of *Fahrenheit 9/11*, namely, that of using visual images to both negate the commentaries and discourses emanating from the Bush administration, and affirm those which represent Moore's point of view. Here, visual material is used in a *revising* manner in support of aspects of the film's theoretical network which have a *deconstructive* function in negating antithetical points of view (i.e., those voiced by the administration); and in a *confirmatory* manner in support of aspects of the network which play a legitimizing role in consolidating the core ideological discourse of the network (i.e., that voiced by Moore, in the commentary). However, as in the prologue, *Fahrenheit 9/11* is not always successful in managing and demarcating the signifying potential of its empirical visual materials in support of the film's core underlying premises here, and the attempt to orchestrate these materials within a partisan dialectic of repudiation and confirmation over the major division of the film also meets with similarly qualified success. The key point is that this incomplete conclusion has the consequence that *Fahrenheit 9/11* comes to present a series of complex, sometimes ambivalent, rather than entirely coherent patterns of such repudiation and conformation, once more bringing the film into closer correspondence with a realist model than at first sight might seem to be the case.

After the opening sections of the main body of the film *Fahrenheit 9/11* proceeds to address a range of issues. These are, in the order in which they are broached within this section of the film: (a) The question of the nature of the financial relationships which existed between the Bush family and Saudi dignitaries, and the role such relationships played in the decision to allow aircraft carrying the bin-Laden family to leave the US after 9/11; (b) the administration's attempt to foster a climate of fear amongst the American public in order to garner support for the "war on terror"; (c) the question of why the attack on Afghanistan was carried out in such a "desultory" fashion; and (d) the institution of the Patriot Act. In these sections of the film the approach to the use of commentary and visuals changes from that adopted within the prologue. Whereas, within the prologue, a range of brief units of commentary and reinforcing visuals are employed, here, each issue is addressed to a larger extent. The collage-type orientation of the prologue, with its over-abundance of concepts, and tapestry of empirical material, is forsaken here in favour of a course suggesting that a more in-depth investigation of the issues, and more sophisticated elaboration of points made earlier, is now being carried through. Nevertheless, these sections of the film still embody the characteristic structural penchant of *Fahrenheit 9/11*, which is to employ visual empirical material to both negate the rationalizations of the Bush camp, and affirm Moore's own, which, *in this section of the film*, make the case that the Bush administration's reasons for engaging in the "war on terror" were essentially financial, and related to an aspiration to control the international supply of oil.

However, one consequence of this focus is that, here at least, *Fahrenheit 9/11* does not particularly address the arguably more imperative *political* reasons for the invasions of Afghanistan and Iraq, and this, in turn, gives this section of the film, like those sequences set within Congress, an insubstantial feel. Up till this point, the theoretical network of *Fahrenheit 9/11* has

324

extended and honed its internal causal models in the "stratified" manner of a realist critique. However, a fissure now appears to open up within these models, because some essential (political) relationships are overlooked. These perceptible breaches could be regarded as the outcome of structural flaws within the film, or as emblematic of the way in which *Fahrenheit 9/11* persistently excludes that which does not fit with its ideological objectives, as those objectives unfold across the course of the narrative. On the other hand, it could also be argued that, according to a revelatory and intuitionist model of aesthetic realism, *Fahrenheit 9/11* should not be required to be inclusive in the manner of an entirely rational, cognate enquiry.

However, even if this argument is accepted, that which is debarred here still seems to diminish the overall explanatory power of the causal models mobilized within *Fahrenheit 9/11*, and, from a realist perspective, this is a deeply regressive move. It is not, therefore, the exclusions themselves which are at issue, but the impact these have upon an already weakening causal framework; and, here, the conceptual dimension of *Fahrenheit 9/11* undercuts positive analogies already destabilized by the empirical dimension of the film. In general, and from a realist perspective, such undercutting of positive analogies would be perceived to be a positive quality of the film. However, the problem is that it occurs at the expense of a diminution of the abstract dimension of the causal models in *Fahrenheit 9/11*. In addition to such diminution, this section of the film also contains a noteworthy number of determinate "truth claims," rather than merely "interesting candidates for truth claims," and this has the effect of forcing the empirical materials to reinforce the film's ideological objectives. Such fortification, taken together with the sense of exclusion, over-certainty, absence of important abstract causal features, and one-dimensional use of evidence apparent in these sequences, makes this section of *Fahrenheit 9/11* one of the least effectual within the film.

If the opening acts of the main division of *Fahrenheit 9/11* are concerned with the aftermath of the attack on the World Trade Centre, the invasion of Afghanistan, and the financial links between the Bush camp and various Arab elites; the remainder of that division is taken up with the invasion of Iraq. This final part of the film is also divided into four sections. The first of these sets out and caricatures official rationalizations for the prosecution of the war, whilst the second focuses upon the military recruitment of disadvantaged African-Americans. The third then returns to the issues of corporate sleaze addressed during the prologue and beginning of the main division of the film—but this time focussing principally on the role played by the Haliburton corporation. Finally, the film ends on a personalized note, in following the emotional rites of passage undertaken by the grieving mother of a soldier killed in Iraq.

In many respects, the Iraq incursion lies at the heart of *Fahrenheit 9/11*, and, perhaps because of this, this section of the film is also marked by a discernibly distinctive stylistic, and use of theory and evidence, dissimilar to that employed both in the prologue and beginning of the main division of the film, yet including features drawn from both these subdivisions. Here, Moore attempts to use both the inexplicit and highly charged collage-like style of the prologue, and more linear approach adopted at the beginning of the major division of the film; and this section of *Fahrenheit 9/11* frequently alternates between these two stratagems, first, by displaying a series of epi-grammatic units of linked commentary and visuals which have no overall coherence, and then by engaging in more lengthy interviews and com-mentaries, which provide more articulate accounts of the subject. At the level of film form, this final segment of *Fahrenheit 9/11* endows the film with an overall structural unity, as the two different stratagems adopted in the prologue and beginning of the main division of the film now re-appear together in concord. At the same time, this formal structural closure is accompanied by thematic closure, as the film's over-arching explanation of its problematic, namely, that the so-called "war on terror" is merely a pretext for a set of political, economic and military objectives formulated well before the events of 2000, is reasserted. Nevertheless, and as elsewhere in *Fahrenheit 9/11*, these aspects related to closure are also accompanied by others which tend to open up the connotation levels generated by the film. This final section of the film also brings new levels of "stratified" description and causality to bear on the subject of enquiry, and concludes with a general air of mystified scepticism, rather than firmly stated propo-sition, in a manner consonant with a realist approach.

conclusions

Although *Fahrenheit 9/11* is sometimes characterized as an ideologically tendentious work, the film is best understood as predominantly so at the conceptual level, but less so at the more empirical, non-conceptual level. From the perspective of a philosophical realist network model of theory formation, the *conceptual* theoretical network of *Fahrenheit 9/11* is exemplified by a "self-interested," rather than "disinterested" rationality, by a propen-sity to issue too many absolute, rather than "interesting candidate for" truth claims; and by an interior theoretical model containing too many "positive," and too few "neutral" and "negative" analogies. From the per-spective of an intuitionist cinematic realist model of theory formation, the conceptual theoretical network of *Fahrenheit 9/11* is also exemplified by forms of "propaganda [rather than indeterminate realism] steeped in physical reality" (Kracauer 211); and, so, contains too many "unfortunately heavily didactic scenes" (Bazin 158).

However, although a theorist of intuitionist realism such as Bazin would undoubtedly have censured *Fahrenheit 9/11* as an ideologically "organized film," he might also have endorsed the auspicious role played by the "faults" in such organization: the "negative imprints" established by the film's realist empirical base (Bazin 162); for, if the *conceptual* theoretical network of *Fahrenheit 9/11* inclines towards a spirit of anti-realism, the film's extensive and multifaceted *empirical* theoretical network predisposes more towards the quality of a realist model of theory formation. It is at this level that the interior theoretical model of *Fahrenheit 9/11* presents neutral and negative, as well as positive analogies; because, in addition to playing the roles of guaranteeing the truth claims of Moore's ideological perspective, and negating the truth claims made by the Bush Administration, the non-linguistic empirical materials evident within *Fahrenheit 9/11* sometimes undercut or muddle both these shaping assignments. Further to an accountability for most of the negative and neutral analogies manifest within the film, the highly diverse and intermittently incongruent continuum of empirical materials in *Fahrenheit 9/11* also cedes the film an "empirical adequacy," which, whilst superficially serving to legitimate the theoretical account advanced, more noteworthily challenges and unsettles that account. Whilst these unformulated and tenuous materials may not possess sufficient authority to topple the film's hegemonic ideology, their essentially provisional, rather than established status, *is* sufficient to create fissures—what Bazin refers to as "negative imprints"—in that ideology; so inserting a degree of equivocation into the film. Given all this, it can be argued that, despite the ideological intentionality inscribed into both its authorial "perspective" and conceptual theoretical network, *Fahrenheit 9/11* corresponds more closely to a realist model of theory formation than might at first understanding appear to be so.

If *Fahrenheit 9/11* is considered as a divided film, in which an authoritarian, narrowly-focussed ideological dimension is on occasion transported by a visual empirical foundation more inclined to indeterminate expression and tentative allusion, that division is also most perceptible in the prologue, and less so in those sections of the film which cover the invasions of Iraq and Afghanistan. This is partly because, whereas, in the prologue, a relatively unsystematic conjoining of empirical materials tends to off-set and undercut ideological discourse; in these later sections, the increasingly organized use of such materials within a more rationalized, linear and perceptually "realist" fashion of film-making tends to re-centre and underline them. In these sequences, "self-interested" explanatory accounts are ceded a superior measure of exposition, and one consequence of this conceptual corroboration is that the empirical takes on an ancillary and naturalising *function*, rather than more self-governing and revising *outlook*. From the perspectives of both philosophical and intuitionist realism such a function would be characterized as anti-realist, because it bears self-interested truth claims rather than disinterested "candidate for truth" claims, and so closes down the areas of more connotative implication indispensable to realist theory formation.

During the period of "screen theory" styles of film-making grounded in perceptual realism, or "naturalism," were frequently criticized on the grounds of a presumed capacity to "naturalize" ideology.[4] This is, for example, the basis of the critique of the "classic realist text," mounted by Colin MacCabe in his dismissal of Ken Loach's *Days of Hope* (1975) as inopportunely naturalist (MacCabe 12). Today, such blanket and blinkered repudiations of naturalism have now chiefly disappeared, perhaps because so many excellent and important "naturalist" films emerged during the 1980s and 1990s, including Loach's own *The Gamekeeper* (1980) and *The Wind that Shakes the Barley* (2006). Nevertheless, from the perspectives of philosophical and intuitionist realism, an important point remains to be clarified concerning the alleged, inexorably "naturalizing" propensity of naturalism; and this is that, whilst "naturalism" *may* possess a naturalizing predilection, it *categorically* possesses a contrary and more munificent *representational* inclination, which *should* bring the naturalizing function into question, and *should,* therefore, enable an authentically philosophical and intuitionist realist form of aesthetic expression and reception to transpire.

The experience of aesthetic realism in film is based upon the active contemplation of "candidate for truth claims" about the world, which are expressed within representational forms and techniques corresponding to our perception and memory, and which are assessed against the experience of the spectator. To judge that a film is "realistic" is, therefore, to make a twofold judgement, the first part of which concerns what it is that the film depicts, and the second what life is like. Whilst the spectator is making this dual judgement the film meanders onwards both synchronically and diachronically, and the spectator's judgements concerning the truth or falsity of any particular truth claim are persistently deferred (Aitken *European Film Theory* 256). This process of realist expression and reception is both inherently indeterminate, and also grounded in the *representational realist*, rather than naturalizing capabilities of naturalism, because representational forms which correspond to our perception and memory provide the foundation upon which "interesting candidate for truth claims" can be assessed, and the realist double-judgement freely exercised.

However, it is the naturalizing, rather than representational realist imperative which gains ascendancy in the Iraq sequences of *Fahrenheit 9/11.* In these sequences, the use of techniques such as linear narrative, propositional explication, real-time temporo-spatial continuity, and logical conceptual enlargement *should,* notionally, enable the realist representational imperative to come into sight. However, such an outcome does not materialize, because the naturalizing tendency of these sequences governs that imperative. Nevertheless, this is not the case with those sequences in which the empirical theoretical network of *Fahrenheit 9/11* unhinges its own conceptual theoretical network, and in which, accordingly, the film comes closer to meeting the demands of philosophical and intuitionist realism.

Here, *Fahrenheit 9/11* succeeds in throwing off the envelope of conceptual anti-realism, and in setting out an impressionistic analogical model, accommodating both reason and intuition, in order to answer that "deepest of all … questions, what is there really in the world?" (Harré 178). Finally, the analysis undertaken here suggests that concepts taken from philosophical realism can be productively aligned with others derived from "continental" intuitionist realism, and this, in turn, suggests a way forward for future studies.

notes

1. I have developed the notion of "intuitionist realism," a term which covers the ideas of John Grierson, Siegfried Kracauer, André Bazin and Georg Lukács, in earlier work. This includes *European Film Theory and Cinema: A Critical Introduction* (2001); *Realist Film Theory and Cinema: The Nineteenth-Century, Lukácsian and Intuitionist Realist Traditions* (2006); "The European Realist Tradition." *Studies in European Cinema* (2007); and "Physical Reality: The Role of the Empirical in the Film Theory of Siegfried Kracauer, John Grierson, André Bazin and Georg Lukács." *Studies in Documentary Film* (2007).
2. See my *Realist Film Theory and Cinema: the Nineteenth-Century, Lukácsian and Intuitionist Realist Traditions*; and "Realism, Philosophy and the Documentary Film," in Aitken (ed.) *The Encyclopedia of the Documentary Film* (2006).
3. I am not concerned here with whether or not pragmatism should be classed as a form of anti-realism, but with a distinction which can be made between pragmatist and philosophical realist approaches.
4. The term "screen theory" refers to the body of film theory associated with the journal *Screen* during the 1960s and 1970s. (See the editor's introduction to this volume for more details.)

works cited

Aitken, Ian. *European Film Theory and Cinema: A Critical Introduction*. Edinburgh: Edinburgh University Press, 2001.

——. *Realist Film Theory and Cinema: The Nineteenth-Century Lukácsian and Intuitionist Realist Traditions*. Manchester: Manchester University Press, 2006.

——. "The European Realist Tradition." *Studies in European Cinema* 3.3 (2007): 175–88.

—— "Physical Reality: The Role of the Empirical in the Film Theory of Siegfried Kracauer, John Grierson, André Bazin and Georg Lukács." *Studies in Documentary Film* 1.2 (2007): 105–22.

—— "Realism, Philosophy and the Documentary Film." *The Encyclopedia of the Documentary Film*. Ed. Ian Aitken. New York; London: Routledge, 2006.

Allen, Robert C., and Gomery, Douglas. *Film History: Theory and Practice*. New York: Alfred A. Knopf, 1985.

Bazin, André. *What is Cinema?* Volume I. Trans. Hugh Gray. Berkeley: University of California Press, 1967.

Beardsley, Monroe C. *Aesthetics: Problems in the Philosophy of Criticism*. 2nd edition. Indianapolis: Hackett Publishing Co, Inc, 1981.

Bhaskar, Roy. *A Realist Theory of Science*. Atlantic Highlands, NJ: Humanities Press, 1978.

—— *The Possibility of Naturalism: A Philosophical Critique of the Contemporary Human Sciences*. Brighton: The Harvester Press, 1979.

Bordwell, David and Carroll, Noël (eds.). *Post-Theory: Reconstructing Film Studies*. Madison and London: University of Wisconsin Press, 1996.

Carroll, Noël. *Theorising the Moving Image*. Cambridge: Cambridge University Press, 1996.

Devitt, Michael. *Realism and Truth*. Princeton: Princeton University Press, 1997.

Harré, Rom. *The Philosophies of Science: An Introductory Survey*. Oxford: Oxford University Press, 1972.

Hesse, Mary. *Models and Analogies in Science*. Notre Dame: University of Notre Dame Press, 1966.

—— *Revolutions and Reconstructions in the Philosophy of Science*. Bloomington and London: Indiana University Press, 1980.

—— "Duhem, Quine, and a New Empiricism." *Challenges to Empiricism*. Ed. Harold Morick. Indianapolis: Hackett Publishing Company Inc., 1980.

Keat, Robert and Urry, John. *Social Theory as Science*. London: Routledge and Kegan Paul, 1975.

Kracauer, Siegfried. *Theory of Film: The Redemption of Physical Reality*. Princeton: Princeton University Press, 1997.

Kuhn, Thomas. *The Essential Tension: Selected Studies in Scientific Tradition and Change*. Chicago and London: Chicago University Press, 1977.

Lovell, Terry. *Pictures of Reality*. London: British Film Institute, 1980.

MacCabe, Colin. "Realism and the Cinema: Notes on some Brechtian Theses." *Screen* 15.2 (Summer 1974): 7–27.

Morick, Harold (ed.). *Challenges to Empiricism*. London: Methuen, 1980.

Papineau, David. *Reality and Representation*. Oxford: Basil Blackwell, 1987.

Passmore, John. *Recent Philosophers: A Supplement to A Hundred Years of Philosophy*. London: Duckworth, 1985.

—— *Serious Art*. London: Duckworth, 1991.

Psillos, Stathis. *Scientific Realism: How Science Tracks Truth*. London: Routledge, 1999.

Putnam, Hilary. *Reason, Truth and History*. Cambridge: Cambridge University Press, 1981.

—— *The Many Faces of Realism*. La Salle, Illinois: Open Court, 1987.

—— *Realism with a Human Face*. Cambridge, MA and London: Harvard University Press, 1992.

Rescher, Nicholas. *Conceptual Idealism*. Oxford: Basil Blackwell, 1973.

Rorty, Richard. "The World Well Lost." *Journal of Philosophy* 69 (1972): 649–665.

Trigg, Roger. *Reality at Risk: A Defence of Realism in Philosophy and the Sciences*. London: Harvester Wheatsheaf, 1989.

contributors

Ian Aitken is Professor of Film Studies at Hong Kong Baptist University. He is the author of *Film and Reform: John Grierson and the Documentary Film Movement* (1990); *The Documentary Film Movement: An Anthology* (ed., 1998); *Alberto Cavalcanti* (2000); *European Film Theory and Cine   ma* (2001); *The Encyclopedia of the Documentary Film* (ed., 2006); *Realist Film Theory and Cinema* (2006); and *Lukacsian Film Theory and Cinema* (2009).

Martin Barker is Professor of Film & Television Studies at Aberystwyth University. He has researched and published in a number of fields, including comic books, censorship controversies, methodologies of research, film analysis, and most particularly audience research. He directed the 2003–4 international project on the reception of the film of *The Lord of the Rings*. In 2006 he directed a commissioned project for the British Board of Film Classification into audience responses to screened sexual violence. His books include *The Lasting of the Mohicans: History of an American Myth* (with Roger Sabin, 1996); *Knowing Audiences: Judge Dredd, its Friends, Fans and Foes* (with Kate Brooks, 1998); *From Antz to Titanic: Reinventing Film Analysis* (with Thomas Austin, 2000); and *The Crash Controversy: Censorship Campaigns and Film Reception* (with Jane Arthurs and Ramaswami Harindranath, 2001).

Harry M. Benshoff is an Associate Professor of Radio, Television, and Film at the University of North Texas. His research interests include topics in film genres, film history, film theory, and multiculturalism. He has published essays on Dark Shadows fan cultures, blaxploitation horror films, Hollywood LSD films, and *The Talented Mr. Ripley* (1999). He is the author of *Monsters in the Closet: Homosexuality and the Horror Film* (1997). With Sean Griffin he co-authored *America on Film: Representing Race, Class, Gender and Sexuality at the Movies* (2004) and *Queer Images: A History of Gay and Lesbian Film in America* (2006).

Douglas Brown is a videogame theorist and lecturer at Brunel University, London. He is currently writing a PhD focusing on how the suspension of disbelief functions in ludic environments. His work has been published in several books and journals, and he has also worked on games for Square-Enix, contributing to many titles including *Final Fantasy XII* and *Valkyrie Profile*. His favourite game is *Alpha Centauri*, but he can usually be found playing far too much *World of Warcraft*.

William Brown is a Teaching Fellow in Film Studies at the University of St Andrews. He has published work on contemporary American, French and British cinema, and his research interests include the effects of digital technology on film in a variety of different national contexts, together with cognitive/neuroscientific approaches to cinema.

Warren Buckland is Reader in Film Studies at Oxford Brookes University. He is author of *Directed by Steven Spielberg: Poetics of the Contemporary Hollywood Cinema* (2006); *Studying Contemporary American Film: A Guide to Movie Analysis* (2002) (with Thomas Elsaesser); *The Cognitive Semiotics of Film* (2000); and editor of *The Film Spectator* (1995) and *Puzzle Films: Complex Storytelling in Contemporary Cinema* (2009). He also edits the journal the *New Review of Film and Television Studies*.

Sean Cubitt is Director of the Program in Media and Communications at the University of Melbourne, and Honorary Professor at the University of Dundee. His publications include *Timeshift: On Video Culture* (1991); *Videography: Video Media as Art and Culture* (1993); *Digital Aesthetics* (1998); *Simulation and Social Theory* (2000); *The Cinema Effect* (2004); and *EcoMedia* (2005). He is the series editor for Leonardo Books at MIT Press. His current research is on public screens and the transformation of public space; and on genealogies of digital light.

332   **K.J. Donnelly** is Reader in Film at the University of Southampton. He is author of *British Film Music and Film Musicals* (2007); *The Spectre of Sound* (2005); and *Pop Music in British Cinema* (2001). He also edited *Film Music: Critical Approaches* (2001). Although a member of the film faculty he also works with Southampton University's music faculty and physicists at the Institute of Sound and Vibrations Research.

Thomas Elsaesser is Emeritus Professor of Film and Television Studies at the University of Amsterdam. His essays on European cinema, film history and media archaeology, American cinema and contemporary media theory have been translated in more than 15 languages and published in over 200 collections. He has been visiting professor and research fellow at UC Berkeley, IFK Vienna, Sackler Institute Tel Aviv, NYU and Yale. In 2006 he was Ingmar Bergman Professor at the University of Stockholm and in 2007 Leverhulme Professor at Churchill College, Cambridge.

Most recent books as (co-) editor include: *Cinema Futures: Cain, Abel or Cable?* (1998); *The BFI Companion to German Cinema* (1999); *The Last Great American Picture Show* (2004); and *Harun Farocki: Working on the Sightlines* (2004). His books as author include *Fassbinder's Germany: History, Identity, Subject* (1996); *Weimar Cinema and After* (2000); *Metropolis* (2000); *Studying Contemporary American Film* (2002, with Warren Buckland); *Filmgeschichte und Frühes Kino* (2002); *Terror, Mythes et Representation* (2005); *European Cinema: Face to Face with Hollywood* (2005); *Filmheorie: eine Einfuehrung* (2007, with Malte Hagener; English edition and Italian translation forthcoming); and *Hollywood Heute* (2008).

Volker Ferenz has a Masters of Arts in Theatre Studies, Philosophy and German Literature at the University of Munich, Germany (2002) and a Ph.D. in Film Studies from the University of Gloucestershire, UK, on the unreliable narrator in contemporary cinema (2005). He has publications on narrative theory in both Germany and the UK. He is now based in Munich working as script consultant for a variety of film production and distribution companies.

Tanya Krzywinska is Professor in Screen Studies at Brunel University. She is the author of several books and many articles on different aspects of videogames, horror, and fantasy and is particularly interested in occult fiction and fantasy worlds. She is the co-author of *Tomb Raiders and Space Invaders: Videogames Forms and Meanings* (2006); *Sex and the Cinema* (2006); *A Skin for Dancing In: Witchcraft, Possession and Voodoo in Film* (2001); and co-editor of *ScreenPlay: Cinema/Videogames/Interfaces* (2002); and *videogame/player/text* (2007). She convenes a Masters programme in Digital Games: Theory and Design at Brunel University, London, and is President of the Digital Games Research Association.

David Martin-Jones lectures in Film Studies at the University of St Andrews, Scotland. He is the author of *Deleuze, Cinema and National Identity* (2006), has published articles in a number of international journals (including *Cinema Journal*, *Screen*, and *CineAction*) and is on the editorial boards of *Film-Philosophy* and *A/V: The Journal of Deleuzian Studies*.

Carl Plantinga is Professor of Film Studies in the Communication Arts and Sciences Department at Calvin College. He is the author of *Rhetoric and Representation in Nonfiction Film* (1997) and *Moving Viewers: American Film and the Spectator's Experience* (2009); and co-editor of *Passionate Views: Film, Cognition, and Emotion* (1999) and *The Routledge Companion to Philosophy and Film* (2008).

Barry Salt is a Term Tutor at the London Film School. He has a B.Sc. and Ph.D. in Theoretical Physics and has been a ballet dancer, computer programmer, and film lighting cameraman. He has taught at the Slade School, University College and the Royal College of Art. He is the author of *Film Style and Technology: History and Analysis* (second edition, 1992); *Moving into Pictures: More on Film History, Style and Analysis* (2006), plus many articles on film history.

Thomas Schatz is Mary Gibbs Jones Centennial Chair in Communication and former Chairman of the Radio-Television-Film Department at the University of Texas, where he has been on the faculty since 1976. His books include *Hollywood Genres, The Genius of the System: Hollywood Filmmaking in the Studio Era* and *Boom and Bust: American Cinema in the 1940s*. He also edited a recent four-volume collection on Hollywood for Routledge. Schatz's writing on film has also appeared in numerous magazines, newspapers and academic journals, including the *New York Times*, the *Los Angeles Times*, *Premiere*, *The Nation, Film Comment, Film Quarterly* and *Cineaste*. Schatz is the founder and Executive Director of the UT Film Institute, a program devoted to training students in narrative and digital filmmaking, and the production of feature-length independent films.

Saša Vojković is Associate Professor of Film and Media at the Department of Cultural Studies, Faculty of Philosophy, University of Rijeka. She was the recipient of the ASCA Ph.D. Fellowship (Amsterdam School for Cultural Analysis, Theory and Interpretation) awarded by the Faculty of Letters, University of Amsterdam. She also won a YK Pao three-year postdoctoral teaching fellowship awarded by the Department of Humanities, at the Hong Kong University of Science and Technology. She is author of *Yuen Woo Ping's Wing Chun* (2009); *Filmski medij kao transkulturalni spektakl: Hollywood, Europa, Azija* (*Filmic Medium as [Trans] Cultural Spectacle: Hollywood, Europe, Asia*) (2008); and *Subjectivity in the New Hollywood Cinema: Fathers, Sons and Other Ghosts* (2001).

index

Page numbers followed by *n* refer to notes

343

345